The Jamaican People
1880–1902

The Jamaican People
1880–1902
Race, Class and Social Control

Patrick Bryan

The University of the West Indies Press

Barbados • Jamaica • Trinidad and Tobago

The University of the West Indies Press
1A Aqueduct Flats
Kingston 7 Jamaica

Printed by Stephensons Litho Press Ltd
ISBN 976-640-094-6

04   5 4 3 2

CATALOGUING IN PUBLICATION DATA

Bryan, Patrick E.
   The Jamaican people 1880–1902: race, class and social
   control / Patrick Bryan

   p.cm.
   Previously published: London: Macmillan Caribbean, 1991.
   Includes bibliographical references and index.
   ISBN: 976–640–094–6

   1. Social classes – Jamaica – History. 2. Jamaica – Social
   conditions. 3. Jamaica – History – To 1902. I. Title.

HN223.B79 2000   972.92'20 – dc.20

Cover design by Adlib Studio, Kingston, Jamaica

Contents

List of abbreviations

CO	Colonial Office
DG	*Daily Gleaner*
HBJ	*Handbook of Jamaica*
JA	*Jamaica Advocate*
JBB	*Blue Books Island of Jamaica*
JCM	*Jamaica Minutes* of the Legislative Council
JDR	*Jamaica Annual General Report* with Departmental Reports.
JG	*Jamaica Gazette*
JM	*Jamaica Memories*. A Collection of Essays on Life in Jamaica at the end of the nineteenth and early-twentieth century
NLJ	National Library of Jamaica
WIRC	West Indian Royal Commission

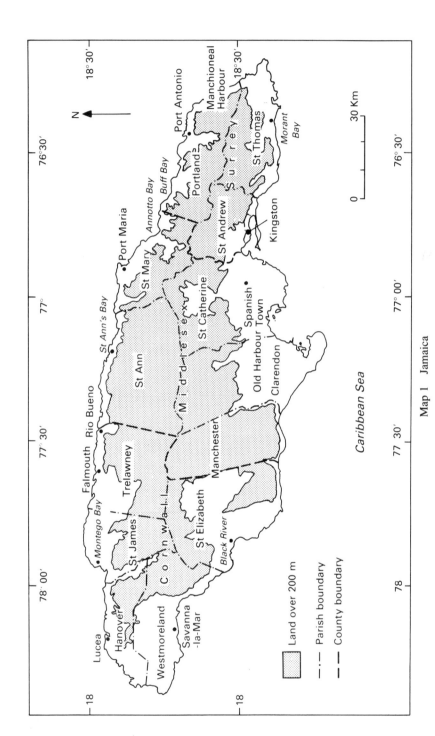

Map 1   Jamaica

Introduction

The strategy of the white ruling class in Jamaica had always been to maintain their dominion over the black and coloured population. That strategy was partly a response to the turbulence of Jamaican slave society, pockmarked with protest and rebellion. Although white dominion or white hegemony also came to be seen as part of the order of society, it is also clear that the white population of Jamaica viewed the colony before and after the abolition of slavery as volatile, potentially unstable, subject to incendiary and insurrectionary action by 'combustible' blacks and coloured. Whatever the disagreements between whites they were all agreed that the maintenance of an ordered society necessitated policies that took into serious consideration the supposed propensity of blacks for violence.

It is clear that coercion was considered to be an important mechanism for the maintenance of white social and political authority; yet within the ranks of white society were those who believed it to be prudent to create a regime which rested not only on force but on consent and on co-optation. The hegemony of the ruling class was then assured by the manipulation of the law, the control or influence upon the political and constitutional order, by the control of land resources, and by the projection of the concept of the indispensability of white leadership for the progress of the colony. In the latter respect, the white leadership was far from reluctant to cite, for black consumption, the Republic of Haiti as an example of black incapacity for self-government.

The minority leadership of Jamaica assumed a cultural chasm between the white and the black. The assumption was to some extent overstated in the sense that the cultural differences between one sector of the population and the other were not quite as deep as the elite leadership believed. The bridges between the 'Two Jamaicas', not least the sexual bridges, were numerous. But it is precisely this conception of a chasm that encouraged whites to formulate policies that would have anglicised (the word used was 'civilised') the population. They assumed that a well-ordered society was more sure of achievement by fostering common norms than by encouraging diversity. Cultural homogeneity would and could coexist, in any case, with racial heterogeneity and racial hierarchy. Habits of thought that had emerged out of the particular social relations of slavery continued to influence society well after slavery had been abolished, for hegemony during the slave period had involved not only the legal ownership of slaves but also a whole belief system that entrenched the white oligarchy as the economic, political and cultural leaders of colonial society in Jamaica. In the late-nineteenth century blacks were, of course, no longer slaves. A new definition of blacks had emerged. They were now the 'subject people' to be systematically 'civilised', their environment had become the 'mission frontier'.

The idea that blacks were a constituency for white civilisation was certainly not new. But whereas that idea had been principally the province of Nonconformist missionaries prior to emancipation, the idea became far more secularised at the end of the nineteenth century. By then, too, the concept of 'civilisation' of the barbarous had gained wider respectability in the context of the rapid expansion of empire and imperialism that justified itself with the pretence of philanthropy.

Among the ideological tools used to justify empire, to civilise the heathen, and to control society were social Darwinism and positivism. Positivism, with its adherence to the joint principles of order and progress insisted on a justification of the social order, and the accommodation of change to that social order. The moral order of society rather than the social order was what positivists placed on the agenda of change. The moral order has an appearance of neutrality, of course, even though it is mainly a mirror of the economic, political and general order of society. Social Darwinism was an apt companion of positivism, since the former could explain white hegemony as a product of biological 'fitness' to survive and dominate, while the latter justified the given social structure.

Thus racism, which had emerged from the slave plantation system as a hegemonic weapon, found itself with an intellectual legitimacy that was used to justify class domination, and white social authority. Differences of lifestyle were interpreted as indications or proofs of biological rather than cultural differences. Cultural differences, when they were recognised as such, were not considered to be a function of social inequities. The working classes were broadly regarded as racially inferior, children of a child race who, to some extent, were to be shielded from political demagogues. One consequence of that pattern of thought was that it projected a paternalism that reinforced and endorsed inequalities between classes and groups. Paternalism's virtue is that it helps to generate consent within inequity, and who knows, iniquity.

For the whites of Jamaica and elsewhere where slavery had been abolished, the challenge of emancipation consisted in organising production around free labour while keeping alive the spirit of inequality that had marked the plantation system. Inseparable from that spirit were the caste and class distinctions between people. These distinctions are very evident in contrasting patterns of marriage, courtship and family life, as well as in patterns of leisure. At the level of sexual relations interaction between the races assumed an unequal relationship between them. Yet the inability of the oligarchy to extract the traditional levels of obedience and subservience that slavery had made possible (at least in theory and in spite of slave insubordination and revolt) led them to adopt policies that would ensure consent, and project a principle of tolerance and the sanctity of British legal institutions. The black population, as the subject people, were the objects of the law, and never the formulators of it. But the provision of poor relief and charity institutions – private and public – and the provision of health services, however inadequate and grudgingly given, were important means of providing some legitimacy for the elite.

Of course, control could be exercised by other means as well – such as the firm control of land resources, precarious tenancies, and the swelling of the surplus labour force by East Indian immigration. But control and consent could also be generated by the provision of a system of education that promoted opportunities for individual social mobility, and encouraged values that legitimated the system of domination. Anglicisation, internalisation of hegemonic values, the belief that there were two Jamaicas, the one civilised, the other uncivilised, was to drive a wedge between the educated (anglicised) black middle class and the masses of black labourers whose universe was composed of a Christian God, coexisting with beliefs and practices (such as obeah, revivalism and myalism) construed as inimical to an ordered and civilised society. The story of the black middle class demonstrates in part that ethnic groups do not necessarily have a 'high degree of internal solidarity' and that an ethnic group 'is likely to be split along religious, class, and political lines'.[1] The evolution of a black middle class was not an anomaly in the pattern of hegemony. On the contrary, the achievement of European culture and education became an end in itself for probably most members of the black middle class. And the few who dared to challenge the hegemonic system in principle could offer little more than sympathetic applause from the sidelines when the black masses took to the streets in riots, and otherwise disturbed the 'public peace'. Blacks such as Robert Love were isolated because they could not develop values separate or distinct from the white hegemonic ones without frankly denying their hard-earned respectability.

Thus, while white hegemony was questioned by Robert Love and by Theophilus Scholes (from London), the challenge was undertaken within the framework of an appeal to an abstract British justice and fairplay, and an appeal to the concept of the equality of man. They could challenge the idea of racial inferiority, condemn racism, or the existing structure of society, even doing so in alliance with whites who sympathised with black causes. But the reality was that analysis of the inequalities of Jamaican society, or of empire, could not easily be transformed into political or anti-hegemonic action. It should be noted, however, that the school system was never sufficiently pervasive to influence the entire population, so that the weaknesses of the system combined with the resistance to hegemonic values by the black masses ensured a significant continuation of folk values, especially religion.

Religion may be viewed, on the one hand, as an indication of the cultural gap between European and African Jamaica. On the other hand, it can also be viewed as a force for the maintenance of consent. It would be an error to believe that outstanding clergymen, in their policy of anglicisation or civilisation, assumed, universally, that conversion had to be complete. On the contrary, there was a flexibility that allowed for the adoption of what was regarded as African religious expression in the formal Christian Churches. Such a policy, it was expected, would attract the black constituency to the formal Churches, and even make blacks partners in the conversion of the African heathen. For Archbishop Nuttall, the strengthening of the Christian Church would cement the British Empire. The maintenance of hegemony assumed the creation of 'openings' for the black population in an ecclesiastical edifice ruled and dominated by whites.

The symbolic universe of empire crowned the legitimation of white authority. Jamaicans belonged, perhaps, to the 'slums of empire' but presence in the slums could not conceal the imperial glitter which shone across race and class lines. It has been noted that 'subordinate groups may participate in maintaining a symbolic universe, even if it serves to legitimate their domination'.[2]

We have said that hegemony seeks legitimation of the social order – even at the expense of limited concessions – but consensus, consent, or legitimation do not remove the need for force. The law, and instruments of coercion such as the Jamaica constabulary, the militia and the British army and navy were of extreme importance in the maintenance of law and order, which were inseparable from white hegemony. Hence Mr Chamberlain's insistence that Jamaica pay its share in the costs of imperial defence. The riots in Montego Bay, in 1902, demonstrated the importance of the forces of coercion. In the elite vision, the action of the black constabulary in suppressing (albeit under white leadership) the riots in Montego Bay, was crucially important. Their action demonstrated that a black constabulary would train its guns on rioting black Jamaicans. That action was a victory for white hegemony (and white ethnicity), and proved the essential limitations of ethnicity as a binding tie between blacks.

I wish to thank the staff of the following libraries, collections and archives for their courteous assistance: The National Library of Jamaica, the West Indian Collection of the University of the West Indies, at Mona; the Jamaica Archives; the Public Record Office in London; the Milton S.

Eisenhower Library of the Johns Hopkins University; the National Archives and the Library of Congress in Washington, DC.

Thanks, too, to the Department of History of Johns Hopkins University, and the Program in Atlantic History, Culture and Society at Johns Hopkins who hosted me from April to September, 1986, during which time I wrote the first draft of this study. I thank Professor David Cohen for assisting me to settle into Baltimore.

My stay at Johns Hopkins was made possible by leave granted to me by the UWI, Mona, and by funding from the Council for International Exchange of Scholars, and from the UWI.

On a more personal note, I wish to thank the versatile Dr Karl Watson of the Department of History, UWI for completing my teaching and examination duties while I was away.

A special word of thanks to Professor Franklin Knight (of Johns Hopkins) who was not only very hospitable to me and my family in Baltimore, but who read and commented on a draft of the manuscript. I thank him for his very valuable comments and insights. Finally, thanks to my family for giving me time off.

Notes

1   T.J. Jackson-Lears, 'Concept of Cultural Hegemony', in *American Historical Review*, Vol. 90, No. 3, 1985, p. 573.
2   *Ibid.*

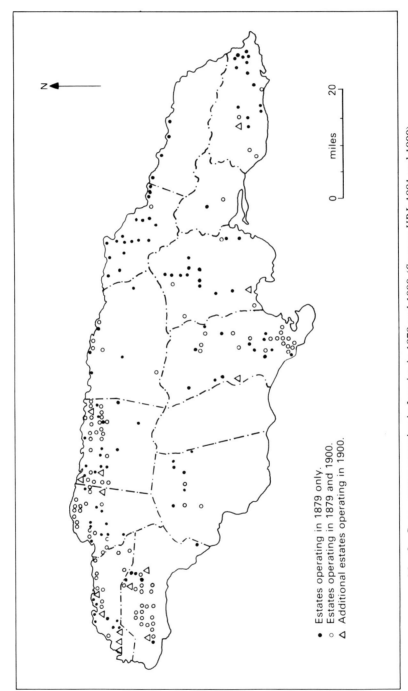

N

0   miles   20

• Estates operating in 1879 only.
○ Estates operating in 1879 and 1900.
△ Additional estates operating in 1900.

Map 2   Sugar estates operating in Jamaica in 1879 and 1900 (*Source: HBJ*, 1881 and 1900).

CHAPTER 1 | The plantation economy

The latifundist sugar industry had been for nearly two centuries the axis around which the Jamaican economy turned. But it was more than that. It was also the primary institution which shaped Creole society in Jamaica, since, to a considerable extent the formation of social classes was directly linked to plantation production. The ownership of capital in the sugar industry, the administration of plantation enterprises, and the structure of the labour force came to correspond to important class and racial divisions in society. It was also the plantation economy which helped to forge the relationship between the Jamaican colony and the British metropolis.

Therefore, the historical relationship between the fortunes of the sugar industry and the welfare of Jamaica makes necessary an assessment of the economic prospects of that industry in the late-nineteenth century when the fortunes of sugar were in decline. Sugar, slavery and British colonialism had been linked in a mercantilist structure which, in the second half of the nineteenth century, steadily surrendered to the British rejection of protectionism and the consequent adoption of free trade policies.

Free trade policy, which removed in 1846 the protection given to British West Indian sugar, was only one additional factor which made the struggle for survival of the British West Indian sugar industry difficult. The industry experienced a shortage of capital and credit, in the absence of which there was no significant improvement in techniques of production, or systematic establishment of central factories. Unlike the old mercantilist order, liberal capitalism offered no support to the inefficient producer.

The difficulties of the sugar industry did not arise because of declining demand for sugar as such. On the contrary the consumption of sugar in Britain, for example, increased from 695,000 tons in 1870 to 1,424,000 tons in 1896, or an increase of over 100 per cent.[1] In the United States, the 'consumption of sugar from all sources, including home production, increased from 993,532 tons in 1881 to 2,767,162 tons in 1904'.[2] These figures indicate for the United States a per capita increase in consumption of from 44 lb in 1881 to 75.3 lb in 1904. In 1897, the United States imported 84 per cent of the sugar which it consumed despite the increase of production at home.[3]

1

The fact is that cane-sugar producers faced keen competition from beet-sugar producers. By doubling bounties on exports Germany, for example, increased exports of beet sugar from 594,360 tons in 1880 to 848,124 tons in 1882 and in 1884 to 1,154,816 tons.[4] Britain increased its consumption of beet sugar from 376,909 tons in 1880–2 to 611,590 tons in 1886–8.[5] There was, on the other hand, a matching sharp decline in cane sugar imports, from 700,000 tons in 1875 to 344,000 tons in 1896.[6] In 1897, 37 per cent of sugar consumed in the United States was beet sugar. Meanwhile, prices for cane sugar fell from 25/6d per cwt in 1873 to 11/3d in 1900.

In Jamaica sugar estates fell into bankruptcy and were either sold or abandoned. Between 1879 and 1887 39 estates were abandoned, and between 1887 and 1900, 57. The crisis in sugar showed itself in the decline from 316 estates in 1867 to 122 in 1900. Sugar cane acreage declined from 42,413 acres in 1884 to 26,121 acres in 1900.[7] Output declined from 483,000 cwt in 1874 to 399,000 in 1894 and to 295,000 in 1900. In 1870 sugar had contributed 44.5 per cent to total agricultural exports, by 1884 that contribution had fallen to 26.1 per cent, by 1895 to 12.9 per cent, and in 1900 to 10.8 per cent.[8]

The highest rate of abandonment of estates occurred in the parishes of St Andrew, St Thomas, Portland, St Mary, St Ann, St Catherine and St Elizabeth. The lowest rate was in Hanover, Westmoreland, Trelawny, St James and Clarendon.[9] Sugar production until the end of the nineteenth century continued to hold its own in the latter western parishes and sections of Clarendon.

The abandonment of estates was only one response to the problems of the sugar industry. Planters also mounted vigorous protests against British free trade policies, without success as it turned out, since British policy continued to favour the importation of cheap sugar, both in the form of bounty-fed beet sugar and in the form of the 'falling price for such quantities of British West Indian sugar as were exported to Britain between 1874 and 1901'. That policy contributed to the 'profitability of re-exporting refined sugar at reduced prices'.[10] The Colonial Office recognised the problems facing the British West Indian sugar planters but ruled out a revival of the preferential market for West Indian produce. (The British saw no inconsistency in their own insistence that the Jamaican and British West Indian markets be kept open to British imports on favourable terms to Britain).

A second response by planters was to exploit the expanding United States market, whither, in fact, most of Jamaica's sugar was exported between the 1880s and 1900. The Colonial Office accepted as a matter of course that the British Caribbean would become more dependent commercially on the United States.[11] The rapidly expanding United States economy opened up new opportunities for commercial agriculture in Jamaica. The United States population had tripled between 1815 and 1860. Urban population growth, responding to increased industrialisation, was reflected in the multiplication of urban centres from 52 cities with populations over 25,000 people in 1872 to 160 such centres by 1900.[12] There was also an estimated 50 per cent increase of per capita income in the second half of the nineteenth century.[13]

The difficulty of the United States market was the erratic nature of the tariffs, though it was clear that, at its worst, it was more promising than the British market at its best. In addition, whatever the problems of sugar, the fact was that the United States market was open to imports of bananas, coconuts, cacao, rum and coffee, on favourable terms to Jamaica. Sugar, in any case, was also directed towards the US market, which was much closer to Jamaica. It is probably in this context that Jamaicans discussed, between 1880 and 1884 and again between 1898 and 1900, the possibilities of annexation to the United States.

Sugar planters had continued to regard Jamaica as a plantation out of which it was convenient for Her Majesty's subjects to earn money, and the question of loyalty to empire sometimes took second place to the need to have secure and profitable markets. In 1898, planters were especially concerned that the establishment of a United States Protectorate over Cuba and the acquisition of Puerto Rico in the same year as a colonial possession of the United States, would give to the latter a potentially large area of sugar land. The possession of plantations in Cuba and Puerto Rico would, it was anticipated, lead to a tariff policy that would discriminate against Jamaican sugar in favour of Cuba and Puerto Rico.

All discussions of annexation to the United States, however, foundered on the question of institutional racism in the latter country. Given that Jamaica was, officially, a racial democracy (despite a lethal informal racism) it was thought that to encourage US-type institutional racism would be to expose the racial contradictions in Jamaican society. Up to 1910 the *Jamaica Times* was commenting on the dangers, in this respect, of US influence in Jamaica.[14] In 1884 and again in 1890–2 there were experiments with reciprocity conventions between the United States and the British West Indies. Reciprocity conventions hopefully would achieve similar objectives to annexation. Yet, in reality, Jamaica imposed discriminatory tariffs on United States goods.[15] In 1890 the United States trade negotiator even complained: 'You people run your Government on the taxes you levy on American products'. In 1889, the US consul, Mr Louis Dent, used the services of the *Daily Telegraph*'s editor, Mr Guy, to wage a campaign against the new tariff which promised, as usual, to impose higher duties on US imports. He also pressed Mr Gideon, an important banana trader and entrepreneur (viewed by Mr Dent as the leader of the elected element in the

Legislative Council) to represent the United States interest in that Council. Dent's conspiracy failed partly because some of his supporters were convinced that Dent was involved in a game of bluff, in which he was essentially acting on his own.[16]

The Colonial Office was well aware of how adverse the tariff was to US goods, but chose to stick to its policy of 'scraping along'. Referring to the 1890 reciprocity negotiations, the Colonial Office commented:

> First of all for many years the United States has been taking a steadily and rapidly increasing proportion of produce of the West Indies, while the West Indies in return have only to a small extent and in some cases not at all increased their purchase of US goods, the difference being doubtless paid with bills of England which takes vastly more from the US than it sends to it. The US naturally doesn't like this, and knows that the West Indies cannot do without their market; they put a pistol to their heads, and threaten them with sudden death as an alternative to altering their tariff.[17]

In their strategy of diversifying trading partners the Jamaican planters looked to Canada as well. Between 1882–5 consideration was given both to a confederation with Canada, and failing that, to a reciprocity convention in which, hopefully, the Canadians would take over from the United States market. The attraction of Canada rested in the ability of the latter to supply foods normally obtained from the United States, and in the reality that Canada's was an expanding economy within the British Empire. The Canadians showed relatively little interest in confederation, and negotiations for reciprocity failed, for two main reasons. Firstly, there was no substantial shipping between Canada and the West Indies, and secondly, Jamaica would probably lose £27,555 in revenue from the removal of duties contingent on a reciprocity convention.[18] Reciprocity, then, would be brought about by a sacrifice of government revenues for the benefit primarily of the sugar interests.

Finally, the Empire itself struck back. The position of the Colonial Office was that any such agreement with Canada should embrace all the British West Indies and not Jamaica alone. That constraint made a commercial arrangement impossible since Canada, while being able to absorb most of Jamaica's sugar, could not do the same for the combined British West Indies.[19] The United States would then, perhaps, not prove co-operative:

> An essential part of the present proposal is that Canada should have the benefit of a differential duty. This would at once excite the wrath of the United States, and induce the exclusion of the West Indies from the American markets. That would not matter

if Canada could replace the States or if Great Britain gave her West Indian colonies a closer market – but this is far from being the case.[20]

In the first few years of the twentieth century the problem found partial solution through the Brussels Convention. Between 1904–9 Canada became the major purchaser of Jamaican sugar (74.9 per cent in 1904–5) compared with 2.2 per cent for the United States in the same year. But in the twenty years between 1880 and 1900 Jamaica had to rely on the US market for most of its sugar exports.[21]

Diversification

Diversification of production was a pragmatic and necessary response to the crisis in the sugar industry. At the same time, such diversification as did occur was possible principally because of the generation of demand for agricultural products in the late-nineteenth century in the metropolitan economies.

Some planters developed their logwood and pimento production. Peak production for logwood was 115,000 tons in 1889. There was a decline in the 1890s until a new low of 34,000 tons was reached in 1900.[22] The value of logwood exports fell from £448,678 in 1894 to £98,618 in 1901.[23] Pimento production tended to fluctuate from a low of 4,866 tons in 1866 to a high of 13,888 in 1899/1900.[24] Export earnings from pimento ranged from £76,786 in 1894 to £173,562 in 1900.[25] The cost of production of logwood did not require a high capital investment, and most labour went into chipping logwood.

> The worker might get 12/-, 16/-, 20/- per ton chipping logwood. If the wood is plentiful it takes a man seven or eight days to chip one ton of twenty-four hundredweight at 12/- per ton, sometimes more. If he (the proprietor) pays 12/- drayage to the wharf and 16/- labour in all his costs are 28/-, his profit 52/-. This he gets without expenditure of a penny in cultivation.[26]

As with logwood, so too with pimento and grazing, labour could be used much more sparingly than in sugar production. Cattle pens had often been attached to estates. However, some estates were converted into cattle-breeding pens.[27] Livestock was needed for transportation, mules fetched good prices, and they were also believed to be less vulnerable to ticks and other grass parasites.[28] Anthony Musgrave, in 1880, at least, thought that the penkeeping industry could prove profitable in Jamaica because there were markets in the Caribbean, particularly Cuba, for livestock. There was a tendency, however, claimed Musgrave, for Jamaicans never to admit that anything was profitable.

Musgrave made the assumption that, given the amount of capital invested in cattle farms (that is the amount for which pens had been bought), there was good reason to think that 'they afford on an average of years a very fair amount of interest on investment'. While some planters turned to penkeeping, it appears from Governor Musgrave's comments, that there were other planters who passively opposed penkeeping, causing a re-tardation in the development of the export industry to 'adjacent places' (Cuba, presumably). He referred to the:

> astonishing want of sympathy on the part of the sugar planters in any project which, if successful, might result in raising prices of cattle which were required for the sugar plantations . . . And it is the fact that the passive opposition of the sugar planting section of the community, at one time dominant and still influential, especially in England, has impeded the development of any in-dustries which seemed to create a demand for labour which would withdraw it from the sugar estates.[29]

One of the major stock-raising parishes was St Ann. Pens varied in size from 200 to 2,000 acres. They were subdivided into guinea grass pastures, commons, woodland, and on the larger pens lands were rented to tenants who paid for their leases either in cash or in labour.[30]

Some planters resorted to mixed cultivation of sections of their estates, while leaving whole areas abandoned (the usual term used was 'ruinate').[31] In other cases sections of the estates were leased to tenants. In 1892, of five estates owned by the absentee planter, Henry Sewell, two continued to be sugar estates (Cave Valley 1,080 acres, and Drax Hall 1,438 acres), while three were in pimento and grazing (Hyde Park 1,614 acres, Home Castle 4,042 acres and Richmond Pen, 3,000 acres). Of 11,174 acres owned by Sewell, then, some 8,654 acres were in pimento and grazing and only 2,528 in sugar.

The resident planter, E.G. Barrett, dedicated 7,698 acres to pimento and grazing. Indeed for the parish of St Ann, for estates of over 1,000 acres, there were 81,678 acres dedicated to pimento and grazing, 15,325 acres to sugar, and 4,000 acres rented to peasants. Similarly, in St Elizabeth there were 30,195 acres in sugar and 58,759 dedicated to logwood and grazing. In Clarendon, for estates over 1,000 acres in area, there were 46,281 acres in sugar, 9,353 acres in grazing, 19,677 acres in grazing and 'ruinate'. In Westmoreland, there were 43,732 acres in sugar, 27,098 acres in pimento and grazing. In Manchester, where the emphasis was on mixed crops there was a common combination of coffee, and grazing. In Trelawny there were 40,596 acres in sugar, 30,340 dedicated to grazing and another 25,000 acres abandoned. (These figures refer only to lands over 1,000 acres).[32]

The banana plantations

Some planters also added bananas as a new crop on their sugar estates. But more generally bananas were being grown in areas, particularly the parishes of Portland and St Mary, where there had been large-scale abandonment of sugar estates. The demand for bananas in the United States, the favourable tariff for bananas and other fruit exports including citrus, coconuts and cacao (at this time the world demand for cacao outstripped supply), the proximity of the United States market, and the availability of shipping, facilitated the banana trade. Steamships made for rapid transport.

Export of bananas increased from 329,000 stems in 1879 to 1,843,000 in 1884 to nearly 3,000,000 stems in 1889, and by 1900 had grown to 8,000,000 stems.[33] The banana had, up to the 1870s, at least, been grown mainly by the peasantry but during the 1880s bananas became an estate crop. The banana is, of course, convenient for small-scale cultivators as well, since it can be conveniently grown with other crops in a pattern of mixed cultivation, with coffee and cacao for example, which it amply shades. It also provided small farmers with a cash income. The banana, unlike coffee or cacao which take several years to reach maturity, is ready for reaping between nine and twelve months after planting.

By 1900 plantation bananas accounted for 74 per cent of land under banana cultivation.[34] The export value of bananas rose from £32,895 in 1879 to £603,480 in 1900. By 1890 bananas had outstripped sugar as Jamaica's major export. In 1900 bananas contributed 25.6 per cent compared to sugar's 10.8 per cent of exports.[35]

The emergence of the banana industry, was, in a sense, the revival of the parishes of Portland and St Mary which had gone out of sugar production. St Catherine, St Andrew and St Thomas produced bananas as well. In the western districts of the island sugar continued to predominate. Manchester and St Elizabeth perhaps predominated in mixed cultivation.

Coffee, a crop cultivated by large proprietors and small settlers experienced severe fluctuations in price during the nineteenth century. Between 1870 and 1900, however, coffee prices stood at an average 85/- per cwt.[36] A large quantity of coffee was produced by small settlers, but in the late-nineteenth century there was an increase in large units of coffee production, mainly in the parish of St Thomas.

The major consequence of the presence of the US market was that it made possible the maintenance and expansion of commercial agriculture. The traditional sugar planters held their own in western Jamaica and in parts of Clarendon, while new entrepreneurs, emerging at first from the mercantile sector and professional groups, directed their energies to the banana industry in the parishes of St Mary, Portland and St Thomas. In short, the economic crisis of the late-nineteenth century did not lead to the complete economic collapse of plantation Jamaica, or of the plantocracy.

One of the important consequences of emancipation in 1838 had been the growth of small-farmer communities in the island. Small farmers, producing goods for subsistence, for the local and international market, had grown in number. But their access to land was limited partly by the preference of planters and government to sell land in large units. Limited access to land ownership was underlined with the emergence of banana plantations in Jamaica. Tenancies became more precarious. In addition, small farmers were adversely affected by the sugar crisis which reduced the ability of wage-starved sugar labourers to consume their goods. In spite of the growth of the small-farmer complex in Jamaica, the farmers were to a considerable extent still dependent on the plantations for temporary or permanent wage labour in several districts. Small farmers were, after all, still in need of a cash income.

Between the traditional planter segment and the new entrepreneurs (the banana producers especially) there was one thing in common. They shared most of the island's resources between them, so that land resources continued to be dominated by a small elite. This elite included non-whites.

In summary, the Jamaican planter class continued to be substantial landowners, exporters, and employers of labour. In the western parishes, especially, their sway over landownership was unchallenged. Even if it is conceded that their material resources were reduced by the trade crisis their relative power remained undiminished. Their political power was restrained by the structure of Crown Colony government since 1866, and even after 1884, but it is a bit romantic to assume that Governor Henry Blake who regarded Jamaican blacks as 'ignorant' and backward was serious about an 'agrarian democracy' in Jamaica.[37] No one seriously envisaged a shift in political or economic power from planter to peasant or black masses. And, at that time, the social authority of whites remained as intact as their domination of land resources. As Juan Bosch has noted, 'in any human collectivity social authority is in the final analysis stronger than authority of the political sort'.[38]

Emancipation and the exodus from the plantations by the ex-slaves, and the latter's seeming independence of the plantations did appear to have 'jeopardised the accepted, and to the whites, acceptable, social distinctions between various groups of men'.[39] This concern was not allowed to become reality. The asset of slave society to the whites had been the ability to 'disguise social class differences by emphasising racial caste differences'.[40] This asset continued to be used in the late-nineteenth century. White hegemony was sustained by the constitutional order as well.

Economic change at the end of the nineteenth century did not alter, but rather reinforced the structure of plantation Creole society. White hegemony was assured by relative wealth, by the political and constitutional order, and by that special authority which had been associated with skin colour in a multi-ethnic community dominated by one segment. The experience of the late-nineteenth century demonstrated that the plantation ethos had not died.

Notes

1 CO, 318/292, 1898, Vol. 2. 'Consumption of Sugar in the United Kingdom'.
2 Paul L. Vogt, *The Sugar Refining Industry in the United States: Its Development and Present Condition*, Philadelphia, 1908, p. 2.
3 United States Department of Agriculture (Pamphlet), 17 January, 1898, Doc. No. 63. Quoted in CO, 318/292, 1898, Vol. 2.
4 R.W. Beachey, *The British West Indies Sugar Industry in the late-Nineteenth Century*, Oxford: Basil Blackwell, 1957, p. 58.
5 *Ibid*, p. 59.
6 US Department of Agriculture, Doc. No. 63, January 1898.
7 Veront Satchell, 'Rural Land Transactions in Jamaica, 1866–1900'. M.Phil., History, UWI Mona, 1986, p. 73.
8 *Ibid*. p. 77. Table 3.4, 'Contribution of Major Staples to Total Agricultural Export, Jamaica 1870–1900 (% Value)'.
9 *Ibid*., p. 82. Table 3.5, 'Number of Sugar Estates Abandoned in Jamaica 1867–1900'.
10 William E. Gordon, 'Imperial Policy Decisions in the Economic History of Jamaica, 1664–1934', *Social and Economic Studies*, Vol. 6, No. 1, March 1957, p. 13.
11 CO, 137/544, 1890, Vol. 3. Blake to Knutsford, 15 December, 1890, No. 101. Colonial Office Minute, 17 January, 1891.
12 Glenn Porter and Harold Livesay, *Merchants and Manufacturers: Studies in the Changing Structure of Nineteenth Century Marketing*, Baltimore: Johns Hopkins University Press, 1971, p. 155.
13 William P. Glade, *The Latin American Economies: A Study of their Institutional Evolution*, Van Nostrand, 1969, p. 211.
14 *Jamaica Times*, 27 July, 1912.
15 CO, 137/544, 1890, Vol. 3, 19 January, 1890.
16 Department of State, T–31 Vol. 37. Louis Dent to Department of State No. 255, 13 May, 1899.
17 CO, 137/544, 1890, Vol. 3. Colonial Office Minute (Anderson), 19 January, 1890.
18 CO, 137/528, 1886, Vol. 4. Norman to Granville, No. 367, October 1886.
19 CO, 137/544, 1890. Blake (Confidential) to Knutsford 15 December, 1890. Colonial Office Minute, Mr Harris. See also George Baden Powell, *The Times*, London, 1 October and 2 October, 1884.
20 *Ibid*. Minute by Mr Harris.
21 William Gordon, 'Imperial Policy Decisions'. pp. 18–19.
22 Veront Satchell, 'Land Transactions'. p. 76. Table 3.3: Agricultural Output: Jamaica 1866–1900.
23 *JBB*, 1904, p. 239, 'Value and Quantity of Logwood ... exported during the ten years 1894–1903'.

24 Satchell, 'Land Transactions', p. 76. Table 3.3.
25 *JBB*, 1904, p. 237 'Value and Quantity of Pimento ... Exported during ten years, 1894–1903'.
26 *DG*, 4 April, 1896. Albert DaCosta to Editor.
27 Department of State, T–31 Roll 28. Dispatches from US Consuls in Kingston, 1726–1906. Enclosure to No. 173, Hoskinson 12 October, 1878. 'Third Annual Report on the Trade, Navigation, Production and Economic Condition of This Island'.
28 Frank Cundall, *Jamaica in 1912*, Kingston, 1912, p. 123.
29 Sir Anthony Musgrave, 'Jamaica: Now and Fifteen Years Since'. A paper read before the Royal Colonial Institute on 20 April, 1880; NLJ: *Jamaica Pamphlets*, No. 9, p. 25.
30 Cundall, *Jamaica in 1912*, pp. 122–3; and Sir Henry Blake, 'Opportunities for young men in Jamaica', 1892.
31 *JCM* 1894, Appendix 15, 'Return of all sugar estates, pens and other properties of 1,000 acres and upwards in each parish showing name, description of the property; names of proprietors and whether resident or absentee. Number of acres of each property.' Presented to Council at request of Rev. Henry Clarke, p. 37.
32 *Ibid.*
33 Satchell 'Land Transactions'. Table 3.10, p. 97. 'Quantities and Values of Banana Exports: Jamaica 1872–1900'.
34 *Ibid.* p. 96.
35 *Ibid.* p. 77, Table 3.4.
36 *Ibid.* p. 88.
37 Arthur E. Burt, 'Genesis of an Agrarian Democracy under a Colonial Governor in Jamaica, 1888–98', in *Journal of Ethnic Studies*, Vol. VIII, No. 1, November 1979.
38 Juan Bosch, *Composición Social Dominicana: Historia e Interpretación*, Santo Domingo: Alfa y Omega, 1983, p. 133.
39 Franklin Knight, *The Caribbean: Genesis of a Fragmented Nationalism*, New York: Oxford University Press, 1978, pp. 131–32.
40 *Ibid.* pp. 131–32.

CHAPTER 2 | Crown Colony government

Crown Colony government was introduced into Jamaica in 1866 following the Morant Bay Rebellion of the previous year. A Legislative Council consisting of the Governor, nominees of the Governor and ex-officio members, replaced the old Assembly which had been for a long time the political instrument of the planter class and its allies. And so, elections on a limited franchise gave way after 1866 to the nominating and veto powers of the Governor, who was, as usual, appointed by the Crown.

In some respects, the 1866 constitution had given to the oligarchs what they wanted – a strong government capable, they thought, of maintaining white rule. Crown Colony government, therefore, had strong support, especially among those who continued to fear that a Morant Bay type rebellion was always in danger of repeating itself elsewhere. The drastic action of Governor Eyre in 1865 against the black population continued to enjoy the approval of Jamaica's elite. Indeed, in 1903, thirty-eight years after Morant Bay, one citizen was calling for the erection of a statue to honour Governor Eyre and his heroic act of salvation at Morant Bay.[1] Since, also, Crown Colony government promised to be a benevolent paternalism it attracted support from segments of the black population, against whom, ironically, the whole constitutional manoeuvre had been directed.

From the perspective of the Crown the new form of government would be both efficient and impartial. It would presumably provide the buffer between contending factions, classes and interests. It would also, presumably, be able to remove the most blatant causes of distress among the masses while protecting and advancing the interest of the oligarchy. The arrangements made in 1866 would in the long term provide the basis for 're-sponsible' government:

> The claim that it would provide impartial government and protect the interests of the poor and ignorant, can be stated as a promise to bring the society into equilibrium. Then, when the contending classes were in equipoise Crown Colony government would come to an end. During the time that the poor were being developed and the rich restrained, the whole society would have learned the style of responsible politics appropriate to a free society.[2]

Another attraction of Crown Colony government was that while it reduced the constitutional power of the oligarchy, it posed no threat to their social power and authority, their economic power, or their domination of land resources. Thus, 'the theory of the constitution asserted autocracy. The practice of politics assumed an oligarchy'.[3] As propertied men the oligarchs surrounded the imported administrators. There was a reinforcement of racial prejudices inherent in the society, 'by restoring whiteness as a necessary qualification for jobs at the top of the administration'.[4]

Yet, by the end of the Sir John Peter Grant regime (1866–74) there was muted protest against Crown Colony rule. The truth is that the 1866 constitution had effectively disfranchised blacks and browns without offering to whites hegemonic power in the colony. The oligarchy were not convinced that Crown Colony rule especially favoured their interests. One criticism of Crown Colony government was that it was expensive and imposed heavy tax burdens on agriculture and commerce. A second was that tax revenue was used for the benefit of those who paid least. The third criticism was that Crown Colony government was autocratic. A fourth criticism was that the government bought supplies directly from overseas rather than from local merchants. Fifthly, the expanded colonial bureaucracy deprived Jamaicans of experience in administration.

The first two charges are essentially false, because the heaviest tax burdens fell not on the oligarchy but on the mass of Jamaicans whether through land taxes, house taxes, or taxes on food consumed by the labouring classes.[5] A high proportion of the limited tax paid by planters into general revenue was redirected into funding East Indian immigration. Absentee planters also escaped most taxes except for local, parochial dues. Tax revenues were also pumped into costly projects such as the Rio Cobre irrigation scheme, designed to assist commercial agriculture. Revenues were also directed into the formation of a para-military police force. The third criticism is accurate only for the rule of Sir John Peter Grant who initiated Crown Colony rule in Jamaica.[6] The fourth criticism was clearly based on sectional interests. The fifth charge was undoubtedly true. Indeed, Crown Colony administration very self-consciously, and without conscience, showed marked preference for bureaucrats imported from England. The British bureaucracy was truly the mechanism through which Jamaica paid its tribute to the empire, by way of salaries and positions.

It was the question of the extent to which Jamaica was to share the cost of imperial defence which put the revision of the 1866 constitution at the top of the political agenda. In 1882 the detention of the ship, *The Florence*, by the imperial authorities in Jamaica led to legal action which resulted in the imposition of damages and costs upon Jamaica. The Colonial Office insisted that Jamaica pay a part of the expenses arising from the episode since the incident occurred in Jamaican waters.[7]

The Jamaican opposition argued that the act of seizing *The Florence* 'was done in furtherance of the foreign policy of the Imperial government, in supposed assertion of the neutrality laws. And the principle contended for . . . is that the costs of proceedings under such circumstances are properly payable by the Imperial government and cannot justly or reasonably be charged upon the Colonial revenues'.[8] The demand note of the Colonial Office reaffirmed the conviction of the reformers that the colony was being sacrificed on the altar of metropolitan self-interest. The *Florence* incident created the opportunity to agitate for greater involvement in government by Jamaicans.

Yet for all its noisiness, the island-wide agitation for constitutional change lacked social depth, because it could seek nothing more than a greater involvement of a minority towards greater autonomy. The reformers and critics of the 1866 constitution were agitating not for political independence, but rather for representation and involvement in the local decision-making process. There was no one so foolish as not to recognise that the current social and racial order rested in the naval and military power of Britain. The franchise could not be broadened to encourage extensive black and coloured participation in government, since to do so would be to initiate the surrender of constitutional power to blacks and coloureds. That was not on the agenda.

Underlying political-constitutional thinking in 1883–4 was the concern about how more power could be vested in the oligarchy without restoring the pre-1866 status quo; and how to adjust the franchise without generally enfranchising the black population. It is true that the social and racial cleavages of Jamaican society had a direct impact on the constitutional order. Yet, also, at the Colonial Office, there was an effort to adapt Crown Colony government to meet local needs as far as those were compatible with imperial interests.[9]

The political agitation continued for nearly two years, after which an Order in Council in 1884 finally carved out the new order. The Legislative Council would consist of the Governor, four ex-officio members, and two nominated members. There were to be nine *elected* members, any six of whom could veto financial proposals. Thus, in theory, the elected members by voting together could exercise some influence over financial matters. However, the Order in Council provided that in exceptional situations the Governor could increase the official side of the house by nominating three additional officials, and he could exercise veto powers by declaring a matter to be of 'paramount' importance. For the period 1884–95 neither Sir Henry Norman nor Sir Henry Blake ever exercised this power, and certainly under Norman's administration the assumption was that the elected members would not behave as an opposition.

The modification of Crown Colony government was therefore cautious. The constitutional changes of 1884 did not alter the structure of government by way of reducing the power of the Crown. Rather, the constitutional change of that year emerged out of a backward-looking conservative political-constitutional movement which was converted by the Colonial Office into constitutional advance by introducing the electoral principle. This principle allowed oligarchs to be elected rather than nominated, and offered a share in government which was constitutional but not democratic since it vested veto powers in the hands of the expatriate governor.

Caution also dictated the approach to the franchise. All adult males who occupied a house assessed for poor rates, or who paid parochial taxes of not less than £1 per annum, or who paid a minimum of £1 – 10 per annum on taxable property were eligible to be registered voters. In 1886 this meant 7,443 electors in a population of half-a-million; 3,766 blacks out of a black population of 444,186; 98 East Indians out of an East Indian population of 11,016; 1,001 whites out of a population of 15,000; 2,578 coloured out of a mixed race population of 109,946.[10]

It is clear from the evidence that Crown control and the limited franchise were directed towards the principle of social control. A low franchise, it was thought, would increase the risk of 'collision between classes – too much risk of excitement and agitation'.[11] A further response in the British Parliament came through Sergeant Simon:

> It is very desirable that steps should be taken at this juncture by those interested in property and plantations in Jamaica how they speak with regard to the reforms being introduced. If they join the opposition in the Island, they will prevent liberal changes which are being made from having a fair chance and the ultimate result must be a serious collision with the people followed perhaps by *surrender of power to the Negroes.*

The response of the Colonial Office was not to deny the truth of Simon's statement but to indicate that such a statement should not have been made in public:

> It is most undesirable to state publicly that if the new constitution is not allowed a fair trial it can only be altered in the direction of giving the Negroes control over the Legislature.[12]

Those who favoured a high franchise in order to reduce black and coloured participation appear to have outdone themselves in 1884. The decision was taken in late 1885 to amend the franchise to include householders who paid 10/- in direct taxes, and male adults earning a salary of over £50. In August 1887 there were 42,266 voters. The sequel was predictable. In 1893, the facilities to assist illiterate voters to cast their votes were removed, thus effectively disfranchising them. A literacy test was imposed.[13] Governor Blake confided to the Colonial Office that the purpose of Law 39 of 1893 was to deprive the illiterate voter of assistance without which he could not, presumably, record his vote. Blake insisted that the illiterate voter was 'venal' and easily 'led astray'. But in fact his real aim was to reduce the coloured and black men eligible to vote to under 20,000:

> The illiterate voter is not well spoken of. He is said to be venal and easily led astray, though I have received no definition of the latter backsliding. The truth seems to be that many voters who take no interest in elections refuse to devote a day to going to poll, except for a consideration, and the illiterate voter alone supplies the assurance to the candidate or his agent that value has been received for money spent. But if he be eliminated we may find a very attenuated electorate *even though* 20,000 remain on the register.[14]

The combination of the literacy test and hard times, which made it difficult for prospective voters to pay their taxes, effectively reduced the number of registered voters to 16,256 by 1900–1.[15] The narrowing of the franchise in the 1890s was partly a confession, however, that black voters could exercise some influence through the franchise. It was also sometimes bluntly stated that the black vote could be manipulated by 'designing men'.

Not surprisingly, representation in the Legislative Council was dominated by spokesmen of the landed and business interests, which is exactly what Governor Blake and his oligarchical allies desired. 'It will always be necessary', claimed Blake, 'in a mixed community where the Negro population enjoys so wide a franchise that the ultimate power as regards legislation shall remain with the Crown'.[16] For Henry Blake, the black population was 'ignorant' and potentially dangerous. After five years in Jamaica, and a few riots, Henry Blake's thought was perhaps no longer distinct from that of the white oligarchs.

Political liberalism, which in effect meant including the white oligarchy in local decision-making, lost its force during Joseph Chamberlain's tenure at the Colonial Office, starting in 1895.[17] Chamberlain had convinced himself that 'liberal constitutions are not really suited to a black population' and that local government in the West Indies 'means only the rule of a local oligarchy of whites and half-breeds – always incapable and frequently corrupt'.[18] British policy at the end of the nineteenth century did not envisage coloured domination of political administration anywhere in the Empire. There was a clear distinction, for example, between the white colonies (dominions) such as Australia and Canada and the coloured colonies in the Caribbean, India and Africa. However, the fact that Chamberlain reasserted the dominance of the metropolis in the partnership between

Whitehall and the local oligarchy (to the annoyance of the latter) does not disprove the fact that there was a coincidence, if not a linear relationship, between the social structure of empire and that of the remote island colony of Jamaica. Both realities assumed white hegemony.

Chamberlain abolished the financial veto of the elected members and reasserted the Crown's right, implicit in the 1884 Derby constitution, to appoint the full number of nominated members, thereby moderating Derby's 'moderate step in advance'. If the Chamberlain period was marked by an increase in Crown power, or by a greater sense of imperial trusteeship, it was also marked by unapologetic demands that Jamaica pay its way in the Empire. In March 1898 he recommended to Governor Hemming that, 'Notwithstanding the immediate financial difficulties of the Colony' an 'increase in the militia vote should be urged on the Legislative Council'. He also made it abundantly clear that the imperial government expected Jamaica to pay its share of the expense of imperial defence.

> I am to add that having regard to the fact pointed out by the Colonial Defence Committee that Jamaica contributes towards her defence a much smaller sum in proportion to revenue than do the other West Indian islands it is difficult to imagine that inhabitants of so loyal a colony will continue to be backward in accepting their share of the financial responsibilities of local defence; they will no doubt have in mind that on the imperial government falls not only the expenses of maintaining the local garrison of imperial troops, but also the entire cost of the Navy, on the supremacy of which the safety of Jamaica in common with that of all other parts of the Empire ultimately rests.[19]

Chamberlain's modifications after 1895 amounted to a right incline, rather than a right about turn. Firstly, the oligarchy did continue to have a voice in government; and secondly, blacks continued to be excluded from government. Even if the attitudes of the Colonial Office were influenced by the belief that liberal constitutions were not suitable for coloured tropical colonies, yet in Jamaica there had never been a liberal constitution which would truly have put to the test the belief that blacks were incapable of conducting themselves like keen British Parliamentarians. Thirdly, the objectives of 1866 whereby the Crown would act paternalistically on behalf of the 'unrepresented classes' were reasserted by Chamberlain. Crown paternalism was also present in the 1866 and 1884 arrangements. Fourthly, the function of Crown Colony government, or at least one of its main functions, was to ensure social stability and to maintain imperial interests in Jamaica. This social stability was in theory to be assured by a structure of government which enabled the Colonial Office to balance contending interests in the island, to permit flexibility in resolving social and other issues, and to employ the tools of co-optation.

Crown Colony government even appeared contradictory in its policies. It discouraged Jamaican emigration to Panama and Central America (in the interests of planters and their labour supplies), but never absolutely prohibited it (out of its obligations to the 'subject people'). It enforced the laws against squatters but in the 1890s provided marginal land to rural farmers. For agrarian reform, such as it was, was brought about not because the Crown wished to alter the balance of class relationships but rather to maintain the essence of those relationships by making land concessions. In accordance with developments in Britain itself, it endorsed mass education but left it mainly to the Churches and private individuals to provide buildings and teachers. The Colonial Office had extremely strong reservations about the agreement between Jamaica and the West India Improvement Company concerning the construction of the railroad extensions to the north coast; and even identified serious conflicts of interest. Yet, it bowed to the pressure from the local oligarchy. The Crown's reservations were, as it turned out, justified when the Company went bankrupt and Jamaica was faced with huge debt.[20]

Crown Colony administration was always sensitive to the possibility of racial conflict though the Colonial Office was somewhat sceptical about the theory of Jamaica as a land of combustible blacks. Jamaicans dealt with the possibility of racial conflict by declaring that Jamaica had no racial problem, and that, officially, no distinctions were to be made between Her Majesty's subjects on grounds of colour. Since, also, the objective overall was to keep power out of the hands of the coloured sector – brown and black – the rising economic power of those groups had to be accommodated, but every possible obstacle had to be placed in the way of constitutional and political equality. The constitution in theory and practice had of necessity to be congruent with the inegalitarian social structure of Jamaica. The reduction of inequalities would have produced, it was believed, the same result as voluntarily handing power over to blacks. Hence imperial paternalism suited blacks better in the short term than political liberalism which was weighted in favour of local white hegemony.

Plantation Creole society had demonstrated that however strong the links to the metropolis that the internal structures of a colony possess that colonies have 'a logic of their own which cannot be reduced to their external ties to the Atlantic trade and the political Metropolis'.[21] Yet it is also true that Jamaica's experience in the late-nineteenth century is inseparable from its membership in the British Empire. The concept of nation was yet young, or at least retarded by the racially based class structure. The concept of empire was far stronger than nation.

It was the concept of empire which bridged the gap between the races and classes in Jamaica. British civilisation, pride in empire and in monarchy were driven home with mammoth demonstrations in honour of Queen Victoria's Golden Jubilee in 1887 and Diamond Jubilee in 1897. Balls, church services, addresses of loyalty to Victoria, pride in imperial affiliation, and spectacular fireworks, much of it paid for out of local resources, (private and public), a holiday for Queen Victoria (1902) were aimed to produce, in Jamaicans, an unshakable loyalty to empire, and an appreciation of imperial benevolence.

Jamaican and West Indian migrants to Santo Domingo's sugar plantations in their plea for consular representation in 1884 ended their petition with a prayer for the Queen; a British consular officer in Costa Rica insisted that he had controlled the mercurial conduct of Jamaican migrants by appealing to them as responsible subjects of the British Empire. The attitude of workers in the Panama Canal Zone, Costa Rica, Santo Domingo and Cuba, suggest that there was a devotion to empire which swept down to the masses of the population.

The Great Exhibition of 1891, while not a royal occasion as such, was opened by the Prince of Wales, and was intended in the minds of the Colonial Governor and his colleagues to foster a spirit of empire. The immediate aim of the Exhibition was to promote Jamaica's foreign trade. However, according to Blake's boast, it was fully supported by all classes and proved that the 'old' antagonisms of Jamaican society were no hindrance to the country's bright future, as all races and colours were united in their sentiment of respect and love of empire. For the rural black Jamaican it was Queen Victoria who had freed them; for middle and upper-class Jamaicans it was monarchy, armed with fleets and forts, which protected them from the people whom Victoria had 'freed'. The glitter of empire had a broad appeal and served, just as Crown Colony government did, to reinforce a continued belief in white leadership.

Crown Colony government enjoyed great legitimacy, partly because there was no alternative in sight. Perhaps Rev. Carey Berry summarised the views of other whites when he suggested that whites were not opposed to self-government as such. Rather, they feared that self-government would 'make it too hot for any white people to remain here'.[22] For a Mr Joyce, in a prize-winning essay published in the *Daily Gleaner*, Crown Colony government was relatively impartial whatever its defects. A self-governing Jamaica would be 'another Haiti'.[23] A return to 1866 was undesirable, a moderate step from 1884 would give power to blacks. Had not J.A. Froude pointed out the ridiculous spectacle of a black parliament?

It was not purely coincidence that most statements made in favour of self-government came from certain black spokesmen. Mr J.H. Reid, an educated black and frequent contributor to the *Jamaica Advocate* (the only newspaper to articulate a 'black position') called Crown Colony government a 'hired government'. Since national life, argued Reid, was the aggregate expression of the moral and intellectual forces of the community 'a hired government could not promote national sentiment'. Crown Colony government was one in which 'much of the legislation . . . was in diametrical opposition to the best interests of the majority of the population, in spite of the skill displayed in the arrangement of the words of which the laws are made'. Jamaicans, in Reid's opinion, were not being afforded the opportunity to practise the arts of citizenship. Also, the coercive system of slavery had been succeeded by the 'craft' which was in operation, with the 'same end in view, viz to keep the spirit of serfdom in the breast of the Negro'.[24] For Robert Love, editor of the *Jamaica Advocate*, Crown Colony government ignored the 'idea of mutual obligation, as between governors and governed'.[25]

In his study of Crown Colony politics in Jamaica, Arthur Burt suggested that race was not a factor in elections. Insofar as race was not made an issue in elections, this analysis is correct.[26] But in reality the thinking of the oligarchy and of the Colonial Office (exaggeratedly so under Chamberlain) saw race as crucial, insofar as it was thought that at all costs blacks and coloureds were to have only a rigidly circumscribed participation in government. The structure of Jamaican politics made it possible and necessary for white candidates to articulate some of the interests of blacks within the oligarchical framework, made possible by the reality that oligarchical representatives were sensitive to those issues which could influence black voters on their behalf. One such issue was education. Insofar as members of the black middle class gave political support to whites and conversely did not support black candidates by virtue of their blackness one might conclude that there were no black politics as such.[27] Yet the vigorous efforts of Dr Robert Love, the editor of the *Jamaica Advocate*, demonstrate not only the articulation of a 'black' position, but that it is misleading to assume that blacks were apathetic. Robert Love and his supporters threw their weight behind white candidates who supported black issues. Brown politicians such as R.H. Jackson adopted populist positions. But then, the 'black' position was influenced both by ethnicity and by class position. To the extent that some black politicians tended to see black progress as identical with the manipulation of British culture there was no substantial difference between them and liberal elements within the white segment of the population. But it would be untrue to suggest that spokesmen for the black population did not attempt to identify specific black interests.

Despite the limitations of Crown Colony government and the concern that the current Jamaican leadership did not have the 'largeness of view' necessary for the comprehension of a national as opposed to a class interest, it is true that even among the white sector Crown Colony government was seen as a transitional period during which blacks would be prepared to inherit the political kingdom.

The gentle fluctuations in Crown Colony rule affected the political relationship between Jamaica and Britain more than the political, social, economic relationships between classes and races. Those relationships were confirmed in the structure of the law. They were mirrored in a positivist/ social Darwinist ideology which rationalised the status quo. They were present, as well, in the structure of marriage, family and sexual relations, in the nature of social welfare institutions, in the use of leisure, and in the system of education. To these we now turn.

Notes

1 NLJ, MST 59, *Livingstone Collection*, Vol. 1, 1898–1903; H.P. Deans to Editor, *Daily Gleaner*.
2 Roy Augier, 'Before and After 1865', New *World Quarterly*, Crop Time, Vol. 2, No. 2, 1966, pp. 38–9.
3 *Ibid*. p. 33 and pp. 37–8.
4 *Ibid*. pp. 38–9.
5 *Ibid*. pp. 33–4. The question of taxes was often at the centre of political argument in Jamaica. While the ruling oligarchy were quick to condemn any new imposition, and complained of old ones, the reality is that the heaviest burden of taxation fell on the labouring classes. There was a land tax, for example, in which the small holder paid at the rate of two shillings per acre, while the large landowner paid at a farthing per acre, or if over 1500 acres, nothing at all. Absentee proprietors escaped most taxes, except for parochial dues. It was calculated in 1896, that of the £11,635 contributed in tax revenue by large proprietors, some £9,251 was taken to subsidise East Indian immigration. Also, a large sum was dedicated to repay old immigration loans. (See *Jamaica Advocate*, 28 March, 1896) Most of the revenue for poor relief came from a house tax much of which came from the poorer segments of the community. Governor Norman admitted that it was an 'inequitable and oppressive' arrangement, but that there was no alternative.
6 Ronald Sires, 'The Jamaican Constitution of 1884', in *Social and Economic Studies*, Vol. 3, No. 1, June 1954, pp. 67–8.
7 H.A. Will, *Constitutional Change in the British West Indies, 1880–1903*, Oxford, 1970, pp. 16–45.
8 CO, 137/512 XCA 012705. 'Speeches delivered by A. Lindo at a Public Meeting held in Falmouth on 17 October 1882, and a letter addressed by him to the Editor of the Trelawny and Public Advertiser', Jamaica: *Trelawny and Public Advertiser*, 1882, p. 2.
9 H.A. Will, C*onstitutional Change*, p. 45.
10 *Ibid*. p. 64.
11 *Ibid*. p. 52, quoting Mr Ashley's speech in the House of Commons, 25 April, 1884.
12 CO, 137/519, 1884. Public and Miscellaneous Offices and Individuals, 19 February, 1884. Extract from Mr Sergeant Simon's speech in the House of Commons and Minute of RWH, 20 February, 1884.
13 H.A. Will, *Constitutional Change*, p. 64.
14 Jamaica Archives, 1B/5/18, Vol. 47. Blake to Ripon No. 197, 16 May, 1893.

15 H.A. Will, *Constitutional Change*, pp. 62–3.
16 Jamaica Archives, 1B/5/18, Vol. 47. Blake to Ripon, No. 74, 13 March, 1894.
17 H.A. Will, *Constitutional Change*, p. 253.
18 *Ibid.* p. 232.
19 Jamaica Archives, 1B 5/8/31. Chamberlain to Blake, 5 March, 1898.
20 CO, 137/537. CO Minute 25302, 22 December, 1888 and Report of Crown agents to CO, 5 January, 1888.
21 Magnus Morner, 'Economic Factors and Stratification in Colonial Spanish America with Special Regard to Elites', *Hispanic American Historical Review*, Vol. 63, No. 2, May 1983, p. 340.
22 *JA*, Rev. Carey B. Berry to Editor, 17 August, 1895.
23 *DG*, 24 December, 1903. Essay competition. 'The Best Form of Government for Jamaica'. The winning essays, those of Mr M.F. Johns (a schoolmaster) and Mr M.A. Joyce, were published in full by the *Daily Gleaner*.
24 J.H. Reid, 'The Negro Slave' in *JA*, 25 May, 1895.
25 *JA*, 8 August, 1896. Editorial, 'Some of the Functions of a Government'.
26 Arthur Burt, 'The Development of Self-Government in Jamaica, 1884–1913', Ph. D. (Toronto) 1960.
27 In the 1889 elections the white planter and merchant, Col. Ward, was strongly supported by Mr Matthew Josephs, Mr Smickle, both relatively well known black teachers. His opponent was Richard Hill Jackson (a coloured politician) whose platform was radical enough to encourage the *Gleaner* to accuse him of 'setting class against class' and of 'attempting disintegration instead of promoting harmony'. *DG*, 13 March, 1889.

CHAPTER 3 | Law and order

Since one of the major concerns of Crown Colony government was the maintenance of order rather than the correction of social injustices, it followed that the law and its operation were central as a guide to existing class relations. The law may be used, in an ideal sense, to protect the weak, but it was the intimidatory aspect of the law which stood out most sharply in an ethnically divided society. With the legal abolition of slavery in 1834, the law and the system of justice became more essential as a mechanism for controlling 'combustible' blacks.

It is true that the ex-slave plantation colony of Jamaica became the recipient of district courts (abolished in the 1880s), magistrates courts, and the jury system. Yet, the ends of justice (which admittedly are not coterminous with law) could be frustrated by having oligarchs or their representatives sit in judgement over those who had, allegedly, offended them.

Black spokesmen were sometimes wary of official and semi-official propaganda which claimed an Olympian impartiality for the system of justice. Robert Love frequently referred to 'class legislation', while J.H. Reid observed that colonial legislation was 'in diametrical opposition to the best interests of the majority of the population, in spite of the skill displayed in the arrangement of the words of which the laws are made. The venom is in the operation of the laws'.[1]

One cannot sustain the commonly held view that Jamaica was a peaceful colony at the end of the nineteenth century. That view is misleading because it gives the impression that there was a passive submission to the legal institutions of the colonial state. It is also misleading because it ignores the enhancement of levels of state violence directed specifically against the black population, which was regarded as genetically 'combustible'.

Apart from the general question of violence there was the question of the perception of law, not as a regulatory mechanism but as a punitive and vindictive instrument. This view of the law was not confined to the oligarchy. In 1897 J.H. Reid, in one of his interpretive articles published in the *Jamaica Advocate*, observed that Jamaica could be more aptly described as law-loving rather than law abiding:

When inquiry is directed towards the discovery of the reason for this love of law, it will be found that it is the evil, and not the good, in the law that has won for it such a degree of attachment from the people. The benefits to be derived from the operation of the law seem to receive little less consideration than the advantages that may be received from its power . . . It is the *vindictive* and *punitive* character of the law that recommends it to the admiration of the people . . . The primary consideration in the various business transactions between individuals seems to be, not what is honest, fair and right, but rather what is legal – that is how far the more astute may go in his attempts to overreach, or the powerful in oppressing, his neighbours, without bringing himself under the penalties of the law.[2]

Reports often indicate the litigiousness of the Jamaican peasantry. If J.H. Reid is correct, then we have before us a supreme example of socialisation among people who associated law with vindictiveness and with punishment, not with justice.

The Morant Bay Rebellion of 1865 had demonstrated that old patterns of coercion would be inadequate to maintain law and order, which was defined after Morant Bay to mean keeping blacks in control. The Jamaica Constabulary which came into existence in 1867 was, therefore, paramilitary in its use of drill, arms, occupation of barracks and forms of discipline.[3] The dispersal of Jamaica's population over the interior of the island created a demand, not only for a centralised police force, but for a supplementary Rural Police which was especially established 'for the purpose of connecting the main police system with the remote recesses of the island'.[4] The Rural Police Force, which was under the supervision and control of Officers of the Constabulary, was empowered to search, without warrant, any person suspected to be in possession of stolen goods.

If disorder is examined in relation to crimes of violence such as murder and manslaughter, then Jamaica was probably less violent than other colonies in the Caribbean.[5] Most manslaughter cases were associated with jealousy, as were attempts at murder and poisoning, use of acid by jealous women, and arson.[6] The most common act of violence was cutting and wounding, using the all-purpose machete. Cutting and wounding declined from 835 cases in 1896 to 508 in 1905–6, with a record low of 338 cases in 1901. Assaults occasioning bodily harm fluctuated between 50 and 70 convictions between 1896 and 1905. Cutting and wounding was as popular an offence among women as among men.[7] Evidently, as long as blacks directed violent tendencies against each other rather than against the state or against whites the colonial authorities could afford to bask in sunny complacency.

The police were kept busiest imposing some restraint on the violent, exuberant and obscene language of the Jamaican people. Perhaps because of more rigorous prosecution by the police and greater care taken by citizens to watch their language when within ear-shot of a constable the prosecuted offences showed a marked decline from 4,247 in 1893 to 3,585 in 1896–7 and to 2,660 in 1905–6. (We could also conclude that the police showed less inclination to prosecute for that offence). Abusive and indecent language merged easily with disorderly conduct. The latter offence remained at an average of 4,000 per year between 1893 and 1905. Police reports generally credit the island's 'tranquility' to the relative absence of drunkenness among the labouring classes, compared, at least, to England.[8]

Praedial larceny

The law showed itself at its most intimidatory with respect to the problem of praedial larceny, viewed by the leaders of the community as a major obstacle to production in the countryside. The structure of landownership in the countryside whereby farmers did not always own or cultivate contiguous plots of land, or owned plots which were distant from their place of residence, facilitated praedial larceny. Since the cost of going to court was often not worth the price for a busy small farmer it is probable that there were more cases of praedial larceny than the court records suggest.

Gisela Eisner, however, rightly demonstrates considerable scepticism with respect to the supposed seriousness of praedial larceny. She notes that in 1905 'the average value assigned to the stolen property in 2,349 cases brought into court amounted to only 1.03s.[9] Some contemporary observers were equally sceptical. A Baptist minister, offering evidence to the 1897 Royal Commission, observed that the problem was not as serious as the complainers suggested, citing the large acreages of canes, bananas and coconuts left unprotected in all parts of the island, and yet rarely touched by the poor.[10]

Praedial larceny was sometimes attributed to ignorance, sometimes to hunger, but it is naïve to assume that people stole only to supply immediate nourishment. Supporters of the hunger thesis point to the decline of praedial larceny when crops were good, and the rise of praedial larceny during periods of severe drought.[11] Yet some evidence points to the marketability of stolen produce as a major incentive to praedial larceny, including citrus, logwood and pimento, all export commodities. As a planter, Mr Gossett emphasised, his grapefruits were never touched until a market for them appeared in the United States.[12]

In 1886 Justice Gibbons exposed the relationship between logwood stealing and local merchants. According to Gibbons:

> Since I required the production of the wharf books in a case of
> logwood stealing at May Pen, when I was informed by an over-
> seer of Denbeigh, that Lord Penrhyn had been robbed of 60 tons
> [£300] during the then season I have observed that no prosecu-
> tions have been instituted. There is no disguising the fact that Mr
> W.C., the Custos, is a large shipper of logwood . . . I have
> observed a suspicious connection between larceny of produce,
> particularly logwood and pimento, and the business of the mer-
> chant. In one case of larceny of pimento from a small cultivator
> tried before me there was no doubt of the thief having sold the
> stolen pimento to a local buyer who was himself the employer of
> the buyer and the party who ultimately profited by the theft of
> pimento . . . So, too, in several cases of logwood stealing it has
> appeared that the stolen logwood was readily purchased at the
> local wharf belonging in almost every case to a magistrate. These
> facts which have only casually come to my notice are doubtless
> well known to the bulk of the people.[13]

Yet praedial larceny was consistently regarded as an offence typically
committed by members of the working classes, and was treated in law as
such. Thus Act 32 of 1889 disallowed causal roadside buying and selling of
produce, though instead of fulfilling its purpose, it 'tended to restrict legitimate trade'.[14] Law 37 of 1896 (the Produce Protection Law) tried to check
the offence from the receiving end.

Praedial larceny continued to be regarded as a typically black perver-
sion although the structural problems of the countryside and what one
observer called the 'rotten and unscientific state of the relations between
labour and capital',[15] lay at the root of the problem.

The punishment for praedial larceny was flogging. In 1886 the Attorney General observed that the temporary abolition of flogging for praedial
larceny had not led to an increase in the offence.[16] In spite of the bureaucrat's
observation which implied that flogging was not a deterrent to praedial
larceny flogging was the punishment most consistently applied right up to
the end of the nineteenth century, with obvious approval. In 1896, Mr R.B.
Braham, a member of the Legislative Council and a wealthy banana producer and shopkeeper, pronounced with fiery conviction, 'Flog the Negro';
that is the only thing they are afraid of . . . '.[17] In 1896, a boy was given
twelve lashes for stealing one orange. Adults were beaten with the cat-o'-
nine-tails designed to produce serious laceration of the skin. Flogging was
an important method of intimidating and terrorising the black population
into obedience.

Legislation which proposed the continuation of flogging for praedial larceny provoked an extremely angry retort from Robert Love in 1896. The basis of Love's retort was that flogging was yet another example of class legislation since it was well known that only blacks were likely to be victims of the lash. The principle was also wrong, not only because flogging had proved ineffective in removing the problem of praedial larceny, but because the lash which had been used as an instrument of degradation of the black could not be effectively used to correct that degradation. In a brisk editorial Love declared:

> Whilst a thief who lifts a shop, or robs a bank, may be punished by a few months imprisonment, the poor wretch who steals a 2lb yam, or a stick of logwood, must, besides imprisonment, be lacerated by a cat-'o-nine-tails . . . We hate this law because we are convinced that it was intended to operate on a class only. How many *white* men will be whipped for praedial larceny? Not one. Why? Because the circumstances are such that they are not exposed to the commission of the offence. We hate this law because, while its penalty will brutalise the offender, it will leave him no less an offender . . . By a strange species of reasoning they propose to drive out of us by the lash, the evil which they had driven into us, by the lash, for nearly 300 years.[18]

The formulators of law do not necessarily take their cue from abstract or ideal constructs, but from the social and economic power realities of a society. Since the ethnically divided community of Jamaica operated on the basis of differential access to power and resources on the part of whites and blacks, it followed that the dominant minority used the law to reinforce their social and political authority over blacks. The latter were victims of the twin jeopardies of being black and working class.

Prisons

In 1884 the Inspector of Prisons had declared proudly that 'from the point of view of the English Wardens and that of the convicts themselves, the General Penitentiaries were no "longer a place of refuge"'.[19] Public sympathy is not oriented towards social deviants, and in the Jamaican situation where, inevitably, the majority of prisoners were black, the idea that prisons were designed to punish held sway. Jamaican cynicism was displayed in the architecture of prisons where the cubic footage of cells ranged between 330 and 375 cubic feet. The minimum standard was, in Britain, regarded as 800 cubic feet.[20] Yet, there is no proof that Jamaican prisoners at the time were half the size of Englishmen.

It was the metropolitan concern with prison reform which convinced Jamaicans to turn their attention to the welfare of prisoners. In 1885 the Colonial Office asked for a reconsideration of the dietary regime of prisoners. A school for prisoners at the General Penitentiary was opened in 1885. The concern of the Colonial Office about the absence of education in Jamaican prisons was at least partly addressed in 1886 with the establishment of a library at the General Penitentiary, though the almost universal illiteracy of prisoners limited the use and the utility of the library.

Churchmen, such as Enos Nuttall, were also keen on prison reform, though there may have been greater concern with ministration to the spiritual needs of prisoners than with the material circumstances which destined people born in certain situations to prison. This is not to deny the importance of moral or spiritual regeneration.

The two largest prisons in the colony were the General Penitentiary and St Catherine District Prison, the former located on eleven acres of land within the walls and with a special area marked off for female prisoners. The General Penitentiary was designed to accommodate 580 prisoners, but overcrowding was already evident by the end of the nineteenth century. In 1897 the General Penitentiary was accommodating 22 per cent more prisoners than was intended, and in 1905 and 1906 42 per cent more and 24 per cent more, respectively. Prisoners, often condemned to hard labour, worked on roads, quarries, and in brickmaking. Prison labour went some way towards paying for prisoner upkeep. In 1900, for example, the gross expenditure on the General Penitentiary compared with income was in the proportion of £18,780 to £6,275, leaving a net cost of £12,505.[21]

The Gladstone Report of 1895 in England had placed emphasis on reformation as well as deterrence, and had condemned 'non-productive' labour such as the crank and the treadmill, while recommending greater attention to the individual needs of prisoners and the provision of libraries and communal workshops.[22] Up to 1908, however, Jamaican prisoners were still employed on the treadmill, though they were also engaged in quarrying, burning bricks, breaking stones, and in one or other of the trades.[23] Ironically, the productivity of prison labour was such that the *Daily Gleaner* was moved to editorialise on the question of whether prisoners should be allowed to produce goods and services which could be performed profitably by the hardworking artisans of Jamaica.[24]

Prison discipline was generally regarded as good, with the help of flogging. For women, it was decided that the most effective way to ensure discipline was to crop the hair, since it was thought that nothing alarmed black women more than the fear of having their hair shorn.[25]

Vagrancy

Vagrancy laws are especially important in an urban setting, when employment opportunities are limited. While Eisner sees the truly great movement into Kingston and St Andrew as beginning after 1921,[26] there had been a steady movement into Kingston and St Andrew during the late-nineteenth century. The population of Kingston grew rapidly during the 1880s, as more and more workers migrated to the urban zones in search of employment. The number of domestic servants and self-employed increased.[27] The movement into Kingston was partly influenced by opportunities for employment arising from the expansion of government services (Kingston succeeded Spanish Town as capital of Jamaica in 1872), perhaps by returning immigrants, but generally there was little development in the city to 'correspond to the magnitude of the influx'.[28]

The censuses of 1891 and 1911 report a rise in Kingston's population from 46,542 to 57,379 and for St Andrew (including Half Way Tree and its vicinity) from 9,702 to 23,322.[29] The 1879 Royal Commission reported that migrants into Kingston did not have skills which could be used in the city; there was no constant demand for such services as they could render. Men, women and children of several families occupied the same room; children were neglected and turned into the streets to pick up a living as best they could. There were large numbers of women who were left alone with families of children to support. Wives or concubines deserted by their husbands or paramours, women with children of more casual encounters all formed part of the most depressed layer of Kingston's population.

There was a host of urban occupations, but these were not sufficient to provide occupation for all seekers. There were carpenters, bricklayers and masons, blacksmiths, coachmakers and coachtrimmers, higglers and hucksters and milliners and seamstresses; there were potters and painters, printers, saddlers, sailors and stevedores, merchant seamen, domestic servants, gardeners, wharfingers, store servants; there were tanners and cabinet makers, coopers, and coppersmiths, draymen and druggists, farriers and fishermen, bamboo fibre manufacturers, bakers, butchers, dogcatchers, and goatherders. Not listed in the census for the sake of decency and propriety, but a vibrant class of over 300 women, were the prostitutes, aggressive in the retailing of their wares, contemptuous of the police, and irrepressible. Then there were the gamblers, the vagabonds, pickpockets, hangers-on, beggars, tricksters and pimps and men who, imitating a Spanish accent, passed off as gold bangles cheap brass bangles to gullible customers.[30]

One of the few people to propose solutions for the poverty, overcrowding, unemployment and destitution in Kingston was Enos Nuttall. Unlike other people who suggested that the solution rested in a more rigorous vagrancy law, such as that of the French and Danish West Indies 'which forces people to show they are earning an honest livelihood, and in default treated as criminal, and in some way compelled to labour', Nuttall proposed an educational programme for the benefit of juvenile vagrants, neglected children, and a work/study programme for the young of Kingston. He recommended agro-industry resting on local products (such as ginger and guava) and initiated with the co-operation of government and private enterprise. Nuttall's view was that vagrancy laws should follow, not pre-cede, the creation of job opportunities, and an education which could provide the necessary equipment for productive work.[31]

At the time when Nuttall made his proposals (1897) the Jamaica Legislature was in the mood for retrenchment, and one of the targets for reduction of expenditure was education. Since idleness, like praedial lar-ceny, was viewed as a weakness of the black population, it is not surprising that the colonial state viewed repression rather than reform as the solution to Quashie's inveterate idleness.

The vagrancy laws were tightened during this period, and vagrancy itself was given a broader definition in law. The law included 'idle and disorderly persons as well as rogues and incorrigible rogues'. The new vagrancy law was passed in 1902 just after the Montego Bay riots of that year. The definition of vagrant was broad enough to include all individuals who could not offer a 'proper' account of themselves. It was meant to cover the idle, unemployed, prostitutes and obeahmen. The term vagrant meant all persons who, though able to work did not. Idle and disorderly persons meant:

> every person who shall be found wandering abroad, or placing himself in any public place to beg or gather alms, or causing any child to do so. Every common prostitute who shall be found wandering in any public place and behaving in a riotous or indecent manner, or annoying passers-by soliciting them . . . Every person pretending to use any subtle craft or device by palmistry or any such superstitious means to deceive or impose on any person.[32]

Vagrants and disorderly persons also included those found wandering, lodging in piazzas, outhouses, sheds, mills, trackhouses . . . not having any visible means of subsistence and not giving a satisfactory account of him-self. Under the vagrancy law fell people who exposed obscene books, pictures or prints, in public, or who exposed themselves. Included, also, were persons 'wandering abroad and endeavouring by the exposure of wounds or deformities to obtain alms'.[33]

The vagrancy law was so comprehensive that the healthy who had no employment and the wounded and deformed who could not work and therefore begged for a living, were equally guilty of vagrancy. In practice if not in theory, homelessness was punishable by the vagrancy law.

The vagrancy law provided one of the most able descriptions of depressed urban life. It points to the growth of begging, abandonment of children and spouses, and housebreaking. There were, of course, habitual vagrants. The conduct of some female vagrants suggests a sincere effort on their part to get into rather than stay out of gaol. For example:

1   assaulting an arresting constable,
2   biting a constable *in court,*
3   assaulting another woman while in process of being arrested by the constable,
4   using abusive and indecent language in court, while being tried for indecent language in the first place.

The evolution of the Jamaican economy in the second half of the nineteenth century influenced the way in which the society was policed, since Jamaica became, in economic terms even less of a plantation society, than before. Yet, it was the characteristic approaches and attitudes of the plantation society which dictated the structure of policing and the application of the law. One of the assumptions of the plantation society was that blacks had to be controlled because they were 'combustible' and susceptible to violence. The assumption of the presence of a violent streak in the black personality passed beyond the general concerns of an elite to ensure mass control.

The social authority of whites was to be ensured as far as possible by placing the coercive levers of power in the hands of whites. Following the Cumberland Pen Riots of 1894, Governor Blake even removed coloureds and blacks from the sergeant ranks. The militia had to be captained by whites, even if the footsoldiers were black and coloured. Authority, clothed in white, was represented by white magistrates, some of them imported.

Authority, however, was exercised by means other than the law or armed forces. Just as important was the exercise of ideological controls. Most important in this respect is the function of the Church and Christianity as socialising agents. It is undoubtedly true that the political system, and the forces of coercion and the law, were very important institutions which ensured general domination of society. But, they were not the only ones. Also important was the encouragement of a values consensus, in particular with respect to religion, and through religion, westernisation of culture.

Notes

1 *JA*, 17 April, 1897. J.H. Reid, 'Legality'.

2 *Ibid.*

3 *HBJ*, 1900, p. 199. See also Howard Johnson, 'Social Control and the Colonial State: The Reorganisation of the Police Force in the Bahamas 1888–1893', in *Slavery and Abolition*, Vol. 7, No. 1, May 1986, pp. 46–58. Regrettably this useful article which discusses a similar situation for the Bahamas came to my attention when it was no longer possible to comment on it.

4 *HBJ*, 1902, p. 185. Inspector Knollys acknowledged the importance of avoiding that the police become 'dependants of individuals or parties among local authorities' as had happened in the 'history of the old police force'. *JCM*, Vol. 25, 1888. Police patrols however, were given special duties to visit estates and pens. Rural headmen were to take action to prevent the larceny of rum, etc. In St Thomas there were special night patrols during harvest against sugar and rum larceny from estates. *JCM*, 1887, Appendix XVI.

5 For a brief study of murder in Jamaica, see Michelle Johnson, 'A History of Murder in Jamaica', UWI, Mona, Caribbean Study, 1986.

6 *JCM*, Vol. 25, 1888, Appendix XXXlll. Report of James John Bowrey, Government Analytical Chemist.

7 *JCM*, 1887, Appendix XV. Annual Report of Inspector-General of Police for the year ended 30 August, 1886.

8 *JCM*, Vol. 25, 1888. Report of Inspector-General of Police 23 July, 1887.

9 Gisela Eisner, *Jamaica 1830–1930*, p. 233.

10 *WIRC*, 1897. Evidence of Rev. S.C. Morris (Baptist), 5 April, 1897, p. 334/342.

11 CO, 137/513, Vol. 1, 1884. Enclosure of Attorney General's Report, 7 February, 1884. Also Despatch No. 59, 21 February, 1888 and No. 109, 4 April, 1889 of CO, 137/538.

12 *WIRC*, 1897. Evidence of Mr B.S. Gossett, p. 293/301.

13 CO, 137/518, Enclosure to Norman (No. 469) enclosing Gibbons to Governor Norman, 23 April, 1884.

14 Eisner, *Jamaica*, p. 231.

15 *DG*, 4 April, 1896. Albert DaCosta to Editor.

16 CO, 137/525, No. 49, 22 February, 1886.

17 *JA*, 17 October, 1896. Godfrey Hull to Editor quoting Mr Braham.

18 *JA*, 4 July, 1896. 'The Lash as Education and a Deterrent'.

19 CO, 137/520, 1885. Norman (No. 39) 2 February, 1885, enclosing report of Inspector of Prisons, 28 October, 1884.

20 CO, 137/520, 1885. Norman (No. 39) 4 February, 1885.

21 *HBJ*, 1900, p. 105 and *HBJ*, 1908, p. 186.

22 John Stevenson, *British Society 1914–45*, Harmondsworth: Pelican Books, 1984, p. 376.

23 *HBJ*, 1900, p. 103 and *HBJ*, 1909, p. 185.

24 *DG*, 14 December, 1899.

25 CO, 137/525, 1886. Norman (No. 49) 15 February, 1886, enclosing Report of Director of Prisons, 10 November, 1885.

26 Eisner, *Jamaica*, p. 187.

27 *Ibid.* p. 188.

28 *Ibid.* p. 188.

29   Jamaica Census, 1911, 'Population of Chief Towns, 1891 and 1911'. The indications are that certain districts or communities grew rapidly during this period:

	1891	*1911*
Smith's Village	661	2553
Allman Town	1825	2807
Fletcher's Town	1011	1437
Pasmore Town	723	1919
Hannah Town	829	2074
Brown's Town	766	1429

30   Report of Royal Commission upon the Conditions of the Juvenile Population, 1879. Evidence of Mr Berry.
31   Enos Nuttall, *Some Present Needs of Jamaica*, Kingston, 1897, p. 14.
32   *Laws of Jamaica, 1902–5*. Law 12, 1902, 'A Law to consolidate and amend the Laws relating to Vagrancy, 1902'.
33   *Ibid.*

CHAPTER 4 | Nuttall and the religious orientation

Eminent colonial figures such as Archbishop Enos Nuttall understood that religion was inseparable from the daily life of the Afro-Jamaican working classes, and that their religious world-view was an important, perhaps the most crucial, variable in what he termed their 'mental construction'. Social control could not be separated from the orientation of African religious thought. For Nuttall, Jamaica was a 'mission frontier' where the Afro-Jamaican population were to be persuaded to accept 'Anglo-Saxon' Christianity and so to move closer to the supposed norms of white society. Paget-Henry notes comparable elite action in Antigua: 'to detach the Africans from their magical systems of symbolic support and reattach them to Christian ones', and to 'make colonial schooling their authoritative source of information'.[1]

The aim was to justify the order of society, not to change it. Social Darwinism, positivism, and Christian philosophy provided justification for the principle underlying the aim. Force was the ultimate guarantee of order in the society, yet there had to be an equilibrium of consent to ensure the dominance of the elite, and to give that elite, old and new, some legitimacy. Ideological control consisted of making Afro-Jamaicans Englishmen – the Anglo-Saxon of the far West. Cultural conformity equalled social equilibrium. Social equilibrium would postpone the next riot.

Afro-Jamaican beliefs and revivalism

In contrast to elite culture which adapted European ways to life in Jamaica, in as pure a manner as possible, there existed a lifestyle among Jamaica's working classes which had evolved over some four centuries – if we include the period of Spanish rule which ended formally in 1670. It is not unusual, of course, for the working classes to practise or to hold beliefs which are not shared by the elite. In his study of the *Making of the English working class*, for example, E.P. Thompson refers to the continuing tales of witches and boggarts, to traditional celebrations such as 'Mischief-neet' and specifically working-class practices at celebrations of Christmas, shrove-tide, 'Cymbalin Sunday', and so on.[2]

In the case of Jamaica, folk customs were partly drawn from the African cultural heritage, and partly from the latter's modifications in response to the dominant European culture. Folk wisdom, poetry, song, and folk tales were part of the cultural landscape, of the rural folk in particular. That folk tradition had been partly moulded by the adoption of Judaeo-Christian practice during the nineteenth century when Nonconformist Christian preachers exercised substantial Christian influence over the black slave population. The adoption of Christianity has been discussed at length by Mary Turner, Edward Brathwaite and Monica Schuler, who also analyses the impact of African religious practice in the island following the importation of African indentured labourers after emancipation.[3] Schuler observes that 'the experience of Christianisation revealed that the Afro-Jamaican religious tradition . . . had consistently reinterpreted Christianity in African, not European cultural terms'. Myalism, for instance, absorbed certain 'congenial aspects of the Baptist version of Christianity – such as the infiltration of the Holy Spirit and baptism by immersion'. Pukkumina is Christian with a strong affinity for African beliefs in obeah and magic.

The interaction between European and African religion in Jamaica showed itself in the adoption of 'subtle' tendencies in theological doctrine, and erratic practices in regard to ecclesiastical discipline. Nor could these tendencies be completely controlled. The Anglican clergyman, Rev. Horace Scotland commented on 'the gross anthropomorphism . . . in regard to religious convictions or conjecture' among the non-European races of Jamaica. He saw this evidence of anthropomorphism in 'the language and sentiments of our West Indian peasantry; in those of many members of the Christian Churches who have been of long standing and according to their lights, of consistent moral character and social respectability, not only with their own class, but also with their betters'. According to Scotland, it was 'very difficult to divest our people in the West Indies of the idea of materiality in regard to the Divine attributes'.

Scotland noted that in 1885 some 50,000 adult males (8 per cent of the total population) had not indicated in the census (1891) affiliation to 'any religion whatever'.[5] Apart from the fact that women, not men, have tended to be the major church-goers, Scotland's comment is worth looking at more closely. Church attendance as registered in formal censuses could not be used as a measure of religious involvement. These 50,000 men could have been attached to any number of 'nativist' churches. Many adventurous men – entrepreneurs of religion – broke away from established or non-established Churches and established their own tents and their own congregations. It is noteworthy that the Colonial Office almost invariably refused to give those gentlemen the right to be named 'marriage officers'. They were called 'locust' preachers and had rather chequered reputations, occasionally expelled by other denominations. According to Scotland:

> South Carolina Camp revival evangelists and the Jamaica 'Locust' preachers have also served fitly and fully as illustrators of ethnological idiosyncrasies when applied to Christian hermeneutics and exegesis.[6]

Scotland then quoted from a local preacher:

> God gave Moses ten Commandments but God so good, me bred'ren, dat Him say if we keep five, Him will keep de odder five for we.

The episcopalian clergyman observed with some puzzlement that the 'emancipated classes' move freely from one denomination to the other according to 'passing sentiments' or 'present convenience'. The significance of this transiency was lost on Scotland, buried in his 'hermeneutics' and 'exegesis'!

While there are no revealing statistics on the subject, the general evidence points to a continuation, if not an expansion of Afro-Jamaican Creole religion, despite the efforts of the Churches. One suggestion was that the Salvation Army, which attracted a great following in Jamaica, may have given the 'movement' of emotional, evangelical type religion great impetus.

> The advent of the Salvation Army, some six or seven years ago, gave to the movement a big impetus. Thousands joined the Army, and the 'invasion' became a triumphant march through the island. The value of street preaching, however, became better understood and more appreciated, and in a short time the whole of the northern part of Kingston became a field for the Evangelists who set up, without organisation of any sort, but purely on individualistic principles, an opposition religious party.

The same correspondent insists that not only Kingston but all of Jamaica in 1895 was a 'very hotbed of most grossly perverted religious fervour'. The sort of stuff that was preached by these prophets, male and female, was both 'blasphemous and amusing'. Others among the elite were opposed to Afro-religious expression nominally on the grounds that revivals, for example, disturbed the peace. Indeed, two women were brought before the court in 1895 for disturbing the peace. One had actually announced the coming of the Kingdom of God, pleaded for repentance, and had heard the Holy Spirit in a voice of thunder. She quietly submitted to arrest and imprisonment: 'I will go to prison, for I suffer for my Lord, my Master He suffered for me'. A second woman had had a vision (on her sick bed) of the pierced feet and side of the Saviour. Having been cured during her vision (she was partly paralysed) she had been commissioned to go to Kingston to deliver a warning of the coming of the judgement. Even more famous, however, were the St Mary Warners, prophetesses of the 'wrath to come'.[7]

The efforts to integrate the rural population into European norms of culture did not succeed fully, not necessarily because there was resistance to it, (though that was also the case), but because the formal institutions of Church and school did not touch the majority of the population.

There has been a substantial amount of writing on Jamaican customs relating to death and burial. For the late-nineteenth century period Afro-Jamaican customs and practices obviously differed from European customs and practices. In rural Jamaica death had its special ceremonies:

> [The] whole community turn out to help the bereaved family. Some would come only to weep and wail, but others would go to Lucea to buy boards to make the coffin while others would sew the shroud, which in the case of a woman would be a long, straight white dress completely covering the feet of the dead and trimmed with yards of white lace and tiny bows. Two bits of board would be set against each cheek of the deceased and the lower jaw bandaged to the rest of the face to keep the mouth shut. The less educated people would 'pass' the small children over the dead to ward off evil spirits, and in some cases the small children were even bathed in water used for washing the dead, to ensure that the dead would protect them![8]

After describing the preparations for feeding the mourners – huge pots of yams and meat – our source continues:

> The grave was dug by willing workers and the coffin made by skilled carpenters. The local preacher would conduct a service in the yard of the deceased and the coffin carried to the grave, which was usually a few yards away from the house. [There was] another service at the graveside . . . All would repair to the home of the deceased to eat and drink, sing hymns, and speak in glowing terms of the dead. A few neighbours would sleep with the bereaved family until the 'Ninth Night' when there would be a wake – a get together provided with fried fish and bread and copious cups of coffee. [There was] hymn singing and small talk until 12.00 p.m. when a regular service was conducted and the good deeds of the dead extolled. Chairs would be turned about and other movable articles of furniture, while children of the deceased would be spun completely around. To this day I have been unable to grasp the significance of all this activity but I entirely enjoyed the excitement.

Herbert George deLisser who witnessed a Ninth Night ceremony in the early-twentieth century confirmed most of this account by Mrs Carter. In deLisser's account there is story-telling, games, and wrestling until morning.[9] The singing was led by one appointed to do so, one who could carry the refrain above the contending claims of rival harmonisers. 'In solemn recitative, he repeats each couplet . . . No matter how well the words are known, this recitative must never be omitted'.[10]

Funerals were in the fullest sense community affairs. Writing in 1870 Gardner notes: 'When a person of any kind of importance died, preparation was made for the wake. If the family was not able to bear the expense, plates enveloped in black crape were sent round from house to house, and gifts of those kindly disposed collected. All who chose to come to the wake (were) freely welcomed'. 'Gardner sees the wake as a grand time for gossip, feasting and too often drunkenness'.[11] DeLisser and Carter do not mention drunkenness.

Given that the Churches in Jamaica had been endeavouring to 'civilise' Jamaicans by discouraging many of the practices associated with the 'mental construction' of the Afro-Jamaican, how did Church members respond to the traditions of wakes, obeah, etc.? We can assume that non-Churchgoers continued their practices as usual – and there were many people who were not associated with the formal Christian Churches. The answer is to be found partly in Joseph Williams' account. We quote Williams, a Jesuit priest:

> In the case of Church members in the Jamaican 'bush', much of the farcical carrying on is perforce omitted. But even in their case, at times, when they wake the dead, and incidentally the entire neighbourhood, not a few of the time-honoured superstitions will creep out, in spite of all the clergymen say or do. In general, the Church member will feign to be above these remnants of the days of slavery. No matter what his belief or lack of belief may be, to have a minister of religion officiate at the funeral is all-important – to provide a grave spot.[12]

The clergyman, according to Williams, was needed to provide a grave spot, to lead the procession from home to cemetery (called a 'heading'), to conduct a service in the house (called a 'Churching'), and at the church, and then to lead the procession to the cemetery. The observant Jesuit priest noted relapses of the converted:

> But even in the case of professed Church members, there is occasionally a reversion to type, at least on the part of some of those who attend the obsequies and follow the cortège to the burying ground.[13]

Williams also notes that some of the customs were related to old Ashanti customs, such as raising and lowering the coffin three times before leaving for the burial ground. The coffin and corpses were also used as an effective means of collecting debts owed to the deceased.[14]

Williams was inclined to view the Afro-Jamaican population as light-hearted in respect of funerals, and to illustrate his point he offered the example of the funeral of the Bugler of the Salvation Army Corps at Montego Bay:

> He had been a really likeable lad and universally respected. As a consequence, his funeral was attended by the community at large, and the Town Band led the procession to the grave. [There was] proper solemn music, well-executed. But no sooner was the service at the grave concluded, when the black population proceeded to escort the Band back to town . . . to the tune of *Tipperary*. Whereupon men, women, and children, in long lines joined arms, and proceeded to cavort and prance along in dance formation.[15]

Williams suggested that this action was not a consequence of lack of respect, but the response of a 'light-hearted' people. We need not agree with Williams about the light-heartedness, but it is interesting that Mrs Carter in her account spoke of enjoying the excitement.

From the Church's point of view the eradiction of 'superstition' was a far way away with respect to the masses of the population. But the Church, often mirroring the conviction of white cultural superiority, did not pay due attention to the fact that what was in their view superstition constituted a whole structure of beliefs. For example, African medicine, with its use of herbal remedies, and dismissed contemptuously by white doctors as 'bush remedies', worked in association with mystical beliefs and rituals.[16] Nuttall came closest to recognising this factor when he suggested that the removal of superstition amounted to the destruction of 'integral parts of native African life'. The examples of Bedward and others mentioned later demonstrate an extremely close relationship, indeed the integration, of healing (medicine) and religion. (Sheridan has also established very clearly that during slavery black doctors and doctresses gave the necessary nursing care to ailing slaves in hothouses or slave hospitals, and further that in the treatment of the scourge of yaws certain white doctors 'came to acknowledge that African remedies [herbal based] were more efficacious than those [mercury based] of European origin). Eugene Genovese also identified religion with black folk medicine, 'in its function as an agency for the transmission of black religious sensibility into a defence against the psychological assaults of slavery and racial oppression'.[17] During slavery, myal practitioners, who understood the medicinal value of certain plants and had built up a body of knowledge of herb medicine that was of real service in {curing the sick, were mobilised for work in the plantation hospitals.[18]}

African medicine 'embodied the principles of good and evil'. The good medicine man used a combination of herbs and white magic for good purposes, whereas the bad medicine man or sorcerer used poisons and black magic to hurt and destroy people.[19] These realities were not eliminated by emancipation. In the late-nineteenth century Church and State continued to suppress the practice of obeah (black magic). Expulsion of obeah-practising members of the Church from the communion of the Christian Church meant the loss of potential converts to 'civilisation'. Keeping them within the body of the Church was an endorsement of sin. The Anglican Church appears to have wavered between expulsion and other forms of punishment, such as suspension, exclusion from communion and 'excision' from the Church register.[20] Accusations were, however, not easy to prove. In the late-nineteenth century obeah was placed under the vagrancy laws. Obeahmen, by exercising some considerable influence over the black population, had traditionally challenged white domination over their black slaves.[21] A magistrate, L.L. Samuels, in St Thomas released an obeahman on the grounds of 'first offence'. The white population was scandalised. Another defiant obeahman, charged with the illegal practice, protested to the court that the State was standing in his way of earning a livelihood.[22]

In 1898 the fine for consulting an obeahman was increased from 40/- to £10, and obeahism became an offence under the vagrancy law. The alternative was 12 months in prison.[23]

A member of the Legislative Council, Dr Johnston, insisted that he had known 'eleven people in a yard consulting a boy nine years of age and ready with goats and all sorts of presents to him in recompense for his good services as 'obeah boy'. Evidently, the obeahmen were advertising their skills, since there were in circulation pamphlets being widely sold – such as the 'Confession of John Hoffman' or 'the Dying Story of Rock Salt' or 'other great obeahmen who never lived. They (the pamphlets) were more believed in than the Bible'.[24]

Not only Afro-Jamaican adults and children proved amenable to obeah. East Indians enjoyed an outstanding reputation as well.[25] The perdurability of obeah in Jamaica was a consequence of secrecy, belief, and probably the craftiness of the obeahman himself. As Rev. Emerick noted: 'You will not be able to understand obi-ism and account for influences of the obeahman unless you consider obi-ism as a religion and the obi-man as a priest. The real genuine obi-man is not often trapped, he is too cunning for that'.[26]

The tradition of employing the services of elderly women as healers, which Sheridan notes for the slave period continued in the late-nineteenth century. It was the obeahman who was most feared because, as Mrs Zelia Fraser observed, 'in a country where vegetable poisons of unknown virulence abound (obeah) is no laughing matter'.

In 1894 Alice Spinner (Mrs Fraser) wrote an account of the Afro-Jamaican belief in 'duppies'. Alice Spinner, a novelist married to the Director of the Railroad, had a lively interest in Creole life, and her account of 'duppies' is matter-of-fact and obviously gleaned from the Afro-Jamaican citizens with whom she came into contact. The 'duppy' was neither a ghost nor the spirit or soul, but only the 'shadow' of the departed; the soul being perfectly distinct from its 'duppy', and going to heaven or hell, as the case may be, leaving its shadow or 'duppy' to linger behind on earth. The soul of a notorious evil-doer – a noted obeahman, for example, – is supposed to go straight to hell for his crimes, but his 'duppy' will remain behind him. Only being the shadow of a bad man, it will partake of his vicious qualities, probably a 'Rolling Calf'. Spinner noted that the Negroes wore charms against 'duppies', 'indeed many coloured people, if the truth were known. A little bag tied round the neck is no great trouble . . . A silver penny, or quattie in the bag and a piece of garlic. "Yes, missus, an' a grain of corn an' something else, but what that something else is I do not know," I was told by a brown girl. Perhaps the 'something' was *assafoetida*, for an English nurse in the hospital assured me that little bags containing that evil-smelling drug are often found on the patients, and the reason for their use is always the same, 'duppies''.[27]

> Many 'duppies' are themselves highly scented with such essences, so that they may be plainly traced as they walk along, although otherwise invisible. This is universally believed, and oddly enough, has some foundation, for often myself, when I have been out walking in the early morning, I have been puzzled by meeting a sudden whiff of strange, sweet scent, apparently from nowhere. It lasted an instant and was gone, but the curious sensation it gave me made one understand how it strengthened the popular belief, and I remembered how easily, in this country of sudden currents and gusts of wind, a strong breeze, loaded with scent of some far-off blossom, may chance to come your way. A sudden hot gust of wind also betokens a 'duppy's' presence, for they are not like our chilly northern ghosts, but on the contrary give out a great heat . . . 'Duppies' haunt the banks of rivers where people have drowned. Hospitals are filled with 'duppies', for naturally, although many deaths must occur, none of the subsequent ceremonies can be gone through . . . A little boy I knew, called Josiah, was supposed to have the gift of seeing 'duppies' ''cos he born wid a caul, missus, an' oftentimes I get 3d for a lilly bit, for people know 'bout Josiah an' dat I hab it, an' so come an' buy lilly bits as a charm against 'duppies' . . .' the Ceiba or cotton tree was the haunt of 'duppies' . . . mischievous

house-spirits. They will upset and hide things, and most especially delight in throwing sand and gravel on the roof. Unchristened children [are] dressed in blue [as a] safeguard. Blue was the Virgin's colour.[28]

Spinner argues that belief in 'duppies' was all-pervasive among the black population ('Truly in these islands 'duppies' are a power'). The author also refers to inexplicable deaths through fear, and to 'Duppy Gate' at the soldiers' 'Camp' where 'no Negro has yet been found to face the "duppies" that infest this particular spot'. (These were the 'duppies' of English officers who died there of yellow fever). No Negro sentries could be found.[29]

Spinner also describes wakes and Ninth Night ceremonies, the positioning of food 'outside in the little yard which every Negro possesses and where cooking and washing is done – to feed the departed'.[30]

Religion was the cement of the social life of the Afro-Jamaican population, to the extent that to separate religious beliefs and practices from education, leisure, labour, and other aspects of material life can be unrewarding.

Cultural imperialists made serious efforts to integrate the population and thereby create greater social and possibly racial harmony within the overall framework of oligarchical domination. African culture was viewed, intransigently, as primitive. There were two primary methods used to integrate the population – the school and the Church. As we shall see, financial constraints, racial prejudice, and difficulties of communication among other things made resistance on the part of the Afro-Jamaican population to the civilisation stream easier and probably, for the most part, successful. Resistance did not assume rejection, outright, but adaptation. By the end of the nineteenth century while myalism continued, for example, to be important, it was revivalism which caught the elite eye, demonstrating once again the continuing integration or syncretism between European based Christianity and Afro-Jamaican religious belief.

The Bedwardian revival

The Jamaican upper and middle classes shared a profound dislike and fear of Afro-Jamaican religious expression, even more so because there was an association between the Morant Bay Rebellion of 1865 and one of the most vigorous revivals in Jamaican history. There had also been revivals in 1831 and 1840 and there was to be another in 1883.

The conclusion that revivalist movements sometimes serve the function of a 'cathartic emotional outlet' and are in part the consequence of 'unsatisfied longing for vital religious experiences' bears some validity to the Jamaican situation given that the Churches of Jamaica had, by the 1880s, lost some of the evangelical vitality of the earlier decades.[31]

To the extent that revivalist movements are 'spontaneous' outbursts in search of vital religion and are safety valves for the expression of discontent they are movements which conserve rather than change or challenge society. They can also have the effect of splintering religious structures, on the basis of the 'revelations' experienced. Thus, on the one hand, they prevent the organic integration of religious expression in the hands of the elite, but also shatter (in the case of Jamaica) the collectivity of religious expression among the poor.

The major outburst of religion which attracted most attention and comment was the Bedwardian revival of the 1890s. The Bedwardian movement was, however, more than a spontaneous outburst of religion. In every sense of the word it was a formal Church, with a theology defined. Contrary to the supposed Old Testament consciousness of which Nuttall had spoken there was a very strong 'New Testament' consciousness. Bedwardian theology accepted the Trinity: 'The Trinity indivisibly yet each in His own function is manifested in Man's Redemption and Salvation. God gave his Son, the Son took upon himself our frail humanity, and died our souls to save'. The coming of the Holy Ghost, the Comforter, as described in the Acts of the Apostles was important to Bedwardian theology:

> Yet after all His wonderful teachings, the disciples must wait till
> He sent the Holy Ghost, proceeding from the Father Himself.
> When the Holy Ghost came, then only was there perfect prepar-
> edness for our grand work in favour of Man's Salvation.

In Bedwardian theology there were three heavens. There was also great emphasis placed on fasting.[32]

Bedwardism also embraced beliefs which, despite the acceptance of the New Covenant, for the guardians of European culture and civilisation were unacceptable. This is what Nuttall says on the matter:

> In the West Indies this popular belief often takes the form of
> expecting miraculous healing through the application of some
> crude medicament or the drinking of some bush water, or the
> bathing in some stream which has been blessed by a native
> prophet or preacher. These various operations attract large crowds,
> and are usually accompanied by prolonged religious exercises.
> Such things are frequently pointed to as evidence of the deep
> degradation of the Negro. But I have often publicly called atten-
> tion in Jamaica to the fact that these practices do not differ
> essentially, or even in most of the concomitants from what is to
> be witnessed even yet at sacred shrines in European countries, or

in the temples of the Christian Scientists in America.[33]

Those practices could not be encouraged in the Anglican Church, and not in any formal Christian Church for that matter; but Nuttall, who was inclined to see the religious conduct of Jamaica's working classes as comparable in many respects to the conduct of the labouring classes in England, for example, was less severe in his condemnation of these practices. Such practices would eventually die out with 'proper guidance'. Other Jamaicans did not share his views on the subject, and Bedwardism continued to be regarded, as Nuttall himself said, as evidence of the 'deep degradation' of the blacks. Despite his problem with the law Alexander Bedward continued to bless the waters of the Hope River and to baptise the ailing, healing them in body and spirit to the accompaniment of the vigorous song:

> Dip dem Bedward, Dip dem
> Dip dem in the Healing stream.

Before the Synod of 1894 Nuttall stressed that the very existence of the Bedwardian cult was an indication of the great need for more effort to be made on the part of the clergy and laity 'to go out into the highways and hedges . . . and compel them to come in'. Many had been converted but as yet unreached were the 'ignorant multitudes from whom (come) in the main, the occasional outbursts of superstition like August Town and Haddo and the Moneague water . . .'[34] To the Governor (Blake) he confided:

> I have in fact advised those of our clergy who have consulted me on the subject to avoid harshness in those references to the subject which are inevitable. It is much easier to fan the flame of excitement than to put it out. Unless there be some new features developed I do not see the wisdom of interference on the part of myself and our clergy beyond what we are doing in the quiet way I have indicated. The people will see for themselves bye and bye that there are no real results.[35]

But people continued to flock to Bedward's healing stream. In 1904 the *Daily Gleaner*, in a long editorial, compared Bedward's religious movement with comparable practices in Europe. The editor saw the Bedward movement, as well as the dedication to shrines in Europe and Russia, as an indication of a particular level of cultural development. Jamaicans (presumably the upper and middle class) were inconsistent in accepting European 'superstition' and rejecting Jamaican 'superstition':

> But after all, Bedward is not one whit different from the average faith healer . . . We have been to August Town, and have seen what takes place there; and bad as the 'ceremonies' are there, they are surpassed by what takes place at the healing waters of St

> Seraphim in Russia. Bedward, too, can lay claim to an undoubted
> number of cures, many people have been made whole through his
> ministration . . . Yet many of those who will solemnly relate to
> you certain miraculous occurrences of which they have heard,
> would be greatly shocked if you mentioned that Bedward had
> also performed miracles. In other words, Bedward is an imposter,
> but St Seraphim or some other worthy is not . . . We cannot see
> why a healing stream in one part of the world should be of
> superior efficacy to a similar stream in any other part.[36]

It is not by any means that the *Gleaner's* editor supported Bedward. Rather
he saw Bedwardism as the manifestation of a particular stage of mental and
cultural development. Bedwardism would be cured through the greater
'civilisation' of its practitioners:

> In any community may be found thousands of persons corre-
> sponding to the different stages of culture society has passed
> through. Outwardly, we may all seem to be much alike, the
> difference is in the constitution of our minds.[37]

When Governor Blake reported to the Colonial Office on the Bedward
movement he insisted that there was nothing to fear from Bedward himself
but more so from 'saner and more designing men' who might seek to use
the movement to create disturbance among the people who are so 'excitable
and ignorant as our population'.[38] Not surprisingly, Bedward's movement
was anxiously watched for any evidence of sedition. The evidence of
sedition was found in his declarations that it was time for the 'black wall'
to knock the 'white wall' down, and that he was 'master of the black' and
'master of the white'. A correspondent to the *New York Times* in 1895
commented (perhaps with some exaggeration) on the fact that Bedward
discussed the colour question and politics, 'declaring that the time is at hand
when the blacks must rise up and crush the whites and assume the government, as their brothers have done in Haiti . . . His mad career goes un-
checked. Worse yet, the island is now overrun by prophets with rival
healing streams, and all draw big followings and make money'.[39] Bedward,
inevitably, was put away in the lunatic asylum which was the destination of
many religious Afro-Jamaicans who were certified 'insane through revivalism, obeah or other religious excitement'.[40] The evidence does not really
point to Alexander Bedward as leader of a political movement though the
statements attributed to him do suggest a perception of a relationship
between religion, political power and the question of race in Jamaican
society. Bedwardism as religious practice showed considerable affinity to
religious orthodoxy of a Christian, New Testament kind. Bedward himself
dressed as an Episcopalian minister of religion. On the other hand, his

healing stream and general activities at the Hope River demonstrate an obvious continuity with the Native Baptist and African-Jamaican tradition. The Bedwardite movement also bears striking similarities to certain millenarian movements in South America. It may not have been as spectacular as the movement of Padre Cicero (Ceara, 1889), or of Antonio Conselheiro at Canudos (1893–7) in Brazil. It is striking though that Bedward's movement saw an association between white rule and misery, in the same way as did certain tribes of Indians in the Amazon.

> In the tribes deculturated by missionaries and explorers, the Indians developed a syncretic religion, part Roman Catholic, part that of their ancestors. They turned to that religion for unity and hope. Messianic movements flourished which denounced 'white civilisation' as the source of local misery and announced a new and perfect life in which the whites would not be present. The masses often conceived of the millenium as a world without whites, whom they equated with exploitation and associated with their misery.[41]

Bedward, in 1895, described white men as hypocrites, robbers, thieves, liars:

> The Pharisees and Sadducees are the white men; we are the true people . . . Brethren, hell will be your portion if you do not rise up, and crush the white man . . . The Government passes laws that oppress the black people, rob them of their bread . . . Let them remember the Morant War . . . The Constables and the Inspectors are Scoundrels . . . [42]

As we have indicated, Bedward's movement was only the largest and most sustained, Creole religious movement, with a colonial-wide organisation. Other movements like Bedward's attracted attention mainly when an act or acts alerted the police. In June 1896, for example, the police intervened in a case where a man named Harrison, but who went by the designation Jesus of Nazareth, was to have reenacted the raising of Lazarus, using one of his female disciples, Lydia Edwards, in the role of Lazarus.[43] In October of the same year a 'convince Doctor', Dr Walker, had his appliances dismantled by a priest; his specialty was the blessing of water, effecting of cures, and the casting out of evil spirits.[44]

Elite attitudes

Afro-Jamaican religion was, in the view of the elite, a denial of civilisation:

> It appears to me that although we are living in an advanced state
> of civilisation in this country, yet there are many who seem to be
> at the lowest ebb of an uncivilised type, especially in their relig-
> ious worshipping . . . Last week, for four nights in succession
> these religious Arabs had it all their own way.[45]

This particular observer was especially upset that the constable – whom he
described as a 'red seam automaton' – was watching the revival, not
restraining it. The *Daily Gleaner* in support of 'Taxpayer' commented on
the annoyance occasioned by the unseeming and noisy orgies miscalled
'revival meetings'. It is 'perfectly true that there seems to be no law to stop
the holding of these scenes of debauchery and hideous caterwauling . . . The
police have not orders to interfere, and when they do, the parties interfered
with, under the advice of some pettifogging lawyer, bring actions against
the constabulary and get damages, as in the case of Loza vs. the Church,
from the mistaken sympathies of an ignorant or prejudiced jury'.[46] The
Gleaner goes on to establish (not intentionally) that the protest was not so
much against the noise as against the culture:

> Of course, we know the argument used in favour of non-interfer-
> ence. It is that if you interfere you are arbitrarily infringing the
> rights of the citizen to meet and amuse himself or seek salvation
> in his own way, and if you do not stop a ball in the house of a
> well-to-do citizen or the choral service of the Parish Church, you
> cannot in common justice silence the howling and drumming of
> a jumba dance, or the vociferous squalling of a revival meeting
> . . . But are respectable citizens to be kept awake night after night
> in some otherwise quiet neighbourhood by a congregation of the
> lowest and most disreputable idlers of the community, who meet
> together to indulge in debauchery and obscenity of the vilest
> description and who make night hideous by yelling and scream-
> ing at the top of their voices like a saturnalia of demons of the
> pit?[47]

Culture was a matter for the police, when non-European culture was the
issue. The comment made by the *Gleaner* on wakes was not unusual, and
was a good representation of how Afro-Jamaican religious expression was
viewed by the middle and upper class.

All respectable people believed that blacks could make progress only
under the guidance of the white man, and by extension the white man's
example. So informed a work as Livingstone's *Black Jamaica* rests on this
hypothesis, and so acute an observer as Herbert George deLisser takes it for
granted. 'The Negro', deLisser wrote in February 1900, 'if left altogether to
himself will make no progress'. The feeling which blacks had for progress

came from the example of their superiors. 'In Hayti there had [been] no such class to set such an example'.[48] And deLisser did not belong to that group of whites who thought that blacks were chronically lazy and had to be coerced into manual labour.

This orientation probably partly informed the policy of white immigration, though there were definitely other reasons for such a policy – such as reducing the availability of the highlands to black cultivators. Up to 1890 Governor Blake was advocating white immigration – but particularly Englishmen with capital. But he goes on to say that the 'highlands [were] admirably suited for colonisation' by whites:

> I should not advise the advent of white agriculturists except in communities, on such a scale that the colonists would find themselves a part of homogeneous society, with a sufficient number of white neighbours to form their own social public opinion and standard of morals. Isolated white labouring agriculturists among a black population would certainly fail.[49]

The idea that progress was linked to population and to race was widespread in the Americas in the late-nineteenth century. The profound industrial growth, physical expansion and general prosperity of the United States was seen to be the result of liberal policies of white immigration. Jamaica, in the nineteenth century, was regarded as underpopulated. By the late 1890s Blake was no longer as sure about the policy of white immigration. Responding to a recommendation by one Mr S.H. Wheeldon of Brown's Town, advocating the settlement of Englishmen in the highlands of Jamaica, Blake summarised for the Colonial Office the 'failure' of the Seaford Town settlement of Germans and of the Scottish settlement at Altamont. The problems were climate, sun, and rainfall.

> Seaford Town still exists . . . some of the original immigrants and their descendants . . . cultivate ginger and arrowroot, etc. and are in a few cases fairly well off, but the majority are poor and settlement can in no sense be construed a success.[50]

Furthermore, the white communities did not surpass 'in intelligence the adjoining black communities nor does their energy compare favourably with the latter'. Sir Henry did not see the light.

Even J.T. Palache, whose record as a social reformer is moderately good, concluded (in the debate for raising the school-leaving age) that the age should be raised on the basis that the intelligence of children in 'tropical climates' did not develop as quickly as European children and therefore it was thought a stronger reason to keep the age at 16 years and give the children the advantage of getting the rudiments of education. It was the British inspector of schools who intervened, to come to the defence of the children of Jamaica. He claimed that perhaps they did not develop physically as swiftly, 'but in intelligence [they] would find the great weight of authority showed that during the early years the children have progressed much more quickly than children in England, when they are properly taught'.[51]

W.P. Livingstone, who had been editor of the *Daily Gleaner* and who wrote *Black Jamaica*, thought that the Jamaica black could progress only under the guidance of the white man.[52] Here are a few of Livingstone's views, which were certainly not intended to be malicious. On racial mixture he claims: 'the intelligence of the one [whites] meets and amalgamates with the animalism of the other, producing a strange nature, the good which is perpetually reaching . . . to higher things, and the evil, like an unseen hand, perpetually dragging it back to savagery'.[53] Secondly, the black started out the equal of the white but his environment proved too much for him. Social advancement of man depends upon temperature.[54] According to Livingstone, there were three groups of blacks; the masses, those who have risen above the common level, and the few who have arrived at the highest stage of development. The first group are like children, the moral faculties are dormant, they are not vicious, they know no law, and therefore, know no transgression, they are religious but not pious. They face the world with a smile, but it often covers the agony of want or pain. They are timid and dependent . . . yet 'none so brave' when they forget their position and behave simply as men. This group is responsive to sympathy and justice, and ready where these are given to form passionate attachments to the superior race. They are quick to detect unkindness, and they can range from sullenness to paroxysms of rage.[55]

The other two categories are assessed in relation to the extent that they have become culturally 'Europeanised'. Yet, in Livingstone's view:

> It is simply that the blacks must be recognised as having entered
> into full possession of the country. It is inevitably theirs, its
> history will henceforward be their history, its fortune their
> fortune.[56]

Livingstone finds Britain's relationship with her 'black subjects' a 'passive' one, and the blacks have, without special imperial assistance, developed up to a certain point. But they are still a child race, ignorant and impressionable.[57]

Livingstone's view corresponded more or less with those of the paternal imperialists, and those who saw the cultural assimilation of the period as a preparation for full citizenship. They were at least ahead of Professor Froude. Oscar Marescaux was not. Here are his views:

> The higher you tax Quashie the better it will be for the community. If he has to pay a tax of one shilling he has to work so much

the more for it, and the planter gains by his labour. Without being forced, the Negro will not work, it is a delusion to think it, it is useless to appeal to his sense of comfort.[58]

The author's comments on Mr Marescaux's person and attitudes are, I believe, worth quoting:

> Going east we pass the Colonial Bank, where Mr Oscar Marescaux lorded it and lost much money for the bank in irrecoverable loans to sugar estates. Mr Marescaux was a very tall man, over six feet, long thin legs, hunched-up shoulders with a growth of beard after the style of a Frenchman. Irascible and arrogant. His views on natives of the country were narrow but not peculiar to himself. They still survive among many of our great landowners today.

General attitudes of the elite of Jamaica to blacks and coloureds were conditioned to a considerable extent by the persistence of the social structure of the island which left whites in a superordinate and blacks in a subordinate social position. Economic change, even where it adversely affected whites, did not diminish their cultural authority. The emergence of social Darwinism as the new prism through which to view the evolution of human societies reinforced white social authority and confirmed the subordination of blacks within the racial and class structure. Quasi-scientific racism and its growing association with imperialism solidified the traditional socio-racial structure of Jamaica.

It is clear that W.P. Livingstone, whose work *Black Jamaica* was received with intense hostility by leaders of opinion in Jamaica, was influenced by the evolutionary theory of social Darwinism. Public opinion was scandalised not so much by what he said about blacks, but by his accurate observations about white and brown morality.

Enos Nuttall

One of the most outstanding personalities in Jamaica was Enos Nuttall who arrived in the island in 1862 as a Methodist lay preacher. He entered the Anglican Church, became Bishop of Jamaica in 1880, Primate of the West Indies in 1894, Archbishop of the West Indies in 1897, and died in Jamaica in 1916 after over 50 years uninterrupted service to the Church and to the Jamaican community. Though the Anglican Church had been disestablished in 1870 by Governor John Peter Grant, with the eager support of the Nonconformist Churches, Nuttall's leadership served to make the Anglican Church one of the most dynamic institutions in the island with a focus on the religious, educational and moral welfare of the mass of Jamaicans, at least as Nuttall himself understood that welfare. Anglican activity reflected Nuttall's ideas, which were shaped not only by Christian humanism, but by positivism, social Darwinism, and by his belief in 'Anglo-Saxon' civilisation. His influence was particularly prominent in religion and education, and there was no question that his voice was listened to by all the Governors of the period and by the Colonial Office as well.

Archbishop Nuttall epitomised in his person and career the idea of imperial paternalism. His biographer, Frank Cundall, cheerfully records that Nuttall was a 'keen imperialist', and so does Bishop E.L. Evans.[59] Nuttall embodied the new sensibility to empire enlarged and enriched by the addition of India.

Imperial paternalism was a system of ideas, more or less benignly expressed, fundamentally conservative, which sought through reform to maintain the status quo by offering hope of progress within the imperial framework. The underlying assumption was that progress would be encouraged among (not imposed upon) the 'subject races' of the Empire (subject races were usually coloured) by the white man. Adolphe Roberts correctly refers to Nuttall's innate conservatism.[60] He accepted as a man with a conservative mind, social hierarchy, but insisted upon moral equality. Historical evolution was governed by the divine will which was never to be questioned under the most trying of circumstances.[61] Like Edmund Burke, Nuttall believed that a spirit of piety was essential for the maintenance of society.

These views of society or social evolution are an aspect of positivism, most methodically expounded by the French philosopher Auguste Comte. The French philosopher linked the new sociology to the existing social order and, 'though it will not reject the need for correction and improvement, it will exclude any move to overthrow or negate that order'.[62] Positivists viewed society as governed by rational laws. Nuttall, like some positivists, substituted 'divine will' for rational laws. The social order, in the positivist creed of the latter nineteenth century was justified in itself. All social effort should be concentrated on 'moral renovation' not revolution. Similarly, Nuttall spoke of the promotion of the 'mental and moral elevation' of the African race, by those who had an interest in their welfare.[63]

Comte had insisted that 'the principal social difficulties are today essentially not political but moral ones' and their solutions required a change in 'opinions and morals' rather than in institutions. Furthermore, 'the social order stands under external laws against which none may transgress without punishment'.[64] Thus in Nuttall's view, while freedom was the 'birthright of man' slavery was not an aberration, or an abuse of freedom, but rather an act of Divine Providence which gave the black man his first opportunity to witness free conditions:

> The system of steady work, regular food, clothing and rest . . .
> safeguarded and developed the physical life of the Negro, and
> served, in the providence of God, as a stepping stone to free
> conditions.[65]

The positivists saw institutions of government as self-adjusting in the face
of progress. Nuttall, it seems, considered the colonial system as lasting until
such time as the leaders of the Jamaican community had progressed enough
to ensure their succession. It is not that positivists rejected mass welfare. On
the contrary, the 'condition of the lower classes', should be improved, so
long as that improvement did not disturb 'the indispensable economic
order'.[66] Nuttall showed his dedication to the positivist political order in
1884, when he pointed out to political agitator R.H. Jackson the continuing
need for 'the controlling hand of the British Government on our affairs':

> And so the confidence of those who have had good reason in the
> past, on our own showing, to doubt our capacity so to govern as
> to promote the welfare and development of 400,000 at the lower
> end of the social scale, might be retained during the period in
> which we were at once educating ourselves to the practical use of
> political privileges and proving ourselves capable of caring fully
> and well for all sections and interests in the community, and thus
> surely and safely leading on to the inevitable complete political
> emancipation . . . I think a mistake is being made in any public
> agitation which goes beyond a clear assertion that the proposed
> concessions are only accepted as instalments of more complete
> representative Institutions which it is hoped the duly elected
> Representatives of the people will be in a position effectively to
> claim the Crown to concede at no very distant day.[67]

Here again Nuttall represents the positivist viewpoint that order and progress were inextricably linked in the march towards the future. Progress was
possible without a rupture of the given order. Order was the precondition
for progress: 'all progress ultimately tends to consolidate order'.[68]

Positivists, then, did not deny the possibility of progress, but believed
that improvement must come gradually, that progress was gradual but
inevitable, that social order was a 'necessary basis of social progress'.[69]
Comte himself held a 'profound preoccupation with the problem of social
control and the re-establishment of social consensus'.[70] Comtian analysis
offered, simultaneously, assurance and justification to the holders of power,
and hope for their opposites.

In the late-nineteenth century positivism became associated with
social Darwinism,[71] and, again in Nuttall's thought there was obvious evidence of Darwinism, a Spencerian interpretation of Charles Darwin's

theory of evolution. Social Darwinism supposed that some races would eventually die out, unfit to survive in a world of keen competition. Nuttall, applying the notion of the survival of the fittest, concluded that the African race in the Caribbean was 'likely to continue and increase' and that the race had 'responded to the claims of Christianity'. Even in the southern USA where Nuttall doubted that 'the black man has had opportunities, proportionate to his numbers, of coming really under the influence of various forms of Christianity, that in the case of those who have yielded to that influence and become active members of the Christian Church, there is evidence of the more permanent traits of Christian character and life which will be exhibited by Negro people on a large scale, when they become subject to the influences of Christianity and Christian civilisation'.[72]

The progress of blacks in the western hemisphere was proof, for Nuttall, that blacks would not be among the races which would prove 'unfit'.

It remains for us to examine more fully the way in which Nuttall applied or adapted this thought to Jamaican conditions, and particularly to the concepts of religion and empire. Marcuse has observed the positivist tendency to view 'each historical level as a higher stage of development than the one preceding, by force of the fact that the latter is the necessary product of the earlier one and contains a plus of experience and new knowledge'.[73] The Archbishop, adapting the premise to the evolution of Christendom, saw the latter as moving towards a unity of organisation and a synthesis of belief, enriched by the spiritual experiences of non-Europeans insofar, of course, as those experiences did not conflict with basic doctrine.

Nuttall regarded Jamaica as a missionary frontier where the 'ignorant' black multitudes had to be brought into the mainstream of the Christian community while maintaining the position that black religious expression could be used to strengthen Christianity.[74] It was his conviction that Christianity had a universal message which took precedence over the artificial divisions into multiple denominations of Christians. He accepted, in principle, that there should be one Church, 'with essential beliefs one, essential organisation one, and free inter-communion maintained between all its ministers and all its members. In my view essentials of doctrine and organisation are few and simple, and such as will be ascertained without much difficulty when we have realised that unity of the Church is the most pressing question of Christendom'.[75] African religion in Jamaica did not, for Nuttall, constitute piety, but rather a barbarous expression of awareness of God in nature, the product of primitive superstition.

Though his views were highly critical of those who concentrated on the insular rather than the universal Church, those views were not precisely based on a concept of ecumenicism. They were grounded in the belief that the advancement of worldwide Christian civilisation necessitated the joint work of all Christians against the forces of evil which could be detected in the barbarous practices of non-Christians. Where the exercise of primitive religion in such a community as Jamaica had features which could be absorbed into the wider practice of Christianity without causing contamination of fundamental doctrine, such practices should be absorbed, the better to attract the 'subject' people to the demands of Christendom. Tolerance, indeed, gave some legitimacy to authority. The conversion of the heathen, and of the semi-heathen in Jamaica was part of the international process to make Christendom universal. The Church, in short, had one foundation. The religious order of Christendom was entirely capable of harmonious evolution, paralleling the harmonious evolution of the social order in general historical development.

The dilemma for the Church was really to determine the extent to which 'non-European' religious practice should be absorbed into the 'Christian' Church. Permitting some degree of absorption would strengthen the membership, but to allow it free play would be to weaken the western Church and its companion, western civilisation. The solution was to view African beliefs or Creole beliefs as superstition and to encourage Afro-Jamaican expression which was not incompatible with that of the formal Church. As Nuttall said:

> The correction of superstitious tendencies must be kept constantly in view. There is a tendency among the Negroes to transfer into their Christian associations that superstitious element which is an integral part of native African life, as in fact, it forms a part of the life of all undeveloped races, and of the ignorant sections of the more advanced races.[76]

The Archbishop associated, then, African 'superstition' with an 'integral part' of native African life, recognising as he did the intimate association between religion and daily life. To remove the one – superstition – was to reduce the other – the integral parts of native African life. Nuttall's positivist creed, however, insisted that change should be slow, quiet and directed.

The three elements which Nuttall identified as possible contributions of black religious expression to Christianity were, firstly, the importance which blacks attached to music; second, the importance of participation in a service by the entire congregation; third, was the strong 'realisation by the Negro Christian of a personal God, and His immediate connection with the events of human life – physical and spiritual'. Among Afro-Jamaicans 'isolation in Church life is repugnant'.[77] These three features would probably have applied equally well to any ardent Methodist of the period (and Nuttall had considerable experience of Methodism prior to his coming to Jamaica). It was not so much the fact that these were independent attributes of Afro-Jamaican religious expression as that these attributes were already accepted in Christian practice:

> The Negro manifests his religious social instincts in his love of religious services in which he can take a share. In every form of worship this social instinct has the opportunity to manifest itself in hymn-singing, which is usually joined in with great fervour. As regards the Church of England, both the responses in the prayers and litanies and the canticles and hymns, are joined in with earnestness and a fullness seldom realised in other communities . . . The Church which does not exhibit the brotherhood of Christians will have little prospect of real progress among black people.[78]

The Church had the responsibility to encourage not only music as such but music which 'appealed to the sympathies of the Negro'. The Archbishop seems to have been particularly impressed by Jamaican digging songs which demonstrated not only love of music, but a sense of community – clearly an ideal addition to Christian brotherhood:

> So fond are Negroes of music that even out of scanty wages they will manage to buy some sort of musical instrument. In digging yam-hills and other field work, the hoes descend in regular time to the 'song without words', which echoes from mountain to mountain in pleasing harmony – solo and chorus, and also extra parts added (at their sweet will) which never seem to mar the melody or jar the ear. They appear to possess an intuitive knowledge of harmony, and they have a remarkable capacity of adding impromptu parts, or single notes which emphasise the melody and produce no discord, in such simple rhythms as a music-loving but uncultured people naturally furnish; though some of their tunes are not lacking in dramatic effect at times.[79]

Nuttall's belief that the Christian should demonstrate in daily life the impact of the Lord on personal consciousness found affirmation in Afro-Jamaican religious perception of the power of God in 'all nature, in all life, in all circumstances'.[80] The evolution of Christianity would be best assured if the contributions of all races or cultures were co-opted and integrated. If diverse perceptions of religion were integrated into the Christian whole, universal Christianity would be enriched, and become more vibrant, even perfect. The positivist conception (albeit conservative) of development, order and progress, did not rule out perfection. As Christianity, therefore, responded to diversity:

> What one emphasises and another neglects will, as time passes

and intercommunication increases, tell upon the whole body of Christian thought, defects will be remedied, excrescences removed, and Christianity will tend more and more to become a perfect expression of the whole of the Divine teaching as interpreted by the thoughts, experiences and needs of the whole human race.[81]

The practical and realistic bent of the Negro and the philosophical, abstract and idealisitic religious perception of the East Indian would add to the experience, knowledge, and dissemination of Christianity. Nuttall also contributed to the positivist notion of relativity by recognising that exposure to education and the trend of modern (secular) thought would modify some of the wholesome elements in Afro-Jamaican religious perception. In positivism 'all social forms and institutions are provisional in the sense that, as intellectual culture advances, they will pass into others that will correspond with intellectual capacities of an advanced type'.[82]

Just as in secular society Comte's reverence for established authority was reconciled with the principle of tolerance, so too in the ecclesiastical domain there was room for tolerance. One of the tests of Nuttall's episcopal and positivist tolerance came in 1883 when Jamaica experienced one of its periodic revivals. Nuttall was not unmindful of white, elite fears of the potential disruption which a revivalist movement could bring about in Jamaica. But he nevertheless reiterated the view that the gradual, quiet exposure of Afro-Jamaicans to Christianity and western civilisation in general would eventually remove from Jamaica experiences such as the revival of the 1860s and of 1883.

The responses of Nuttall, who had come to Jamaica at the time of the 1862 revival in response to that revival, was interesting because it demonstrated his concern from the beginning with the 'upliftment' of the 'subject peoples'. Nuttall always insisted that outbursts of emotion among black congregations were not qualitatively different from what he had seen among the more 'ignorant sections' of the 'advanced races', and in the working class districts of England. His role was to offer a 'sympathetic and steadying influence'. He also showed the underlying policy of co-optation of Afro-Jamaican religious practice into the Christian (formal) Church.

Nuttall's response to the revival was questioned by two of his clergy who worked very closely with him. On the one hand Rev. D.B. Panton in Manchester found Nuttall lacking in enthusiasm for the revival, while Rev. Ramson found him too enthusiastic. In a letter to Panton, Nuttall expressed the view that revivalism was 'vital religion', but he feared for the status quo. The dilemma was how to preserve 'vital religion', and not allow it to pose a threat to the status quo.

In his words:

The revival in your parish, if a revival of pure religion, is something I should like to witness and share – even if there are some things about it I should not like. You know the danger of these things in Jamaica. But I see clearly that we are all so in danger of guarding against the evils of enthusiasm in religion as these develop in this country, that we are in *greater* danger of losing the power of vital religion.[83]

Rev. Ramson condemned revivalism, and Nuttall replied to him in August 1883 showing some limited support for the revival, and showing less concern about the status quo:

I am obliged to differ from you in this matter as much as I differ from Mr Panton. Because he sees such a vast preponderance of good in what is taking place under his close observation in Manchester, he is disposed to astonishment at what he deems the spiritual blindness of those clergy and others who are doubtful about Jamaican revival movements. Because what had been brought under your notice has been spurious excitement and probably resulted in immorality, you are disposed to think I speak of revival work as contrary to the Church and to Christ ... Here is a matter in which we have to learn to distinguish and discriminate. What is going on in Manchester is in kind and degree as like as can be to what takes place in most of those missions in English parishes conducted by men of different Church views under the direct sanction and often with the personal help of one or other of the bishops. [But] what has been done frequently in many parts of Jamaica in the name of revivalism is too abominable to be even named.[84]

While Nuttall was warning Rev. Panton of the 'dangers' of revivalism in Jamaica he was at the same time reassuring Rev. Ramson that there was no need to fear since revivalist movements in Jamaica were not substantially different from what transpired in English parishes with the approval of English bishops. He made reference to the immorality contingent upon revivalism, but since these things were 'too abominable to be named', we are left in the dark as to what immoral practices accompanied revivalism. In another letter to Rev. Panton the Bishop complained:

It is one of my present crosses (only emphasising the habit of my life) to be obliged to differ from many with whom I would see eye to eye because I feel compelled to look at all sides of the facts. Mr Ramson has written me very strongly against revival movements. You think and speak as if I were steeped in the spirit of worldly opposition to what is truly spiritual because I cannot be so enthusiastically confident as you are to the ultimate and abiding good.[85]

The Bishop continued to show far more concern about 'immoral practices' within revivalism than about the dangers to social stability. Though no one identified these immoral practices they were referred to from time to time.[86] At the same time Nuttall thought that the response of the clergy was important in determining the course of the revivalist movement. Harsh words and statements, he believed, could do more harm than good by fanning the fires of excitement. But sound Christian leadership would, on the other hand, have the desirable effect of incorporating local religious expression into the formal Church. Nuttall criticised the response of churchmen to the revivalist movement which spread to the western parishes, or as he called it 'the recent religious excitement there'. The responses of churchmen were influenced by their recollection of Morant Bay, and the danger of a general revolt based on race:

> No doubt they have clearly in mind the undoubted and serious evils connected with the revival 20 years ago. But I believe that general excitement, like the present more local manifestation thereof, needed above all things the firm sympathetic guidance of intelligent, strongminded Christian ministers. I should expect these movements to develop fanaticism and all kinds of folly and vice, without such guidance; and with such guidance I should expect these movements to become the occasion and partly the means of great social, moral and spiritual improvement. This is the lesson I draw from the history of the last 1800 years, and the only difference needing to be made in applying to Jamaica lessons drawn from the history of other countries and ages, is that the Jamaican people are more easily led, for good or evil, than is the case with many other people.[87]

Nuttall did not accept the elements of racist thought that blacks were irredeemable, and that there were genetically inherited characteristics which condemned the coloured races to perpetual savagery or irrevocable decline. The Archbishop made distinctions between the races, but like his acquaintance Theodore Roosevelt, used the terms race and culture almost interchangeably. Society, that is, could be changed by altering the social environment. Culture was not static. He referred to 'features in the native African religion' as amounting to a 'race characteristic'. He also refers to 'fundamental differences' between the races arising from 'mental construction'.[88] Evidently, however, this 'mental construction' was not the supposed Lamarkian theory of acquired characteristics, but rather a theory of acquired culture.[89] Because he goes on to say, 'it is important to remember that part, at least, of this fundamental difference (of races) is the result of culture, or the absence of it, and that all special race tendencies will be modified by time and culture'.[90] As far as Afro-Jamaican religion was concerned, the problem was to alter the 'mental construction' and specifically to convert a recalcitrant 'Old Testament' consciousness into a 'New Testament consciousness',[91] and remove the features of African 'superstition' which impeded full absorption into the Christian Church and western civilisation.

The history of religion and society in Jamaica facilitated the integration of blacks in the formal Christian Churches. A significant difference between Afro-Jamaican religious experience and similar experience among black communities in the United States lies in the solidarity of black Churches in the USA contingent upon institutional racism. Racism enforced the formation of black Churches under black institutional leadership which led ultimately to greater black racial solidarity, or reinforced black solidarity. In Jamaica, there was never quite the same experience, in spite of the presence of the Native Baptist Church which had the closest association with Afro-Jamaican religious perception. But the formal Baptist Church was still under white leadership, and Native Baptist Churches were not organically linked. For the rest, the relationship between Christian Churches and the masses of the population represented a continuum of beliefs ranging from the most 'formal' patterns of worship to African Zionism, Pukkumina, myalism and revivalism at the other end of the continuum. Thus religion, like marriage patterns, revealed the complex mechanisms by which segments of society were linked and held together. A 'Black' Church in Jamaica, institutionally speaking, would have found survival difficult since the official policy was one of co-optation and assimilation.

The positivist state was hierarchical, assumed governance by a 'cultural elite' and inequality. The German positivist, F.J. Stahl, even insisted that the distribution of wealth was the work of God's will.[92] In Jamaica the cultural elite was not exclusively white, but it was whites who ruled, and who set standards, good or bad. Thus Nuttall's priesthood would consist of men of all races, but leadership belonged to whites.

Education was high on the agenda of social action, set by positivists for the State.[93] Nuttall, despite the great efforts which he dedicated to education, through the Anglican Church, considered that primary responsibility for education rested with the State. The Church's function was entirely a question of moral commitment. So, at least, he reminded the Inspector of Schools. Secular education was a useful mechanism in the positivist mind to eliminate superstition, that is to say traditional religion.[94] All citizens were to be educated but levels of education corresponded to social hierarchy. In Nuttall's view people should be educated 'according to their requirement', and subjects at elementary school level should be taught in terms of their 'practical usefulness' in the future lives of the people. Secondary education was the province of the upper and middle classes, though 'every facility should be provided for further teaching to specially capable boys and girls'.[95] The Belmont Orphanage was for the education of good domestic servants, the nursing profession was carved out for coloured women.

All citizens, in the positivist tradition, had duties. There is a duty resting upon every man to give some of his time and interest and effort, 'to the active promotion of some monument or institution intended to benefit the whole community'.[96] Nuttall's positivist orientation led him to the inevitable conclusion that the duty of the clergyman encompassed 'everything that appertains to the welfare of our people' who:

> will respond none the less, but all the more to our efforts for their
> spiritual welfare, if they know that in a time of stress and strain
> . . . we have cared for their temporal things.[97]

Workers, then, would receive moral and spiritual guidance, education and work. Education was an instrument for the preparation of skilled workers.

The flag of Nuttall's positivist state fluttered well above that of the locally elected or nominated Legislative Council of Jamaica. Nuttall identified vital links between Christianity and empire. Imperial unity required not just a coexistence of cultures, but a limited integration of European and other 'subject' cultures. Such a policy would strengthen the Church's membership and simultaneously the Empire and Christendom. Also, once elements of the subject empire had been absorbed into the Church on the basis of a limited assimilation of their own religious experiences and expressions it would become practical for the leaders of Christendom to utilise them to win over other elements within the Empire.

> In these qualities Christianised sections of the race may assist the
> growth in the Christian community generally of sound ideas as to
> due subordination to wise ecclesiastical authority.[98]

One of the over-riding considerations of the Bishop was the 'mischief resulting from the divisions of Christendom; the waste of energy, the overlapping of work, the weakening of discipline, all this needed a practical remedy. Where is the remedy to be found? It is needed in order to secure the true and rapid progress of Christianity in the wide fields of heathenism'.[99] The Archbishop encouraged and prepared Jamaicans for missionary work in the Pongas Mission in Africa. The Baptists also set up a mission in New Calabar. The comment of the Bishop of Sierra Leone on a visit to Jamaica in about 1892 suggests that by then Jamaican missionaries had become a familiar sight:

> On several occasions we heard the Bishop [Nuttall] remind his
> black congregation that the Jamaican is commonly called the
> Anglo-Saxon of the Far West. He is emphatically a colonizer.[100]

The torch of civilisation and of Christianity was to be carried, eventually,
not only by the white Christian but by the black convert thoroughly trained
in Christian religion and western life, an agent for the spread of western
civilisation. The western civilisation which Nuttall desired to spread was
first and foremost the British way of life but more typically he spoke of
Anglo-Saxon civilisation, which would embrace the United States as well.
For Nuttall, who was on fairly close personal terms with the United States'
President, Theodore Roosevelt, was an ardent advocate of an Anglo-Ameri-
can alliance.[101]

It was not so much the Anglican Church that Nuttall believed in, as W.
Adolphe Roberts suggests,[102] as the British Empire and Anglo-Saxon civilisation. The rule of Britain, the Bishop said, had been intended (despite
some weaknesses) to benefit and raise subject races, and to a 'wonderful
extent it has succeeded in this. Our people are becoming . . . more and more
fit to exercise the rights of empire, and I trust they will show that they are
proud of their connection with the Empire, and are ready to sustain . . . the
Queen's dominion'.[103] A significant proportion of the cultural transfer of
British Anglo-Saxon civilisation was British Christianity.[104] The Archbishop, as he was in 1897, envisaged one Christian community dominated
by British Christianity.

Nuttall's views on empire were conditioned in part by the movement
for imperial unity and imperial community which reached its peak during
the Joseph Chamberlain years. But his general views on empire had been
shaped before then. The concern for the competitiveness of the British
Empire, with respect to Germany and the United States, stimulated programmes for efficiency and unity.[105] Self-reliance had always been emphasised, since no one expected the Empire to cost the British taxpayer
anything.

There was no doubt that significant numbers of the Afro-Jamaican
population supported the Churches, and the growth of new settlements was
also always followed by the establishment of churches and schools in those
areas, by rival denominations. The construction of churches and schools
was, in the late-nineteenth century, a result of the labour and the financial
contributions of the Afro-Jamaican population – albeit in the case of the
Anglicans with some assistance from the Society for the Propagation of
Christian Knowledge. The Baptists established Calabar College, the Anglicans St Peter's Seminary, and the Presbyterians a theological school to train
a local ministry to facilitate the spread of Christianity in rural Jamaica. In
fact, the concentration on rural Jamaica led almost to neglect of Kingston,

which in the view of so many people was becoming a den of all iniquities. Again, Nuttall endeavoured to fill the gap in Kingston. Part of the problem of the established Churches was that funding for their efforts which traditionally came from overseas was curtailed, as parent bodies became more interested and involved in the wider mission fields of Asia and Africa. Within Jamaica, by 1892 there were 100 Anglican clergy and approximately 150 catechists. In that year the Church Army was established, consisting of men who could reach the population not easily reached by 'ordinary agencies'. The Church Army of the Anglican Church equipped itself with a Gazette which was a paper 'for working folk containing simple Gospel, and Church teaching of a kind which they need and can understand'.[106]

The number of Anglican churches increased from 92 in 1884 to 212 in 1900. In 1868, prior to disestablishment there had been 89 only. There were, by 1900, 96 mission stations in the fourteen parishes. Accommodation increased from at least 32,340 in 1884 to 71,970 in 1900. Average attendance was approximately two-thirds of seating capacity.[107]

The Churches, after much inter-denominational competition, recognised the need for co-operative effort in the Jamaican mission, but clergymen and other observers saw a declining enthusiasm for Church attendance on the part of the Afro-Jamaican population. Writing in 1905, the Presbyterian, Rev. C.A. Wilson, lamented that 'Religion has not the hold on the heart of the people to make it the mainstream of action. Men look at the Minister and speak of owing him money'.[108] The conscientious clergyman complained that the bane of religion in Jamaica was hypocrisy, that perhaps half of the Church members were not Christians. They profess not and believe not. They gamble on Saturday, take the Lord's Supper on Sunday, pray on Sunday and swear on Monday.[109] Other clergymen mourned the fact that the Afro-Jamaican population stayed away from Church, and that their absence was not on account of poverty, since it was obvious that they could afford beautiful attire.

Falling attendance was attributed to 'indifference, unbelief or religious reasons'.[110] In the first category were those who had been baptised but no longer indulged the fashion of going to Church on Sunday. 'A man, especially of the lower class, who did not attend Divine Service was looked at askance by his neighbours. So he went. At present no one thinks any the worse of a man for staying home on the Sabbath day. So he follows his natural inclinations and stays home. Indifference was also a product of the kind of education which consists of a smattering of everything. Others stay home because they dislike the poor sermons'.[110]

Clergymen were accused of being too busy doing too many other things outside their strictly spiritual functions – sitting on Parochial Boards, or organising fund-raising events. This particular criticism of the clergy is

an ironical tribute to the role which clergymen had been playing for so
many years. Priests were indeed active on Parochial Boards, and sat on the
Legislative Council, (their numbers destined to increase) partly because
they viewed themselves as the representatives of black voters, and were
among the sectors of society which showed most concern for the welfare of
the Afro-Jamaican population. The fund-raising activity of the Church was
a response to declining subsidies from abroad and the declining ability of
the rural population in particular to support their Churches.

The criticism of the clergy notwithstanding, their work was acknowledged, at least in the negative sense, in that without their efforts the social
situation would have been far worse. The limited 'civilisation' which Jamaica
was privileged to enjoy was entirely on account of their efforts. So, at least,
argued Herbert George deLisser.

The role of the Church complemented that of administrators and of the
dominant class in transforming the ex-slaves and their descendants into 'a
stable, obedient and hard-working class of wage-labourers; that is, to try to
preserve the basic structure of relations of production by deploying ideological, rather than physical, means of coercion'.[111] In practice, the role of
the clerical element is best understood as a bargaining one which sought to
balance the interests of employers and workers. For certain segments of the
elite mass education was not particularly desirable, because it 'spoiled'
labour. But, for Nuttall and others, education was linked to order and
progress. Dr John Hall, a member of the Legislative Council, saw education
as social guidance, 'guidance (of the unlettered) in respect for the law and
in recognition of conscience are not merely duties inherent in the brotherhood of man. They are safeguards demanded by the welfare of the society.
It is by these means that the hydra of anarchy can be overcome. It is by
better education of the people and increased guidance by their *natural*
leaders that an end can be put to the loss and misery of strikes and lockouts
and boycotting . . .' [112]

The activity of the Church was constrained by limited resources, and
churchgoing became, probably, as much an activity to demonstrate 'respectability' as to prepare for the Kingdom of God. The reality that the
mission frontiers of obeah, Kumina, Bedwardism, had not been brought
fully under the control of the Church militant did not reflect a lack of
commitment by churchmen. Rather, it is a testimony to the resilience of
Afro-Jamaican working-class religious expression, which, ever creative,
syncretised rather than accepted or rejected. Yet, the evidence points to the
continuation of some of these traditions among Afro-Jamaicans who had
attained some 'social respectability'. Subtle differences in religious expression suggest not sharp differences in the practice of religion but subtle
gradations. The positivists would have seen this as an act of Divine Providence, and the hope of progress within order.

Notes

1 Paget Henry, *Peripheral Capitalism And Underdevelopment in Antigua*, New Brunswick and Oxford: Transaction Books, 1985, p. 61.
2 E.P. Thompson, *The Making of the English Working Class*, Harmondsworth: Penguin Books, 1977, p. 446.
3 Mary Turner, *Slaves and Missionaries: The Disintegration of Jamaican Slave Society, 1787 – 1834*, Urbana and London: University of Illinois Press, 1982; Monica Schuler, *Alas! Alas! Kongo: A Social History of Indentured African Immigration to Jamaica, 1841–1865*, Baltimore and London, 1980; Margaret E. Crahan and Franklin W. Knight, *Africa and the Caribbean: The Legacies of a Link*, Baltimore and London: Johns Hopkins University Press, 1979.
4 Monica Schuler, *Alas! Alas! Kongo*, pp. 34–5.
5 Rev. Horace Scotland, 'Modern Infidelity considered in respect to the Middle and Lower Class in the British West Indies', *West Indian Quarterly*, 1886–7 p. 7 and p.13.
6 *Ibid*. p. 13.
7 *New York Times*, 10 December, 1895. 'Piety Among Jamaican Blacks', Dateline, Kingston, 25 November 1895, p. 16.
8 *Jamaica Memories*, Sarah Carter.
9 Herbert George deLisser, *Twentieth Century Jamaica*, Kingston: The Jamaica Times, 1913, p. 130.
10 Rev. Joseph Williams, (S.J.), *Whisperings of the Caribbean: Reflections of a Missionary*, New York: Benziger Bros. 1925, p. 225.
11 W. Gardner, quoted in *ibid*. p. 229.
12 *Ibid*. p. 237.
13 *Ibid*. p. 239.
14 *Ibid*. p. 282.
15 *Ibid*. p. 239.
16 Richard Sheridan, *Doctors and Slaves. A Medical and Demographic History of Slavery in the British West Indies, 1680–1834*, Cambridge: Cambridge University Press, 1985, p. 72.
17 Eugene Genovese, quoted in *ibid*. p. 97.
18 *Ibid*. p. 79.
19 *Ibid*. p. 75.
20 NLJ, MS 209a, Vol. 32b, *Douet Letter Book*. Douet to Rev. J.S. Fraser (locovia) 2 October, 1894.
21 Sheridan, *Doctors and Slaves*, p. 78.
22 JDR, 1905–7, p. 140 and Jamaica Archives, 1B/5/18, Vol. 47, Blake No. 162, 23 May 1892 to Knutsford.
23 Proceeding of the Legislative Council, Kingston, Jamaica, 1898, pp. 11ff. Debate on Obeah Law.
24 *Ibid*. p. 11.
25 Alice Spinner, *The Reluctant Evangelist and other Stories*, London: Edward Arnold, 1896, p. 320.
26 Rev. Abraham J. Emerick, S.J., *Jamaica Superstitions: Obeah and Duppyism in Jamaica*, Woodstock, Maryland: Woodstock Letters 1915–16, p. 37.
27 Alice Spinner, *The Reluctant Evangelist*, p. 319.
28 *Ibid*. pp. 321–5.
29 *Ibid*. p. 319.
30 *Ibid*. p. 315.

31   David O. Moberg, *The Church as a Social Institution, The Sociology of American Religion*, New Jersey: Prentice Hall, 1962, p. 440 and p. 449.

32   A.A. Brooks, *History of the Jamaica Native Baptist Church*, Kingston: Daily Gleaner, p. 16.

33   Enos Nuttall, 'Negro Christianity', in Rev. J. Ellison (ed.), *Church and Empire*, Longman: London, 1907.

34   Frank Cundall, *Life of Enos Nuttall*, London: SPCK, 1922, p. 108.

35   NLJ, MS 209a, *Bishop's Letter Book*, Nuttall to Sir Henry Blake, 25 September, 1983.

36   *DG*, 3 October, 1904. 'Faith Healing'.

37   *Ibid*.

38   Jamaica Archives, 1B/5/18, Vol. 49. Blake to Ripon No. 165, 28 May, 1895.

39   *New York Times*, 10 December, 1895. 'Piety Among Jamaican Blacks', p. 16.

40   CO, 137/514, XC/A 012699. Report of Dr Allen on Lunatic Asylum, 1883. Table 12. Enclosure to Despatch, Norman to Derby, No. 107, 13 March, 1884.

41   E.B. Burns, *The Poverty of Progress, Latin America in the Nineteenth Century*, Berkeley: University of California Press, 1980, p. 122.

42   *JA*, 2 February, 1895, 'Bedward's Trial'.

43   *JA*, 27 June, 1896.

44   *JA*, 17 October, 1896.

45   *DG*, 21 March, 1889, 'Taxpayer' to Editor, on 'Revival'.

46   *DG*, 21 March, 1889, 'Revivals and Wakes'.

47   *Ibid*.

48   H.G. deLisser, 'White Man in the Tropics', *Century Review*, February 1900, NLJ, *Jamaica Pamphlets*.

49   Sir Henry Blake, *The Awakening of Jamaica*, NLJ, *Jamaica Pamphlets*, No. 22, 1890.

50   Jamaica Archives, 1B 5/18, Vol. 49. Blake to Chamberlain, No. 372, 14 November, 1895.

51   Legislative Council of Jamaica. *Proceedings of the Third Session*, 1894, pp. 87–89.

52   W.P. Livingstone, *Black Jamaica: A Study in Evolution*, London: Sampson Low, Marston and Co., 1900, p. 15.

53   *Ibid*. p. 6.

54   *Ibid*. pp. 9–10.

55   *Ibid*. p. 227.

56   *Ibid*. p. 241.

57   *Ibid*. p. 242.

58   'J.B.', *Jamaica Pie: Being Tales of Past and Present*, Pt. 1, 'Glimpses of Old Jamaica', Kingston, *Daily Gleaner*, 1943, p. 4.

59   Frank Cundall, *Life*, p. 213; and Bishop E.L. Evans, *A History of the Diocese of Jamaica*, Kingston, C-1976.

60   W. Adolphe Roberts, *Six Great Jamaicans*, Kingston, Pioneer Press, 1952, p. 52.

61   *NLJ*, MS 209a, Vol. 29, *Bishop's Letter Book*. Nuttall to William Klein, 31 July, 1893.

62   H. Marcuse, *Reason and Revolution: Hegel and the Rise of Social Theory*, Boston: Beacon Press, 1960, p. 341.

63   Enos Nuttall, 'Characteristics of the Negro' in Rev. J. Ellison, (ed.) *Church and Empire*, p. 103.

64   Marcuse, *Reason and Revolution*, p. 346.

65 Enos Nuttall, 'The Negro Race' in Ellison (ed.) *Church and Empire*, London: Longman, 1907, p. 87.
66 Marcuse, *Reason and Revolution*, p. 347.
67 NLJ, MS 209a, *Bishop's Letter Book* Vol. VIII. Nuttall to R.H. Jackson, 21 January, 1884.
68 Marcuse, *Reason and Revolution*, p. 357.
69 H.E. Davis, *Latin American Social Thought*, Washington D.C.: University Press of Washington D.C. 1963, p. 189.
70. H.E. Barnes and Howard Becker, *Social Thought: From Lore to Science*, New York, Dover Publications, 3rd edition, 1961, Vol. 3, pp. 825–6.
71 Davis, *Latin American Social Thought*, p. 193.
72 Enos Nuttall, 'Characteristics of the Negro', p. 93.
73 Marcuse, *Reason and Revolution*, p. 354.
74 Enos Nuttall, 'Negro Christianity', p. 115; and Enos Nuttall, 'Characteristics of the Negro', p. 103.
75 NLJ, MS 209a, *Bishop's Letter Book*. Nuttall to Rev. James Roberts, 26 August, 1893.
76 Nuttall, 'Negro Christianity', p. 116.
77 Nuttall, 'Characteristics of the Negro', p. 97.
78 *Ibid.* p. 104.
79 *Ibid.* p. 104.
80 *Ibid.* p. 97.
81 *Ibid.* p. 113.
82 Marcuse, *Reason and Revolution*, p. 354.
83 *NLJ*, MS 209a, *Bishop's Letter Book*, Vols. VI–VII. Nuttall to Rev. Panton, 14 April, 1883, and Nuttall to Rev. Ramson, 28 August, 1883.
84 *Ibid.*
85 *Ibid.* Nuttall to Panton, 28 August, 1883.
86 Rev. Dingwall, *Jamaica's Greatest Need*, London: Lennon and Co. 1892. Dingwall, p. 28, refers to 'unclean types of revivalism'.
87 *NLJ*, MS 209a, *Bishop's Letter Book*. Nuttall (Unofficial) to Hon. E.N. Walker, 30 July, 1883.
88 Nuttall, 'Characteristics of the Negro', p. 113.
89 T.G. Dyer, *Theodore Roosevelt and the Idea of Race*, Baton Rouge and London: Louisiana State University Press, 1980, pp. 7–39.
90 Nuttall, 'Characteristics of the Negro', p. 112.
91 *Ibid.* p. 98.
92 Marcuse, *Reason and Revolution*, p. 369.
93 H.E. Davis, *Latin American Social Thought*, p. 190.
94 *Ibid.* p. 190.
95 Enos Nuttall, 'Some Present Needs of Jamaica as specified in an Address delivered at the Opening Meeting of the Diocesan Synod', 9 February, 1897. p. 7.
96 *Ibid.* p. 14.
97 *Ibid.* p. 14.
98 Nuttall, 'Characteristics of the Negro', p. 112.
99 Nuttall, 'Negro Christianity', p. 116.
100 E.G. Ingham, *The African in the West Indies by the Bishop of Sierra Leone*, c.1892, p. 21.
101 Frank Cundall, *Life*, p. 213. For Roosevelt's views on race and culture see T.G. Dyer, *Theodore Roosevelt and the Idea of Race, op. cit.*

102   W. Adolphe Roberts, *Six Great Jamaicans*, p. 52.
103   F. Cundall, *Life*, p. 77.
104   Nuttall, 'Some Present Needs', p. 3.
105   J.G. Greenlee, 'Imperial Studies and the Unity of the Empire', *Journal of Imperial and Commonwealth History*, Vol. VII, No. 3, 18 May, 1979, p. 321.
106   NLJ, MS 209a, *Bishop's Letter Book*, Vol. 29.
107   *HBJ*, 1900.
108   Rev. C.A. Wilson, *Men with Backbone and other pleas for Progress*, Kingston: Educational Supply Co, 1913, p. 73.
109   *Ibid*, p. 74.
110   *DG*, 22 December 1900. Essay by Mr A.S. Roberts, Newport P.O., 'Why are the Churches not better attended?'
111   Raymond T. Smith, 'Race and Class in the Post-Emancipation Caribbean', in Robert Ross, *Racism and Colonialism: Essays on Ideology and Social Structure*, The Hague: Leiden, Martinus Nijhoff, 1982.
112   *DG*, 8 February, 1886. Editorial comment on speech of Dr John Hall.

CHAPTER 5 | The ranks of society

From a total of 506,154 people in 1871, Jamaica's population grew to 588,804 in 1881. In spite of emigration during the 1880s the population grew to 639,491 in 1891 and to 831,383 in 1911. In 1871 there were 13,101 whites, 100,346 coloureds, and 392,767 blacks. The census of 1891 shows only a marginal increase in the white population – up to 14,692. Of these 14,692 as many as 5,962 lived in Kingston, and another 2,510 in St Andrew and St Catherine. More than half of the white population lived in the urban zones, then, of Kingston, St Andrew and St Catherine.[1]

Whites declined as a percentage of population from 2.29 per cent in 1891 to 1.88 per cent in 1911. The coloured population proved to be the most rapidly expanding segment, showing a growth of 33.8 per cent between 1891 and 1911. The black population grew by 28.9 per cent. The census of 1911 put the black and coloured population at 75.8 and 19.6 per cent of total population. In 1891 the black population had stood at 76.41 per cent and the coloured at 19.07 per cent.[2]

The differential access to the economic resources of the island concentrated economic and ultimately political power in the hands of the white minority. The social and political, bureaucratic and cultural authority of the white segment was partly assured by the fact that 'a society may perpetuate social inequalities far more effectively when the maldistribution of income is buttressed by phenotype'.[3]

Social differences between the racial segments were not, however, entirely conditional on the perception of racial differences between people. Distinctions between people and groups could also be made in terms of occupation, speech, dress, general life chances, income, property, religion and levels of education. But such differences do not assume the existence of 'incompatible cultural institutions', they are, rather, a commentary on the opportunity structure in a society which essentially enjoyed a continuum of shared beliefs and customs.

White society accepted a certain level of equality among whites, not because they believed that all whites were equal but because being white in the Caribbean has special meaning. Being white in the Caribbean means, above all, *not* being black. Thus, the ideas and values that develop in this so-called 'cultural section' will be 'permeated by the necessity of defining

{ itself against its despised and feared opposite'.[4] }

Ethnic 'unity' within the white segment did not deny the differences in wealth, privilege, and status between whites. Colonial administration itself created social distinctions. In their discussion of Iberian colonial administration, Stanley and Barbara Stein observe that colonial 'administration provided a highly visible structure of command and a framework which encloses the more formless processes of social, economic, and cultural change'.[5] Within white society the colonial bureaucrats collectively represented British imperial power and served to foster the legitimacy of British rule. This is why, in the colonial setting, the bureaucrat enjoyed a status which he never enjoyed at home. As Frank Cundall, himself a bureaucrat, expresses it:

> In England, a man may serve the State all his life and never come
> under public notice. In the West Indies his every action is noted.
> His salary is freely commented on, his holidays duly chronicled,
> his promotions recorded, and his personality freely criticised.[6]

The bureaucrat, a white administrator in a land of dark men, was expected to be the champion in the smallest detail of everyday life of white, British, cultural supremacy. At the same time, he helped to ensure that domination of the bureaucracy by whites would reinforce pre-existing class, racial and cultural distinctions, between people.

The expatriate bureaucrat's associations and interactions were primarily with the ranks of white society. It was generally acknowledged that however open-minded the bureaucrat was at the time of his arrival in the island, his attitude came to resemble closely those of the dominant white segment, especially with regard to the black and coloured population.[7] There was, in addition, a certain measure of integration into the economy. Despite their transiency, colonial bureaucrats, from governors to second-class clerks, invested in grazing pens, cinchona plantations, and other economic enterprises. A survey conducted in 1884 revealed that land ownership among colonial bureaucrats ranged from 200 acres to over 2,300 acres.[8] Governor Henry Blake admitted his interest in land ownership in the island.

Social interaction did not rule out conflict between the top segments of the white population. The colonial bureaucrat was considered by the local white establishment as transient, uncommitted, opportunistic; he was often viewed as without merit by the white Jamaican upper class who described him sometimes as the 'aristocratic destitute' or as 'third rate'. The root of that conflict was precisely the domination of the bureaucracy by expatriates who deprived 'worthy' locals of prestigious office. White Jamaicans lamented that there was a drain of the financial resources of the colony to support high salaries and pensions. They believed that lack of knowledge of the vernacular by expatriate magistrates could frustrate the ends of justice. Hence the following story:

Overheard in court
A prisoner was before Justice Judge Little, charged with the theft of a pig.

> Judge: What did you do with the pig?
> Prisoner: John Cro' tek 'im, sah!
> Judge: Call up Mr John Crow![9]

The power of white Jamaican society over the bureaucrat rested in the power of white Jamaica to ostracise socially the bureaucrat who violated the social code, or otherwise conducted himself in a way which showed antagonism to the superordinate whites (and coloureds). Hence, Justice Gibbons who used the law to protect farmers who had been victims of dishonest conveyancing, and who uncovered the link between big business and praedial larceny, was to have been black-balled if he had attempted to join the white Manchester Club. The residents of Mandeville refused to make social calls on Justice Gibbons.[10]

Yet, the appeal to local symbolism (such as the vernacular) to establish, perhaps, that they could control the 'natives' better, could not conceal the reality that Jamaican whites viewed themselves no less as Englishmen than their rivals in the bureaucracy freshly arrived in the island. The point was made forcibly by a black Jamaican that whites identified with 'the soil and less so with the people of the land'.

> The Jamaican white man has his peculiarities as well as man everywhere under the influence of climate, local needs, blessings, thought, feeling . . . At once he is the least Jamaican of everything pertaining to the country. He longs to return to England, if he is a native Englishman; and if he is not, he thinks at least he ought to visit that country; and he speaks of it as 'home', even when he has never visited it. There are, however, some families among them, who, on account of their 'stake' in the country have become identified with this land for generations, but it is for the greater part an identification with the *soil*, and less so with the *people* of the land.[11]

Ultimately, the power of white Jamaican society rested not in noble birth but in a centuries old tradition of dominance associated with the wealth extracted from sugar and other plantations. Whites maintained their position by the habit of power and by the power of habit. The decline of the sugar plantations did not reduce their social authority. The white planter class may be divided into the two categories of resident and absentee planters. The majority of estates over 1,000 acres in 1895 were owned by resident planters, but proportionately the absentee proprietors still held considerable acreages. There were also partnerships between absentees and resident planters. Planters discussed seriously the possibility of annexation to the United States, or confederation with Canada in 1884, to protect their economic interests.

The traditional planter class was joined after the 1880s at the top of the socio-economic ladder by the banana entrepreneurs. The great banana entrepreneurs had originated in the mercantile segment and in the professional areas of Jamaican life. J.E. Kerr, for example, who started a business in Montego Bay in the 1870s, shipped logwood to Boston, then loaded a cargo of flour from New York for shipment to Jamaica.[12] In the early 1880s he became interested in the export fruit business (bananas and oranges) in Montego Bay and Lucea, and was soon to have branches at Falmouth, St Ann's Bay and Port Maria. J.E. Kerr became one of the biggest shippers, and from the 1880s his fleet of ships, including steamships, were transporting oranges and bananas to New York. Kerr's first fruit boat was the *Edith Godden*. Later he added the *Pemona*, the *Vertumnus*, the *Neptune*, the *Argonaut*, the *Jason*, the *Golden Fleece* (wrecked in 1896) and the *Atlanta*, capable of eighteen knots and 'doing the trip from Montego Bay to New York in four days or less'.[13] J.E. Kerr, in 1887, was also a producer of some 350 acres of bananas at Llanrumny.

Dr (later Sir John) Pringle, a Scottish medical officer who subsequently became a member of the governor's Privy Council, became one of the foremost banana entrepreneurs. Owner of Trinity and Brimmer Hall estates Pringle purchased Nonsuch (2,500 acres), Nuffield, Newry, Tulloch Castle and Green Castle on a thousand-year leasehold, all for the sum of £6,500. Some of the properties purchased by Pringle had been owned by his father-in-law. Most of those purchases had been made in 1887, but by 1912 the Pringle properties were 'continuously developed until in 1912 the Hon. Sir John Pringle had under cultivation in St Mary and St James nearly 5,000 acres in bananas and with associates 1,000 acres in St Thomas. Later the Pringle holdings in St Mary were to form almost the entire holding of banana cultivation in Jamaica of the Atlantic Fruit Company and afterwards of the Standard Fruit Company'.[14]

Other significant banana producers were A.L. DaCosta who had been growing bananas since 1881 on 200 acres at Fontabelle and Pemberton Valley, and 300 acres at Quebec. In 1893 a partnership between Robert Butler Braham, the Hon. John Powell Clark, William Peploe Forwood, and Francis Bather laid the foundation for the Jamaica Fruit Company (Dove Hall) when they appeared as mortgagees 'having the power of sale to have certificate of title of James Celeste Lecesne (Harker's Hall, St Catherine) of a plantation or sugar works called Dove Hall Estate and Grey's Hill, St Thomas in the Vale'.[15] Dove Hall had approximately 2,300 acres. A.L.

DaCosta was a major merchant, R.B. Braham was a storekeeper and stock-raiser, W.B. Forwood was the director of the Atlas Steamship Company.

The mercantile sector, then, entered banana production. Other merchants were to link their import business with the export of bananas to the United States. In 1893, for example, the association between Charles E. DeMercado (a merchant of Kingston and also a shareholder of the *Daily Gleaner*, and a partner of Lascelles in New York) and David Gideon (D.S. Gideon and Nephew, General Importers and Commission Merchants of Port Antonio) began when DeMercado proposed a shipment of bananas to New Orleans to cover the return trip of boats bringing his merchandise to Kingston. This association bloomed into a larger one between DeMercado, Gideon, Di Giorgio, Johnston and the Atlantic Fruit Company.[16]

The banana industry helped to blur even further the distinctions between planters and merchants; though at one level the sugar men were victims of the vigorous banana entrepreneurs. Some sugar planters eventually converted to banana production.

The link between merchant and planter capital was not confined to the banana industry. For example, Alfred Pawsey, a prominent merchant of Kingston, was also the proprietor of Gibbons Estate in Clarendon and of Bog Estate. He cultivated 470 acres of cane, produced 470 hogsheads of sugar and 424 puncheons of rum in 1900. William Malabre, another prominent merchant and customs broker, was also a substantial planter.[17] Colonel Ward – he held office in the militia and donated the Ward Theatre to the city of Kingston – had interests in sugar (Monymusk), coffee (Abbey Green in St Thomas), but was also the major retailer of spirituous liquors in Kingston.[18]

Planter and merchant capital also went into transportation. In 1897, for example, the West India Electric Company was initiated with a capital of $750,000 (*sic*) divided into shares of $100 each, with authority to increase the same to $1,250,000. The company received the franchise to operate an electric tramway or tramways, a power house, factories, and stations associated with the tramway. The directorship included Samuel Constantine Burke (lawyer), Peter Elicio Auvray (druggist), Louis Verley (planter and merchant); Sigismund Schloss (merchant), Ronald McPherson (gentleman), William Andrews (solicitor), and Arthur Rich Saunders (medical practitioner).[19]

Planter and mercantile interests linked themselves into the Jamaica Society of Agriculture in 1885. In the following year the organisation added Merchants' Exchange to its title and received the patronage of the Governor, together with a small annual subsidy.[20] (The Governor pointed out for the benefit of the Colonial Office that the organisation was not intended to be a political one.) In 1895 the organisation became the Royal Jamaica Society of Agriculture and Commerce and Merchants' Exchange.[21] During the twentieth century it evolved into the Jamaica Chamber of Commerce. Prominent members of the Society were William Malabre, Colonel James Ward, James Verley, Captain Forwood, P.E. Auvray, J.E. Kerr, J.M. Farquharson, F.B. Lyons, J.L. Ashenheim, all merchants, planters or a combination of both.

Ten members were added between 1894 and 1900, in which latter year there was a distinction drawn between town and country members. Among the new country members were Lorenzo D. Baker of the Boston Fruit Company. Other new members were F.L. Myers of rum fame, Thomas Aguilar and Isaac Brandon. Colonel Ward served for a long time as president of the organisation. Ward was also one of the Board of Directors of the Kingston Ice Making Company, he was a director of the Jamaica Co-operative Fire Insurance Company and he was a long time president of the Jamaica Club, an exclusive organisation of 'gentlemen' (£5–5–0 entrance fee and £3–3–0 annual subscription). Alfred Pawsey, while not listed as a member of the Merchants' Exchange, sat on the Board of Directors of the Kingston Ice Making Company, the Jamaica Co-operative Fire Insurance Company, the Jamaica Marine Insurance Company Ltd., and sat on the Managing Committee of the Jamaica Club.[22]

Jamaica's elite also sought association with each other in social clubs. While clubs are important as sports (or other) associations, they can be important instruments of social interaction, and equally, social exclusion. Ostracism in society generally could be reflected in exclusion from a club. As such, the club can serve the function not only of excluding large numbers of potential members, it can also discipline or enforce the conformity of members of the elite group through the fear of ostracism. A British observer commented on the fear which whites had of being ostracised: 'for a white man to champion the cause of his black fellow citizens is to risk social ostracism; and where culture and intelligence and everything that makes life of a refined and educated man worth living is confined to a limited circle, such a penalty is too great'.[23]

We do not know what examples this observer had in mind, but the evidence surrounding the example of Justice Gibbons illustrates the point well enough. Gibbons had alienated certain elements of the elite by his personal intervention in the credit relationship between shopkeepers and rural farmers, by exposing the relationship between logwood theft, big business and the magistracy. Originally posted in St Ann, Gibbons, who was a magistrate of the District Court, was transferred to Mandeville. Gibbons takes up the story:

> I had no acquaintances in Mandeville, and with very few exceptions, no one called on me. W. Coke called and I returned his call, but finding his wife would not call on my daughter because, I

have since been informed, my sister, who was in the island some years ago, had not called on her, the acquaintance dropped and Mr Coke assumed an attitude of hostility towards me . . .

His relationship with Mr J.T. Palache was also influenced by the following incident:

It may be that my having held the inquest on the body of his brother Gilbert Palache who destroyed himself with strychnine, in which the jury on the evidence of Mr Coke, found a verdict of death by misadventure, whilst all the other evidence pointed to *felo de se*. In this case I afterwards learned that all the jurors, with but one exception, were creditors of the deceased, who had died hopelessly involved, but one of them was the agent of a foreign Insurance Company in which the life of the deceased had been insured a few months previously, the amount of the policy was afterwards received by Mr J.T. Palache, as administrator . . . but . . . none of the creditors have yet been paid. [I have heard] Mr Lewis say that he intends to get his money.[24]

Mr Gibbons was to have been blackballed if he had sought application for membership of the Manchester Club.

The Jamaica Club was an organisation of elite men, including Colonel Ward, Mr Baggett-Gray, and the Hon. Jonathan Pringle (MBE, CMG), the latter two being members of the Managing Committee.[25] In Porus, in May 1894, a gentleman's Social Club was founded. The President of the Porus Club – consisting of 25 'gentlemen' – was businessman H.S. Braham.

White Jamaicans who had entered the island from Great Britain continued to maintain ethnic identities. Both the Scottish and Irish population maintained organisations which supposedly addressed themselves to their specific interests. In reality, though, these clubs were perhaps more important for the purposes of social intercourse. There was both a Jamaica Scottish Society and a Jamaica Caledonian Society. The rules of the Jamaica Scottish Society were drawn up in about 1914 and while in theory a reflection of 'Scottish' ethnic consciousness in Jamaican society it was really another exclusive social club. The objectives of the society did encompass mutual aid, such as rendering assistance to deserving natives of Scotland who were in need, to maintain a benevolent fund, to encourage the study of Scottish literature, music, sports, and to celebrate St Andrew's day. Membership was open to natives of Scotland and to Jamaicans of Scottish extraction. The annual subscription was 10/-.[26]

It is an indication of the ethnic divisions of Jamaican society and the desperate urge for social acceptance by some members of it, that an aspiring member of the Jamaica Caledonian Society could plead in a letter to the press for acceptance of coloured Jamaicans into the society. Someone signing himself as *Nemo me impune lacessit* pointed out that 'there were many loyal Scotchmen in Jamaica even though they have African blood; they are two-thirds Scottish, and as proud of the "auld countrie" as of the land of their birth. There were many loyal Scotchmen, claimed Nemo, among the coloured population'.[27] The plea for acceptance by browns continued a long, albeit not distinguished, tradition in Jamaica.

In December 1900, the Jamaica Caledonian Society celebrated St Andrew's Day at the Myrtle Bank Hotel.

> The dining hall had been very prettily decorated by some braw Scottish lassies, who had also placed a sprig of heather before each guest. The dinner was most appropriate to the occasion, beginning with Cockie Leckie soup and ending with Grampian pudding, all the chief delicacies of the land o' cakes coming between. The great dish, of course, was the Haggis, which was solemnly carried round the table to the strains of the bag-pipes, and was followed by the inevitable 'wee drappie o't''.

The programme ended with Scottish airs.[28]

The white oligarchy was, at the end of the nineteenth century, linked together in interest group organisations. But they also held strategically important positions as directors of insurance companies and building societies which mushroomed at the end of the nineteenth century. No doubt, Rev. Henry Clarke who established the Westmoreland Building Society, and the founders of the Trelawny and St Elizabeth Benefit Building Societies had originally intended that these societies 'provide for the improvement of the dwellings of the working classes'. Apparently, however, the building societies grew out of the reach of the working classes.[29] The directorships of the societies were to repeat names such as Colonel Ward, E.X. Leon, P. Elicio Auvray, Louis Verley, S.L. Schloss and John E. Kerr.

There were also white professionals, lawyers and doctors, who were also what we might term 'medium' farmers. The easiest professionals to identify are medical doctors. Dr J.L. Cox had an estate at Content in St Ann with 50 acres of bananas. Dr J.L. Edwards had 23 acres of land in bananas in St Catherine. Dr J.A.L. Calder acting as attorney for Marian Calder ran a 60 acre banana business at Aberdeen, while he ran on his own account a cacao farm of 10 acres.[30]

It is true that sugar planters, faced with the continuing problems of the sugar industry, sometimes sold their land, or perhaps even went into bankruptcy. But two points need to be noted. The first is that sugar estates in parishes such as Westmoreland and Hanover held their own. The second point is that where sugar planters thought it wise to sell their land they sold it intact, so that Jamaica's elite remained rooted in landownership.[31] The sale of sugar land, such as in Portland, St Mary and St Thomas to banana producers, far from weakening the oligarchical structure served to strengthen it. As we note elsewhere, planters also dedicated themselves to other forms of commercial production – such as pimento, citrus, logwood and pen-keeping.

Whatever the links of ethnicity between whites there were important economic and social divisions between them. There were the overseers and bookkeepers, many of them imported but not sharing the same prestige or power as the *grands blancs* plantation men or planter-merchants, and certainly not enjoying the influence of the bureaucrats to whom citizens tipped their caps or hats. In 1884 an overseer could earn an annual income of between £150 and £200. The main problem for the overseer, and it was a major drawback, was that he could be dismissed without notice. 'It is dangerous', commented Rev. Clarke, 'for a man of family to hold the position'.[32] There were, in addition to overseers, planting attorneys whose income was derived on a commission basis but whose prestige was higher than that of the overseer.

One of the most exploited sections of the white labour force was the bookkeepers whose existence, based upon an income of between £30 and £60 per year, and on 'the hardest work and roughest treatment imaginable', was precarious.[33] An 86-year-old overseer, recalling his days as a book-keeper observed that when he arrived in Jamaica in 1893 (having paid his own fare from England) he received an income of £36 per annum. He was not allowed to ride. During a three-month illness he received no salary. He had as many as thirty or forty tasks to get through each day. He eventually became an overseer at £160 per annum, a position which turned out to be much superior to the one he had had as a bookkeeper on the absentee Sewell sugar estates.[34] Banana plantations also employed bookkeepers, and life seemed just as difficult as on sugar estates. One bookkeeper pointed to the disparity between his income and the profits of the estate, to the absence of medical assistance, and to the shortage of sanitary conveniences:

> Bookkeeper, in any case, is a misnomer as far as using the term on banana estates is concerned. I kept books for half a day out of seven, and the balance of time was either sitting down on a heap of damp banana trash waiting for drays, or riding a mule in the capacity of *private detective* or *professional slave driver*. The estate I was employed on [made a] profit of £2,000 per annum. My wages were 30/- per week, one pound of which I never saw as it went to pay for my two meals a day . . . I had fever and outbreaks which unfitted me for work and I had to pay the doctor myself. [There was] no bath or bathroom on the estate, and no water except in the streams a mile off where I was told I must

bathe. I did so at first and got ringworms thereby from the Negroes who also used nature's tub as a laundry. After that I could only get a bath once a week in the nearest town, which was not too often for an Englishman's comfort even in his own land.[35]

Bookkeepers were not encouraged to marry, since the estate had a vested interest in collecting a portion of their salary for room and board. This portion of salary would be lost if the bookkeeper married. And so, not surprisingly, the bookkeeper sought other compensations, having been deprived of matrimonial bliss. The headman on the estates (an updated version of the slave driver) provided bookkeepers with women on the estate. Pressure could be placed not only on the women but on their families:

I have known of girls to hold out a long time . . . others run away. The 'weaker vessel' knows, alas!, that her whole family is dependent on the only Sugar Estate.[36]

The bookkeeper's sweethearts, once they had been secured, were paid through the Blotter (i.e. the Pay Book) for work they had never done. Finally, there were cases where bookkeepers kept, in polygamous style, both mother and daughter.

Whites were employed in the upper ranks of the police force. There were also white professionals such as medical officers, some of them imported, and school inspectors some of whom strengthened their economic position by investments in land. There were, finally, poor whites, immigrants who had been encouraged to come to Jamaica on the basis of promises of land ownership and other blandishments. In the 1840s encouragement had been given to the importation of Germans with the intention of settling them in the highlands to cut off access of blacks to those highlands, and thereby force blacks to remain on the lowland plantations. The official reason, or published reason, was that the 'civilisation' of blacks made it necessary to keep them close to whites on plantations.[37]

German settlers did not live up to the expectations of white elite society. The poverty of many of the settlers, and the realisation that whiteness at the level of German community settlement failed to demonstrate white superiority, led Governor Blake to conclude that the Seaford Town German community could not be construed a success. In truth, the Germans lived very much like the blacks in their adjoining communities, cultivating ginger and arrowroot. 'In intelligence', complained Blake, 'they did not surpass the adjoining communities nor do their energy compare favourably with the latter'. The conclusion was that 'isolated white labouring agriculturists among a black population would certainly fail'.[38]

But the social use to which these poor white farmers put their ethnic inheritance is nicely described by J.H. Reid:

> But there are other whites not included in the Backra [class], especially when it is used in connection with intellectual and social greatness. They are described by the term 'white laba', an abbreviation of and corruption of 'white labourer'. [They] include later immigrants of English, Irish, German origin, and a few Portuguese commonly called 'poto' who all take rank side by side of the ordinary peasant, but take advantage of their native connection to appropriate to themselves all they can of the status of their more favoured kindred.[39]

Social class differences between whites could be bridged by common ethnicity, a factor which the historian Bryan Edwards noted for the late-eighteenth century.[40] As in the earlier period, however, there were opportunities for bookkeepers, or overseers, to improve their positions in society by promotions, for example, to more lofty occupational categories.

Wealth was not the monopoly of whites. On the contrary, some members of the mixed population had acquired or inherited wealth and gradually they were to achieve levels of political representation in accordance with their status as property holders. During the period under review, P.A. Moodie was one of the more significant banana producers and traders in Portland. Moodie was consignee to Messrs Warner and Merritt of Philadelphia for the shipment of bananas. He cultivated some 24 acres of bananas at Snow Hill, and leased Golden Grove Estate (5,000 acres) which was planted in bananas. He was also chairman of his Parochial Board and manager of the Co-operative Fruit Company, as well as US consul in Port Antonio.[41] George Steibel, who had acquired his fortune overseas, was one of the wealthiest Jamaicans of the time. Moodie was described as a brown man, Steibel's race is not described clearly, but he was definitely coloured. He was sometimes described as a gentleman of leisure. Minority layers of the coloured population extended their participation in landowning, trading, and dominated such professions as law, to the extent that Henry Blake always envisaged himself as being in perpetual conflict with the coloured solicitors of Kingston. The coloured Solicitor-General of Jamaica, William Baggett-Gray, was a Commodore of the prestigious Royal Jamaica Yacht Club, and a member of other 'exclusive' clubs such as The Jamaica Club. In 1902 it was reported that:

> The white people of the island constitute, roughly speaking, the classes; but on the same footing as these, and mingling with them on terms of perfect equality are numbers of well-to-do coloured people, of various shades of complexion, well-educated, cultured

and travelled, many of them occupying high positions in the public service, practising as lawyers, doctors [and in] church office.[42]

There is little doubt that the wealthier and more educated layers of 'brown' men enjoyed high prestige but it would be untrue to suggest, as Inspector Thomas did, that there was 'perfect equality'. Indeed, the greater the material prosperity of the coloured population the greater the social discrimination against them.[43] The old assumption that in a situation of conflict browns could support blacks over whites continued to have some force.

The underlying and largely unvoiced conflict between whites and browns emerged during discussions on the reorganisation of the Jamaican militia in 1891. The militia had been reorganised in 1886 under Governor Henry Norman's administration (1884–9) at the request of Mr William Malabre and 262 other 'influential Jamaicans'. By 16 June, 1886 Downing Street had accepted the recommendation that a Volunteer Militia be organised on the basis of the 1879 Volunteer Militia Law. The act of loyalty had been promoted by the fear that the deployment of British troops in the Sudan would have resulted in the withdrawal of British troops from the island. The militia was established as a supplementary force to the regular British militia. It was agreed that the British troops should not be withdrawn since Jamaica was 'the recognised centre of British interests in the West Indies'.[44]

The militia was intended to be an elite corps of 'respectable' Jamaicans. Membership was open to all male inhabitants over 18 and under 46 years who had a minimum annual income of £30, or paid £2 or more in direct taxes, or who possessed a freehold of the value of not less than £50. Probably in order to recruit whites who did not qualify through property ownership, taxes or income, the Governor was granted the discretion to 'accept the services of persons who, though not qualified or not liable to be called upon to serve under this section are nevertheless willing to serve as Volunteer Members of the Militia Forces . . . ' The militia recruit who wished to join the mounted corps was required to possess a horse of the value of £20 or upwards. Governor Norman assured the Colonial Office that members of the force 'shall be persons interested in the maintenance of order and in the welfare and security of the island'.[45]

In effect, membership of the Volunteer Militia required a property qualification, and such people presumably were the ones who had an interest in the maintenance of 'order and in the welfare of and security of the island'. It is not explicitly stated whether Mr William Malabre and his gentlemen were influenced purely by sentiments of loyalty to the British Empire (Norman's official interpretation of their action) or by concern that the absence of British troops would leave the island unsafe for the elite.

What is clear is that enthusiasm for the militia rapidly died when it became apparent that British troops would not be withdrawn after all. A mere five years later Governor Henry Blake pointed out that 'although on paper there were 600 militia men that the militia had really almost ceased to exist'.[46]

The presence of blacks and coloureds in the militia also contributed to the declining enthusiasm. For example, having decided to disband the militia as it stood then, Blake suggested that the 'Falmouth Mounted Corps which is the best corps in the island and is composed of owners of property and overseers' should not be disbanded, since in the event of necessity, 'they would be worth two companies of black militia'.[47] Quite obviously there were coloureds in the militia who could not be excluded, since their property qualifications were impeccable. The acceptance of coloured leadership within the militia was, however, also a function of how the white oligarchy viewed the coloureds.

The Militia Bill of 1891 was opposed in the Legislative Council on the grounds of expense, though the underlying reasons were not financial, but social. Messrs. Farquharson, Craig and Clark of the Legislative Council made it clear to Governor Blake that they were 'afraid to increase the country corps of militia as they *could not trust the people* and would prefer to pay £100,000 to the Imperial Government to secure the presence of the headquarters of a whole regiment here'.[48] These prominent members of the Legislative Council informally confided to Henry Blake that this particular point of view could not have been voiced in Council discreetly. The elected members of the Council, representing the views of parts of the white establishment, were averse to the creation of a militia which would put arms into the hands of people whom they viewed as their race or class enemies. It was not only the possession of arms by blacks which was feared, but the access to arms by coloured people. This attitude was expressed more forcefully by the white planter Mr W. Bancroft Espeut, who made a statement to the Colonial Office on the matter.[49]

The message of Espeut, the violence of whose language had been 'trimmed' by Mr Wingfield of the Colonial Office, was that the militia was putting arms into the possession of the 'deadly enemies of the whites, and this would be used one day against them'. Espeut claimed that the creation of a military corps *officered by coloureds* would be dangerous.[50] It is true that Espeut was concerned about the 100 black men who annually retired from the police and others who retired from the West India regiments who might constitute a nucleus of armed violence against the white dominated state. Yet Espeut's concern was, interestingly enough, not directed so much at the blacks ('in themselves they are not dangerous'), but at the brown element which would lead them.

He [Espeut] wished to know whether HM's Government were

really committed to such a policy as that of raising local militias
and whether they knew what such a policy meant. He pointed out
that annually some 100 men retire from the police and others
from the West India regiments – that these formed a nucleus of a
force which we were now teaching the coloured man to organise
and lead . . . It was better that these 'black' men should go to their
plots of land and forget as soon as possible all the training they
ever knew; in themselves they are not dangerous, but once teach
the 'coloured' men to lead them and the community would never
be safe. This was just what the militia was doing; it was giving
instruction to the deadly enemies of the whites, and this would be
used one day against them. There was clearly hatred between
'coloured' people and the whites and it would never be removed.
Herein was the real meaning of opposition of the Legislative
Council to the Militia Bill, and they intended to oppose it in
every legitimate way. At the same time, *they would not for a
moment venture to let the colour question come up or even be
suspected*, it was too dangerous.[51]

The recommendation of the Colonial Office was that black militias
should and could be established, but under white officers. Blake's own
response was that Espeut had exaggerated the situation, but that his views
were shared by other members of the Council. The Governor also pointed
out that members of the coloured population 'chafe under much of the
social inferiority which is nonetheless real that it is not *officially* acknowledged'. The Governor endorsed the loyalty of 'coloured men' and their
political sense. The coloured men probably realised that 'to get rid of the
whites would be the knell of their own destruction'.[52] The views of Espeut
and others demonstrate a continuing preoccupation with racial issues as
they affected the security of white Jamaican society. The militia movement
was one further illustration of the problem of race and colour in Jamaican
society. With more economic power falling into the hands of the coloured
population white hegemony seemed under threat, both through the franchise and through armaments.

As with white society, so too with 'brown' society there were considerable variations in the ability to acquire wealth and exercise power. The
coloured population cannot simply be regarded as an intermediate class
between white and black. In cultural terms they cannot, at the upper level,
be distinguished from whites; and at the lowest levels of society they can
hardly be separated from the black working classes. Given the reality that
much of the coloured population emerged out of 'illicit' or casual liaisons
between white and coloured, or white and black it would have been surprising if parts of the coloured population did not occupy the anonymous ranks

of the dangerous classes of the urban zones. In 1879 it was observed that the poor juvenile population of Kingston was largely of mixed blood.

The social standing, the history and the experience of the mixed bloods of Jamaica are central to the invention of the tradition of shade prejudice as opposed to race prejudice. The browns were described as the 'most intensely Jamaican of the whole population' and as particularly sensitive on the subject of colour 'the more so the farther they recede from the white man'.[53]

> At one extreme [the coloured] can be distinguished from white men in colour only by mathematical reasoning, or by philosophical tests, and, except in the matter of favour and general estimation, are in every way equal to their white brethren; and at the other by some having such a small tinge of whiteness in them, that but for the same aids they could never be known to possess the remotest blood-relationship to the white man.[54]

The black population was also stratified along lines of occupation, income, and status. Social divisions between blacks had always been strong, ranging from the ethnic or inter-tribal divisions between them when they first arrived in Jamaica as slaves to the occupational distinctions which emerged with the maturation of the slave plantation system. The latter induced a varied occupational structure of headmen, slave-drivers, field, factory and household workers, as well as artisans and manual agricultural labourers. Status divisions inevitably operated within the broader framework of a growing black ethnic consciousness, generated by its opposite, white ethnicity.

Emancipation in 1838 had helped to make more complex the social structure of black society, with the establishment of small settlers in the hinterland, the expansion of the internal marketing system, the growth of an educated black professional class, and of a relatively prosperous segment of independent rural farmers. An important professional group within the black population was the constables, some 700 in number during our period, in their uniforms of plain white tunic and dark blue trousers with red stripe, a simple white helmet, and plain black leatherboots. The constabulary had been established in 1867 under the regime of Sir John Peter Grant.

The forces of coercion – at least the militia and the constabulary – were shared by all colour segments of the population, but the arrangement of office was made to correspond to the general ranking of society – whites at the top, blacks at the bottom, and browns in the middle. Membership of the constabulary offered rank and status but not a significant income for the bulk of constables. The rank and file of the constabulary were recruited from among families of the more prosperous rural farmers – the same social layers from which the teachers and artisans came. A first class constable, which was about the ceiling for blacks in the force, earned between £40 and £45 per annum. This salary compared with £900 earned by the Inspector-General in 1879, and £300 earned by first class inspectors, £250 earned by second class and £200 by third class inspectors. The Deputy Inspector-General earned £300 per annum plus £1 per day travelling.[55] A second class constable earned one penny (1d) more per day (2/4d) than the daily allowance for the sub-inspector's horse.[56]

It has been observed in another context that 'police forces have often been ladders of mobility for less advantaged ethnic communities when the career of policeman has been shunned by those groups that enjoy greater access to more prestigious and financially rewarding jobs'.[57] In Jamaica's case ascent in rank was circumscribed by the colonial limitation on the levels to which a black constable could climb. After the Cumberland Pen Riots in 1893, blacks were removed from the Sergeant ranks and replaced by recruits from the Irish Constabulary.

The black middle class, whose cultural attainments gave them some status, were conscious of the distinctions between themselves and the mass of poor blacks. According to Dr Theophilus Scholes:

> Inasmuch as some of these people, from a desire to emulate have, by means of sustained industry and its results, the acquisition of property, education, and other accomplishments, qualified and are qualifying themselves for the larger sphere, or larger responsibility, the entire division ought to be considered as consisting of two distinct classes – civilised and uncivilised – occupying separate and precise spheres. Hence, the practice of referring to and of treating Ethiopian communities – British, American, and others – as though they all belong to the uncivilised class is arbitrary and unjust.[58]

Yet, as we shall see, Theophilus Scholes was not lacking in sympathy for the poor blacks of the Empire whom he viewed as an oppressed class.

The ever-vigilant and generous-spirited Dr Robert Love was particularly disturbed at efforts by Jamaican blacks to draw distinctions of superiority and inferiority between themselves and Africans. The ancient tradition whereby the enslaved Creole black described the fresh African slave recruit as 'Guinea-bird', and 'salt-water nigger' continued to haunt the island. Robert Love was commenting on a statement that 'the blacks from West Africa are not in any respect worthy mess mates for the West Indian Negro, who in every way showed his superiority'.

> Considering the recent history and actual surroundings of the Negro, one would think that it would be impossible for him [the Negro] to be a snob . . . The Negro who attempts to disassociate

himself from his Race, as someone superior to it, is the worst kind of snob . . . Nigger snobbery's unspeakable meanness is visible in the fact that members of this Contingent [West India Regiment] would have accepted, and digested the white man's haughtiness and scorn on condition that they were allowed to scorn someone else.[59]

Within the ranks of society were the Chinese shopkeepers and Lebanese (called Syrians in Jamaica) Dry Goods merchants who migrated to Jamaica in the last few years of the nineteenth century. The Chinese community became leaders in the grocery trade, while the Lebanese, who were not ethnically distinct from the whites, became involved in the drogher business and in peddling of dry goods in both rural and urban areas. The Chinese were distinct, ethnically, from the upper layers of the merchant segment which was white and coloured, and they were more engaged in the local retail market than in the import/export and wholesale trade. It is probable that the cool reception which Chinese and Lebanese merchants received in Jamaica was partly a consequence of business competition, made possible by systems of credit which were not, on the surface anyway, as exploitative as those used by the traditional shopkeepers. Chinese and Lebanese communities demonstrated a high level of cohesiveness within the larger mercantile segment.

With the exception of the Chinese and Lebanese communities, each ethnic segment was divided by class, representing almost the entire gamut of occupational activity, property-ownership, and professional attainment. The importance of wealth as a defining characteristic of class – and it was wealth which had initially provided status in slave plantation society – was cynically commented on by Dr Robert Love in October 1902:

As far as this world goes, money is everything. Nothing shows the hollowness of human (civilised and Christianised) society, as money does. The possession of it works wonderful and rapid changes. If a man is black, as soon as he has it, he is declared white; if ignorant, he is declared learned, if vicious he is declared eccentric, if ugly he is declared handsome . . . The Remedy for the Black Man's Burden is *money*. Let the Negro strive to have more business at the Tax Office, than in the Police Court.[60]

Wealth and occupational categories are a useful basis upon which to begin an assessment of class differences, but culture, speech, dress, place of residence, quality of housing, educational opportunities, morbidity, diet are also important variables. But central to class distinctions is the concept of *distance* which H. Hoetink, taking his cue from Mannheim, discusses for the Dominican Republic:

> The concept of distance, horizontal and vertical as well as temporal and, in certain cases, mythical, is emphasised heavily in all layers of society. In regard to social stratification, such a society imposes upon its members an *image* of social hierarchy in which the social categories are precisely defined and allocated. Such an image need not correspond at all closely to social reality, nor need it prevent social mobility. In the Dominican Republic the image of social stratification was based on a dichotomy: *la gente bien, la gente culta, la clase pensante vs. el pueblo, el vulgo, la plebe.*[61]

In Jamaica members of the white elite were described, sometimes perhaps with sarcasm, sometimes not, as the aristocracy, which at least suggests how 'non-aristocrats' viewed the elite of the community. Terms such as 'elite' were used unashamedly, or 'fashionable society' in contrast to the 'humbler classes'. Distance could, of course, be bridged and perhaps more often than not in the terms used by Dante Bellegarde for Haiti in 1901: 'Everyone has two faces – one for those above and one for those below'.

In a society where inequality of citizens was accepted as the basic principle of social organisation, distinctions between classes were affirmed not only through wealth, or occupation as such, but through education, language and dress. Language and speech were clear social indicators. In a racially homogenous society clothes and speech are the most obvious badges of class 'difficult to gauge accurately at the margins, but clear enough for the great majority of people to be able to assign themselves to "upper", "middle" and "working class"'.[62] In a racially mixed society colour and ethnicity were also useful guides to class position.

Speech and dress

The speech of the majority of the population was a Creole which utilised an English lexicon within a structure influenced by African languages.[63] That of the middle and upper classes was English which bore as close an affinity to the 'Queen's English' as they could make it. There was, and is, probably no easier way than language to identify differences of class, and to some extent differences of race, in Jamaica. The language of the Jamaican masses was the conduit through which they expressed their folklore, proverbs and song, and the primary vehicle for religious expression as well. The ability to speak 'good English' was a measure of the extent to which a citizen was conversant with British culture.

In the late-nineteenth century British culture was aggressively reasserted in Jamaica, to affect, for example, leisure patterns. European culture, via the *Pax Britannica*, was advancing relentlessly throughout the world, into areas which had not experienced the extent of political and cultural domination to which Jamaica had been exposed since 1655. The evolution of a national consciousness was expressed through a recognition of a folk-idiom which could be appropriated without violating the principle that Jamaica's culture was British.

This is why language could remain both as an indicator of class, and also in the case of the Creole, as a 'quaint' Jamaican invention. The Presbyterian clergyman, Rev. Radcliff, gave a series of lectures on the lessons contained in Jamaican proverbs; the poet, Tom Redcam (Thomas McDermot) wrote his first poem in Creole in 1902. Claude McKay's Creole poems were collected and published by Walter Jekyll, and the poet from the hills of Clarendon received a gold medal from the Institute of Jamaica. W.C. Murray ('Funny' Murray) commented on local issues, people and events through the medium of the Creole. The middle and upper class used English as their principal means of communication, but employed Creole as part of that awareness of the existence of distinct 'local colour'. Their very use of Creole, however, was an ironical comment on the social distance which separated them from the Creole-speaking masses of the population. It was this sense of local colour which led Jamaicans to sponsor competitions for the 'best doll' of a 'peasant' woman, or for the composition of a Jamaican 'national' anthem which sang of the Jamaican landscape to the tune of 'God Save our Gracious Queen'.

The fashions worn by elite women reflected a leisured lifestyle, and levels of income. They wore stiff corsets, high-necked blouses, long sleeves, dresses falling over the ankles. In contrast working women made a clear distinction between 'working clothes' and 'Sunday best'. A visitor to the island in 1876, however, described the working women, on their way to work, as generally well-dressed:

> when proceeding to their work, tie a handkerchief round their hips, and draw their skirts through it thus forming a furbelow round their waists not unbecoming . . . Their legs are thus bared from the knee downwards, and they step out in a style which would gladden the heart of the most exacting drill-sergeant.[64]

But the working woman was conscious of the fact that clothes went a long way towards making the lady. Just prior to the 1891 Exhibition, a street vendor was overheard making the following comment to a friend:

> When a lick on me silk frock and fling me parasol over me shoulder and drop into Exhibition Ground you will know wedder I is a lady or not.[65]

Among men, as well, dress was an important indication of rank and class. Solicitors, tradesmen and other businessmen wore morning coats, waistcoats, and Derby hats. Physicians often wore black top hats. Members of the Legislative Council wore top hats and coats in imitation of Westminister. The opening of the Legislative Council was something of a spectacle for the crowds of Spanish Town. While ladies had their riding habits, men for that pursuit put on leggings and riding breeches. The ability to own them at all was viewed as an indication of affluence, prominence and importance.[66] Collars were high and stiffly starched. Whiskers and beards were an important part of the dress of the male species, who also waxed their moustaches. Some beards were of formidable length, breadth, and thickness.

The working man was, on workday, dressed in a Jippi-Jappa hat and wore coarse blue dungarees with large patch pockets (called a 'Shall I' or Old Iron). When he was not barefooted he wore a 'bull-dog', a cheap make of rope-soled slipper of Chinese manufacture which sold at 1/6d per pair.[67] (Top boots were for gentlemen). Many workers went to their places of work with undershirts ('merinos') and no shirt. White shirts and standing collars, like regulation cricket bats and balls were for gentlemen. On market day, however, the working man donned his jacket.

Dress, even when very smart, could be a visible indication of servant status. Coachmen, for example, who served elite households were liveried, wearing 'tall boots, white tightkneed pants, a long black coat, top hat and gloves'.[68] Jockeys were put into uniform in the 1890s, a far cry from the casual dress earlier, and the fork which served as a spur. The emphasis on dress among the elite was such that even for informal gatherings men wore tails or dinner jackets and women evening dresses. Voluminous clothing proved no obstacle to vigorous all-night dancing at society balls.

The Governor's dress served not only the ordinary functions of covering the body decently and fashionably. As the representative of Her Majesty, the bureaucratic projection of Queen Victoria, his public attire was a symbolic representation of the might of the British Empire. At the opening of the Jubilee Market in 1887, the Governor appeared in his Windsor uniform, which distinguished him from the 'several hundred gentlemen in full evening dress with officers of the army and navy in their uniforms, and the several orders of Foresters, Good Samaritans and Odd Fellows with their Aprons and Sashes, trimmed with gold lace . . .'[69] 'At the Grand Review of the Naval Brigade, the Regulars and the Volunteers at Up Park Camp before an estimated 20,000 people, (a special pavilion had been erected for the accommodation of the "fair guests" of the day), Sir Henry Wylie Norman appeared in the full uniform of a British general, seated on a handsome charger, his orders and decorations on his breast, his cocked hat and plume on his head and looking every inch the gallant soldier'.[70]

Up to the end of the nineteenth century dress could also be an indicator of ethnic origin. Neither East Indians, Chinese, nor Lebanese/Syrians immediately surrendered their patterns of dress. The East Indians, wearing their dhotis and pugarees, were contemptuously viewed as half nude and a bad moral influence; the long-haired Chinese were hostilely described as wearing 'oil skin pajamas'. The colourful dresses (like 'gypsies') of the 'Syrian' women met with greater approval.[71]

The relationship between social groups was determined partly by class differences, demonstrated by wealth, occupation, culture, performance or non-performance of manual labour, speech, dress, general life chances. There were clearly sharp contrasts between Jamaica's social classes. But the relationship was much affected by racial factors. Certainly, a US visitor to the island was convinced that the 'Negro is admitted to the charmed circle of society', only through a 'sort of superior toleration'.[72] Attitudes toward the black were partly conditioned by the traditional relationship between whites as an employer class and blacks as the employed class, and partly by the quasi-scientific racism of the late-nineteenth century.

The official position of the colonial government was that racial distinctions between Her Majesty's subjects should not be made, but it would be extraordinarily naïve to believe that race was not an important factor in social relations. A planter confessed that the 'would be whites and the money-made whites, sit in the front pew of the Church, so that their lips may touch the wine cup . . . before it becomes blackened by Ethiopian lips'.[73] An employee of the Public Works Department in Morant Bay received two weeks notice of dismissal following his refusal to address the DMO's son as 'Mr'. The child addressed the black artisan, Mr Friend, only by the name 'Friend'.[74]

A black clergyman was refused a clean cabin aboard a coastal steamer for racial reasons.[75] A black minister of religion (Presbyterian) was refused burial at the church where he had once ministered. Another clergyman described the demonstration of prejudice as a special kind of snobbery, and cowardice:

> Prejudice is cowardice pure and simple. Men who are 'hail fellow' with the dark man at certain times, affect not to know him at certain other times, because of the company they may be in. They will give the black man a brother's grip under certain circumstances, and recognise him with a distant bow when in another circle.[76]

Rev. C.A. Wilson concluded that displays of racial prejudice hampered the growth of the Jamaican community, which was subject to an 'irritating and silly caste system'.

The mix-up of colours does not make for patriotism. Colour is an asset too highly esteemed in Jamaica. Clear skin and straight hair are amongst the best recommendations . . . To a nauseating extent does the idea prevail that whatever pertains to the white man is good, that what is connected with the black man is evil, or of little consequence.[77]

We indicated earlier that prejudice was not only directed against the black population, but also against the brown population. In essence, as David Thompson has suggested, racialist theories can be viewed as a modern variant of 'those principles of exclusion, intolerance, absolutism, and claims to *elitism* which have been persistent throughout the experience of European civilisation'.[78] White ethnic identification which unified whites across class had, as one of its fruits, discrimination against the black and coloured population. Racism, as expressed by white society, served the function of consolidating the specific interests of the superordinate white oligarchy against encroachment by subjected groups. However irrational racism was, it had functional value in daily life.

In the following chapters I will attempt to indicate how the various segments interacted; to identify institutions which were shared in part or fully. Class distinctions, in our view, were given greater depth by racial distinctions which in turn corresponded or coincided with varied cultural practices. That Jamaica did not enjoy a homogeneous culture is attributable to the fact that there existed sharp contrasts between the economic standards and educational opportunities of different classes.

Notes

1   Jamaica Censuses, 1881, 1891, 1911.
2   Jamaica Census, 1911.
3   Stanley and Barbara Stein, *The Colonial Heritage of Latin America: Essays on Economic Dependence in Perspective*, New York: Oxford University Press, 1970, p. 57.
4   Charles W. Mills, 'Race and Class: Conflicting or Reconcilable Paradigms?', *Social and Economic Studies*, Vol. 36, No. 2, 1987, p. 100.
5   Stein and Stein, *Colonial Heritage*, p. 69.
6   Frank Cundall, *Jamaica in 1912*, Kingston, 1912.
7   Edward Brathwaite, *Contradictory Omens, Cultural Diversity and Integration in the Caribbean*, Jamaica: Savacou Publications, 1985, p. 92.
8   CO, 137/517, 1884. Norman to Earl of Derby, (No. 348) 24 September, 1884. Enclosure showing estates owned by civil servants.
9   *DG*, 22 December, 1899. 'Gleaner Christmas Competition for the Best Local Original Joke'.
10   CO, 137/518, 1884. Norman to Derby, (No. 469), 8 November, 1884.
11   J.H. Reid, *The People of Jamaica Described*, p. 87 (Italics original).
12   Department of State, C8.1/22, 3593/30, Miscellaneous Correspondence.

J.E. Viera to United States Consul, 28 March, 1877.

13 Ansell Hart, 'The Banana Industry in Jamaica', *Social and Economic Studies*, Vol. 3, No. 2, September 1954, p. 217.

14 *Ibid.* p. 216.

15 *JG*, Vol. 17, No. 39, 27 September, 1894, p. 288.

16 Hart, 'The Banana in Jamaica', p. 219.

17 *JCM*, 1894, Appendix 15. 'Return of the Total Number of Sugar Estates, Pens and other properties of 1,000 acres and upwards in each parish showing name, description of the property, property names of proprietors and whether resident or absentee. Number of acres of each property'. Presented to Council at the request of Rev. Henry Clarke, p. 11.

18 *Ibid.* p. 11.

19 Jamaica, *Laws of Jamaica*. Law 33, 1897. West India Electric Company's Law, 28 May, 1897.

20 *JCM*, Vol. 23, 1886. Governor's Message (No. 7) on 'Jamaica Society of Agriculture and Commerce'.

21 NLJ, MS 317, *Casserly Collection*.

22 *HBJ*, 1908, p. 493 and p. 503.

23 John William Root, *The British West Indies and the Sugar Industry*, Liverpool: J.W. Root, Commerce Chambers, 1899, p. 131.

24 CO, 137/518, 1884. Norman to Derby, (No. 469) enclosing Gibbons' letter of defence.

25 *DG*, 18 May, 1894.

26 NLJ, 'Rules of the Jamaica Scottish Society' (about 1914).

27 *DG*, 3 December, 1900. Annual Dinner, Caledonia Society.

29 Law 27 of 1888 which amended the Law of 27 October, 1886 addressed itself to the problem: 'Whereas many Societies have been established under the Benefit Building Societies Act, 1865, and their usefulness has extended beyond the industrious poor and middle classes whose benefit was contemplated at the time of the passing of the said act, all mortgages granted to Trustees of a Building or Benefit Building Society for any sum not exceeding £500 shall be exempt from Stamp Duty'.

30 *JCM*, 1894, Appendix 15.

31 Veront Satchell, 'Rural Land Transactions in Jamaica, 1866–1900', M. Phil. History, UWI, Mona, 1986, pp. 205, 225 and 246.

32 *Colonial Standard*, 7 October, 1884. Rev. Henry Clarke to Editor of the *Times*, London reproduced in *Colonial Standard*, 7 October, 1884.

33 *Ibid.*

34 *JM*, Essay of H.T. Steele.

35 NLJ, MST 59, *Livingston Collection*.

36 *JA*, 6 September, 1902. Felix Holt, 'Confessions'.

37 Douglas Hall, 'Bountied European Immigration into Jamaica with special reference to the German Settlement at Seaford Town up to 1850'. *Jamaica Journal*, Vol. 8, No. 4, 1974.

38 Henry Blake, 'The Awakening of Jamaica'.

39 J.H. Reid, *'The People of Jamaica Described'*, p. 87.

40 Bryan Edwards, *The History, Civil and Commercial, of the British Colonies in the West Indies*, (3 Vols), London, 1801, Vol. 2, pp. 7–8.

41 Department of State Microseries, T 31, Roll 28. Hoskinson to Seward (private), 14 October, 1879. 'Mr. Moodie is decidedly the best agent you could select. He is a brown man, has great influence with the natives, transacts a large fruit

business and bears a reputation of an honest, able and intelligent merchant'.

42   Herbert Thomas's lecture on Jamaica published in *Journal of the Society of Arts*, No. 2568, 7 February, 1902, p. 221. (See NLJ Pamphlets).

43   J.A. Froude, *The English in the West Indies: or the Bow of Ulisses*, p. 213.

44   CO, 137/521, 1885. Norman to Derby, (No. 176) 9 May, 1885, 'Formation of a Volunteer Militia Force'.

45   *Ibid*. (No. 406) 3 October, 1884.

46   CO, 137/545, 1891. Blake to Knutsford, 5 August, 1891.

47   *Ibid*.

48   Jamaica, Archives, 1B/5/18, Vol. 46. Blake to Knutsford, No. 106, 4 May, 1891.

49   CO, 137/545, 1891. E. Wingfield's summary of Mr Espeut's statement at Colonial Office.

50   *Ibid*.

51   *Ibid*.

52   CO, 137/549, 1892. Blake to Knutsford (Confidential), 7 July, 1892.

53   J.H. Reid, *The People of Jamaica*, p. 88.

54   *Ibid*. p. 87.

55   *HBJ*, p. 203.

56   CO, 137/514, XC/AO52699. Memorandum of Matthew Joseph, to Colonial Office.

57   Cynthia Enloe, *Police, Military and Ethnicity, Foundations of State power*, New Brunswick and London: Transaction Books, 1980, p. 144.

58   Theophilus Scholes, *Glimpses of the Ages or the 'Superior' and 'Inferior' Races so-called, discussed in the light of Science and History*, London: John Long, 1905, (2 vols), Vol. 1. p. 211.

59   *JA*, 8 November, 1902, 'Nigger Snobbery'.

60   *JA*, 4 October, 1902.

61   Harmannus Hoetink, 'The Dominican Republic in the Nineteenth Century. Some Notes on Stratification, Immigration and Race', in Magnus Morner, (ed.), *Race and Class in Latin America*, New York and London: Columbia University Press, 1971, p. 112.

62   John Stevenson, *British Society, 1914 – 1945*, Harmondsworth: Pelican Books, 1984.

63   Maureen Warner Lewis, 'The African Impact on Language and Literature in the English-Speaking Caribbean', in Franklin Knight and Margaret Crahan (eds.) *Africa and the Caribbean: The Legacies of a Link*, Baltimore and London: Johns Hopkins University Press, 1979, pp. 101–123.

64   Sir David Sibbald Scott, *To Jamaica and Back*, London: Chapman and Hall, 1870, p. 79.

65   *JM*, Essay of May Jeffrey Smith.

66   *JM*, Essays of Mrs Florence Buckley and Mr H.R. Milliner.

67   *JM*, Essay of Mr William Martin.

68   *JM*, Essay of Mr Gladstone Burke.

69   W.A. Feurtado, *The Jubilee Reign of Queen Victoria in Jamaica*, 1837 – 1887, Kingston, 1896, p. 151.

70   *Ibid*. p. 178.

71   *JM*, Essay of Mr F.M. Goldsworthy.

72   Julius Moritzen, 'Has Jamaica Solved the Color Problem?' from *Gunter's Magazine*, January 1901, p. 39 (NLJ Pamphlet No. 49)

73   *JA*, 4 October, 1902. Felix Holt, 'Confessions of a Planter'.

74   *JA*, 16 May, 1896.
75   *JA*, 21 September, 1895.
76   Rev. C.A. Wilson, *Men With Backbone and other Pleas for Progress*, King-
      ston: Educational Supply Co., 1913, p. 80.
77   *Ibid.* p. 84.
78   David Thompson (ed.), *Political Ideas*, Harmondsworth: Pelican Books, 1978,
      p. 195.

CHAPTER 6 | Marriage and family

It is useful to begin this discussion of marriage and family in late-nineteenth century Jamaica by making the distinction between families which were founded on the basis of the civil, Christian or Jewish rites of marriage, on the one hand, and on the other the pragmatic, functional marriage often referred to as 'faithful concubinage'. The first forms were the property of the middle and upper classes, the second form was widely practised among the black and coloured working classes of Jamaica. The former were re-garded as good, the latter as bad for the moral integrity and civilisation of Jamaica. By law, the children of the first forms of marriage were legitimate, the offspring of the second illegitimate.

There were social reformers who recognised the permanency and faithfulness of peasant concubinage, but who were much grieved by the reality that the rates of illegitimacy were exceptionally high, approximately 60 per cent, since faithful concubinage had no validity in law. There were only two alternatives. The first was to encourage concubines to 'legalise' their relationship. The second was to modify the law. Clergymen, who had already compromised on the question of illegitimacy by agreeing to baptise illegitimate children, encouraged, when they could, the first alternative. In 1902 Rev. Webb recommended in the Legislative Council the second alternative, 'to amend the marriage law, legalising the union of such per-sons without publication of banns and under well-defined conditions, and legitimatising their children'.[1] Rev. Webb may have been aware of the reservations of many Afro-Jamaicans about publication of banns, but at the same time his proposal's effectiveness would have been restrained by what constituted 'well-defined conditions'. Rev. Webb's well-intended reform did not alter the structure of marriage in Jamaica.

Despite the legal disparity, both systems of marriage had in common some commitment to permanence, except that one was a permanence based upon a contract, the other was a permanence based upon a pragmatic commitment until further notice. It is not known whether the non-legal basis of separation described by Gardner, writing in 1870, continued in the later nineteenth century. A decision by faithful concubines to part was marked by the division of the 'cotta' into two parts, with one half going to each party.[2] In any case, the frequent comment made on the solid commitments of

Creole marriage, and the incidence of manslaughter arising out of these commitments when they were violated, and the dedication to the offspring arising out of these marriages testify to a seriousness of commitment.

Non-legal marriage is not, of itself, a denial of commitment to family, any more than 'legal marriage' creates in itself an ideal situation for the raising of families. But Victorians believed that formal marriage was the foundation of the moral integrity of society, just as illegitimacy was the social evil from which other social evils flowed. With the concept of legal marriage went numerous assumptions, many of which were the inevitable assumptions of a white elite who constituted themselves into a kind of local aristocracy which set the 'tone' for social behaviour, and of a rising middle class whose values were shaped and fashioned by a desire to conduct themselves respectably, in accordance with the standards of their 'aristocratic superiors'.

These standards or assumptions rested on a well-defined position and role for women in Victorian Jamaica. The extent to which the two systems of marriage coincided or differed, therefore, was a measure of the extent to which the working woman of Jamaica and her male counterpart could materially support a lifestyle which was an intrinsic part of middle and upper class respectability.

Of the 79,365 wives mentioned in the 1911 census, most were not listed among the employed. The first principle of Victorian marriage was that married women did not work outside the home. This principle, whether imposed by men or not, was thoroughly internalised by women who issued paeans of poetic prose in praise of their 'subordinate' position. Working outside the home was 'unsexing', women should not 'invade the domains of men', high aims and ambitions could be 'gratified in the home'. Men went out into the world to witness the daily ebb and flow 'in human affairs – to fight the battle of life and women should build up a little world in her home'.[3] The virtues of woman rested in devotion to duty, patience, subordination of will. Men agreed.

Whatever the abilities of women, they were best as 'queens of the throne of the home, and ministering and giving relief and tranquility to the sick and suffering'.[4] It may be true, then, to suggest that 'Victorian women were guided into domestic confinement by members of their own sex'.[5] Yet, we cannot overlook the ultimate concern of the Victorians – the integrity of the family. The woman's place was determined above all by the fact that 'by her physical reproductive capacity the female ensures the continuity of the family, the central social institution and vehicle for the preservation and orderly transfer of property'.[6] So it was that most young ladies of the elite and middle classes did not go to work, 'but sat at home and sewed fine seams while their parents gave parties to find them suitable husbands'.[7] It may be, as D.H. Lawrence has suggested, that 'no woman does her house-

work with real joy unless she is in love'.[8] Yet, in Jamaican society the
existence of a large domestic work force went a far way toward reducing a
housewife's chores. The domestic staff could include a cook, a cook's
assistant, and a nursemaid.

Women were expected to be virtuous and chaste; and, just as important, to appear to have a reputation for chastity. The chastity of women was
an aspect of family honour. The Slander of Women Law was not passed
until 1905, but its declaration that:

> Words spoken and published after the passing of this law, which
> impute unchastity or adultery to any woman or girl, shall not
> require special damage to render them actionable,

was a stern statement of intent of the Victorian age.

Courtship among the elite, in principle and practice, was designed to
hinder pre-marital sexual encounters. In her later teens the female adoles-
cent performed the remnants of what seemed a puberty rite. She 'went into'
stays and corsets, then into long dresses. Her hair 'went up' and skirts were
let down to the ankles. The eighteenth birthday signified full acceptance
into womanhood. Courtship was formal and chaperoned. Young women
were anxiously watched by their matronly chaperones who had to be present at balls or dances, where etiquette was very strict.[9]

Married women were specially protected in law from husbands who
failed to support their wives financially. The Maintenance Laws of 1881
and 1887 'provided a ready means of enabling wives to get an order for the
payment of weekly sums by their husbands for their maintenance in which
respect the previous law was defective. These laws, together, provided that
husbands were obligated in law to maintain their wives, whether or not
those wives had the ability to maintain themselves. Men who abandoned
their wives and children to public charity 'will be declared rogues and
vagabonds'. Laws of 1870, 1886 and 1887 separated women's property
from the property of husbands, offered some independence with respect to
personal property, and protected women from the consequences of indiscre-
tions committed prior to marriage with respect to property.

> A husband shall be liable for the debts his wife contracted, and
> for all contracts entered into and wrongs committed by her before
> marriage, including any liabilities to which she may be so subject
> under any Acts or Laws relating to Joint Stock Companies.[10]

Married women, then, were to be protected in law. The defence of the
married woman was simultaneously the protection of the family, and specific enactments existed to ensure, as far as possible, that a husband's
responsibility to his wife would assure the integrity of the family.

The integrity of marriage and the family was associated in Jamaica with the maintenance of the boundaries of class and colour, and in the case of white society, of caste. Individual choice was, naturally, permitted, but within the confines of race, since racial intermarriage was not countenanced. The theme of inter-racial marriage was a sub-plot in Alice Spinner's novel *Lucilla: an Experiment*. The lesson was simple. Such interracial marriages were best lived out overseas, out of reach of the coloured family of the coloured bride or bridegroom.[11] Definitely, the maintenance of white hegemony dictated marriage within the white group as a general rule. Where individual choice was frustrated the avenue of elopement could be, and at least in one case we know of was, used; in this case an Inspector of Police eloped to Baltimore, with the daughter of a Stipendiary Magistrate.[12]

The wedding day, with its white bridal gown (purity) and its orange blossoms (fertility), wedding ring (captivity or eternal love), secrecy of honeymoon, tossing of the bouquet, the bridal cake with its doves, bells, cupids, roses and horseshoes (all known from Roman imperial times), demonstrated the absorption of ancient European and British folk custom into a ritual of respectability for Euro-centred Jamaica. Some day between 1898 and 1903 a Jamaican bride:

> . . . looked marvellously attractive, was attired in a dress of white
> silk and accordion-plaited chiffon with natural orange blossoms
> and shower-bouquet of lilies and maidenhair fern.

The wedding presents were numerous and costly.[13] A Jewish wedding in 1902 included as gifts a pianoforte (a vital piece of equipment for the middle and upper class ladies), a renaissance bedspread, oil-paintings, and numerous items of silver.[14]

Despite protective legislation drafted by men who in legal and social terms accorded a high degree of respect and consideration for women as the respected column upon which family-life and, indeed, civilisation rested, it remains true that the male of the upper and middle class was an autocrat who broke the rules which he had formulated. This tendency was reinforced by the reality that in the context of elite marriage he was the sole breadwinner, 'and in very truth the Head of the Household (to whom) wife and children paid due homage'.[15] Since the Victorian *pater* was able, by ingenuity, to draw a line of demarcation between his sexual life and his obligations as *pater-familias*, he was able, despite an increasingly strident public opinion against it, to indulge his sexual appetites (possibly made more demanding by Dr W.H. Saunders' (Chicago) formulas for the restoration of sexual potency[16]) outside the bosom of the family.

Naturally some women complained anonymously to the press:

> He likes variety after a little time and seeks it; he then neglects
> his wife, makes her unhappy by his discontented humours, or

debauched manner, and tries to find faults in the home when in reality it is only to excuse his own conscience. Worse yet, he forgets his earnings belong to her.

And finally:

What woman with any spirit or self-respect can love, honour, much less obey, in many instances.[17]

Some wives, however, in their quest for vengeance may have won Pyrrhic victories, such as the clergyman's wife in southern Manchester who gave birth to twin children whom she had borne for a gentleman in the district[18] or Mrs E.A. whose husband sued for divorce on the ground of adultery in 1886 demanding £200 in damages from Mr. N.M.[19]

The queen on the throne of the home was sometimes the victim of kingly violence. An erring husband who habitually beat his wife appeared before the court in 1886 and that erstwhile gentleman was ironically saved from the Magistrate's sentence only 'at the instance of his wife'. He was held, all the same, 'to keep the peace for six months'.[20] How many wives would have liked to take such action against husbands will never be known. It is probable that some women returned to take up residence with their families.

Up to 1870 at least, infidelity, like subordination of will, and a courtly appreciation of female kind, was sometimes an unstated part of the contract. According to Gardner:

It is wonderful that in other respects the character of the white Creole ladies proved so excellent and amiable, as their position was a trying one. It was rarely that an offer of marriage was received from anyone who did not maintain at least one coloured or black housekeeper, for so in the colony it was customary to designate a concubine. This all but universal appendage of a bachelor's household would in most cases retain her position until a few days before the marriage. If a good natured person, as was usually the case, she would prepare the home she was quitting for the expected bride; while that lady would often take an interest in the future welfare of herself and children, astonishing to any woman trained amidst other associations. It was well for her domestic peace if she had not to submit to the existence of one or more establishments other than that of which she was head.[21]

What the historian, Gardner, was describing was a system of elite concubinage which differed qualitatively from, say, peasant concubinage. Elite concubinage was an arrangement normally between a white (and possibly coloured) male and a coloured or black woman, the length of time of which was determined by the decision of the male to take a (presumably white) bride. White/coloured concubinage therefore allowed for the continuation of marriage exclusively among whites, while permitting semi-permanent liaisons with coloured women. Gardner's account suggests that white and coloured concubinage led to the existence of multiple families.

What changed in the twilight years of the nineteenth century was not the practice of extra-marital liaisons, or concubinage but the emergence of a very strong public opinion against it. Gentlemen were accused of keeping mistresses during Legislative Council Sessions in Spanish Town; other gentlemen were accused of leading lives of open shame or of siring numerous illegitimate progeny. A public official who died in 1889 left substantial property for his seven 'natural children' (three girls and four boys) as well as to his two legitimate children. Yet another gentleman left his property to his two natural daughters in 1882.[22] Others left property for their 'reputed' children.

Since faithful concubinage (to be distinguished from elite concubinage) existed outside the law, and was usually raised as an issue of illegitimacy, it is difficult to gain any insight into the structure of these non-legal, non-documented unions. Nor can we assume that they functioned in the late-nineteenth century in the same way that they do now. Yet, there are conclusions which can be drawn from the limited evidence. The first is that they represented as much a qualitative as legal difference in the relationship between men and women of different classes. Secondly, this qualitative difference was, in part, a consequence of the fact that 'faithful concubines' unlike married parties of the middle and upper classes were, nearly universally, members of the labour force. There was little possibility here that the working woman's main purpose in life was to provide 'gentleness' and 'softness'. Thirdly, faithful concubinage approximated a social and economic reality in which men and women of the working classes were economic partners in day to day survival.

Where women performed wage labour they received less remuneration, it is true. But it is more important that they were earners. The female population figured prominently (183,696) in the agricultural labour force of 271,296 in 1891. In that year, in Portland, there were 1,080 women working in the banana industry compared with 1,095 men; and in St Mary 1,132 women to 1,186 men. In the pens, there were 31,594 labourers of whom 15,769 were women. In the sugar industry there were 19,639 women and 18,784 men. The census figures may have exaggerated the number of women in agriculture but they are good enough for us to conclude that women were a significant part of the workforce. In 1891, approximately 35 per cent or 9,503 of the ground provision planters were women, though it is not clear the extent to which they planted on their own or worked in partnership with men. The low wages of the labourer and the limited earning capacity of small farmers made partnership rather than domination (based on the man as sole breadwinner) perhaps the typical relationship between men and women of the working classes.

For the United States, Robert Staples concludes:

> Their [the men] own lowly position has effectively prevented them from suppressing their women in the same manner that white males have dominated white females. They have been forced to adopt more egalitarian views towards the role of women as a result of certain historical and social forces.[23]

The woman's important role as breadwinner stood in such tangible contrast to the leisured lifestyle of middle and upper class women, that the black man's reputation for laziness increased, and he was given little credit for what he did. Referring to the working women of Jamaica, W.P. Livingstone has this to say:

> They appear unconscious of any hardship in the arrangement which transfers to them so large a part of the burden of life. It gives them a certain power, apart from sex, over the men, which in the circumstances is perhaps essential.[24]

Livingstone, dedicated as he was to measuring lifestyles by a strictly European yardstick which assessed behaviour in terms of elite behaviour in Jamaica, was comparing elite women with working women. That the working women appeared 'unconscious of any hardship in the arrangement which transfers to them so large a part of the burden of life' was an indication that here was a lifestyle which varied from elite lifestyle. Livingstone's comment is perhaps more significant than he realised. He goes on to speak of the power which working women exercised over their men, a clear indication of an association more closely based on partnership than on male domination. The prevailing concept of femininity, domesticity, the woman's role as mother, regulated by the daily rhythm of the household, was completely denied by the position of working women whose place was as much outside the home as within it. Inevitably, the Afro-Jamaican working woman had far more in common with her male class counterpart than with the elite woman who was a beneficiary of the class inequalities of Jamaican society. The cult of womanhood and domesticity was class bound, and was facilitated by the expanding domestic services which provided the labour power needed to maintain that cult.

The rate of marriage in Jamaica witnessed a rise and fall during this period 1881–97; though the rate was never very high. The rate of marriage per thousand of population was 3.7 in 1881–2 and reached a high of 5.5 in 1890–1. It fell to 3.7 in 1897–8 and returned to 5.0 in 1899–1900. In 1900–1 it was 4.2 per thousand.[25] These rates cannot be said to reflect any growing popularity of the marriage institution. In 1890–1, when Jamaica reached its peak of 5.5 per thousand, the equivalent figure for the United Kingdom was 6.9, for France 7.1, New Zealand 6.0, Queensland 7.7. Jamaica was ahead of Ireland (4.5) in that year.

The national average also conceals regional variations. The rural-urban variation is just as notable as the variation between the depressed sugar plantation areas on the one hand and the non-sugar areas such as Portland, St Mary or St Thomas. The conclusions of the Registrar General that a higher rate of marriage was the companion of greater prosperity has, therefore, some validity. The higher rates of marriage in urban Kingston and St Andrew were, also, probably influenced by the fact that a high proportion of the elite lived in these parishes.

Table 6.1   Marriage rates in parishes 1890–1

Parish	No. of marriages	Rate per thousand
Kingston	315	6.4
St Andrew	217	5.7
St Thomas	215	6.6
Portland	237	7.4
St Mary	257	5.9
St Ann	317	5.8
Trelawny	185	5.9
St James	142	4.0
Hanover	131	4.0
Westmoreland	238	4.4
St Elizabeth	372	5.9
Manchester	276	4.9
Clarendon	294	5.1
St Catherine	364	5.5
Whole Island	3560	5.5

Source: JBB, 1891

The figures in Table 6.1 are for 1890–1 when the marriage rate peaked in Jamaica as a whole. Urban Kingston had one of the highest rates for the island. But it was the banana parish of Portland which showed the highest rate of marriage, at 7.4 per thousand. St Thomas, another banana parish, showed the second highest rate at 6.6 per thousand. The lowest rates of 4.0 and 4.4 are recorded for the sugar parishes of Hanover, St James and Westmoreland. Between 1891 and 1900 there was a tendency for the island rate to fall, as we have noted, including the banana parish of Portland, but the sugar parishes, with the exception of Trelawny, continued to fall as well.[26] If marriage was not a popular institution in Jamaica as a whole, it was even less popular in Plantation Jamaica, which ironically, was regarded by the planters and their apologists as the nucleus from which blacks would be 'civilised'.

Several explanations were advanced to explain the universal reluctance to marry, ranging from black moral turpitude, to white example, to the breakdown of African family practices, and to the low self-esteem of the black population.

The expense of weddings was viewed as one of the reasons for the reduced number of marriages.[27] Madeline Kerr, writing in 1952, commented on this feature of working class life.[28] The Registrar General in 1911 frankly correlated the prosperity of the banana parishes with the increased number of marriages in those areas. It was also noted from time to time that expenses were not spared for a wedding. A second possibility was that formal marriage would lead to a reduction of female independence in accordance with the pattern of subordination of females in Victorian marriage. In 1902 the *Daily Gleaner* made the following comment which was sensitive to the clash of concepts with regard to marriage:

> The people are not automatons. They think, and have their own ideas about matters, which are often quite an opposite character to the ideas of other races. The Negro woman's remark, 'Is it because you have done away with slavery in the field that you want to establish it in the hut?' represents the opinion of very many in Jamaica. Much, of course, needs to be done to improve the racial view, but one must not mistake the character of the conditions that are seen and the motives that lie behind them.[29]

The view that marriage reduced a woman's independence and could bind her for life to an unsavoury character was again expressed by the Jamaican woman who philosophically stated:

> If we love each other, what need is there of marrying? If we don't we are able to leave each other.

Furthermore,

> As long as they are not married the man works for her, and if he doesn't she is free to get rid of him and have one who does. But directly they marry, it is a generally understood thing that she will have to support *him*.[30]

Livingstone also noted that women of the peasant class are still 'practically independent of the man . . . They prefer a relationship which can, if necessary, give them their freedom at any time'.[31]

Attitudes of reluctance altered, according to Madeline Kerr, 'with the class structure'.[32] With a subtle change of emphasis George Cumper observes that marriage was 'a latent ideal with increased mobility'.[33] A ring of marriage, in this context then, was a sign of individual social mobility.

Marriage was a rite of respectability, which was to be demonstrated by the extent to which the prospective wife could adorn the household, and perhaps her husband as well.

> A Negro of the tradesman or artisan class, otherwise willing to marry . . . is often reluctant to tie himself to a Negress of the same class, because of her lack of training and domestic qualities.[34]

Like Cumper, Roberts and Sinclair observe that 'marriage was regarded as the norm towards which most couples aspire and which in fact more than half attain at the end of the childbearing period'.[35]

People did marry, according to the rites of the Church, and in accordance with civil law. Some faithful concubines married in *articulo mortis*, probably in order to facilitate the transfer of property. Others married after several years of faithful concubinage, with grown children of both parties attending the nuptials.[36]

There were ceremonial differences. If the bride and bridegroom belonged to different Churches, the marriage was often sanctified in both Churches. Three weeks after the first ceremony the couple 'returned thanks' at the groom's church to be followed by a second wedding celebration at the home of the groom's parents. A wedding was not only for a few select guests. Rather it was a community fete. Below is an example of a wedding in the parish of Hanover at the beginning of the twentieth century:

> When a young lady was to be married the husband-to-be had to supply her mother with about 50 yards of brown calico to make up articles for their home. He could not see his bride-to-be for two days before the wedding. Everyone in the district helped in his or her own way. Some brought goats, fowls, pigs, ground provisions, cakes. Music [was] supplied by the local 'fife and drum' band. Some neighbours fixed up the dwelling of the bride and bamboo booths were erected in the yard with numerous seats for the guests. Others sewed for the bride-to-be and the skilled cake-makers baked cakes, which amounted to as much as three tin cases full! The animals were roasted . . . at the home of the groom's parents.[37]

The bride rode to church in a buggy or carriage, while the guests rode behind in pairs to and from the church, each lady escorted by a gentleman. The approach of the bride was sometimes announced by a mounted herald. In some districts there was a pre-wedding celebration on the eve of the wedding when the village assembled – young, old and middle-aged.[38] The celebration consisted of several games, among the most popular of which was 'Jumping'.

Marriage between members of the peasantry demonstrated the principle of partnership. Did this partnership continue after marriage or did male autocracy assert itself? The evidence is limited, but J.H. Reid offers a hint.

> The ordinary wife does not like to join her husband at the family festive board. She may be as careful in presenting him his dinner on as neatly spread a table as anyone can wish, yet she prefers to eat by herself in the kitchen, or in a corner of the room. It is evident she does not believe in equality of the sexes. There are [however] hundreds of families in which, under the impulse of education the wife takes her place with conscious pride by the side of her husband at the family board and every department of life.[39]

The very low rate of divorce in Jamaica suggests the conclusion that marriage was stable, even happy. In 1892 there were three divorces, in 1899 only two. The highest figure for the late-nineteenth century is six in 1897. Between 1905 and 1907 there was an increase to between fifteen and seventeen per annum. Adultery, adultery and desertion, adultery and cruelty, and cruelty were the categories under which divorces were sought and granted. The majority of divorces were on the grounds of adultery. There is no good reason to assume, however, that stability or permanence of marriage meant marital bliss. In a situation where married women were heavily dependent on their breadwinning husbands, there is no doubt that some wives were forced to tolerate high levels of abuse. Furthermore, divorce would have been a cause for 'loss of face', if not social disgrace, in a community where marriage itself was a major indicator of respectability. It is not inconceivable, either, that some women internalised the idea that the wife had a role to play as the suffering Madonna.

Extra-legal sanctions against turbulent marriages also contributed to keeping couples together. A 'respectable' catechist was struck off the list of the Anglican Church because of his propensity to ill-treat his wife.

Patterns of sexual behaviour

Although marriage is, in theory at least, more closely associated with the rearing of families – the bed in which seeds are planted, so to speak – than with sexual relations *per se*, it is clear that patterns of sexual behaviour affect marriage. We have already commented on the formality of courtship

among the elite, a courtship which in the Jamaican context of racial heterogeneity was important for the preservation of white society in a world of
coloureds. Caste-like courtship and marriage patterns among the whites
effectively defended 'aristocratic' status.

At the same time we have observed that, despite the universally
acknowledged principle of Victorian Jamaica that adults of different sexes
living under the same roof and assumed to be indulging in sexual activity
should be married according to the canons of the Church or to the provisions of civil law, that there continued to be in Jamaica 'promiscuous use of
concubine and bride'. As noted earlier, the historian, Gardner, claimed that
men of the upper class enjoyed a system of concubinage with black and
coloured 'housekeepers'. This was a concubinage which was functionally
different from that of the peasantry. White/coloured concubinage assumed
the dependence and subordination of the 'housekeeper', who, incidentally,
was expected to have qualifications over and above the ability to organise
a household and offer sexual services. An advertisement for a housekeeper
specified that the lady must be able to play the pianoforte. The progeny of
such arrangements were destined to receive an education and perhaps
financial and property bequests. The 'advantage' for women rested in
financial security, which, following Gardner's account, was expected to
continue, even after the 'employer' had entered into formal marriage. M.G.
Smith commented on this kind of relationship during the slave period of
Jamaican history.

> Among the coloured population of Jamaica, the women showed
> a clear preference for extramarital associations with whites
> rather than marriage with their own kind . . . Asymmetrical con-
> cubinage rather than marriage was the norm of mating for all
> categories of free persons in Jamaica at this period, . . . coloured
> males by preference also recruited their concubines from women
> of a lower social level.[42]

That these associations continued with some vigour in the late-nineteenth
century is revealed by Livingstone:

> Many parents who resent the bitterness of their own lot make
> every effort to unite their children to mates of a higher shade
> . . . Black girls, no matter how handsome and well-educated, are
> left by suitors of their own class for mulattoes and quadroons,
> who again seek higher alliances; and all will enter at first into
> primitive relations to accomplish their ends . . . Large numbers of
> these (fair skinned) women also live in illegitimate relation with
> whites of *every class*.[43]

Livingstone was also very explicit in his description of the importance of 'racial caste' in the selection of mates in a community where 'the one burning desire is to possess fair skin . . . ' The bleaching process which Livingstone described was related both to the greater material security which a liaison with a lighter racial category could provide or was believed to be able to provide. Social advancement was thus linked to racial dilution.

The ability to exploit, sexually, women of lower 'social and racial status' proved an ideal escape for those who preferred to postpone the responsibilities of family life, *à la Victoria*.

> The average white does not look at the black girl as he does at one of his own race; if he regards her favourably at all, it is usually with the eye of lust . . . [44]

'Well-built creatures', 'perfectly supple', 'nature's wild daughters' were some of the terms used to describe the black woman.[45] Rev. Dingwall lamented that the society had become 'womanised' and that one sinner of fair colour 'can undo' much of what the clergyman had tried to achieve.[46]

The formal structures of colonial administration also encouraged casual non-marital relations. A constable was not allowed to marry before four years of service; before marriage he had to receive permission, and the character of his bride had to be assessed by his superiors.[47] The structure of plantation society, albeit no longer all-pervasive, also encouraged tenuous linkages.[48]

In 1902, the *Daily Gleaner*, whose opinions represented those of white society, editorialised on the question of hypersexuality in Jamaica, but sought to identify that hypersexuality with black male sexuality. 'Here is Jamaica's paramount need – the training and disciplining of the black race . . . Let them practise self-control'. 'The average black man', the editorial continued, 'is not as highly developed in mind and character as most white men, for the same reason that many white men are stunted in intellect and will as compared with their fellows – because they do not discipline themselves and keep their passions in subjection'.[49]

The very righteous Mr Dingwall was concerned that courtship among professedly Christian families encouraged 'the secret breach of God's command by the young people previous to marriage [regarding] such action as not exactly partaking of the nature of sin, but rather as the *necessary preliminary* to all marriage'. Rev. Dingwall insisted that 'many of the so-called "falls" are due not so much to seducers as to young seductresses trained by their parents, and also that women demonstrated far too much initiative and aggression in courtship'.[50] On the other hand Rev. Wilson pointed out that 'Womanhood is so beset with temptation . . . That she who has not her own will and fixedness of purpose *must* go to the wall. Men tempt with gold and mislead with fair speeches and large promises . . . The serpent in the man can be detected by the twinkle in the eye, the attempt at familiarity, or the careless, or slightly rude remark'. Wilson also observed that young women, as soon as they were engaged, expected to be 'supported by their sweethearts. This mistake often leads to serious results'.[51] Courtship and its consequences were often initiated by letters.

Prostitution

In its own perverse way, prostitution is not antagonistic but rather complementary to marriage. As David McCreery has observed in a recent study, 'by her degradation the prostitute reinforces the approved social role for women of "virgin-mother" evident in the Catholic world in the cult of the Virgin. Her ready availability protects "honest" women by venting or diverting socially dangerous male sexual aggressiveness while reinforcing established moral values and stereotypes of male dominance'.[52]

Jamaica had its share of *demi-mondaines* at the end of the nineteenth century. In 1886 a 'Voice from the North-East' referred to the lack of employment among women which causes some women to make an 'illicit living'. More importantly, however, the correspondent observed that the clients of these women were 'men of means' who were taking advantage of the poverty of the women.[53] Perhaps it was the expansion of the banana ports of the island which provided these 'opportunities' for women.

Kingston appears to have been well supplied with prostitutes. There were houses of prostitution on Fleet Street, and Peter's Lane. Provisions were made for the monitoring of the health of prostitutes. In 1891 information was laid against 364 women under the Contagious Diseases Law in Kingston and Port Royal. Of these, 133 were sent to the Lock Hospital for treatment, 'having been found diseased'. Fifteen were sent to prison for non-compliance with the law. In a memorandum on 'Disorderly Houses' the Inspector General of Police, Mr Knollys, defended the continued existence of brothels without which there would be a 'great increase in immorality'.[54]

In his comment in 1893 on prostitution the Bishop of Jamaica expressed the view that Jamaica did not have a large prostitute class. The real problem rested in a more generalised sexual immorality. 'A large section of our population [were] not living morally, but at the same time [were] not to be classed with prostitutes'.[55]

The dominant group within the society – the whites – used the institution of marriage to maintain the boundary between themselves and the coloured majority classes. At the same time sexual practices were conditioned by the desire to achieve a white somatic norm image, which was made possible by sexual relationships outside marriage between the white (males) and non-white (females). In this way 'purity of blood' could be maintained among the ruling class, while 'impurity of blood', cloaked in illegitimacy among the masses in itself, reinforced and sharpened the distinction between the classes and the masses. Asymmetrical concubinage was economically functional. In a different sense, so was 'faithful concubinage' among the 'mountain Negroes'. For the rising middle class marriage placed a legal seal on respectability.

Marriage, concubinage and courtship patterns appear to differ from one segment to another. Concubinage, as practised by the elite, was functionally and qualitatively different from the faithful concubinage of the lower classes. It did not rest on assumptions of equal partnership, but rather on the ability of elite males to use their social position to exploit sexually women of lower social, economic and racial status. Elite concubinage did not, then, overlap institutionally with peasant concubinage. Nor can it be denied that 'the monogamous marriage pattern of the ostensibly Christian West Indian upper class is very significantly modified by the conditions of West Indian life'.[56]

Yet, the evidence points to an equation between social mobility and marriage on the one hand, and respectability on the other. Socially mobile blacks, as they assumed the patterns of life of the Eurocentric community, also adopted marriage, which was a feature of life of the black lower middle class and middle class. Ultimately, the prevalence of concubinage among the lower classes was interconnected with class position. Of course, it may also be true that the pew was less frightened of hell-fire than the pulpit would have liked.

Social policy framers emphasised marriage because, among other things, they believed that illegitimacy was the 'great social evil', which presumably adversely affected the life chances of children. Shrewder observers, such as Rev. Webb and Rev. East recognised that the 'mountain Negroes' had functional family units, and attentively looked after the welfare of their children. This was why Webb advocated that faithful concubines should be encouraged to formalise their relationship in conventional marriage.

The leadership of Jamaican society, however, became so obsessed with illegitimacy that the harsh social and economic realities of rural life were given scant attention as explanatory factors which determined the life chances of children. Indeed, as we have noted, illegitimate children of the elite (we cannot say all) were recipients of valuable property bequests or of education – a fact which should have indicated to the 'civilisers' and uplifters of the 'subject people' that the progress of children was determined not so much by marriage or illegitimacy but by poverty or wealth, by opportunity or lack of opportunity.

Notes

1   *JCM*, 1902, p. 23.
2   W. Gardner, *History of Jamaica*, London, 1873, p. 182.
3   *DG*, 23 December, 1899, Essays by 'Princess Alice' and 'L.H.H.', on 'Should Women Work outside the Home?'
4   Rev. William Graham, *Woman: Her Sphere and Opportunities*, Kingston: Educational Supply Co. 1899, p. 8.
5   Mary P. Ryan, 'The Power of Women's Networks', in Judith Newton, Mary Ryan, *et al., Sex and Class in Women's History*, London, Boston: Routledge and Kegan Paul, 1983, p. 183.
6   David McCreery, "This Life of Misery and Shame",: Female Prostitution in Guatemala City, 1880–1920', *Journal of Latin American Studies*, Vol. 18, Pt. 2, November, 1986, p. 334.
7   *JM*, M.A. Robinson.
8   Laws of Jamaica, 1902–5. Law 8, 1905. 'A law to amend the law relating to the slander of women', 13 April, 1905.
9   *JM*, Daisy Jeffrey Smith.
10 Laws of Jamaica, 1884–1887. Law 21, 1886.
11 Alice Spinner, *Lucilla: An Experiment*, London: Kegan Paul, 1896 p. 112.
12 CO, 137/520, 1885, Vol. 1. Norman No. 31.
13 NLJ, MST 59, *Livingstone Collection*. 'Wedding Bells'.
14 *DG*, 12 December, 1902.
15 *JM*, Daisy Jeffrey Smith.
16 *DG*, 2 December, 1900 (Advertisement).
17 *DG*, 14 December, 1903, 'Women's Way: Love, Marriage and the Divorce Problem'. Essay by 'Only a Woman'.
18 NLJ, MST 209, Box 1. Rev. C.L.B. to Nuttall, 20 August, 1886.
19 *DG*, 15 July, 1886.
20 *DG*, 22 July, 1886.
21 W. Gardner, *History of Jamaica*, p. 377.
22 Island Record Office, Jamaica. Wills probated in the Supreme Court, Vol. 135. Will of H.S.S., entered 6 March 1890 and of J.U.M.D. entered 22 February, 1890.
23 Robert Staples, 'Masculinity and Race: The Dual Dilemma of Black Men', *Journal of Social Issues*, Vol. 34, No. 1, 1978, p. 171.
24 Livingstone, *Black Jamaica*, quoted in Mintz, 'The Jamaican Internal Marketing Pattern', p. 97.
25 *JDR*, 1900–1. Number of marriages and rate per 1,000 of population, 1891–2 to 1900–1. Report of Registrar General, p. 293.
26 JBB, 1891. Marriage Rates in the Parishes, 1890–1 and JDR, 1900–1 (p. 293). Marriage Rates per thousand of population 1891–2 to 1900–1.
27 *Royal Commission on the Juvenile Population*, Nuttall's evidence, p. 13.
28 Madeline Kerr, 'The Victorian Family pattern needs an all-powerful father, a secure economic background, plenty of snobbery, but with the possibility through social mobility of making good. It almost seems as if the peasant realises the discrepancies between these concepts because marriage is only desired when a certain economic state had been achieved and generally only when there is enough money so that the wife does not have to go to work. Very

few of those who have attained middle class, or near middle class status have sufficient means to emulate the Victorian family'. Madeline Kerr, *Personality and Conflict in Jamaica*, London: Collins, 1963, p. 95.

29   *DG*, 24 December, 1902.
30   Winnifred James, *The Mulberry Tree*, London: Chapman and Hall, 1913, p. 104.
31   Livingstone, *Black Jamaica*, p. 212.
32   Madeline Kerr, *Personality and Conflict*, p. 86.
33   G.E. Cumper, 'A Modern Jamaican Sugar Estate', *Social and Economic Studies*, Vol. 3, No. 2, September 1954, p. 130.
34   W.P. Livingstone, *Black Jamaica*, p. 212.
35   G.W. Roberts and S. Sinclair, *Women in Jamaica, Patterns of Reproduction and Family*, New York: Kto Press Millwood, 1978, p. 16.
36   The indications are that marriages in *articulo mortis* occurred principally among the labouring population. According to Henry Blake, 'In reply to your Lordship's despatch of Dec. 28, 1891, I have to inform . . . that some 20 or 30 marriages 'in articulo mortis' are performed each year in Jamaica, but considering the *class of people* [italics added] who for the most part take advantage of the provision of Section 29 of Law 15 of 1879 which is only applicable to persons who have lived together in unlawful connection, I do not consider that any hardship or inconvenience as regard the revocation of wills has come about, and that no question in regard thereto has arisen here'. Blake to Knutsford No. 4, 7 January, 1892. *Jamaica Archives*, 1B/5.18, Vol. 46, 1892.
37   *JM*, Sarah Carter.
38   *JM*, A.A. Grant.
39   J.H. Reid, 'The People of Jamaica Described', pp. 97–8.
40   *HBJ*, 1902, p. 256.
41   NLJ, MST, 209, *Bishop's Letter Book*, Vol. 30. Nuttall to Rev. P.D.M. Cornwall, Bath P.O., 18 January, 1893.
42   M.G. Smith, *The Plural Society in the British West Indies*, Berkeley and Los Angeles: University of California Press, 1965, p. 134.
43   Livingstone, *Black Jamaica*, p. 216.
44   *Ibid.*, p. 108.
45   *DG*, 6 December, 1902, 'Pay Day with the Coal Heavers. A Port Royal Sketch'.
46   Rev. R. Dingwall, *Jamaica's Greatest Need*, London: Lennon and Co., 1892, p. 27.
47   *JA*, 25 April, 1896.
48   See Chapter 5.
49   *DG*, 5 December, 1902, 'A Word to the Black Race'.
50   Rev. R. Dingwall, *Jamaica's Greatest Need*, p. 29.
51   Rev. C.A. Wilson, *Men With Backbone*, pp. 30–40.
52   David McCreery, *op. cit.*, p. 335.
53   *DG*, 31 July, 1886, 'Voice from the North-East' to Editor.
54   In 1886–7 information had been 'laid' against 174 women of ill-fame in Kingston. Of these 55 were sent to the Lock Hospital, 28 left Kingston after having been served with magistrate's orders without attending medical examination. Eight left the city after attending medical exam and 10 were sent to prison for non-compliance with the law. *JCM*, Vol. 26, 1888. Report of Inspector General against 364 women under the Contagious Diseases Law in

Kingston including Port Royal. *JCM*, 1887, Appendix XV. Annual Report of Inspector General of Police for year ended 30 August, 1886.

55 NLJ, MS 209, Vol. 30. *Bishop's Letter Book*. Nuttall to Rev. R. Wheler, 10 March, 1893 and to Rev. Osbourne Allen (SPCK), 18 March, 1893.

56 Elsa Goveia, 'The Social Framework', *Savacou II*, September 1970, p. 9.

CHAPTER 7 | Childhood, youth and education

The Lord rested on the Sabbath but not Jamaica's rural children. For many children all Sunday was spent at Church and, during the week, there was a busy round of work and school.[1]

The idea that children were important economic assets was not confined to Jamaica. It was a feature of working class life in Britain at the same period. According to Pamela Horn, 'only very slowly . . . did the old idea of the child as a small worker, who must begin to contribute to family income as soon as possible, begin to disappear for the offspring of labourers and small farmers, as it had already vanished for those in the higher ranks of society'.[2] Jamaica's children, like their parents, were integrated into the colonial economy. The lifestyle of Jamaica's working class children was dictated both by the belief systems of parents and community and by the position of their parents at the bottom of a racially structured class society.

It must also be clear that the lifestyle of children growing up in a small settler household and community varied in quality from that of children of the elite. An elite lifestyle has a large component of leisure, that of workers is closely associated with work and survival. For example, Sir Henry Blake's son kept a pet goat. The peasant child also looked after animals but those were more likely to be used for Sunday dinner than petted. The practice of different institutions is as much a consequence of the limited opportunities offered to children and parents as of cultural preferences.

This point is illustrated by practices surrounding childbirth. Children born in rural Jamaica were most of them delivered by the much maligned 'illiterate' midwife who was presumably little more qualified than her own experiences of childbirth in her earlier period of fertility, and her recollections of oral traditions transmitted from one generation to the next, allowed her to be. Yet, the great distances from hospital – also functionally related to poor transportation – the discomfort of travel by cart or dray and inadequate hospital space, may have advised delivery at home, and hence dictated the use of the midwife's services. The Jamaican government constructed the Victoria Jubilee Hospital partly to honour the fiftieth year of Queen Victoria's reign and partly to dispense with the services of the illiterate mid-wife.[3] Yet, the hospital authorities made it abundantly clear that they preferred as patients the respectable poor *married* women of

Kingston, thereby ruling out the highest percentage of mothers. The hospital had beds for 20 patients only. Not surprisingly, from 89 patients in 1892–3, the hospital had 500 in 1898–9 and expected 600 in 1899–1900. Not only was every bed always occupied but patients were sometimes placed on the floor.[4] Of course, the midwife continued to be needed.

While it is not difficult to accept the view that the ruling classes had a clear concept of ideal conditions (relative to the period) under which infants should be born and raised, it does not follow that their ideas were translated into tangible medical benefits for the working classes. It is not difficult, either, to accept the view that there is some degree of cultural 'autonomy' among the working classes, a system of beliefs which amounts to a 'dialectical pole of resistance . . . grounded in the workers' actual day to day experience'.[5] However, it is a point for discussion whether this autonomy amounts to a voluntary cultural blindfolding or is a consequence of isolation or alienation from institutions created by the ruling ideology. The rulers of society were prone, certainly, to conclude that the black population preferred to exhaust all home remedies prior to attending hospital, without taking into consideration the essentially limited scope of those institutions, limited to a considerable extent by the sparse resources of the colonial economy.

It was easy for the rulers of society to blame the victim; to blame infant mortality on the 'ignorance' of a population which 'resisted' modernisation. High infant mortality may have been a consequence of medical ignorance, of fatalistic superstition among parents. It could also have been a consequence of working mothers returning to work too soon after childbirth, bearing in mind that a child's health is closely related to the mother's. Infanticide, committed by mothers who could not support their children, was a minor, albeit shocking, cause of infant mortality. Jamaican children were particularly susceptible, however, to epidemics of whooping cough which took the lives of 2,297 infants between 1878–81 and 3,626 between 1889–91.[6] In 1895–6, of total deaths (22.7 per 1,000 of mean population) 30.5 per cent were those of children under one year, while 43.4 per cent of that total were those of children under five years.[7] Of every 100 children born in 1895–6, 17.8 failed to reach one year. Some 25.4 per cent of children died before reaching the age of five.[8]

It is not improbable that the magic and ritual associated with childbirth was an effort to resort to supernatural means to protect the life of the child, given the precariousness of that life – such practices as hanging a string of beads around the neck, of placing a Bible and scissors under the pillow until after the christening. Christening or child baptism may very well have been seen as part of the magic and ritual of childbirth.

The naming of children illustrated the continuation of African cultural patterns as well as the influence of Creolisation. The tradition of naming children according to the day of the week on which the child was born – an inheritance of West Africa – continued in muted form. While the children received Christian names they were sometimes given private names – Quashie, Quaco, Qua for boys; Quasheba, Benaba, Fibi for girls. For the rest, names were probably chosen as much for their resonance and beauty lying in the ears of the listener – as for their meaning. Very popular were names associated with the British monarchy – Albert, Edward, George, Alexander, Alexandrina. There were many Princes, and Victorias. Following the Boer War names such as Bobs, Kruger and Buller for boys were used. Church members had a strong preference for names chosen from the Bible. In one case, at least, the name Beelzebub was chosen despite strong discouragement from the officiating priest.

It was not unusual for names to be taken from advertisements – Sunlight Soap, Izal, Vinolia, Cerebros. There were, as well, classical names such as Hannibal, and Xerxes (classical names had often been given to slaves). There were Clements and Leopolds, Mordecai Adonijahs, Triphenes, Ambelzenes and Amandas.

Child labour

The survival of the child destined him or her to a quick integration into a life of work – the world of the parent. During slavery, children had made up the 'pickaninny gangs' on sugar and other estates. That situation did not change with abolition and emancipation. In fact, writing in 1884, Rev. D.J. East pointed out that throughout the whole post-emancipation period, the hardest pressure was put on the labour market for the employment of young children, some of not more than six or seven years. Child and juvenile labour continued in the late-nineteenth century to be used extensively on sugar, coffee and other estates. In the sugar parishes, juvenile gangs – aged 14–16 years – constituted most of the roving gangs who spent a couple of weeks on one plantation or the other.[10] Described as living promiscuously, they earned 4.5d per day, working between 7.00 a.m. and 5.00 p.m.[11] That wage was approximately half of what was paid to women. Obviously, children would have received even lower wages.

Parents, however, were in urgent need of a cash income – whether to purchase foodstuffs imported from overseas, or to pay their taxes; and no matter how small a child's wages they counted for something in the peasant household. As Rev. D.J. East pointed out, 'parents . . . could hardly resist the bait offered to them in the shape of wages for their *children's* labour; such wages at once providing for their maintenance, instead of imposing on them the cost of sending them to school'. Though Rev. East saw some contradiction between the need to educate children and the demand for child and juvenile labour, he admitted the need for the latter 'in order to effect the efficient and profitable working of our sugar estates and coffee plantations'.[12]

Children in rural Jamaica were integrated into the economy not only at the level of wage labour. They also offered unpaid labour services to their parents. It is reasonable to assume that this pattern of labour service developed especially after emancipation when small farmers succeeded in carving out for themselves plots of land for subsistence farming and for the production of a few export commodities. Children were involved at the level of production, harvesting and marketing of commodities.

Child labour was a sufficiently important aspect of the rural economy to ensure that children, without gender differentiation, would be integrated into the functioning of that economy.

The services of children were partly dedicated to tasks and chores, though in a middle class setting such tasks and chores attracted the wage-earning domestic service. Rural children had several tasks to perform before going to school. Water had to be fetched, sometimes at long distances from home, wood and fuel gathered, the house and yard swept, dishes washed, morning coffee prepared. Some girls were involved with doing the laundry, (washing, starching and ironing), cleaning the house and other chores. 'Tiny girls march along with gourds or kerosene tins of water on their heads to the river, tank, or reservoir. At five or six a little boy may be seen careering along on a bare-backed horse, taking it to the river to drink'.[13]

The boys would begin to work on the 'grounds' by the time they were six, so that their value as labourers coincided with their school years. There was heavier demand for the labour of children during harvest – whether of sugar, coffee, ginger, cacao or pimento. Since the rural farmer cultivated a variety of crops there was a steady demand for child labour.

Clearly child labour was confined to the less onerous duties in agriculture such as weeding, sowing grain, cutting anatto, picking coffee, 'rubbing pimento'. Duties such as the grating of cassava flour which went into the making of bammies (cassava cakes), or the manufacture of starch, a vital commodity for Jamaican laundry, were handed over to children.

Just as important, however, was the use of child labour in the marketing of goods. Children, that is, were associated with the internal marketing system of rural Jamaica. Children stayed home from school on Fridays precisely to assist with the marketing of commodities. One rather energetic child, apart from a bewildering variety of chores, sold sugar, coconuts, ripe bananas in the market; another sold her mother's cakes and bammies at 1d or 1½d at the Saturday market.[14]

National attitudes to children are summarised in perhaps a slightly idealistic way by Erna Brodber:

> The Ashanti view of children still persisted – a child as a creature with an obligation to respect elders and a right to their care. By the beginning of the twentieth century the Afro-Jamaican mind had integrated the British and West African views into a perception of the child as a useful being to be shared and cared for by the adults in the community and particularly by those in his parents' kin and friendship network. As such he could be shifted within and without the locale of his primary household group.[15]

We could even add that the home of the minister of religion became part of that network, for 'many of the less privileged children were sent out particularly to ministers' homes, for further training in domestic work'.[16] Training in the home of the minister of religion, however, had a calculated economic intent to ensure that education in a presumably more sophisticated household would maximise opportunities for the higher-paying domestic jobs.

More tragically, perhaps, children were transferred outside these traditional networks. Jamaican children were exported (sold was the word used) to Haiti as domestic servants. (The children may have been imported by Jamaican residents in Port-au-Prince). The parents, so it was reported, were generally in such circumstances that they were 'only too glad to get rid of their children'. The Colonial Office thought that the Jamaican authorities were too disinclined to take action to stop the trade, and suggested that a law be passed to forbid the export of children under 16 years of age. Thus came about the first Emigrant Protection Law (1885) to stop the despatch of children under 16 years to Haiti for domestic service. The Colonial Office took the view that the Haitian Law Courts 'do not afford such persons much protection even when the Consul seems to demand it'.[17] There is, however, little data on the extent of this trade.

Daily life of children

Yet the daily life of children was not without its lighter moments. For amusement boys rode horses, made catapults and traps (springes), calabans to catch rats, mongoose, fowls, and even goats and snakes – a combination of work and fun, and relatively inexpensive. Kite-flying and kite-making were useful ways to pass the time, as was the playing of marbles. Where marbles could not be afforded, children used 'nickels', the seed of a thorny scrub. They huddled together to watch fights between the snake and the mongoose.[18] At school and presumably in the community boys played cricket, shaping their bats from local wood or from scraps of lumber, or bamboo. Green mangoes or young lemons were used for balls.

There were home games, guessing games, ring games. Equipment for games was basic, including the fingers, each of which had its own name: Tumpy, Lickpot, Longman, Ringman, and Little Didymus. Girls made their own dolls by simply sewing wool on to the top of corn cobs and clothing them, or dressing up little bottles. If the girls' games amounted to an early preparation for maternity, the boys conversely were prepared for the masculine world of toughness, aggression, mobility and domination. They played horses, drove teams of oxen, or cantered along on a stick, or wrestled.[19]

Children shared the folk songs and stories of adults, for singing was an important way of passing the time. Some songs were accompanied by games; for example, on moonlight nights they played moonlight or moonshine baby:

> Moonshine baby don't you cry!
> Muma will bring something fe you,
> Some fe you – some fe me
> For we go boil we dirty pot.[20]

An English observer noted that ring games among older girls and boys were very much along English patterns. The words were English but the tunes were usually different, for example 'Little Sally Water'. There were many ball games as well. Writing in 1887, J.H. Reid noted that some of the guessing games such as 'Ship Sail', 'Wagon Load', 'Dribe Off' were still common. Story telling, particularly Anancy stories, was common.[21]

While songs and stories were influenced by Europe, there were still strong African traditions. Augusta Zelia Fraser, the English novelist, who wrote under the pseudonym Alice Spinner, recounted her meetings with an Afro-Jamaican child (Victoria), a nine-year-old girl whose knowledge of folklore and song was extensive. Spinner's description deserves extensive reproduction.

> Her voice was low at first, and her English so clipped and broken, and interspersed with so many Creole words and expressions, that I had difficulty in following her; but she had a sweet, soft little voice, and chanted the little scraps of song with which nearly all the Negro tales are intertwined very prettily. The music of these little airs lies more in their peculiar rhythm than in the notes themselves, and no two that I have heard are alike in this respect. They are mostly sung on two or three notes, only rising

> . . . at the end of each line into a peculiar kind of wail, the music such as it is, being most probably of pure African origin. It certainly is quite distinct from all the other adaptations of European airs. . . . In some of the stories Victoria sang *apparently mere long strings of unknown words*. She sang them none the less carefully and religiously, 'Becos', missus, dey always must be sung so', but she allowed herself that she had no idea of what meaning was attached to them.[22]

Here then was story-telling with music, with religious solemnity, in a language which reflected the continuing African presence in Jamaican culture. 'The child's memory', declares Spinner, 'was inexhaustible. Even now, I have but to shut my eyes to see once more the intelligent small face, the crouching figure, the absurd little black feet, with the wholly unexpected pinky soles thrust from beneath the brief calico skirt'. The English author regretted that she had failed to transcribe all the songs which she had heard from Victoria. She recorded one, however; the story of an orphan whose brothers had gone away to Guinea. After many adventures in which she is rescued by the spiritual intervention of her late mother, her brothers in Guinea hear her song of lamentation and fear, and come rowing across the Atlantic just in time to rescue her from mortal danger.[23]

Education

There was no consensus on what constituted proper education in Jamaica. There were those who doubted that money spent on the education of black people would not be better spent building tramways.[24] There were others who thought that education should be functional, and related to production. Others saw education in the broader sense of educating for citizenship, moral training, and social control, while not ignoring the functional aspects of education. Men such as Enos Nuttall adopted the latter position. Nuttall's Belmont Orphanage was designed to graduate good domestics.[25] His advocacy of agricultural education reflected his concern for functional education and for the agricultural/economic growth of the island.

Among Nuttall's contemporaries were those whose concept of education was inseparable from their own concerns for social control. When the Director of Education, in 1886, recommended that a simple manual on the 'leading principles of Christian Morality' should be introduced into schools, because 'in the present course of instruction there is perhaps not sufficient direct provision for training children in *habits of discipline and subordina-*

tion', he was in effect advocating a system in which the 'masses of the population would give their "spontaneous" consent (*à la* Gramsci) to the general direction imposed on social life'.[26] There were yet others who insisted that the more money spent on education the less would have to be spent on the police. Planters, however, who insisted that education 'spoiled labour' did not win complete political victory at the end of the nineteenth century. As for the advocacy of agricultural education, only rarely was the important observation made that there was a contradiction between favouring practical training in agriculture when the graduating students had only limited access to land resources where their acquired skills could be put to the test.

In the minds of churchmen, at least, religion and education were inseparable; and this marriage of ideological significance, was reflected both in institutional arrangements and in syllabuses. The Churches in the colony had developed an important interest in education, partly because such had been the practice in the metropolis, partly because of the particular relationship which had developed between the Churches and the black population during and after slavery.[27] Nuttall emphasised that the Churches had undertaken to educate the masses of the population out of a moral obligation:

> What the Religious Bodies have done for the primary secular education of the people, they have done of their own free will, being moved thereto by the love of God, and a yearning for the material and mental improvement as well as for the spiritual enlightenment of the people.[28]

By the end of the nineteenth century the conviction that the State should undertake more responsibility for the education of the young was strengthened by the reality that traditional sources of missionary funds from overseas were no longer as abundant. The burden of constructing and maintaining schools and churches fell increasingly upon peasant parents and congregations. Of course, the system whereby the Churches underwrote education in Jamaica eminently suited the colonial administration. However, at the end of the nineteenth century education took on a new dimension outside its traditional moral and spiritual focus. Certainly, the structure of imperialism in the late-nineteenth century demanded education as well; and what was originally a religious affair increasingly became, in Jamaica at least, a partnership between Church and State. In face of competition with the United States and Germany in the 1890s, British imperialists began to associate efficiency with education; an orientation immediately mirrored in Nuttall's statement to Synod in 1897 that education was the 'modern path of progress for all races'. Education was to be widespread, be efficient and to be as practical as circumstances allowed and 'modern circumstances of competition demand intelligence and education of workers; educated men make the best workers in the end'.[29] This was, in part, education for empire's welfare. But for Nuttall as for other clerics, education remained an important tool to maintain social stability. Clergymen continued to associate education and moral training, objectives which were not incompatible with the preparation of children for employment in relation to the socio-economic context in which children grew up. One of the fruits of this orientation was the greater emphasis placed on agricultural training in elementary schools, and the sponsorship of lectures to small farmers on agricultural techniques based on the new scientific agriculture.

The argument that educating blacks made them unfit to undertake the area of life for which they were most suited, i.e. agricultural labour, continued to be upheld by planters such as Robert Craig right down to the beginning of the twentieth century. Other members of the oligarchy, while favouring elementary education for blacks, were opposed to secondary education for them. The more thoughtful Enos Nuttall generally favoured educational opportunities for bright or promising students of whatever race. The hopelessly prejudiced Matthew Farquharson, a storekeeper and landed proprietor, saw no point in educating the lower classes in secondary schools since, in his view, blacks were of limited capability and had, in terms of social development, not yet passed the stage at which the British were at the time of the Norman Conquest.[30]

Conflicting views among the elite on the scope and extent of mass education were complemented by differences of opinion between the colonial authorities and churchmen, such as Enos Nuttall. Essentially the Archbishop had to prod the colonial administration into taking up the challenge of secular education, while trying to ensure that religious education would not fall victim to a secularised syllabus.

In a spirited letter to Mr Thomas Capper, the Inspector of Schools, Nuttall accused the latter of repudiating all responsibility for the education of the masses, and called attention to the fact that 'public opinion in all English-speaking countries, and most other civilised countries, demands that government should consider it an essential part of its duty to provide for the education of the masses'.[31] Nuttall also insisted that mass education was not the fruit of government patronage but rather an entitlement from their status as taxpayers:

> I greatly regret the tone of patronage adopted by Mr Capper in his letter in reference to government grants for education. He does not realise how utterly offensive it is to any people to have it hinted that what is done for them at their own expense by their own servants is done as a favour and a boon.[32]

However, the number of elementary schools in the colony grew from 687 in 1881 to 723 in 1886, to 836 in 1891, and peaked at 962 in 1895. By the turn of the century the colonial government isolated education as the first victim of retrenchment. The number of schools actually declined after 1895. It was agreed that no more denominational schools would be built after that date. Religious education would no longer be linked with a specific denomination (except in the case of Roman Catholic schools), and in essence the Churches accepted the secularisation of syllabuses. The Colonial government had begun to subsidise the construction and maintenance of schools since 1867. Government grants, however, came only after the various denominations had constructed the schools:

> The Inspector of Schools Office has year by year congratulated itself and government on the unusual increase in the number of schools, now 600. But the fact must not be ignored that every one of those 600 had to be established by clerical means, and fostered by clerical care for at least six months, before it could get even an exceptional grant for the actual teaching work done in the schools.[33]

Nuttall also pointed out that 'the amount of school fees collected and the number of children in daily average attendance, is quite as much the result of energy and vigilance on the part of the clergymen as it is the ability and zeal of the teacher'. The co-operation between Churches and Government was demonstrated in the establishment of a Board of Education with the responsibility to oversee the operations of the educational system. On that Board sat representatives of the clergy.

While the debates continued concerning the control of education in the island nearly one-third of children of school age failed to attend school, for a number of reasons. The first was that there were not sufficient schools. The second was that all parents did not send their children to school regularly. A third possibility was that fees, which ranged between 1½d and 6d per week, were too high for some parents. In the 1890s, when fees were abolished, there was a temporary rise in school attendance but the decline after that time suggests that fees were not the crucial variable in attendance or absence.

Rev. East, whom we have mentioned earlier, definitely viewed the demand for child labour as a cause for the poor attendance of some children. In fact, he recommended that 'school-attendance days' should be fixed in relation to the demand for child labour in the particular region of the island, an arrangement which would have been consistent with practice in the United States and in Britain.

The school-attendance days might be fixed according to the

differing circumstances and requirements of different districts. Nor will there be any difficulty in determining these, as custom and necessity already show what they should be.[34]

While East was of the view that child labour was not as urgently needed in the late-nineteenth century as it had been earlier, especially in respect of children under twelve, he yet believed that some accommodation had to be made to ensure full education for children and a constant labour supply from children:

> We are in hearty sympathy with the planter; and we freely admit the necessity for juvenile labour, in order to facilitate the efficient and profitable working of our sugar estates and coffee plantations.[35]

A lack of education on the part of many parents was not necessarily a factor in their failure to send children to school. On the contrary, there is evidence of tremendous efforts by blacks to secure an education for their children. Parents were well aware, at the same time, of the constraints imposed upon the education of their children because of the demand for their services at home.

Even if we concede that schooldays are happy days, it must surely be true that times spent outside the classroom's constraining atmosphere and in the company of friends, are the more satisfying times. It is certain that the classroom in late-nineteenth century Jamaica was not intended to encourage love of learning as much as fear of punishment, under the guise of discipline. The school was, according to Rev. East, an enlightened man of the period, 'really the only sphere in which the child knows truly what discipline is'. School discipline was even more important because

> family discipline, firm and wise, which enforces implicit obedience, and makes the word of the parent law to the young child is what we have most of all to deplore the want of . . .[36]

A few contemporary observers confess that the school system was based, in part, on terror. Indeed one of the main reasons for introducing women into the classroom was to reduce the terror. The colonial authorities, evidently, also tried to reduce the incidence of flogging and brutality. In his report for 1895–6 the Inspector of Schools, George Hicks, said with an almost audible sigh of relief:

> We are getting somewhat farther away from the standard of those old time teachers who used as their daily apparatus for school discipline a surly countenance, a thundering voice, a litany of terms of abuse, a hard fist and a tough stick. Lashes should not be

imposed when a little child is unable to do a recitation or write dictation correctly.[37]

There was, definitely, a growing opinion against the lash as an instrument of education. Lashing did not lead to 'moral improvement' since it tended to degrade and thus humiliate, and to lead to loss of self-respect'.[38] According to the same correspondent, flogging was administered for 'unruly conduct – not always characteristic of the offender; for neglect of lessons; for violation of school regulations. Punishment was meted out by the offended teacher in the open school room as a rule. Flogging, furthermore, apart from being unable to put "brains into a dull boy", served to induce a dislike of studies'.

Whipping at home was sometimes used to supplement and complement (even compliment) the flogging which had taken place at the hands of the teacher. It is not perhaps so much that children were not loved, as that the father's authority rested as much on fear as on the generation of mutual affection. The ferocity of Jamaican mothers has passed down into folklore. This kind of authority was beyond doubt part of the world view of the age, but in the Jamaican context who could draw a distinction between the use of the lash as a corrective mechanism, and the lash as an instrument of degradation? The concentration on enforcing obedience meant that to 'disobey any instruction, however trivial, was a great offence, and respect for parents amounted to fear'.[39] Parental discipline was such that 'it did not necessarily cease when the child grew up'.[40] In the rural communities obedience and respect for the elderly were reinforced by the expectation that children greet their elders by lifting their caps.

Children and the law

In the late-nineteenth century children became a major concern for social reformers in Britain. It is probably under these influences that the Jamaican Legislature passed a law for the prevention of cruelty to children in 1896. The law provided for imprisonment of not more than two years or a fine not exceeding £100 in case of conviction or indictment. For a summary conviction the maximum fine was £25 or six months hard labour (maximum). The law also made provision for places of safety for children which included the poor house and the industrial school.[41] The option between a Jamaican poor house and industrial school, on the one hand, and parental brutality on the other, would have been a grim choice for Jamaican children. The law cautiously reaffirmed the parents' right to punish their children. 'Nothing in the law shall be construed to take away or affect the right of any parent, teacher, or other person having the lawful control or charge of a child to administer punishment to such a child'.[42] There is a notable absence of prosecutions in the police records for cruelty to children, which means either that the police did not care to intervene in private domain, or that misdemeanours of this kind were uncommon in Jamaica, or that the difference between abuse and rigorous parental discipline was far too subtle for a constable to determine. In any event, the provision in law for the punishment of children was so severe that it is difficult to imagine parental punishment approaching that degree of severity.

Juveniles and the law

The records are not sufficiently precise for us to determine the extent to which there was an increase in 'juvenile' crime, partly because it was during this period that the legal differentiation was made with respect to children and young persons as opposed to adults. It is possible that what may seem to have been an increase in juvenile crime was really an increase in the recording of juvenile crimes. By Law 8 of 1896 a young person was defined as someone between the ages of 10 and 16. Law 2 of 1897 revised that law to ages 12 to 16 years. The latter law defined a child as a person under 12 years of age.

It was consistent with a prevention of cruelty to children law (April, 1896) that there should be a law forbidding the whipping of children by the police. Yet, the attempt by the Colonial Secretary to forbid whipping of children under nine years of age (involved in the practice of obeah) was opposed by Dr James Johnston, one of the uplifters of the subject people. By law male children between seven and twelve years of age could be flogged by the police, limited to six strokes of the tamarind switch. For a child, an indictable offence apart from homicide, carried a maximum fine of 40/- or imprisonment with or without hard labour, not exceeding one month. The law did not 'prejudice' sending the child to 'reformatory or industrial school'.[43] Meanwhile, Law 8 of 1896 prescribed whipping not exceeding 36 lashes for young persons (ages 10 – 16). Law 2, 1897, amended that Law declaring that strokes should not exceed six for a child under 16 but over 12 years. Law 25 of 1904, the Young Criminals Punishment Law amended the Laws of 1896 and 1897, and revised the number of lashes downwards. The Christian conscience of the oligarchy would now be satisfied with a maximum of 12 lashes, and be additionally soothed by the presence of the District Medical Officer (DMO) who was to venture his medical opinion as to the physical capacity of a child to endure the lacerating stroke of a tamarind switch.

For the issue here was never whether children and juveniles should be brutally treated. The issue was the permissible extent of brutality and degradation in a supposedly Christian community. Claude McKay, the

Jamaican poet, and once a member of Jamaica's constabulary, observed this aspect of the law's application with agony. In a moral sense the law for the punishment of children (which meant black children in practice), was at variance with the law for the prevention of cruelty to children. McKay commented in verse, and in English, not Creole verse:

> Poor little erring wretch!
> The cutting tamarind switch
> Had left its bloody mark,
> And on his legs were streaks
> That looked like boiling bark.[44]

In an unusual note McKay explained the reasons for the poem:

> No doubt he deserved the flogging administered by order of the court: still, I could not bear to see him – my own flesh – stretched out over the bench . . . I saw his naked bleeding form, and through the terrible ordeal . . . he never cried. But when I spoke to him he broke down, told me between his bursts of tears how he had been led astray by bad companions, and that his mother intended sending him overseas. He could scarcely walk, so I gave him tickets for the tram.[45]

The 'principle' that the 'Negro' should be flogged because the Negro feared nothing else was carried out by the use of the tamarind switch for children, and of the 'cat-o'-nine' for adult males. The law was not necessarily intended to correct, it was intended to do more than punish. It was intended to terrorize the juvenile into submission. In 1896 a boy was given 12 lashes with the tamarind switch, presumably, for stealing one orange.[46]

Social attitudes which had emerged out of the slave plantation system continued to govern society, even when the plantation had ceased to be the central unit of production in several parts of the island. The marvel is that white leaders of society failed to understand why so many blacks were reluctant to be 'civilised' by them.

We have indicated that the violence of the colonial state – even within educational institutions – affected family relations as well, to the extent that violence and degradation could not be separated from the regulation of relationships between people and within families. A boy was apprehended by the police for use of obscene language. Before the court, the boy claimed that he was ignorant of the meaning of the words he had used. He was warned by the magistrate who happily was aware that the boy's father had already given him a sound whipping.[47] Another boy had played a most ingenious prank. He had shouted 'halt' to the night picket, which had halted in response, believing that the order had come from the Sergeant. The Police Court charged him 20/- or 14 days for disorderly conduct. The *Daily*

Gleaner's response was much to the point: 'Much ado about nothing'.[48]

It cannot be denied, of course, that the working classes have traditionally faced the harsher penalties of the law. Yet, in the ethno-cultural complex of Jamaica where the white segment dominated the coloured segment of the population, and at its most generous regarded blacks not so much as citizens but as 'subject' people, the application of the law assumed racial undertones or overtones.

The Jamaican oligarchy imported its humanitarianism, and was always sensitive to ideas coming from abroad. Therefore, the movement for reform of juveniles emerging in Britain, the United States and Canada had some impact on the island.

> The refuge and reformatory movement led to the formalisation of official control over non-criminal juveniles and the exemption of children from the ordinary guarantees of criminal due process ... The reformatory was a crucial intervening variable in the redefinition of children's legal status in the nineteenth century. The institution was the strategic focus of a conservative social reform effort that employed an environmentalist technology of social control ... The reform school organisation served as a vehicle and prerequisite for the formal, legal creation of delinquency as a deviant role for children. The organisation not only required the application of the delinquent label to juveniles who would under any circumstances be considered criminal, but also implied the inclusion of misbehaving and mistreated children and exempted these from the rule of law.[49]

Ideally, the reformatory performed the function not only of reforming children or adolescents but of reforming society through its children.[50] The black rural Jamaican who left school at 14 or 15 years often found his 'secondary' education at the reformatory or industrial school. Ironically, the reformatory may have done more towards equipping the juvenile with an occupation than elementary school had done. As with prisons there was an emphasis on 'practical work' which assisted in financing the cost of the institution. In 1881 the laws relating to reformatories in Jamaica were consolidated and amended.

Apart from reformatories industrial schools were constructed by both government and religious bodies. Industrial schools were established at Alpha (St Mary's Industrial School) in 1881 for girls, and in 1891 a similar school for boys, under the direction of Bishop Gordon of the Roman Catholic Church, was founded. In 1892 Bishop Nuttall established an industrial school at Hope Plantation, with a nucleus of 20 boys transferred from the industrial school for girls started at Shortwood.[51] The industrial schools accommodated both criminal and non-criminal children until about 1892.

As an indication of good intent the industrial schools were removed from the oversight of the police and prison department and placed in the hands of the Inspector of Schools.[52]

It is not easy to determine, despite the institutional division between criminals and paupers, to what extent the distinctions were real ones. Certainly the *Handbook of Jamaica* continued to treat reformatories and industrial schools as one, and secondly, the syllabuses or training programmes were similar. The number of paupers entering industrial schools and reformatories declined, while the number of 'criminals' increased significantly between 1892 and 1907, as the table below indicates:

Table 7.1   Number of criminals and paupers, 1892–1907

Year	Criminals	Paupers	Total
1892	147	68	215
1893	140	74	214
1894	120	80	200
1895	115	85	200
1896	120	87	207
1897	124	99	223
1898	120	77	197
1899	110	66	176
1900	106	60	166
1901	115	49	164
1902	116	43	159
1903	119	34	153
1904	151	34	185
1905	220	44	264
1906	269	47	316
1907	253	46	299

Source: Handbook of Jamaica, 1900, p. 206, and 1908, p. 187.

Other figures for 1899 demonstrate that the largest cohort of criminals and paupers was the age-group 12 to 16 years – children more or less of school age.

Table 7.2   Criminals and paupers under 16 years, 1899.

	Under 9	Age 9–12	Age 12–16	Total
Criminals	–	11	99	110
Paupers	2	19	45	66
Total	2	30	144	176

The boys' and girls' reformatories in Stony Hill were designed to inculcate work habits and skills in delinquent adolescents. The boys at Stony Hill were trained as tailors, carpenters, masons, blacksmiths, tinsmiths, bakers, bricklayers, farmers. By 1900 thirty acres of farmland, compared to half-an-acre in 1878, were being cultivated, encompassing the items which constituted Jamaica's major export crops – sugar, bananas and coffee. The value of the work done by the students at the reformatories amounted to nearly £360 from sales of furniture and their work as masons and bricklayers.

Girls were trained in the 'domestic skills' of needlework and cooking. In 1887 there were 59 girls in the Stony Hill industrial school. 32 of these were listed as criminals, and 15 as paupers. 21 were 'sent away', one as a domestic servant, 11 to relatives, four as servants on license, one to the Clarendon poor house. Four were released on the Governor's authority, and one died.

The director of the institution thought that 'some of the older girls, who are in fact full grown women, appear to feel the necessary restraint somewhat irksome'.[53] Discipline was sometimes maintained by the lash, at other times by cropping of the hair, as in female prisons. When the Marquis of Ripon criticised Governor Blake for reintroducing the whip in the institution, Blake's response was essentially that the 'class of children' in the reformatory made necessary the use of the light rod or cane reintroduced by him in 1890. The Marquis insisted, however, that cropping of the hair was a superior form of discipline.[54]

Of 250 boys discharged from the reformatories between October 1884 and September 1887 only eight had been reconvicted and sent to prison. The Director did not indicate what occupations the 'graduates' pursued, though a number of them seem to have found employment in the Kingston Volunteer Militia Band.[55] Drill and band had been one of the favourite activities of the juveniles at the reformatory.

The passage of juvenile laws was intended partly to reform juveniles, partly to maintain the peace and guarantee social order. The movement of Jamaicans from rural to urban centres had a strong contingent of juveniles. Indeed, it is improbable that there would have been a large number of older people migrating to Kingston or Spanish Town. Rural farmers in possession of land and cottage, for example, would have been among the smallest number of migrants, particularly when such a movement on their part necessitated a change of occupation and a general uprooting. Declining opportunity for land ownership or other access to land in the countryside was no doubt a factor in the migration of youth to the city.

It was reported that as soon as juveniles picked up the smattering of a skill, they sought to set themselves up as skilled labourers – carpenters and bricklayers, or cabinet makers. One witness before the Commission of

Inquiry into the juvenile population in 1879 noted that the young men who floated around Kingston were often between the ages of 12 and 16, 'the worst rips Kingston ever produced'. The 'vagrant children who gravitate to Kingston look after gentleman's horses, hang about the omnibus drivers, each omnibus I think, having fully five boys as hangers on'. The girls gravitated towards domestic service, which offered the occasional advantage of room, board and a small wage. There was little work for women. The cabinet maker, Mr Alexander Dixon, reported that for 'the last four years' he had been employing as many as 20 women and girls at a time, 'and sometimes when I give out that I want 20 I could get five hundred'.[56]

As the nineteenth century drew to a close juvenile crime was on the increase, a testimony to the failure of social policy, of educational policy in particular, to the scanty resources of the colonial state, and to the unfortunate situation of juveniles. The juvenile laws were designed more to guarantee social order than to promote policies which offered dignity to individuals in the society. Dignity and respectability in the late-nineteenth century colonial/imperial framework were not congruent with ideas which the oligarchy cherished about black children or black people. Social reform is not compatible with social tendencies towards dehumanisation of the objects of reform.

It is not possible to indicate the structure of juvenile crime prior to 1896, but clearly between that year and 1906 there was a marked increase in the recorded incidence of juvenile crime. There was also an increase in second offences.

The figures below are for praedial larceny for the parishes of Kingston and St Andrew only:

Table 7.3   Convictions for praedial larceny Kingston and St Andrew

Year	Total convictions	Juveniles 1st offence	Juveniles 2nd offence
1896–7	46	36	5
1897–8	90	60	19
1898–9	85	65	10
1899–1900	96	57	26
1900–1	164	107	24
1901–2	146	99	24
1902–3	76	50	12
1903–4	148	120	15
1904–5	319	244	44
1905–6	186	132	24

Source: JDR, 1905–6, p. 220.

It would be unduly pessimistic to conclude that opportunities were absolutely closed to children of the working classes, since it is clear that a relatively few blacks proved socially mobile through education, at the elementary school level, or at the level of teachers' colleges. Yet it should be understood that secondary education was not designed for the working classes but essentially to solidify class boundaries. The fee structure of secondary schools, their selection process, syllabus and method of evaluation 'helped to rigidify class boundaries and to alienate one group of people from the majority in the society'. Secondary schools were not only few in number but their intake was also small. Elite children continued to be sent overseas, or were educated in a plethora of small private schools. Elite education was intended to equip them for leadership positions in the society. Certainly Nuttall considered that the shortage of candidates for the priesthood in Jamaica was partly a consequence of weaknesses in the secondary educational system.[57]

The socialisation process for young black Jamaicans was, then, a rather complex series of interactions connected with their rural background, the rural economy, and the formal institutions of the colonial state which partly through poverty, but partly through policy, continued to be dedicated to the maintenance of the racially structured class society.

Notes

1 Jamaica Archives. 'Jamaica Memories', by Rev. R.A.L. Knight.
2 Pamela Horn, *The Changing Countryside in Victorian and Edwardian England and Wales*, London: Athlone Press, 1984, p. 165.
3 *DG*, 9 December, 1899, 'Maternity Hospital'.
4 *Ibid.*
5 Charles W. Mills, 'Race and Class: Conflicting or Reconcilable Paradigms?' *Social and Economic Studies*, Vol. 36, No. 2, 1987, p. 80.
6 *JBB*, 1889–91.
7 *JBB*, Governor's Report on the Blue Book and Departmental Reports, 1895.
8 *Ibid.*
9 Isabel MacLean, *Children of Jamaica*, Edinburgh and London: Oliphant, Anderson and Ferrier, 1910, p. 32.
10 Report of the Royal Commission upon the Condition of the Juvenile Population of Jamaica, 1879, p. 22.
11 *Jamaica Memories*, essay by N.W. Fletcher.
12 D.J. East, *Elementary Education. Report of the Royal Commission. A Review*, Kingston: DeCordova and Co., 1884, p. 9.
13 MacLean, *Children of Jamaica*, p. 41.
14 *JM*, by Julia Mullings.
15 Erna Brodbner, 'A Second Generation of Freemen in Jamaica, 1907–44', Ph. D. (History), University of the West Indies, Mona, 1986, p. 73.
16 *JM*, A.B. Lowe.

17   CO, 137/521. Norman to C.O. Derby (No. 172), 8 May, 1885 re-Emigrants' Protection Law (Law 10, 1885).
18   *JM.* A.M. Jackson (Port Antonio).
19   MacLean, *Children of Jamaica*, Chap. 8.
20   *Ibid.*
21   J.H. Reid, 'The People of Jamaica Described', in Rev. R. Gordon, *et al.*, *Jamaica's Jubilee: or What we are and What we hope to be*, London: S.W. Partridge and Co. 1888, p. 101.
22   Alice Spinner, 'A West Indian Fairy Story', in Spinner, A. *A Reluctant Evangelist and Other Stories*, London: Edward Arnold, 1896, pp. 331–2.
23   *Ibid.* p. 332.
24   Mr James Gall's (editor of *Gall's Newsletter*) evidence before Royal Commission on Elementary Education – Digest of Evidence, p. 220. quoted in D.J. East, *Elementary Education*, p. 6.
25   NLJ, MS 209a, Vol. 29, *Bishop's Letter Book*. Nuttall to W.P. Clark (Resident Magistrate, Lucea), 10 April, 1893.
26   Charles Mills, 'Race and Class', p. 75.
27   Mary Turner, *Slaves and Missionaries. The Disintegration of Jamaican Slave Society*, Urbana: University of Illinois Press 1982, *passim.*
28   NLJ, MS 209a, *Bishop's Letter Book*. Nuttall to E.N. Walker (Colonial Secretary), 25 April, 1883, p. 81.
29   Enos Nuttall, *Some Present Needs of Jamaica*, p. 7.
30   Trevor Turner, 'Social Objectives in the Educational Thought of Jamaicans, 1870–1920', p. 156.
31   NLJ, MS 209a, *Bishop's Letter Book*. Nuttall to Walker, 25 April, 1883, p. 81.
32   *Ibid.*
33   *Ibid.*
34   D.J. East, *Elementary Education*, p. 24.
35   *Ibid.* p. 9.
36   *Ibid.* p. 13.
37   *JDR*, 1895–6. Report of Superintending Inspector of Schools, 31 March, 1896, Kingston: Government Printing Office, 1897.
38   *DG*, 19 December, 1903, J.M. Simpson to Editor.
39   *JM*, C.G. Bailey (Spanish Town).
40   *Ibid.* A.B. Lowe (Adelphi).
41   *Laws of Jamaica*, Law 9, 1896, 'Prevention of Cruelty to Children'.
42   *Ibid.*
43   *Ibid.*
44   Claude McKay, *Songs of Jamaica* (introduced by Walter Jekyll) Florida, 1969. First edition, Aston Gardner and Co., Kingston, 1912, p. 111.
45   *Ibid.*
46   *JA*, 17 October, 1896.
47   *DG*, 6 December, 1902.
48   *DG*, 22 March, 1886, 'Much Ado about Nothing'.
49   John R. Sutton, 'Social Structure, Institutions, and the Legal Status of Children in the United States'. *American Journal of Sociology*, Vol. 88: 4–6, 1983, p. 931.
50   *Ibid.* p. 931.
51   *HBJ*, 1900, p. 205.
52   *Ibid.* p. 205.
53   *JCM*, Vol. 26, 1888. Report on Girl's Reformatory and Industrial School (Stony Hill), 30 September, 1887. Appendix XI.

54   Blake to Marquis of Ripon (No. 330), 29 September, 1892, and No. 398, 13 December, 1892.
55   *JCM*, Vol. 26, 1888. Report of Thomas Mair, Director of Industrial School and Reformatory, Stony Hill, 11 November, 1887.
56   Report of Royal Commission upon the Condition of the Juvenile Population, 1879. Evidence of Mr Berry.
57   Trevor Turner, 'Social Objectives', p. 91.

CHAPTER 8

Peasants, tenants and wage-labourers

The access which the ex-slaves and their descendants had to land and economic independence was significantly qualified by the capacity of the oligarchy to constrain that access and curb that independence by manoeuvring the law to defend the class interests of the oligarchs. The ability of rural workers to shape their own destinies was also contingent upon their demand for a cash income, the search for which often forced them into exploitative credit systems organised by, for, and in the interests of shopkeepers who were themselves landlords or planters. The latter linked their businesses with the sale of export crops such as coffee purchased from smallholders at exploitative prices. Pure subsistence production was not viable in a money economy which demanded payment of taxes, duties, fees, and even Church subscriptions. It is possible that the most reactionary part of the white oligarchy linked superexploitation of black labour with taxation.[1] The economic institutions of the colony were entirely compatible with the rigorous exploitation of capitalism on the periphery.

In the post-emancipation period there was an expanding number of small farmers/settlers, more so in some parishes than in others. In some cases small settlers shared their time between plantation work and work on their own account. They stood in contrast to those workers who were heavily dependent on the plantations for employment. The small settler who worked his own land was unwilling to offer his time to planters at the time when his labour was most needed on his own plot or plots of land.

The problems which planters encountered in identifying regular supplies of labour are often expressed in terms of the exodus of the ex-slaves and their descendants from the plantations and their establishment in the interior of the island. The growth of the peasantry and the establishment of free villages has been extensively commented upon, and only the outline will be given here.[2] After emancipation ex-slaves purchased land or squatted. Between 1841 and 1860 alone, the number of holdings under 40 acres increased from 7,919 to 50,000 holdings under 50 acres. In 1902 there were 133,169 properties under 10 acres. In the period after mid-century this growing group of small settlers consolidated itself around the production of staples for export to include coffee, ginger, logwood, and later bananas. In the post-emancipation period the ex-slaves and their descendants contributed to the diversification of the economy. In 1850 approximately 83 per cent, and in 1890 approximately 74 per cent of peasant production was in ground provisions. There was an increase of peasant export production from 11 per cent of peasant production in 1850 to 23 per cent in 1890. Apart from cultivating ground provisions, peasant or small settlers grew sugar-cane, producing some 6,000 of the 12,000 hogsheads of sugar consumed locally in 1871. Peasants produced about two-thirds of Jamaica's coffee exports.[3]

Between 1844 and 1861 internal migration was directed towards St Elizabeth, Manchester and St Ann where land was most available. Population movement had been determined, according to Eisner, 'not so much by the decline of estates as by the availability of undeveloped land. The parishes which attracted people were poorly endowed in cultivable land and because of this they were not only marginal to estate production but also contained much land which had hitherto been neglected completely'. Between 1861 and 1871 there was a temporary increase in migration to Portland, probably because of the start of the export trade in bananas. Between 1891 and 1911 'the eastern parishes of St Mary and Portland now had the maximum rates of growth, while all the western parishes and Manchester gained less than the island average. In the early years banana cultivation was largely carried on by the resident peasantry in the north-east, but with its adoption as an estate crop in the 1890s the demand for labour encouraged the new eastward migration. This labour came largely from the west, where the sugar industry was going through its bleakest period'.[4]

The small settlers could be grouped into three categories: those who had legal title to land; those who squatted on Crown land; and those who leased land in the short or more rarely long term. The growth of the peasantry has been quite appropriately described as 'emancipation in action', rather less appropriately it has been viewed as the shift in the 'balance of class forces [which] changed in favour of the majority classes'. The access to land on the part of the small settlers altered in a fundamental way the structure of land use, but did not affect the structure of land ownership in the same way. For land continued to be concentrated in the hands of the oligarchy who, at the most, were willing to lease but not to sell their lands to small settlers. While it is true that many small settlers obtained lands in such parishes as Manchester, St Elizabeth and St Ann, access to new lands was not an indefinite process. By the 1880s a reverse process had been set in motion. Peasants were by then acquiring less land than they were selling.[5]

From the planter perspective access to land by small farmers radically altered their control of labour. Hence the grim prognostications that Jamaica's existence was in peril with the potential relapse into barbarism of the Afro-

Jamaican population which led to oligarchical propaganda seeking to prove that the sugar industry was the lifeblood of the economy. Hence, too, legal obstacles being placed in the way of land acquisition, such as laws against squatting.

The evidence suggests that it was not true that Jamaican workers were unwilling to migrate from one area of the countryside to another. Rather, labourers could not be persuaded to migrate into sugar plantation areas.

The extent of peasant ownership of land may have been exaggerated. The figures showing the increase of holdings under five or under ten acres over the period 1850–1900 overlook the reality that many people, including professionals, and others who were not peasants, were purchasing small acreages. Secondly, many small settlers who had paid for their lands were losing them because land transfers had not been properly conveyanced. Thirdly, in the western parishes, such as Trelawny, St James and Westmoreland, peasant hold on land was very tenuous. With the expansion of banana production and the increase in the commercial value of land the peasants were pushed out of ownership and land became less available to them. This was particularly noticeable in the banana parishes of St Mary and Portland, noted for their land agitation in the 1890s. The most recent study on land acquisition in Jamaica demonstrated that the expansion of the peasantry had ceased by the 1880s.[6] In the 1890s the Government initiated a programme to sell Crown Lands to small settlers, but the indications are that the land was not always easily accessible, and was outside the reach of farmers from a financial point of view.

Small farmers earned a cash income by selling their products through the internal marketing system. Here the farmer was particularly dependent upon the higgler. In 1881 there were 1,095 higglers in the island. The 1891 census lists 1,011 for the whole island, including one man. An observer of late-nineteenth century Mandeville noted that three-quarters of the number of marketeers in Mandeville were women. 'On that day they wear clean white frocks, stiffly starched pink, white, or a plaid of pink, blue and white, handkerchief . . . around their heads'.[7] It is probable that the census undercounted the number of male 'higglers', though quite obviously it was an occupation dominated by women.

The higgler was not necessarily a woman who enjoyed a purely professional relationship with the small farmer. The higgler could, apparently, just as easily be his wife, creating what Mintz suggests was a 'division of labour within the [slave] family'.[8] There is the case, for example, of the farmer in Manchester who produced coffee, ginger, sweet potatoes, cocos, cassava, and reared pigs. The cassava was converted into starch and 'bammies' by the wife who marketed them in the Balaclava or Mandeville market. The coffee and ginger were sold to local merchants. Sugar 'heads' which he also made, and yams and other ground provisions which the wife did not dispose of at the market were bartered, where possible, for fish, meat or fruit.[9] Mintz, in fact, concludes that the 'pattern of women as marketeers and men as cultivators on the subsistence plots remained consistent both before and after slavery, and this division of labour has probably persisted because there has been no reason for it to change'.[10]

The sexual division of labour was here confined not only to man and wife, but to farmer and professional higgler, whose commercial activity exactly complemented the production of the small farmer. The higgler 'carried a diversified stock of produce so as to avoid being caught in the glut of a single item', in the same way that the small farmer produced a variety of products not only to avoid glut, it is true, but also to provide food at home. The higgler helped the small farmer to transform 'at least part of the products of his labour into cash. This interdependence between higglers and small scale cultivator has never been broken. The small farmer prefers to diversify his tiny farm in order to reduce the risk involved in production of any one item'. Mintz notes the historical/cultural connection with Africa where (in West Africa) women were the marketeers. 'However, the Jamaican pattern could develop and persist only because the slave, and later the freeman, had access both to land and to marketing institutions so that he could produce and exchange food stuffs and craft articles'.[11]

Tenant farmers

One of the major means of utilising the land in rural Jamaica was land lease. There were, inevitably, planters who absolutely refused to lease (much less sell) land, for the obvious reason that every effort had to be made to tap the labour power of prospective tenants by denying them land. This approach was true not only of sugar land but of banana land as well, where peasants could still, up to the 1880s, compete with estate production. Tenancy arrangements by their very nature are insecure because they give the tenant no stake in the soil. Short term leases, in particular, deprive the tenant of opportunities to cultivate permanent crops.

There were broadly speaking two kinds of tenants; those who leased land through cash payment, and those who leased land in exchange for their labour. Tenants also leased more than one parcel of land when they could do so. It was noted that a 'great many of the people who rent land from the large proprietors move about from place to place'.[12] The same observer noted that with the growth of banana estates tenants were losing access to land. 'In the case of where the land has been near the seaport towns, and close to the land of the large proprietors, the latter have forced people to go further back, and have taken their land from them'.[13] Santfleben also suggested that most of the banana farmers who had been cultivating on land rented from the large proprietors, were being pushed into other districts. The growth of the logwood industry did precisely the same thing. 'Some tenants in St Elizabeth were dismissed from lands in some districts because the land was needed for logwood production, logwood having increased in value a few years before. So long as the logwood kept up they did not feel it, but last year logwood dropped in price and the trade stopped, and the labourers have no fields to return to, to fall back on'.[14]

The amount of land leased to tenants cannot be easily determined. How much land a tenant cultivated was sometimes nominal. Some tenants farmed more than the amount of land formally allotted to them. For example, in 1912, tenants were described as renting one acre of land nominally, 'but really for three or four acres, as it is never measured out to them, and they always occupy not only the piece of land they may actually be cultivating at the time, but also the piece they cultivated the previous year and the piece they propose to cultivate during the year to come'.[15]

In 1887 Arthur Prestwidge, who owned 300 acres at Robinson (Annotto Bay area), had twelve tenants 'Nominally renting one acre and growing provisions'. The manager of Shettle and Montpelier Pens reported that Montpelier had 500 or 600 tenants growing bananas and provisions. Eugene Whittingham, a planter with 1,700 acres, reported that with the exception of 600 acres all the land was leased to tenants who grew sugar canes and bananas. Robert Parker, proprietor of Cloves and lessee of All-sides containing 6,000 acres, had 480 tenants all cultivating ginger, 'Say half-an-acre each'.[16] It appeared that tenants may have had access to anything between half-an-acre and five acres of land.

Land leased to tenants was sometimes, but not always, marginal land. Many cattle pens, for example, could have 100 to 200 acres of woodland 'in the more inaccessible hilltops or rocky land, and a portion of it would probably be let to the peasantry for provision grounds paying from 16/- to 24/- per acre, nominally, but really for three or four acres'.[17] One of the criticisms of the system of tenant farming was that tenants were often allowed only hillside land, which, in the absence of terracing and contouring rapidly led to soil erosion.

The cash outlay for the lease paid by the tenant farmer was often quite high in relation to the market value of the land. A critic of the system noted that 'When good land can be bought for £2 and upwards per acre why this nomadic destructive renting at 16/- to £1 per annum?'[18] Tenants were in fact leasing land at a rate equivalent or almost equivalent to the sale price. This was perhaps a sound argument for outright sale of land, were it not that landowners were equally determined not to surrender land ownership.

The tenant was faced with the problem of insecurity of tenure and the length of the lease. Some tenants were not allowed more than one year's lease at a time. The consequences were predictable; tenants could not sensibly plant permanent crops. 'I have known people who were turned off their land when they had planted coffee on it, and they have had to go and break up the coffee'.[19] Another witness before the 1897 Commission confirmed that tenants were usually permitted only one year at a time (in this case at £5.00) but were not 'allowed to plant coffee or guinea grass. As soon as they get their plot of land in order, the owner of the property will say, "you will have to leave" and then gives them notice to leave. He does that in order that the cultivator may leave and then everything comes to the owner of the land'.[20]

Critics of the tenantries viewed the system as wasteful, and inefficient, and were of the view that the sale of land to the peasantry and a system of planting permanent crops under the contract system would be a more viable alternative. Critics of the system did not necessarily see abolition of the tenant system as of any positive merit. Rather, the system of land lease, whatever its weaknesses, did offer some, albeit limited, access to land. As the *Daily Gleaner* pointed out, 'We need not meet trouble halfway by trying to do away with the tenant system on the lines suggested by our correspondent'. The newspaper observed that in St Mary, there was already 'incipient land agitation, arising from the fact that small plots of land can hardly be bought or rented by the peasantry'.[21] The message was that abolition of land lease could aggravate rather than solve the problem of land agitation. Land agitation had been present since the 1890s when black agitators were proclaiming that the land had been given to the 'black man'.

The tense relations between tenants and landlords were aggravated by the failure of some tenants to pay their rent, in whole or in part. The failure to pay was clear grounds for expulsion. At the same time, the regular proclamation that tenants would not pay their rents suggests firstly that some landlords were not avid rent collectors, allowing tenants to get away without payment of rent, except when they wished to find suitable grounds to expel tenants. The second possibility is that rents were set in some cases at an unrealistically high cost to the tenant. Tenants perhaps agreed to pay high rentals in more favourably endowed places. The advantage to the land barons was that they could receive from tenants over and over again the price of a single acre of land.

There were tenants who had been turned off the land after many years. The precariousness of tenancy also had political dimensions, as the following letter to the Editor of the *Jamaica Advocate* suggests:

> Now Mr Editor, do you see what this island has come to? The so-called gentlemen of the Parish, in order to keep out Mr Smickle, have issued circulars to all the tenants on their estates that if they don't vote for Mr Burke, they will be turned off the properties.[22]

Tenants who applied for Crown Lands which became available during the

1890s were sometimes sacked as well. Here is an account of a victim:

> I jest right to inform you about the meeting at Post House about the Crown Land when Bryan Edward was there. Mr Bryan Edward hold and evict against me because I brought you down here, and say that he is an Attorney for the Crown Land, and he is now turning off all the tenants that work upon Mr Verly who sine their name for the Crown Land, and I myself have got a month notice to left where has all our provisions is young and by so doing we had to destroy it on the count of having no where else to work. Dear Sir, we are now walking from place to place to seek work. Sir if we did have our own place to work such advantage could have not taken of us.[23]

Between 1891 and 1892 tenants (in St Thomas) raised a petition against landlords whom they claimed had 'combined' against them to bring about a general eviction. Reporting on the matter the Inspector of Police, Herbert Thomas, denied any conspiracy on the part of landlords, and noted that 'on four of them [estates] there had been no eviction, *except* isolated cases of persistent neglect to pay rent'. In his report, Thomas pointedly noted that black landlords were also evicting tenants:

> *Prospect*: Proprietor James Thompson (blackman) had given fourteen tenants notice 'owing to consistent trouble in respect of cattle trespass'. He must have spent £100 in the courts in the last 12 months.
>
> *Greenwall*: Proprietor George Grossett (black man). These tenants had been offered land lying in the higher part of the property in exchange for what they are now cultivating, as the landlord was about to stock his estate.
>
> *Creighton Hall*: Proprietor W. Baggett-Gray Esq. had given 54 tenants notice to quit as he aimed to stock and cultivate his property himself. The property had been neglected for many years previous to Baggett-Gray's purchase last year, and had practically become the property of the inhabitants of the adjacent village of the White Horse, where most of the signers of the Petition reside. Tenants [who have] nominally one acre are cultivating five or six, some squatted without paying rent at all. One indeed contrived to erect a sugar mill and to grow canes and make sugar for some months before the mill was discovered by a rural headman of the district.
>
> *Rozelle*: E.G. Kerridge Esq. J.P. No general notice; four tenants evicted.
>
> *Mount Rose*: 28 tenants evicted for rent arrears.

Belvidere: 29 tenants evicted for rent arrears.

Shady Spring: Prop. W.L. Mudon Esq. represented by Mr Ker-ridge – five tenants evicted for rent arrears.

Stenton: Prop. I.J. Mordecai, J.S. Marshalleck Esq. Three tenants ejected for rent arrears.

Petersfield: Prop. W.C. Porter Esq. 100 of 114 tenants given notice to quit. Tenants owe upward of £300, and owing to the cattle trespass law repealed last session there has been continual trouble.

Spring Garden: Messrs. D. Marshalleck and Co., General notice of 12 months: reason: Lack of punctuality in paying rent. Notices [have been] long ago revoked except in respect of four or five tenants, who were evicted.

We learn from the Inspector's account that termination of leases arose from non-payment of rent and rent arrears, change in ownership of land, legal questions arising out of the cattle trespass law, the sharing of land tenanted by unauthorised squatters.[24]

There have from time immemorial been differences of opinion between stockholders and farmers. Landlords offered no protection to tenants for the destruction of property by livestock. An article of a printed agreement of 1896 so informs us:

No tenant is entitled to compensation for trespass by the stock of any kind belonging to the property; nor is the stock to be impounded, injured or destroyed.[25]

The cattle trespass law became an issue between tenants and landlords. Many estates in Jamaica which were tenanted combined ruinate and pasture, and many tenants, in exchange for their labour or a rental, were in possession of leased property on cattle pens. It is to be assumed that the law of 1888, amended in 1892, was designed to protect agriculturists, many of whom were tenants. According to the law, it was the duty of the

proprietor of stock [including horsekind, cattle, sheep, pigs, goats and poultry] to take proper and effective measures to prevent such stock from trespassing on the land of other persons and he was responsible in damages in respect of any injury done by such stock trespassing on the land of other persons provided that within 48 hours of the discovery of such injury the party aggrieved gives notice of the nature thereof to the proprietor or person in charge of the stock, and allows him and his valuators free ingress to the land.[26]

The Dividing Fences Law was related to the former in that it sought to place the responsibility for the construction of fences between proprietors. Section 3 of Law 14 of 1888 provided that:

> every occupier of land be liable to bear one half of the expense of erecting and maintaining a sufficient dividing fence to separate their respective holdings.[27]

Section 5 of the same law provided that one party could recover expenses to the extent of half the cost of repairs done to a dividing fence. It is Section 10, however, which addresses itself to tenants in respect of division and demarcation of boundaries. Where the 'occupier of land is not the owner thereof, and is not as between himself and the owner bound by the terms of his tenancy to bear the expenses of erecting or repairing the fence dividing such land from the adjoining land, he shall, on being obliged to defray any such expense under the provisions of this law, be entitled to recover the same from his landlord as money paid at his request, or to deduct the same from his rent as the same falls due'.[28] The spirit of the law was not necessarily unfavourably disposed to the tenant, but at the same time the law could not guard against the eviction of tenants whose insecurity of tenure made resort to the law a suicidal procedure. At the same time, the law permitted a separate contract between tenant and landlord, thus enabling landlords to get around the law.

The claim of the police inspector that the castle trespass law was a factor in eviction of tenants from St Thomas is reflected in the vigorous debate in the Legislative Council on the subject in 1888. The most severe critic of the bill as it had been presented came from W. Bancroft Espeut who protested that the 'onus of fencing rested on the cattle owners. You must remember that ruinate land is cultivated one year and abandoned the next . . . The general principle of the bill which compels a man to keep the cattle which he possesses within bounds is of course a very right and proper one'.[29]

Espeut's objection did not, then, arise from opposition to the principle of the bill, but rather its pragmatic application which could lead to a breach of the principle of the law:

> Some cultivators of land . . . practise a system of levying blackmail on their neighbours by planting a small unfenced area of cultivation, near to where cattle pastured solely with the intent of enticing their neighbours' cattle on the land in order to subsequently recover damage.[30]

The underlying principle of the bill was really that 'good fences make good neighbours' but Espeut was arguing that mutual interest dictated mutual fencing, on the part of the cultivator and cattleowner. The support for mutual fencing also came from Mr J.M. Farquharson.[31] The debate was not presented within the framework of oligarchy versus mass of farmers. The oligarchy knew how to cite the scripture of blackness for its own purposes. A resolution, claimed Mr Farquharson, had been 'moved and seconded by black men'. This is what black men had to say about other black men:

> There is a good deal of jealousy among their people. For instance, one man owns a provision ground and his neighbour keeps one or two horses to carry his provisions to market and possibly a few cows. If the law stands as it is, they would constantly be at variance, as only one of the parties would be responsible for keeping up the terms, his neighbour being at no expense whatever, although the party entitled to damages . . . My opinion of the peasantry of this country is this, when you are prepared to meet them fairly they are always ready to accede to your proposals . . . (Hear! Hear!) I have never found any trouble with them.[32]

The British Attorney-General was not duped by Farquharson and Espeut. He recognised clearly what their position represented: 'an attempt to bring forward a Law to prevent a small settler from recovering damages unless his grounds are fenced'.[33] The bill was passed as proposed, and corresponded to the real social necessity of reducing incidents where animals were wounded in retaliation for injuries sustained.

Efforts were made through legal institutions to facilitate access to land, and to regularise landownership. J. Thompson Palache introduced the 'Further Limitation of Action [Land] Law'. The law was an attempt to correct the exploitation of the law for the deprivation of the small settler. According to Palache:

> There are a number of persons who have bought land and paid their money, get a receipt, and entered into possession for as long as twelve years; the proprietor in England turns up and the poor man is turned off his land. The idea of supporting the interests of people who do not cultivate their lands against those who honestly pay theirs, but unfortunately cannot prove their purchase, is monstrous . . .

In defending the bill Palache insisted that the intention was to settle the rights of those 'honest purchasers, hundreds of whom exist here, who bought their land from dishonest attorneys and whose lands are useless to them because of the existence of the present law, which precludes them from establishing title until after twenty years' possession'. Palache's view was that the limitation should be twelve years not twenty. Palache's motion was carried, but significantly through the overwhelming support of the officials – the Attorney-General, Colonial Secretary, Inspector of Schools, and Director of Public Works. Espeut, who claimed that Palache's bill was legalising squatting, was supported by the elected members – Harvey, Solomon, J.M. Farquharson and Malabre, who had claimed that the bill was asking the Council to 'consider the squatter more entitled to protection than . . . an honest man'.[34]

Since not all squatters were smallholders, the law could have worked to the advantage of large-scale squatters as well. Palache indicated, too, that as a member of two building societies he had an interest in secure titles for the purpose of mortgages.

The growth of the smallholders as a class was therefore constrained by a number of factors, some legal, some associated with the continued land monopoly, high rentals – in 1897 it was reported that rents in St Mary varied from 20/- through 24/- and 28/- per acre and reluctance of planters to lease land (it was noted that the Pringle banana combine refused to lease land because peasant proprietors would compete with it). In 1897, it was concluded that 'considering the class of lands that can be got and all the conditions attached, of taxes, fencing, certain reserved rights of proprietors, and the rentals charged, the people can hardly avail themselves of even such lands as may be said to be in the market for rent or sale'.[35] There had been some access to land it is true, but not necessarily on the basis of firm, secure titles, or on the basis of secure tenancy.

The relationship between labourers and farmers on the one hand, employers and capitalists on the other, was not confined to the distribution of land resources, as important as this was. Also of importance was the system of credit in the countryside which proved a viable means of curtailing the ambitions of farmers and labourers. The attempt of rural shopkeepers to enmesh farmers in a system of credit did not go unnoticed by the administration. Law 2 of 1883 (the Token Prohibition Law, 1883) was designed to put a stop to an 'objectionable practice which was becoming common among country storekeepers of issuing tokens for money which to a great extent compelled the holders to deal with their shops'.[36] The law, while putting an end to one abuse of the credit system, did not terminate the abuse of credit, which was an intimate aspect of the general system of social exploitation in the countryside. That system rested ultimately upon the alliance between the mercantile and the landed interest. This situation was well described by J.H. Reid.

> Labour has been rendered more unproductive through the alliance of the landed with the mercantile interests, in their enterprise of spoliation. In many cases, the people have to reckon with the same individual, both as merchant and landlord. As landlord, he levies contributions through the payment of low wages, and, if the means of escape are sought in the endeavour to cultivate

land on their own account, the people are confronted with high
rents, while the infinitely small profits that may be secured to
themselves through systematic self-denial, are certain to be
completely swallowed up by transactions across the counter.
Being thus driven from one untenable position to another, many
of the weaker minds have abandoned themselves to idleness,
utter despair, to swell the ranks of paupers and criminals in the
course of time.[37]

Merchants loaned money or advanced goods to small farmers until their
crops came in, at a price fixed by the merchant. Even logwood labourers
were forced to depend upon the credit system because logwood magnates
paid their workers only once per month. 'This is a great hardship as
labourers have to live on the credit system; having no cash they must pay an
advanced price and are compelled to take anything that is given them by the
shopkeeper'.[38] When the labourer or small settler proved unable to pay the
merchant could and often did sue. Gibbons in 1884 reported a practice
among local merchants of 'suing for balances of account and relying upon
the absence of the defendant to obtain judgement'.[39]

In dealing with that problem Justice Gibbons, who was to be hounded
out of Jamaica, demanded that the merchants present their books to show
how the balance had been arrived at.

This, so reasonable in itself and so necessary where the defendant
is in almost every case an illiterate and uneducated man, appears
to have given great dissatisfaction and at Falmouth I was presented with a memorial signed by almost every merchant and
shopkeeper there praying that I should forgo the requirement
. . . It was impossible not to see that in many cases advantage had
been taken of the ignorance of the debtor but not in all. There was
one, and only one, merchant (J. Levy of Browns Town) whose
books were produced without hesitation and whose accounts
sustained the fullest scrutiny. *When it is found that the storekeeper supplies goods at his own price to the cultivator on the
credit of his crops and takes produce at his own valuation it will
be manifest that the account between the parties ought to be
examined item by item.* This is the duty of the District Court and
when carried out with fairness cannot contribute to the popularity
of the District Court with the over-reaching merchants.[40]

In an impassioned plea for Agricultural (Loan) Banks, a correspondent
(E. O'Sullivan) condemned the 'Usurers (the blood-sucking vampires) who
charged 1/6 per week interest on a loan of £1. One of these ghouls exacted
£1–10 interest on a loan of £20 for two weeks; tested, it showed that, had the

victim of this human vampire failed to pay for 12 months at the time he should have had to hand the extortioner £56; that is £36 interest on the original loan of £20. This ghoul demands titles to be lodged and a written contract binding the borrower to sell *all* his produce to *him*, the lender'.[41] High interest rates, land as collateral, the merchants' determination of the price of the crop and the price (naturally) of his goods, was a common practice in rural Jamaica, which betrayed intense levels of class exploitation.

It is a speculation worth pursuing that the system of credit introduced by the Chinese based upon the 'trusting' of goods from the grocery shop, which did not necessarily demand such collateral may have contributed to the tremendous volume of trade which the Chinese enjoyed in rural Jamaica. They did not monopolise trade as their detractors were prone to insist.[42] But their volume of business may have reduced the business of traditional shopkeepers. Anti-Chinese sentiment could very well have rested in business competition.

Other aspects of rural labour

Smallholders were also attracted by the cash income which public works offered. A correspondent in February 1886 to the *Gleaner* remarked that 'many of the labourers employed in the railway works, counting it would take years to complete threw up their settlements, depending for support solely on their weekly earnings, very little of which was saved, for often enough goods were taken up at the shop during the week'.[43] While some skilled workers, such as masons, followed the track of the railway (one of the sources of internal migration in the late-nineteenth century) other categories of workers could not do the same, and facing the prospect of returning to their 'thrown-up cultivation' and starting life anew, chose instead to migrate to Colon 'with all the risks'.

The railroad, which had been sold to an American Syndicate – the West India Improvement Company – reached Montego Bay and Port Antonio by 1895. There were, in addition, road works. Main roads in the island, some 70 miles in 1870 increased by 132.5 miles in the 22-year period up to 1892 to 840 miles. Law 17 of 1890 appropriated certain taxes for providing interest and sinking fund on a loan of £140,000 to be expanded in reconstructing the roads taken over as main roads, and also an annuity equal to ʻ.oout £20 per mile per annum for their maintenance. In the succeeding three years an aggregate length of 981 miles was added to the main roads. By Law 4 of 1898 the maintenance of main roads became the province of the General Revenue.

Apart from roads there was expenditure on labour for the construction of bridges over the rivers of the island which, following torrential downpours, were rendered impassable and treacherous. Public expenditure reached the countryside because these roads delved deep into the heart of the rural districts. The public works programme – which many people advocated as a means of discouraging the Panama emigration – was intended partly to provide communication and transportation facilities for goods coming out of the interior, and as such was of benefit to the smallholder.

Road construction, repair, railway construction and bridge building attracted the rural labour force. The railway company never encountered difficulty in finding labourers, and reportedly good relations between capital and labour were accountable to the slightly higher wages and the regularity with which they were paid.

If there were amicable relations between labour and capital in the case of the railroad (though it is impossible not to mention that some 800 Americans were abandoned in Jamaica by the railroad enterprise), the same situation was not repeated with respect to government sponsored road construction. Disturbances were, apparently, always expected on pay-day when workers were often unable to collect their wages. 'This very day', announced a witness before the WIRC, 'at Gordon Town there will be disturbances, and the other day there was quite an affray, and they set fire to a stable'.[44] Wages were, in theory, to be paid fortnightly but yet on payday workers followed 'the gentleman about clamouring for their money, and threatening what they would do if they did not get it'. The problem was that the policy of paying contractors in advance by government gave way to the policy of paying contractors only after the work had been done, since it was thought that contractors were prone to rob labourers. The change aggravated the situation.

> I know of a person who took a contract for two chains of the new road for £25, one for £15 and the other for £10, and he immediately sublet to another contractor one piece for £7, and the other for £8. In that case, if the workmen, after they had put in their labour, did not get their pay, the sub-contractor would not be able to get the money, and the other man could not be held because he was not under any obligation, not having employed the labourers.

These sub-contractors were described as being 'men of the people themselves'. The workers who had a legitimate grievance insisted that appealing to the law was a waste of time, 'and whatever little money they could get out of these men who had nothing would not be worth the trouble'.[45]

Plantation workers

It would be inaccurate to assume that the circumscribed independence of rural farmers which we have described above was common to all Jamaican rural workers. Such an assumption would overlook the regionalism of Jamaica's economy, as well as the resilience of the plantation system. Above all is the fact that in some areas such as Westmoreland, Hanover, Trelawny and sections of Clarendon, the extreme monopoly of land by planters assured a continued commitment by workers to sugar-plantation labour.

The best authorities for this conclusion are the planters themselves. Mr W.C. Shirley, a Trelawny planter, observed in 1897 that workers were dependent upon the estates to provide them with work, partly because the dryness of the parish reduced opportunities for obtaining provision grounds; that labourers cultivated little land of their own, and that 'their cultivation' such as it was, was not profitable. A second planter, Mr Farquharson, observed that workers were, in desperation, seeking employment even at the reduced wage rates arising out of economy measures implemented by planters in response to unfavourable conditions on the international market:

> In task work we used to get 12 chains for 1/-, now it is 20 chains . . . Able-bodied men come to me and ask for work offering to take 9d.[46]

Planters such as Shirley and Farquharson were particularly keen to demonstrate to the WIRC in 1897 that the sugar industry affected the fortunes not only of the oligarchy but labourers and all segments of the population for that matter. That bias clearly does not render untrue his factual statement on wages.

Wages declined, or at best remained static, in the last three decades of the nineteenth century. Yet it must not be overlooked that the wages received were partly determined by the quantity of labour which individual workers could complete. Wages also depended upon whether workers were employed on a ratoon or non-ratoon property, on the nature of the tasks allocated and upon regional variations in the availability of labour. Where labour was abundant, in such parishes as Westmoreland, Hanover and Trelawny, planters had greater control over the wages they paid. The obverse applied where labour was relatively scarce, though planters were prone to make generalisations which suggested that labour was short island-wide.

Table 8.1   Scale of wages and tasks

Task	Wages
1 Digging cane holes (between 2,723 and 2,420 per acre)	4/- to 6/- per acre or 2/3 per hundred
2 Cutting pegs	3d per hundred
3 Planting tops (17 chains)	1/-
4 Picking or drawing tops (5 or 6 cartloads per acre)	9d to 1/- per cartload
5 Good upstanding ratoons on 24 running chains (one task)	1/-
6 Carting manure (7 or 8, sometimes 9 or 10 loads per square chain	3d per load
7 Trenching between the canes	1d per chain
8 Tying canes	$4\frac{1}{2}$–6d per sq. chain
9 Forking land	1/6 per sq. chain
10 Dropping manure per load	3d per load, 8 loads to the sq. chain
11 Moulding	1/- per sq. chain
12 Cleaning and trashing canes in ratooning properties (day labour)	4/- to 8/- per acre
13 Reaping one running chain (task) (Running chains per acre 146.7)	18 chains = 1/6 plant cane
14 Heap and bundle (14 canes each)	1/- for 12–14 heaps
15 146.7 running acre chains per acre	17/- plant cane, 10/7 ratoon

Source: De B. Spencer Heaven, *Handbook of Jamaica*, 1881, pp. 154–161.

Wages also depended upon the personal relations between planter and labourer. The very nature of plantation work gave openings for distrust. Plantations had to operate on the basis of careful management of planting, weeding, reaping. Tasks had to be carefully measured usually by overseers or bookkeepers. However, careful measurement did not alter the fact that planters and their representatives had the power, more or less, to increase the task and pay a lower wage. Reduction of the number of tasks also reduced the availability of employment, and therefore the earning capacity of workers. Planters also withheld wages, presumably on the grounds that labour had not been performed according to specifications. Herbert George deLisser, for a long time editor of the *Daily Gleaner*, noted that the worker could not always depend upon 'getting what he earns', a fact 'abundantly testified by impartial observers'.[47] Withdrawal of wages was not confined to planters. In fact, a clergyman was appropriately reprimanded by his Bishop for indulging in the practice. In the latter case the injured party ended up in court on a charge of assault.[48] Labourers were sometimes not paid for five or six weeks.[49]

Wages were sometimes paid in kind, not by a contractual arrangement between planter and employee, but by unilateral planter imposition. Some planters paid their workers in rum, while no doubt being ardent members of the Temperance Societies. Others paid in estate beef. The 'wages' specifically consisted of the

> cut-up carcass of overworked steers, which often have their throats cut [when dying] 'to save their lives' as the saying is. Half of this beef is sold to labourers fresh and the rest is salted. The salted portion is bought on credit from the estate . . . Every estate keeps a beef book . . . Some workers owe for years, since when they get to owe a few shillings – and perhaps have really been robbed by the estate of a similar amount they go and work elsewhere. This debt is passed on to newcoming labourers.[50]

The beef payments were understandably referred to by workers as the 'Stinking Stuff'.

From the planter's point of view, difficult economic times dictated that workers be saddled with as much as possible of the cost of the planter's inability to compete on international markets. The Jamaican sugar plantation economy was in part a victim of British free trade policies, which, unlike the old mercantile system, offered no support to relatively inefficient producers. Since 1834, certainly, there had been no capital inflows, credit, or improvement in the techniques of production. Wage policy was linked to the necessity, as perceived by planters, of reducing costs.

The day to day operation of an estate demonstrated the policy of extracting as much labour as possible for the smallest possible wage. Hence tasks, for instance, had to be measured with precision, or if not precisely, with an inaccuracy which favoured the planter. The nature of plantation work dictated minute regulation by overseers and attorneys. Supervision was required to ensure that the 'labourer cuts the bottom of each cane hole squarely and deep enough, reaching as far as he can from him with his hoe, and afterwards bringing the bank into a steep ridge, the object being to leave as little undug land under the base of the bank as possible'. Cutting canes by the bundle or heap gave room for cheating on the part of the labourer. 'It is no easy matter to ensure the canes being of the right length, or that the cord is not hollow, however well it may look outwardly, and if by the bundle it is hardly to be expected that all bundles of canes will contain the stipulated number. Whichever system, however, prevails on an estate it must be insisted on that the cane cutters cut the stools at least flush with the ground'. On ratooning estates, 'a watch must be kept on the cartment that the loads carried bear a fair proportion to the liquor yielded, though as many gallons will not be expected from each load as on the more seasonable planting property . . . In cutting and tying by the square chain the manager should see what quantity of cane he gets carried off the land and that he is not paying too high a price per load'. Furthermore, on all estates, there should be rigorous supervision over the work of the tyers, that they do not include in the 'bundles sour or rat eaten canes, which if put through the mill will, as a matter of course, injure the liquor sent to the clarifiers'.[51]

Sugar plantation work, then, meant several items of measurement – cords, bundles, number, shape and depth of holes, methods for laying down manure, and measuring the quantity of work done. From the planter perspective there were several areas in this work where labourers could 'cheat', for example, in harvesting or not packing bundles or cords according to 'specifications', leaving the cord hollow, not weeding meticulously, and so on. From the workers' perspective, the planter and his representative could also cheat by withdrawing wages, or by paying wages in part only, on the pretence that the work had not been done according to specifications.

Economic difficulties reduced the ability of planters to invest in social overheads, but it does not follow that prosperity in the sugar industry would have generated the kind of material incentives, or investment in social overheads which would have attracted labourers to estates in the quantities desired by the planters. The departure of labourers, when they could, from the plantations did not lead planters to re-examine their own social attitudes, or the particular relationship between them and the people whom they employed. It was far easier to blame the victim, to attribute the difficulties of the sugar economy to the laziness of Quashie. The experience of the relationship between black labourers and planters since emancipation suggests that planters believed – such is the force of tradition – that Quashie was being paid what he was worth, which was 'nothing'.

Planters wished to pay the lowest wage possible, labourers sought the highest wage attainable, but that conflict was not resolved on the basis of bargaining or of compromising on wages. Rather, it took the form of swelling the labour force by importing East Indians. The planter argument about shortage of labour was only partly true. Despite the entry of some 37,000 East Indians into the island between the mid-nineteenth century and 1917 when the scheme ended, it remains true that the majority of workers in the sugar industry (calculated at 22,800 by Sir Anthony Musgrave in 1880 or 5 per cent of the population) remained Afro-Jamaicans. Secondly, the majority of East Indians by the 1890s were not employed in the sugar, but in the banana, industry. In 1895 the Protector of Immigrants could proudly proclaim that the depression in the sugar industry did not adversely affect East Indian wages since most of them no longer worked in the sugar industry. In 1883 the report of the Royal Commission reasserted the myth: 'we found that even when task work was the rule and a man could by fair labour thus earn per day double the current wages, the Negro would seldom work more than three or four days in the week, and only at such times and seasons as suited him'. To this charge, Rev. Henry Clarke, the Anglican Minister of Westmoreland responded that all sugar estates which he knew of had more labour than they needed:

> To this I can only say that I know that in my parish for a generation past there have been 5,000 hhds. of sugar produced every year; that to manufacture it the mills have been kept going day and night six days in the week for about six months in the year by the Negroes at very moderate wages too; and that I do not know of one instance during the whole period in which an estate failed to take off its crop for want of labour. Where there is one case of a planter not able to get labour there are a hundred cases of labourers not able to get work.[52]

The reality was that in some areas labour was abundant and in others, scarce. In recognition of this reality Sir Anthony Musgrave proposed the construction of 'homes, or even temporary accommodation of a decent character, such as is provided in Australia for hands at shearing time', in order to facilitate intra-island migration during crop-time.[53] It was not until 1890 that some effort was made to organise internal migration of labour based on a contract system. The idea was to encourage native labourers to work under the protection of the Immigration Department. The arrangement provided for an indentured fee of 50/- to be paid as bonus to the native labourer on expiry of each year's faithful service under contract. The Government charges for mounting the scheme amounted to 10/- per labourer.[54] The system when implemented floundered as a consequence of inadequate wages, at least so claimed the Protector of Immigrants Office.

Love's *Jamaica Advocate* defined the system of contracts as 'semi-slavery', 'misleading and deceptive', 'loaded in favour of the landlord', and a shame to the 'civilisation of the country'.[55]

Planters, therefore, continued to seek the importation of East Indians at a cost to them of between £22 and £25 for each immigrant. Ironical it may appear, but East Indian labour was introduced in order to obtain Afro-Jamaican labour (for which there was always a preference) for the sugar industry.

Reality is often little more than a community perception of that which is real. But it is difficult to determine the extent to which planter perception of reality coincided with the lachrymose propaganda which they fed into the Colonial Office or into the British press. Yet, it must be true that planters came to believe their own propaganda.

The planter argument concerning the shortage of labour was a device to impress upon the Colonial Office the need to import East Indian labour; and secondly, to highlight the disadvantageous terms under which they competed in the British market. Thirdly, the aggressive insistence with which planters argued the merits of the plantation system, as the nucleus from which blacks would be saved for civilisation, appeared to be an appeal to the elusive British conscience which cleverly created the 'white man's burden'. The white man's burden and scientific racism were of paramount importance in Jamaican social life – as it was in British imperial administration – because racial and cultural power offered a social authority to holders of economic power.

Sir Anthony Musgrave, considered a planterphobe, by the planters of course, summarised and countered the myth in 1880:

> I think I am not far wrong in my belief that Jamaica is now generally regarded as a hopelessly ruined community, which was once prosperous, but had become a wreck of its former self; that the Negro population are an idle, thriftless vagabond people, refusing to work and fast lapsing into heathenish savagery; and that if only the civilising influence of the cultivation of the chief staple, which is the sugar cane, should altogether cease or be very much diminished, then nothing can save this once magnificent Colony from utter degradation and the bulk of her people from the condition of their African forefathers . . . The whole of this is an erroneous view . . . It is inconsistent with the fact to suppose that the population [is] dependent for their present well-being or future prosperity upon the cultivation of sugar estates; the truth being that this industry does not afford direct employment to more than about 5 per cent of the total population of the Colony.[56]

Musgrave was not alone in criticising the attitudes of planters. Herbert George deLisser attacked the fierce spirit of animosity that was displayed against the 'Negro character', and argued that 'much of what has been said with respect to the Negro's laziness and aptitude is due to shortsighted ignorance of his past condition, and in many cases, prejudice'. He concluded that 'the planters themselves' were 'largely responsible for the Negro's attitude towards labour'.[57] And deLisser was one of those who believed that the hope for blacks depended on the guiding hand of the white man. In his study of the Jamaican plantocracy, Wesley Roberts observed that the banana estates of the Boston Fruit Company encountered no difficulty in finding labour because of 'more enlightened attitudes' towards labourers; and that workers took employment on banana estates even though wages were not necessarily higher than on sugar estates. Both Musgrave and deLisser agreed that the lack of sufficient material incentives to encourage Jamaicans to work for planters rather than for themselves played an important part in the difficulty which some planters claimed to find in obtaining a steady supply of labour. In truth, planters interpreted the difficulty of obtaining labour at precisely the time they needed it to mean an island-wide labour shortage. Protests by Afro-Jamaican workers against deplorable social conditions and low wages on sugar estates were to encourage planters to find a controllable labour force.

East Indian labour

The most important mechanism for controlling the Afro-Jamaican labour force and forcing wages down was the policy of importation of East Indian labour. It was not so much a shortage of labour as the need to obtain a controllable labour force attached to the plantations which encouraged the policy of importing East Indians. It did not matter whether that labour force was East Indian or Afro-Jamaican. The effect of East Indian migration was to expand the labour force in a labour surplus economy, and thereby force the Afro-Jamaican population to come to terms.

Employers sometimes preferred immigrant labour to 'native' labour because of its greater flexibility or because the immigrant could perform the same task for a lower wage, or because the immigrant could be assigned tasks which the 'native labourer' may have found disagreeable or repugnant. Precisely because East Indian labour was a form of contract labour, that labour force could be assigned tasks which planters chose to assign to them. It did not follow, however, that East Indians were given more difficult or less desirable tasks, for in most areas of labour on plantations Afro-Jamaicans were generally preferred. As a matter of fact, Attorney B. Spencer

Heaven's allocation of tasks in 1881 placed East Indian labour with the juvenile gangs for first weeding – and that only if Creole labour was not available.

East Indian contract labourers were not paid less than Afro-Jamaican labourers either. On the contrary, apart from receiving a fixed wage, they enjoyed such privileges as medical care which was not available to the Afro-Jamaican (Creole) labour force. The fact is, also, that East Indians were employed mostly on banana estates which Afro-Jamaicans, from Roberts' account, had not found undesirable.

It is true, however, that after the period of indentureship there was little to distinguish the East Indian from the Afro-Jamaican labour force – except for ethnic differences. The protection of the office of the Protector of Immigrants ceased, so too did special medical attention and hospital care. The original agreement that land be given to East Indians in lieu of a return passage to India did not always materialise. As a non-indentured labour force the efforts of East Indians to establish some measure of self-sufficiency by embarking on rice cultivation, for example, were discouraged, precisely because the oligarchy insisted upon a monopoly of land and upon control of the labour force.

There is no particular evidence to suggest that the colonial authorities exploited ethnic differences between the East Indians and Afro-Jamaicans. On the contrary, the authorities insisted upon encouraging them to live like 'Christians', and to attend schools which the Jamaican labouring classes attended. Yet, whenever there was immigrant labour which was deemed to compete with native labour for jobs, or where immigrants effectively reduced wages through creating or aggravating the condition of surplus labour, there tended to be conflict between the imported labourer and 'native' labourers, as West Indians themselves discovered when they migrated to the Spanish Caribbean and to Central America.

Nonconformist ministers of religion opposed East Indian immigration, but so too did the Anglican clergyman, Henry Clarke. The US consul, Mr Hoskinson, noted the opposition of the 'religious element' to immigration.[58] Henry Clarke's vociferous opposition to immigration was based on the exploitative nature of the indentureship system (semi-slave labour), on the fact that Jamaica was a surplus labour economy, and that immigration was partly financed by public revenue.

The *Jamaica Advocate* condemned East Indian immigration on the grounds that the native labourer had a prior right to 'live by his labour in his own native land'.[59] A correspondent to the *Jamaica Advocate* saw East Indian immigration as 'taking the people's money to bring labourers thousands of miles from here, to benefit planters at the expense of the people. Is this not class legislation? . . . They do not know how to petition against coolie immigration and the impropriety of the Government allowing those people to walk in the streets almost in a state of nudity, to the disgust of all respectable persons'.[60]

Opponents of East Indian immigration viewed it as contravention of the principle of a free labour market. East Indian immigration also reflected a vengefulness on the part of planters who gloried in abusing Afro-Jamaican labourers.[61] In his comment on 'Negro Isolation' in 1895 J.H. Reid noted that 'Isolation has practically closed the door of almost every calling against the Negro, except that of manual labour, even that is being gradually closed through the operations of a system by which he is taxed to supply the funds necessary for the importation of foreign labour and products, and to drive him out of the market as a producer into the field of vagrancy . . . and lessen his purchasing capacity.[62]

Opponents of East Indian immigration protested that the system was supported by general taxation, most of which was paid for by the very labourers whom the East Indians were intended to displace. In 1880 Musgrave made the following comment:

In April 1867 certain articles formerly charged with duty, consisting mainly of machinery and other things required for the production of staples of the Colony and the development of its industry, were admitted free . . . the absent proprietors of sugar estates or other property escaping (tax) altogether . . . Of 228 sugar properties now under cultivation 114 are owned by persons who make no pretence at residence in the Colony, and except in the small amounts collected for parochial purposes, such as poor relief and parochial roads, are subject to no direct taxes whatever . . . [The public debt] had been increased by the transference to the general revenue of the heavy liabilities on account of the loans for Indian immigration, which up to this time remained a special charge upon the proprietors of sugar estates, to be liquidated by export duties on their produce and some other articles of export, but which are now to be paid from general taxation, contributed chiefly by the mass of the Negro population . . . As a matter of fact, so far from indicating any dependence of the general population upon the prosperity of the sugar-growing interest, it seems to show that proprietors of sugar estates have had to look for assistance to the mass of the population who are not interested in sugar cultivation.[63]

We cannot superimpose the attitudes of black middle class or white spokesmen who were antagonistic to immigration upon the Afro-Jamaican labourer, though it can be assumed that their views were to some extent conditioned by the responses of workers themselves. Workers were aware of the adverse impact of East Indian immigration on their employment and upon their wages, and of the high levels of taxation imposed upon them. The use of such phrases as 'slave coolie' reveals something of an antagonistic attitude to East Indian labourers. 'Perhaps the only reason that could be given why the Indian labourers are preferred is because the proprietors can crush them without opposition, but not so with our Jamaican labourer'.

The evidence points to some measure of adaptation by East Indians despite ethnic particularism. For example, in 1894 the Protector of Immigrants, in a letter to Enos Nuttall, pointed out that of the approximately 11,213 East Indians in the island probably half 'understood English or *rather Creole English*, sufficiently well to benefit by teaching in that language'.[64] Other observers have noted the involvement of East Indians in the practice of obeah, with East Indian obeahmen enjoying high prestige.[65] The Afro-Jamaican population, it has been noted, were to become an integral part of the Indian festival known as Hosay, and the use of marijuana as well as Indian cuisine, and Indian jewellery rapidly became part of Creole life.

The extent to which East Indians were allowed entry into Jamaica is a measure of the influence which planters could successfully exert on the Governor of Jamaica within the modified Crown Colony system. The general revenue subsidised East Indian immigration but planters were eventually forced to pay some of the cost. Conversely, it may be argued that the history of East Indian immigration was a measure of the extent to which the Crown Colony system favoured or acted paternalistically in the interests of Jamaica's rural labourers. The policy of allowing immigration was clearly adverse in its impact on the Afro-Jamaican population. The WIRC of 1897 suspected an act of prestidigitation on the part of the planter class when it observed that most East Indians were working on the banana estates.

Not all planters supported immigration, because the demand for East Indians did not correspond ever to an island need for labourers but to the specific needs of planters in clearly defined regions of the country.

Once the indentureship was over the East Indian was no longer treated as a pampered section of the labour force (and it is true in any case that even as indentured servants planters did not always carry out their side of the contract to the East Indians and arrogantly relegated them to gaol for the most trivial offences). East Indians were to join black workers in the migration to Panama, and they too were victims of the land monopoly which frustrated their attempts to establish independent cultivation. Other East Indians became shopkeepers in the rural townships, and distillers of spirits.[66] A few became substantial landowners as well; yet others migrated to the urban centres, particularly Kingston. They continued the trek away from the plantations. On 19 April, 1902 they revolted in Annotto Bay.

Ultimately, the advantage of East Indian labour to the planters was that as long as indenture lasted East Indian labour could be more flexibly organised. The advantage did not lie in its cheapness, but in the reality that it gave employers some leverage over the Afro-Jamaican workforce.

The planter commission of 1890 had recommended penalties for East Indians who after five years chose to go into shopkeeping. They would, in addition to the ordinary trade licence, pay £2–10–0 per annum for five years as reimbursement for introducing them into the island. This £2–10–0 would go into general revenue. If the East Indian became an independent agriculturist after five years, he would forfeit the right to claim return passage at the end of the second contract. As for incentives to East Indians to own land as a reward for fulfilling their contracts, it appears from recent evidence that they were not among the major recipients of cultivable land.

Barbadian immigration

An effort was made to attract Barbadian immigrants from that 'island's redundant population'. The Barbadians, significantly, were to receive a detached cottage and a small plot of ground – about quarter of an acre, medical attendance and hospital treatment as with East Indians. Wages were put at 1/6d per day for first class labourers, and 1/3d for second class hands. Task work was to be remunerated at the rate of 1/6d per day. Artisans were to receive 2/- and 3/- per day. Women would be paid 10d to 1/- per day, and be given one week's provisions free of charge after allotment. The Barbadians, according to the Gazetted announcement, would have the option of renewing the contract or payment of a bounty of 20/- per year for each renewal.[67]

It is obvious that the intention was to offer Barbadian immigrants advantages not available to the Jamaican labour force. We know that Barbadians came, but in what quantity it is not clear. One account informs us that the masonry for the bridgework across the Negril River – a bridge which lasted until 1932 – was constructed by a Barbadian mason, Philip Corbyn.[68] A second Barbadian was hanged for slitting his East Indian concubine's throat from ear to ear. It is probable that Barbadians preferred other destinations such as Trinidad, Brazil, and Central America.

Conclusion

The history of the island's rural labour force and small farmers cannot be separated from the continuous economic crisis after the middle of the 1880s. For the whole period wages at best remained static, at worst declined. Access to land was definitely reduced during the 1880s and by the 1890s the expansion of the fruit industry reduced even further that access to land.

Tenancies proved a popular way of obtaining access to land but in their very nature tenants are a highly vulnerable sector of the work force, subject to expulsion, short term leases (which limit options) and high rentals when the commercial value of land increased. The latter was particularly true with the introduction of the banana plantations. East Indian immigration reduced the bargaining power of rural labour, while the fragmentation of land by the 1890s made landownership even more difficult.

There was a struggle against social injustice, in the form of strikes, individual protests, and arson, but probably for this period the most effective solution open to workers was emigration to Central America and Cuba, or seeking alternative occupation on public works and on laying railroad tracks.

The East Indians, who had been introduced to ensure a greater level of control over the Afro-Jamaican labour force, were themselves to be victims of the same conditions faced by Afro-Jamaicans once the semi-protective system of indentureship was ended. The creative energies of East Indians in rice cultivation were almost completely stultified. Individual stories or histories of economic success on the part of East Indians do not reveal the reality that East Indians, after indentureship were in a similar situation to the Afro-Jamaican labour force.

The paternal imperialists and the employers of labour had one thing in common – a profound belief that the coloured population was destined to be, for the foreseeable future, the cheap manual labour force. While paternal imperialists such as Archbishop Nuttall never contributed to the idea of Quashie the irredeemable, yet their views strengthened the notion of inferiority of a racial and cultural nature.

It must not be believed that the position of the Jamaican peasant in particular was substantially different, if at all, from other comparable groups in what Eisenstadt has called 'historical bureaucratic polities'.[69] Such peasants Eisenstadt has described as the 'most passive and inarticulate and least organised stratum'. Such groups carried the heaviest burdens of taxation. The governments of such societies often displayed some concern for the welfare of the peasants, though there was a tendency for such governments to yield to the wishes of the rural aristocracy. The major preoccupation of such peasants was the easing of taxation burdens and the strengthening of their economic independence 'by protecting their property against encroachments by large landowners'. Such peasant societies in their village strongholds were 'perpetuators of the various "Little Traditions" and efforts are made to maintain independent cultural traditions'.

The structure of exploitation of rural labour was as much a function of class relations as of racial assumptions. Yet, the reality that the mass of rural workers constituted a race distinct from the employer class, the landowners, and the government itself, strengthened the ability of the ruling class to manoeuvre racial symbolism in order to achieve greater social control. Peasants were poor, not because they had no access to land, or because of the relations between capital and labour in the countryside, but because they belonged to an 'inferior' race. It was even believed that it was best to tax 'Quashie' because he would then need to work harder to pay his taxes. Protests of workers were proof, not as Robert Love would have had it that black people had backbone, but that blacks were easily 'led away' by evil and designing men, and were combustible as a race.

When Dr Love spoke of class legislation, there was always an implication that class legislation was synonymous with racist legislation. He referred to blacks both as 'class' and 'race'.

> Whilst we refuse to regard the Negroes as apart from the general population of our Colony, in their general interests, certain circumstances peculiar to them as a class, made it lawful and necessary for us to address them, as if they were apart. We wish that this was not necessary. We wish that no class ideas, no class distinctions, no class aims, entered into our political life and warped the just spirit of legislation to the advantage of the few and to the disadvantage and hurt of the many. Then the class cry would not be heard among us . . . Let no Negro allow any man to deceive him by saying that there is no class feeling against him. That is a falsehood.[70]

Extreme inequality may weaken the 'capacity for impartial judgement'.[71] It is also self-perpetuating, and influences every facet of daily life. Paternal imperialists endeavoured to encourage a common culture in Jamaica but as Tawney has suggested:

> It [a common culture] must rest upon practical foundations of social organisation. It is incompatible with the existence of sharp contrasts between the economic standards and educational opportunities of different classes, for such contrasts have as their result, not a common culture, but servility or resentment, on the one hand, and patronage or arrogance on the other.[72]

In the following chapter we examine health institutions, morbidity and diet because they are symptoms of the stratified class system of the colony, and demonstrate the effective differences in the standards of physical well-being between classes, the differing opportunity structures, and at the same time the existence of that sense of aristocratic patronage which thrives on the existence of poverty.

Notes

1   J.B., *Jamaica Pie*, p. 4.
2   For example, Hugh Paget, 'The Free Village System in Jamaica', *Caribbean Quarterly*, 1987; 'Apprenticeship and Emancipation', in Gisela Eisner, *Jamaica, 1830–1930*; William Green, *British Slave Emancipation*, Oxford, 1982, among others.
3   Woodville K. Marshall, 'Peasant Development in the West Indies since 1838', in P.I. Gomes (ed.) *Rural Development in the Caribbean*, Kingston: Heinemann Educational Books, 1985, p. 7; and Veront Satchell, 'Land Transactions'.
4   G. Eisner, *Jamaica*, pp. 185–6.
5   Carl Stone, *Power in the Caribbean Basin, A Comparative Study of Political Economy*, Philadelphia: Institute for the Study of Human Issues, 1980, p. 18.
6   Veront Satchell, 'Rural Land Transactions in Jamaica'.
7   NLJ, MST 59, *Livingstone Collection 1898–1903*. 'The Jamaica of Today. Life at Mandeville', extract from *The Morning Post*.
8   Sidney Mintz, 'The Jamaican Internal Marketing System: Some Notes and Hypotheses', in *Social and Economic Studies*, Vol. 4, No. 1, March 1955, p. 97.
9   *JM*, Essay by Julia Mullings.
10   Mintz, 'Internal Marketing', p. 97.
11   *Ibid.* p. 96 and p. 99.
12   WIRC, 1897, p. 313/321 to 314/322. Evidence of Mr D. Santfleben. Santfleben was the District Engineer of the Public Works Department.
13   *Ibid.*
14   WIRC, 1897 p. 307/315. Evidence of Mr Henderson.
15   Frank Cundall, *Jamaica in 1912. A Handbook of Information for intending settlers and visitors with some amount of the islands history*, Kingston, 1912.
16   CO, 137/532, XC/AB13186. Report of George Henderson and Robt. Batten to Governor Norman on the Feasibility of Railroad Extension, Kingston, 22 October, 1887.
17   Frank Cundall, *Jamaica in 1912*.
18   *DG*, 8 December, 1902. J. Hirst to Editor.
19   WIRC, 1897 p. 324/332. Evidence of Mr Matthew Joseph, 5 April, 1897.
20   *Ibid.* Evidence of Mr Andrew Little (a mason and coffee farmer), 5 April, 1897.
21   *DG*, 3 December, 1902, Editorial.
22   *JA*, 11 January, 1896. 'St. Thomas' to Editor.
23   *JA*, 11 January, 1896. Mr Birch to Editor (All *sic*)
24   JCM, Vol. 32, 1891–92, Appendix XLIII. Herbert Thomas to Inspector General of Police 'Report of Inspector of Constabulary for St Thomas as to Petition of Evicted Tenants', 1 August, 1892.
25   *JA*, 25 January, 1896. The *JA* quoted this copy of a printed agreement.
26   *HBJ*, 1894 and 1900, p. 418.
27   *JG*, Vol. XI, 1889.
28   *HBJ*, 1900, p. 420.
29   *JG*, Vol. XI, 1889.
30   *Ibid.*
31   *Ibid.*
32   *Ibid.*
33   *Ibid.*

34 *Ibid.*
35 WIRC, 1897.
36 Papers Relating to Her Majesty's Colonial Possessions. Report of Sir Henry Norman, 30 May, 1884, p. 107.
37 *JA*, 3 April, 1897. J.H. Reid, 'The Bursting of the Clouds'.
38 *DG*, 4 April, 1896. Albert DaCosta to Editor.
39 CO, 137/518, 1884. Norman to Derby, No. 401, enclosing Justice Gibbons' correspondence 'Re-Proposed Abolition of District Courts'.
40 *Ibid.*
41 *JA*, 16 November, 1895. E. O'Sullivan to Editor. Mr O' Sullivan was advocating the establishment of an Agricultural Bank.
42 Jacqueline Levy, 'The Economic Role of the Chinese in Jamaica: The Grocery Retail Trade', *The Jamaican Historical Review*, Vol. XV, 1986.
43 *DG*, 6 February, 1886. 'Vox Populi' to Editor.
44 WIRC, 1897, p. 306/314. Evidence of Rev. Jonathan Reinke.
45 *Ibid.* 306/314.
46 WIRC, 1897, p. 256/264. Evidence of Mr L.C. Shirley (of the Jamaica Sugar Planter's Association), 31 March, 1897.
47 H.G. deLisser, 'The Negro as a Factor in the Future of the West Indies', from the *New Century Review*, No. 37, January 1900. See also NLJ, *Jamaica Pamphlets*, No. 43, p. 3.
48 NLJ, MS 209A, *Bishop's Letter Book*, Vol. 8, Enos Nuttall to Rev. L. Banbury.
49 Felix Holt, 'The Confessions of a Sugar Planter: The Black Man's Burden', in *JA*, 6 September, 1902.
50 Felix Holt, 'Confessions'.
51 The table and the section immediately following are based on De B. Spencer Heaven, *HBJ*, 1881, pp. 154–61.
52 Rev. Henry Clarke to *The Times* (London) reprinted in *Colonial Standard*, 7 October, 1884.
53 Sir Anthony Musgrave, *Jamaica*, p. 18.
54 *JG*, Vol. XIII, 1890, p. 253, 'Report of Commission re-Renewal of Immigration from India'.
55 Quoted in Wesley Roberts, 'The Jamaican Plantocracy: A Study of their Economic Interests, 1866–1914', Ph. D. University of Guelph, 1972, p. 203.
56 Musgrave, *Jamaica*, p. 24.
57 H.G. deLisser, 'The Negro as a Factor', p. 5.
58 National Archives, Washington D.C., Department of State. Microcopy T31, Dispatches of US Consuls from Kingston George E. Hoskinson to Seward, No. 173, 12 October, 1878. 'Third Annual Report on Trade Navigation and Economic Conditions of this Island'.
59 *JA*, 15 June, 1895.
60 *JA*, 23 March, 1895.
61 Felix Holt, 'Confessions', *JA*, 6 September, 1902.
62 *JA*, 15 June, 1895. J.H. Reid, 'Negro Isolation'.
63 Musgrave, *Jamaica* pp. 9–10.
64 NLJ, MS 209a, Vol. 33, *Bishop's Letter Book*. Inspector of immigrants to Nuttall, 9 March, 1894.
65 Alice Spinner, 'On Duppies', in *A Reluctant Evangelist*, London: Edward Arnold, 1896, p. 30.
66 The *Jamaica Gazettes* of 1883–1900 record dozens of spirit licences granted to East Indians.

67   *JG*, 1889.
68   *JM*, Daniel Tait.
69   S.N. Eisenstadt, *Political Systems of Empires*, New York: The Free Press of Glencoe, 1963, pp. 207–8.
70   *JA*, 11 January, 1896, 'Plain Words to the Negro Population'.
71   R.H. Tawney, *Equality*, New York: Capricorn Books, 1961, p. 24.
72   *Ibid*. pp. 31–32.

CHAPTER 9 | Health and poor relief

Among the consequences of poverty are inadequate housing and clothing, poor diet and water supplies, overcrowding and insanitary conditions. These are conditions which encourage both epidemic and non-epidemic diseases. Jamaicans were victims of preventable diseases and of infections which the quality of their lives imposed on them.

Before examining the assorted illnesses which affected the Jamaican population we will look at the institutional arrangements which were designed to alleviate poverty, distress and illness. The health of a population is related not only to diet, nutrition, and the disease environment, but also to the quality and availability of medical services. It is also obvious that poverty, distress and illness are intimately related.

Official poor relief

Since Jamaica was acknowledged to be a Christian community, there were private and public charities which endeavoured to alleviate the problems of material deprivation. After 1880 the administration of poor relief passed from the office of the Governor to his nominated councils, responsible for parochial matters. After the constitutional change of 1884, these powers passed naturally to the elected members of the municipal councils. The popular view that the Parochial Boards were ineffective in the administration of poor relief led to the establishment in 1886 of a Board of Supervision, a body whose aim was to 'establish control over the various parochial boards in their disposal of the funds for Poor Relief vested in them by Law 5 of 1868'.[1] The Governor appointed the members of the Board of Supervision. The new provision of 1886 allowed for the distribution of poor relief to persons who had been affected by natural disaster or by epidemic. Prior to 1886 provision had been made for ministers of religion and members of Parochial Boards to act (gratuitously) as Assistant Inspectors of the Poor, thereby reducing the 'journeying of the poor'. This arrangement was dropped under the new system.

Officially appointed Assistant Inspectors and Inspectors of the Poor were employed to visit and otherwise oversee the welfare of paupers. The

Manchester Parochial Board noted the difficulty inherent in a system where two Inspectors had to oversee 600 paupers. Paupers who were also crippled were expected to travel to get their allowance. To avoid that, some paupers paid a 'commission' to get someone to take their pittance to them, whilst others were told that 'some of the money got lost by the way . . . ' One ticket was found pawned or secured as a pledge at a shopkeepers.[2]

In 1887 there were 4,564 paupers island-wide, in 1895 there were 4,343, in 1899 4,497 and in April 1907 5,321. (The higher figure for 1907 probably arose out of the additional distress resulting from the 1907 earthquake).[3] The author of the *Jamaican Handbook* boasted that there had been a decline of 1.5 per cent in the number of paupers, while the population had increased by 20.6 per cent between 1887 and 1899. The percentage of paupers to population was approximately 0.6 per cent during this period, a figure which the *Handbook*'s editor proudly reported in comparison with England, 2.6 per cent, Scotland 1.5 per cent, Barbados 1.4 per cent and British Guiana 1.0 per cent. Of course, such comparisons mean very little unless the criteria for determining pauper status in each country are clearly set out. Those figures could be used to demonstrate, as the *Handbook* wished to demonstrate, that Jamaica had fewer paupers; or they could be used to show that Jamaica's definition of pauper was much more rigorous than elsewhere.

There were two kinds of relief offered to paupers, outdoor and indoor relief. Indoor relief was offered through a series of poor houses established throughout the country. In 1889 there were plans for new poor houses in St Ann, St Catherine and Spanish Town, while others were being repaired. The cottage system was adopted – the leading principle of which was that there should be buildings with ranges of rooms and that each room should accommodate two inmates in separate beds. The plan allowed for the addition of more buildings when necessary, to allow for proper drainage, ventilation and water supply, an infirmary or sick ward, a mortuary, and bathrooms, nurses and servants' quarters, and concrete floors, recommended because of the 'filthy habits of some of the inmates in some cases arising from illness'.[4]

But precisely who were Jamaica's poor, as defined by the law? In Jamaica, the candidate for poor relief had to establish absolute destitution. A report from the Colonial Secretary's office to the United States Minister demonstrates vividly the spirit in which poor relief was offered. Firstly, it was noted that in Jamaica there was no identifiable group of 'tramps' such as 'is fairly well defined in the United Kingdom'. There was no hereditary pauper class, either.

> It is not known that any particular efforts have been made to prevent the intermarriage of paupers or rather to prevent, what would in Jamaica more correctly express the intention, the co-

habitation of paupers, i.e. outdoor paupers. Owing, however, probably to the peculiar and easy conditions of life in this tropical land, there do not seem as yet any signs as far as I am aware of a separate and hereditary pauper class.[5]

Every effort was made, however, to guarantee that ablebodied people did not qualify for poor relief. Admittance on to the pauper roll necessitated the ability to prove beyond doubt that the applicant was *starving*.

> In case, therefore, of an ablebodied tramp the Inspector is not called on to give relief until he is satisfied that the man is starving and a provision in Section 31 allows the Inspector the period of 24 hours in which to return an answer to an application for relief and it is obvious that a judicious use of this power to postpone a decision would in many cases result in the voluntary removal of the genuine tramp before the decision was given. As an additional means of preventing imposition there is the further power in the hands of the Inspector of Poor, as representing the Parochial Board of his Parish, to decide in what manner relief shall be given and thus is enabled in all doubtful cases to offer relief in a poor house.[6]

There was, then, no hereditary class of paupers, partly because of the prodigality of nature as well as the 'habits and dispositions of the black people'. The Poor Laws were clearly designed to reduce to a minimum the number of people who qualified for poor relief. Jamaica's laws prosecuted as vagabonds those people who had abandoned their wives or husbands or children, leaving them a charge on relief funds. Jamaica's poor, as defined by those who gained admittance to the poor house, were generally 'for the most part aged, infirm, blind, or suffering from chronic or hereditary disease, or the children who are destitute'. In 1883 there were 866 lunatics attached to the alms houses, and as Dr Allen confessed, many of the lunatics should more properly be placed in the poor house.[7]

The Colonial Secretary's office made it clear that poor relief was not intended to rehabilitate. The precise words were that there was 'no provision for converting beggars and tramps into self-supporting members of the society'. Rehabilitation, rather, would come about by the initiative of the pauperised, who would mend their ways and their fortune when relief was refused them:

> The wholesome influence exercised by the restriction of relief to such persons and the refusal of it in most cases to the few who may be designated habitual beggars and tramps no doubt has an indirect salutary influence in converting beggars in *posse* to self-supporting members of the society.[8]

The irony was that revenue for poor relief came mainly from taxing the houses of the poor.[9]

There were regional variations in the pauper rate, though it is not easy to determine the significance of these variations. Firstly, it is not clear whether there was a uniform system of determining who qualified to be a pauper, though the Colonial Secretary's report is quite specific about old people, infirm, chronically ill people, and a number of lunatics. Admittance to the poor house was dependent on the assessment of the Inspector of Poor. It is clear that Kingston remained consistently highest during this period, Manchester was second highest at about 8 per thousand of population. St Mary, Portland and St Thomas, the banana parishes, showed the lower rates. The westernmost parishes, St James, Hanover, and Trelawny (5.8, 6.0, and 6.7) were the highest apart from Kingston and Manchester. St Elizabeth with 1.8 per thousand in 1895 was the lowest. In 1895, Manchester offered only outdoor relief, which was preferred by 'paupers'. In other parishes where indoor relief was offered by the Inspector of Poor, outdoor relief was refused. As the Board of Supervision reported in 1895:

> It is clear that there must be some specially inducing cause for the small percentage of paupers relieved. That cause appears to be that a large number of persons are refused outdoor relief by the Assistant Inspector on the ground that they will not go to the Poor House.[10]

It is significant that a relatively high pauper rate persisted in the sugar parishes and particularly at a time of severe depression in the sugar industry.

The distribution of relief was facilitated by the Churches, by private bequests, and by women's organisations, which focused on both material and moral welfare among distressed women. Among the non-government organisations and bequests which attended to the needs of the poor were the Fletcher's Trust, the Sarah Morris Trust, the D'Espinose Bequest, Wood's Bequest, the St Michael's Church Dorcas Society, the St George's Church Dorcas Society, the Hebrew Benevolent Society and the Jamaica Masonic Benevolence. There was also the Kingston Catholic Association of Ladies of Charity which from annual funds of approximately £54 ministered to fifty needy persons per month. Most of these organisations were established after the middle years of the nineteenth century, and most funds were designated for distribution to the poor of St Andrew and Kingston.[11]

The funds were by no means large. The Fletcher's Trust, for example, amounted to £130 from which the interest was distributed. In 1889, £76 were distributed from the Wood's Bequest to 1,302 persons. The sum of £2,150 was invested from the Sarah Morris Trust under Law 19 of 1880 bearing an interest of 4 per cent to be distributed among the poor of the parishes of Kingston and St Andrew. The Dorcas Societies provided clothing for the needy at Christmas. The Hebrew Benevolent Society ministered to the Jewish poor. The Kingston Sailors Home, established in 1864, received a 'liberal grant' from government after 1879, though it also increased its stock of funds from fund-raising drives.

Women were especially active in charity work, an activity which in some respects was an extension of their nurturative role in the home. The Victorian concept of womanhood reinforced what was believed to be the intuitive, and sensitive nature of women, more inclined to help the needy and the ailing. It was women who distributed charity, in secular and religious institutions, helped to supervise the Sailors Home, ran nurseries for the children of the poor. Charity through the efforts of elite women reinforced the concept of the deferential society.[12]

There were two associations organised and run by women for women. These were the Women's Self-Help Society constituted in 1879 under the patronage of Lady Musgrave, and the Upward and Onward Society founded in 1902, in association with the Moravian Church in Jamaica.[13]

The Women's Self-Help Society was not intended to alter the status of women as such, but to serve as an agency of poor relief among gentlewomen and their 'poorer sisters'. The society offered free needlework classes to all classes of women. The intention was to develop minor resources based on native products for sale to visitors to the country, to find remunerative work for 'poor women of the humbler class, who had a need to supplement their resources'. Needlework was sold to the Vere Alms House, the training college for women, and the 'Committee earnestly solicit orders to enable them to supply even to a small extent the needs of this industrious and suffering class, who seek not for charity but for work, and for the most part are unable to do anything but needlework'.[14]

Needlework had to compete with imported textiles, but the advantage which the poor needleworkers gained from the Society was perhaps the superior marketing intelligence which the Society's elite patrons possessed. By the end of the nineteenth century the Women's Self-Help Society had extended from its headquarters in Kingston to embrace Port Antonio, a branch which received the moral and material assistance of Lorenzo Dowe Baker of the Boston Fruit Company.

The Upward and Onward Society, founded under the presidency of Mrs James Watson, had as its objectives the 'upliftment of womanhood of the island as well as to band them together for mutual help and encouragement'. One of the chief aims of the society was to 'bring about a purer social life' and to challenge the 'debasing immorality so prevalent'.

> Many of our girls succumb to temptation because their lives are empty, narrow and lacking in interest. Ignorance and idleness are the most fruitful causes of moral failure.[15]

The Society printed leaflets, established reading circles, and gave instructions in cooking, sewing, laundry work, the nursing of the sick and provision of first aid.

The elite patrons of these societies directed their attention not only to the material welfare of women but to their moral guidance as well. Both societies accepted the idea that women had a value and function outside the home, and both were essentially rescue operations to prevent women falling into serious levels of material deprivation by offering skills training.

Medical services

The slave plantation owners had provided their slaves with the services of a doctor – perhaps once or twice per week. The extent of medical services, in the countryside in particular, had corresponded to the geographical distribution of the plantations and the hospitals or hothouses constructed on them. Medical services, then, had been essentially decentralised, with doctors directly employed by planters.

Ignorance of the specific challenges to European medicine in the tropics, and the demands of a cosmopolitan disease environment (which reflected the input of three, and later four, continents) had circumscribed the effectiveness of these medical services. But more specific limitations were the relatively short supply of doctors who were unable to cover all the necessary ground; and the fact that the 'doctor often lacked the authority to keep a slave in the hospital for treatment when the master or manager was convinced that the slave was feigning illness to avoid labour'.[16]

At the level of labour, emancipation had reduced the ability of planters to convert the ex-slaves into a permanent labour force tied to the plantation. At the level of health, the ex-slaves and their descendants could no longer rely on planters for medical services. In any case, their handsome incomes reversed by abolition, doctors sought more profitable places than Jamaica to practise their skills.[17] By 1861 there were only 50 qualified doctors in the island, compared to 200 in 1833. In 1900 there were just 100 doctors. In 1890 there was only one doctor to 7,185 people, island-wide. Kingston, which was better served, had 23 doctors in 1890, or one doctor to every 2,109 people. Figures for the colony, omitting Kingston, showed a ratio of one doctor to every 8,803 inhabitants.[18] Kingston's health was no better than the countryside, however. It would be perverse to conclude, though, that the decline in the number of doctors led to a deterioration in the health services. Sheridan thinks that there was a decline in medical services after emancipation.[19]

The fact is that the retreat of the sugar plantation monoculture after emancipation brought with it a need for centralisation of hospital and other medical services. It is difficult to determine whether the centralisation of services compensated for the decline in the number of doctors. Greater levels of centralisation in the hands of government were reflected in increased expenditure on health. Whether this increased expenditure compensated for the former expenditure of planters, pound for pound, is not presently clear. However, government expenditure on health rose to £2,300 in 1852 to £11,325 in 1870–1, and to £31,924 ten years later. In 1889–90 expenditure was £29,890, in 1894–5 it was £34,087, rising to £35,202 in 1897–8. In 1898–9 expenditure fell to £31,390.[20] After almost tripling between 1870–80, perhaps a result of capital expenditure, there were only marginal increases between 1880 and the end of the nineteenth century. Bedspace in the hospitals increased only marginally between 1880 and 1900, from 945 beds in 1880–1 to 1,117 in 1893–4 and to 1,171 in 1899–1900.[21]

While, on the one hand, the colonial government endeavoured to centralise facilities, the ex-slaves and their descendants were helping to decentralise them in their country recesses into the hands of myal men and of 'former slaves who had served as hospital assistants'.[22] It is Sheridan who takes special note of the enormous importance of black and coloured doctresses during the slave period in looking after the ill in the hospitals and hothouses. Apart from the fact that ex-slaves and their descendants must have had good reason to believe that their own doctors could, and did, treat them successfully, it is also true that the departure of doctors from the island after emancipation must have served to increase their dependence on myal men, some of whom, after all, had gained some legitimacy by being employed in slave hospitals. 'Whole districts,' admits William Green, 'were devoid of qualified physicians, and as a result many freedmen who might have been disposed to resort to a white practitioner were unable to do so'.[23]

The ability of the colonial government which was, to be fair to them, committed to a health policy, to institute widespread policies for the improvement of health facilities was hampered by economic crisis, at least in the plantation sector, but probably also by the cynical view that 'the nigger will get well anyhow'.[24]

Careful attention was paid by the colonial authorities to the recruitment of doctors. The recruitment of doctors from Great Britain demonstrated both the importance of colonies in providing employment for metropolitan professionals, and the desire to maintain predictable standards in the medical services of the colony. The medical profession in Jamaica, in fact, exemplified that tendency towards credentialism, as a means of insisting upon the collective socially recognised expertise of the profession.[25] It was not so much the creation of a substantial corps of doctors to provide medical attention for the population that was stressed, so much as the technical efficiency of the profession.

This emphasis was further strengthened by Law 47 of 1872 which established the Medical Council, a body appointed by the Governor for three years in the first instance, and which framed rules with respect to the practice of medicine in Jamaica. Those rules had the force of law after approval by the Governor in Privy Council. The Medical Council, apart from assessing diplomas, certificates and licenses, served a disciplinary function as well. The Jamaica Medical Association, a branch of the British Medical Association (incorporated in 1874) was founded in 1877. Its main functions were to promote 'medical and allied sciences and the maintenance of the honour and interest of the medical profession'.[26]

Doctors were recruited mainly from Britain. In order to ensure, however, that they were well equipped to serve in Jamaica, they were, upon arrival, attached to the Kingston Public Hospital, which was as good an introduction as any to Jamaica's health environment. Doctors were, like their bureaucratic counterparts, privileged. They were offered (and we assume, accepted) free passage from England, six months leave after three years' service, a pension at one-sixtieth of annual salary, the right to private practice even while serving as District Medical Officers (DMOs), and the right to run their own dispensaries. Up to the end of 1889, at least, many of these pharmacies opened only between the hours of 9.00 a.m. and 11.00 a.m., surely a limitation on the availability of medical services.[27] Some consideration was given in 1896 to the establishment of a dispensers' union to be called the 'Jamaica Union of Dispensers' to protect the rights and advance the collective interests of independent dispensers. The editor of the *Jamaica Advocate*, Dr Robert Love, accused physicians of starving out druggists.[28] The high status of doctors based upon the structured inequality of 'professionalism' was reinforced by investment in land and commerce. Since there is a correlation between the availability of medical services and their use by the labouring population, it follows that Afro-Jamaican medical practice, independent of the 'legitimate' and formal medical institutions, was an incidental consequence of the availability of medical services.

It was not humanly possible for doctors to minister, comprehensively, to the needs of the working classes. In 1895, taking the parishes without Kingston, 80 per cent of deaths occurred without medical aid being obtained in the last illness.[29] (It does not follow, however, that the patient had never been seen by a doctor, who may in his medical wisdom have recognised that his skills could not postpone death). In 1890–1, 85.6 per cent of deaths (outside Kingston) were not medically certified. As late as 1906–7, it was reported that of 45 cases of enteric fever reported, 40 patients had died, and that the high rate was attributable to the unavailability of medical practitioners.[30] In 1890, citizens from the Leeward Districts of Hanover, representing some 8,000 people, noted that medical attention was available only once per week, and that fees were exorbitant. The petition was signed by a Justice of the Peace, a Minister of Religion and over 80 others.[31] In the same year, the inhabitants of Porus delivered a similar petition, noting that for medical assistance they either had to travel over the hills for ten miles to Mandeville, or to May Pen which was 15 miles away.[32] Medical attention, was, partly, a function of distance, and relatively short distances by cart or dray for ailing people over abominable road surfaces could seem an eternity of agony. The provision for payment to doctors of a travelling allowance to enable them to visit clients was removed by the Poor Relief Law of 1886 which precluded the 'application of any portion of the poor rate to meet mileage allowance formerly paid to the DMOs for necessary travelling under the Ticket system'.[33] The regulation whereby patients who sought admission into a hospital were required to receive a letter of recommendation from the Custos or Magistrate of the Parish was not withdrawn until the 1890s.[34]

Distance and transportation facilities became crucial variables in medical services. The old sugar plantation slave system had ensured that the doctor visited his clientele on estates once or twice per week. The post-emancipation system required that the patient move to the doctor, and many Jamaicans after emancipation lived out of reach of 'central' facilities.

Transportation, distance and the shortage of medical personnel combined with expense to keep medical facilities out of reach of the labouring classes. In 1883, the maroons complained of the expense of medical attention. 'It is no use', wrote Rev. Stuart to the Colonial Secretary, 'talking to the maroons about receiving medical attendance, poor relief and roads, when one visit of a doctor would cost more than one of them could earn in six months'.[35] However much independence the small settler could achieve by cultivating his own plot, the proceeds of which assisted in feeding himself and family, his cash income was limited. Taxes and medical expenses had to be paid in cash, not in bananas or in ginger. Rev. Stuart noted with respect to the maroons of Accompong, (and the same situation applied to other isolated peasant communities), that 'one person can on average carry only one shilling and sixpence worth of breadkind to market – which is 20 to 24 miles distant . . . they have but small return for their labour'.[36] In 1885–6, the Collector-General, noting the poor health of the inhabitants of St James parish, explained that small settlers 'have felt and are still feeling keenly the tax on their slender resources to provide medical aid, medicines, etc'. Scarcity of money was also a reality for estate labourers, when estate crops were poor. Good crops of ground provisions glutted the market and depressed prices and therefore cash income.[37]

In 1897, Rev. W. Webb cited figures of up to £3–3–0 for medical attention and associated transportation costs.[38] The ticket system reduced costs to poor people by some 50 to 75 per cent, but costs continued to be high especially when travel was involved.

It is in the context of the actual availability of medical attention that we need to examine the widely and uncritically made observations that 'the humbler classes' were reluctant to seek medical attention before illness became terminal; that they preferred their inferior, if not dangerous, home-remedies; and that they demonstrated their 'uncivilised' (African) ways by resorting to magic, superstition, myalism and obeah. The indications are that the labouring population did not attend hospital only when illness was terminal; mortality rates would in that case have been horrendous. Secondly, hospital figures do indicate a large contingent of labourers. In 1884, for example, the Kingston General Hospital records show that of 1,949 cases treated, 591 were labourers, 261 servants, 174 laundresses, 51 seam-stresses and 358 without occupation.[39] Finally, the hospitals were some-times unable to accommodate all potential clients.

The lunatics

The lunatic asylum was completed and first occupied in 1860. In 1861 Dr Bowerbank secured the appointment of a commission to investigate the alleged abuses in the treatment of lunatics. In that year, an Act was passed for the proper supervision and government of the lunatic asylum. Dr Thomas Allen was appointed to the post of Medical Superintendent. In 1893 space at the asylum was expanded to accommodate 450 female luna-tics. These buildings were not completed until 1906.[40]

There was a significant increase in the number of patients admitted and under treatment during the late-nineteenth century, but there was also a higher proportion of recoveries and discharges. The number of patients under treatment increased from 325 in 1872–3, to 512 in 1882–3, to 702 in 1892–3 and to 956 in 1899–1900.[41] Table 9.1 shows the number of patients admitted and treated, the rate of recovery and the death rate for the period 1871–2, to 1905–6.

Table 9.1   Patients admitted to the lunatic asylum, 1871–1906

Year	Admitted	Patients under treatment	Recovery %	Death %
1871–2	80	300	30.00	14.30
1875–6	101	418	37.00	18.30
1885–6	139	561	33.00	18.70
1895–6	174	795	45.95	5.50
1905–6	230	1264	48.20	6.80

Source: *JDR*, 1905–6, Table 10, p. 113.

The occupations of those admitted reveal that 85 or 60.2 per cent of those admitted in 1883 were labourers, and that close to 60 per cent constituted the most active part of the labour force (20 to 40 years).[42] Among the more significant categories of causes of insanity were paralysis and epilepsy (9 and 8 per cent respectively); revivalism, obeah or other religious excitement (7 per cent). In 56.7 per cent of the cases, however, the cause of illness was not known. The largest number of admissions came from Kingston and St Catherine.

Of 68 patients who died in 1900–1, 28 or 41 per cent died of cerebrospinal disease. Another 17 (or 25 per cent) patients died from thoracic disorders, while 15 (or 22 per cent) died from abdominal disorders.[43] In 1883–4 38 patients died of paralysis, brain disease, convulsion and apoplexy, and nine from tuberculosis.

There were more female than male lunatics. In 1885 there were 195 women compared to 172 men, in 1899–1900 some 444 women compared to 405 men,[44] but the difference is neither statistically nor socially significant since the population of females was slightly higher than the male population.

The lunatic asylum could not accommodate all comers. In 1882, Dr Allen reported that there were some 500 known lunatics 'at large' in the island, and there were approximately 866 insane attached to alms houses in the country.[45] Few of the lunatics were criminal lunatics, most were described as 'totally ignorant', and the majority came from the urban zones of Kingston and St Catherine.

An indication of the social origins of the patients – apart from the fact that 73 per cent were black, 20 per cent brown, 2.6 per cent white and 3.7 per cent East Indian – was the fact that of 189 patients admitted in 1899–1900, some 180 were sent to the asylum from prisons and constabulary lockups, and only six from their own homes.[46] There was a proposal (unofficial) that special arrangements be made to house the better off classes so that they would not be in such close – albeit insane contact – with the 'degraded' population.

Societies are particularly fearful of lunatic frenzy which demonstrates itself in violent and sometimes murderous action. In 1884, of 501 lunatics there were only 20 criminal lunatics, five of whom were in custody for murder, four for assorted wounding charges (felonious, unlawful, malicious). Ten of the criminal lunatics had become afflicted with insanity while under sentence in the prisons of the island. In 1899–1900, of 45 criminal lunatics, 29 had been afflicted while serving sentence. The criminal lunatics were all diagnosed as suffering from mania, dementia, or epilepsy.[47] Epilepsy, strokes, and meningitis may all affect the nervous system, so too can nutritional diseases.[48] The result can be severe mental illness whose unhappy result may be murder or other acts of violence. One can only assume that most of Jamaica's lunatics were relatively tranquil. There were certainly twice as many out of, as in, hospital. In the Afro-Jamaican context it is probable that obeahmen and religious healers would have endeavoured to cure the lunatic of 'duppies' or other malevolent emanations.

Housing and diet

Jamaica's medical officers were correctly convinced that the lifestyle of the labouring classes was partly, if not mainly responsible, for illness. Housing and diet were two aspects of lifestyle which they referred to from time to time as causes of morbidity.

The quality of housing obviously varied according to income and preference. Elite homes, whenever we find a description of them, gave the impression of spaciousness and airiness:

> I fancy the houses of the gentry out here are all pretty nearly on the same plan: a habitable verandah all round, and drawing and dining rooms in the centre, and green jalousies at the windows which are unglazed.[49]

The statistics offered by the censuses of 1891 and 1911 do not confirm the widely held view that the labouring classes of Jamaica did not try to improve their housing by flooring them at least, though in 1911 there were as many as 42,241 unfloored houses. Also, in 1911 approximately 42 per cent of houses in Jamaica consisted of one room only.

Table 9.2   Dwelling houses.

		1891	1911
1	Number of dwellings with shingle, metal, or concrete roof and floored.	44,027	91,183
2	Number of dwellings with thatch roof and floored.	35,683	47,637
3	Number of dwellings unfloored and mostly with roofs of thatch.	52,146	42,241
4	Unspecified	2,689	2,873
		134,545	183,934

Source: Jamaican Censuses, 1891 and 1911

The number of dwellings with metal roofs increased from 994 in 1891 to 18,135 in 1911. More houses were built with concrete roofing. Thus the Registrar General concluded that the best class of housing had increased 107.1 per cent, the second best class by 33.5 per cent and the lowest had decreased 18.9 per cent. There were only two cases reported of tent dwellings, and four cases of cave dwellings. In 1911, the number of windowed rooms were recorded for the first time. The Registrar General was of the view that the question may not have been understood by respondents, and that the outrooms occupied by domestic servants may, in some cases, have been omitted. Misunderstood or not, however, the figures in Table 9.3 do indicate something about the stratification of the quality of housing.

Table 9.3   Quality of housing

No. of rooms in dwelling	No. of dwellings
1	75,670
2	72,671
3 and 4	21,627
5, 6 and 7	4,446
8 and over	1,761
Unspecified`	7,759
	183,934

Source: Jamaica Census 1911.

Many rural homes, with their thatched roofs and wattle and daub walls, were earth-floored and constructed without windows. We quote Dr Donovan's report:

> . . . and this brings us to the consideration of the labourer's dwellings, which necessarily vary in size and accommodation, in accordance with the means etc. of the occupant. As a rule, they are constructed with laths, plastered with earth, and a thatched roof; there is no chimney or window, and only one door; but fortunately the walls have generally a good many crevices, which, however, the occupants endeavour pretty successfully to close up with rags etc.; overcrowding is, I believe, the rule, a great portion of those cabins or huts are unfit for human habitation.[50]

Another medical practitioner attributed rheumatism and 'lung affections' to the dampness and stuffiness of the people's dwellings. Other doctors thought that the outbreak of cerebro-spinal fever among children was a consequence of the practice of bedding children on the damp ground.[51]

Social reformers, such as Archbishop Nuttall, proposed a partnership between government and private sector for the construction of lower income housing. The building societies which mushroomed during this period were not generally intended for the labouring classes. Efforts to improve housing conditions among the poor were neither regular nor systematic. In 1864 the Kingston Benefit Building Society established cottages at Rose Lane and later the Garden Cottages on Tower Street. It does not appear that this example was widely followed. Poor gentlewomen were provided with a home by the widow of Mr Louis Verley, 'and is proving a boon to the gentle poor of this community'.[52]

Diet

While overcrowding, poor ventilation and unfloored houses were viewed as responsible for poor health, diet was seen as the cause of several nutritional disorders. 'The diseases due to food are probably the most numerous, which proceed from a single class of causes, and are principally associated with disordered digestion and nutrition, which conditions are brought about by excess or deficiency in quantity or quality'.[53]

There is no systematic study of diet among the Jamaican population during this period. For the elite dining was partly leisure activity and partly nutritional intake. Five course meals were regular, seven course meals were reserved for occasions when guests were present.[54] While Christmas dinner or dinner on such festive occasions cannot be used to determine daily diet, the menu below which won a prize for a 'simple yet suitable' Christmas dinner for the average middle class family must surely be an indication of the standards which the more materially well-endowed set themselves. The menu provided for a family of eight persons – father, mother, six children ranging in age from eight to eighteen: 18, 14, 10 being sons, 17, 12, 8 being daughters, all with healthy appetites. The father's income was £250 per annum.[55]

MENU

Table Decorations

Small glass trays with maidenhair ferns and yellow and white chrysanthemums, dinner service of white and gold. Old silver and glassware.

Entrees	*First Course*
Oyster	Turtle soup
Oyster patties	Boiled snappers and butter sauce
Turtle rissoles	Bread

Second Course	Third Course
Roast beef with York- shire pudding. Chicken pie Boiled ham Baked potatoes Roast white yam Fried plantain Sauce, pickles, mustard	Plum pudding with brandy sauce Custards in glasses Mince pies

Dessert
Raisins, almonds, cheese, oranges, bananas.
The estimated cost of dinner was 30/-.

Quite obviously the labouring classes would not have been able to feed themselves in terms of the above standards. Rev. Wilson noted that domestic workers were underfed.[56] A recent study notes that in the 1890s 'most Jamaican servants (other than nursemaids) were expected to provide their own food, even if they lived in. They were given "findings", food items meant to supplement that purchased out of their money wages, but the practice tended to vary according to the wealth of the employer'.[57] The domestic service, which expanded from 3.2 per cent of the workforce in 1871 to 4.1 per cent and 4.6 per cent in 1881 and 1911, respectively, nominally provided wages of 5/- per week.[58] In Kingston rents paid by domestics amounted to 6/- per month (with water), and 4/- without water, 'but it is a very small room indeed they get for 4/-'.[59] In rural Jamaica the wages were even lower. In a country parsonage (Anglican) the following wages were offered:[60]

One cook and general servant	12/- per month
Another girl about 14 years as cook's assistant	5/- per month
Lad who looks after horses, brings wood, and assists generally	12/- per month

Evidence of the actual diet of the working man in the late-nineteenth century is partly impressionistic. There was also a tendency to generalise about 'Negroes' without always recognising differences in income levels between them. Labourers who were entirely dependent upon the plantations or other similar enterprise for wages were clearly in a different category from those who were only partly dependent on plantations for a wage and/ or worked on their own plots of land. The quality of the diet also varied according to the season since there was a relationship between subsistence production and diet. The independent cultivator was able to supplement his own production with bartering of commodities at the nearest market, or to make purchases through the sale of cash crops such as coffee.

One medical officer noted:

> It is difficult to deal with the question of food; as among the native labourers it varies so much in quantity and quality as well as regularity, according to circumstances, such as wages (regular or intermittent), employment, distance from home, season of the year, locality etc.[61]

The same medical officer was of the opinion that meat and fish were sparingly used from 'economic reasons alone'. The labourer preferred the 'salted article, which he uses in small quantities more as a condiment, but at times he had a gorge of animal food, generally pork'. A description of the daily round of diet by the labouring man was given by Dr Sinclair in 1897:

> The usual diet scale of a labouring man is tea early in the morning; this is made either of plain sugar and water, or of a decoction of herbs sweetened with sugar. He may or may not have a piece of bread with it or the remains of his dinner from the previous night. This is what is called 'choc-la-ta'. Breakfast he takes at about 12.00 noon, and dinner at 6.00 p.m. Both consist typically of yam, cocoa [*sic*] breadfruit or plantain, with a small amount of fresh or salted pork or saltfish. Pork and fish constitute the chief animal food which he eats. For the last few years the people have been eating a good deal of imported food, and now in the room of yam, etc. one frequently sees flour or cornmeal dumplings. It is no uncommon thing for a labouring man to purchase a small barrel of flour, and keep it in his house to feed on . . . At present the food supply is scarce – I mean the native vegetables. There is quite enough flour and cornmeal in the shops, and pigs and fish are plentiful and cheap, but as the people have to buy these, and money is scarce, I do not think they are feeding themselves sufficiently.[62]

Writing in 1887–8 J.H. Reid gives a comparable account of daily diet.

> The first [meal] is his coffee, with which he takes a bit of bread when that is to be had, or in default of that, a roasted plantain, or something similar, and with that he goes to work until breakfast time, about 10.00 or 11.00 a.m. He then has boiled ground provisions – yams, cocos, sweet potatoes, plantain, chochos, being mixed in the same dish. [He has] salted meat and fish in the period of the week between market days, Wednesdays and Satur-

days . . . In towns where there are everyday markets, and villages near the sea, salted provisions are not largely consumed. The last meal of the day is 'dinner' – anytime after returning from work; as early as 5.00 or as late as 9.00 p.m.[63]

Both accounts confirm that diet varied according to location, availability of cash to purchase imported goods, and heavy dependence on locally produced foodstuffs. The diet of labourers was rich in carbohydrates but poor in animal proteins, minerals and vitamins, the absence of which 'can lead to bone deformation and pulmonary and intestinal diseases . . . Generally speaking, there was a close relationship between diarrhoea and other infectious diseases on the one hand and malnutrition on the other'.[64]

For the plantation slave period, Sheridan noted that the diet of Caribbean slaves was low in calcium, deficient in vitamins A and B, and lacking in bovine milk.[65] The reduced use of bovine milk was probably caused in some instances by lactose intolerance among African populations. In addition, too much pork can impair the absorption of calcium.[66] Sickle-cell anaemia, to which Africa-based populations are vulnerable, also requires higher inputs of iron and folic acid in the diet.[67] Malnourished bodies are, of course, much more vulnerable to the ravages of disease and overcrowded conditions in tiny apartments are ideal for the spread of epidemics.

Diseases

Jamaicans were susceptible to malarial diseases, pulmonary and respiratory disorders, bowel complaints or diseases of the digestive system, enteric fevers, kidney diseases, subacute rheumatism, and skin diseases.

Infectious-parasite diseases were a major cause of morbidity and death. Among this category of diseases was dysentery which is transmitted through contaminated faeces to the alimentary canal by flies, dirty hands, contaminated food, water, and fruits. There is a discharge of blood and mucus.[68] Outbreaks of dysentery were often, but not always, localised, for example, in Hanover, in 1882–3, when it claimed several victims.[69] In 1899–1900 it claimed the lives of four of 50 patients at the Hordley hospital in the banana plantation area of St Thomas; in the same year 33 patients were treated for the disease at the Lionel Town Hospital. 54 enteric cases were treated at the Kingston Public General Hospital in 1899–1900; there were 17 deaths. In 1895, there were over 360 cases outside Kingston, leading to three deaths.[70]

Between 1886–8 there were 840 deaths from 8,612 cases of smallpox, reflecting a 9.75 per cent mortality rate. In Kingston alone there were 2,135 cases and 405 deaths (or 18.96 per cent of those infected).[71] The medical authorities observed, however, that the death rate in 'vaccinated areas' was

4.26 per cent compared to 16.04 per cent in 'unvaccinated areas'. The 1886–8 epidemic also affected only one in every 73.75 persons compared to 1874 when one person in every 43.50 persons was affected.[72] While small-pox had not been eliminated the government vaccination programme helped to reduce the incidence of the disease.

From the 1870s infants were compulsorily vaccinated against small-pox. However, revaccination programmes were not undertaken, so that adults suffered a reduced immunity. Secondly, the entire adult population was not vaccinated against smallpox. There was, finally, always the chance that an infected person from overseas would get through quarantine restric-tions. It is not known whether the suggestion that the germ found its way from Panama 'in the dirty clothes forwarded to be washed in Kingston' had any scientific validity.[73] The medical authorities placed much of the blame for the epidemic proportions of the disease in given years to the attitudes, and lifestyle, of Jamaica's labouring classes. Since the Afro-Jamaican population took the fatalistic position that smallpox was 'God's sickness' against which man could not prevail, less enthusiasm was shown for treat-ment or for co-operating with the authorities in the isolation of victims. So, at least, the medical authorities argued. More to the point, however, was that overcrowded housing, poor ventilation, sharing of the same mat, cot, and sleeping under the same roof as infected persons facilitated the spread of the disease.

The conviction that patterns of behaviour among the labouring popu-lation was a hindrance to the effective control of smallpox informed the thinking behind Law 27 of 1873, and Law 3 of 1874. The 1873 Law sought to 'prevent in certain cases, the holding of wakes and other assemblages of a similar nature'. The 1874 Law empowered the Commissioner of Health to take the necessary action to suppress wakes when there was a danger of epidemic:

> The custom which prevails in Kingston among the lower classes
> of holding wakes over their dead, even when persons have died
> of smallpox or other contagious and infectious diseases, on which
> occasions there are large assemblages of people, is one which
> certainly is most dangerous to the public health.[74]

Cases of smallpox were often traceable to a single wake in a particular district. The authorities imposed fines on the convenors of wakes during epidemics, and authorised the police and militia to enforce the policy of isolating victims. In spite of the epidemic of 1886–8 and 1890–1, victory over smallpox was assured, through a policy which emphasised immunisa-tion – though doctors were not satisfied that the colonial authorities were paying sufficient attention to revaccination and isolation of victims in the hospital specially erected for the purpose.

Success against pulmonary disorders was not as assured. Doctors agreed that the Jamaican population was very vulnerable to phthisis, the agent behind pulmonary consumption. In 1882–3 of 45 cases of phthisis treated at the Kingston Public General Hospital there were 21 deaths.[75] In 1899–1900 of 118 cases treated for 'tubercle' there were 37 deaths.[76] There was some variation in the intensity of phthisis in rural parishes between 1880 and 1900, averaging some 77 per year, with a high of 131 in 1884–5.[77] These figures refer only to cases treated in the public hospitals. Island-wide deaths arising from phthisis rose to as high as 2.70 per thousand in 1904–5.[78] The island Medical Department reported in 1882–3 that more than two-thirds of deaths registered in Kingston were the result of consumption and infantile diseases.

It was in 1882 that Robert Koch proved the cause of pulmonary consumption to be the tubercle bacillus, and the X-ray of Wilhelm Roentgen in 1895 became a major source of early detection. The decline in the incidence of tuberculosis is commonly attributed to improvements in hygiene, standards of living, and improved nutrition, in Britain and the United States. The disease was most common in large cities and in the poorer sections of such cities. In this sense, tuberculosis is partly a disease of poverty, related to standards of living, hygiene, sanitation, and overcrowding. The middle classes were not immune from the disease, however. The virus can also be transmitted from milk obtained from infected cattle. In Jamaica, there was little control exercised over itinerant milk sellers, or over milk 'hawked or retailed in dirty little shops'.[79]

There was also the danger that in hospital itself the treatment of tuberculosis in open wards exposed uninfected patients to the disease. The Public General Hospital of Kingston and the lunatic asylum were both mentioned in this respect by Dr Plaxton, the island Medical Officer.[80] Referring specifically to the lunatic asylum Dr Plaxton observed in 1900:

> It is mortifying to see diseases – I refer to tubercular affections – originating in the asylum and at the same time to know that given the means they are largely preventable . . . The remark of Dr Pringle . . . may be applied, *mutato nomine*, to the asylum that 'among the chief causes of sickness and death in an army' the reader will little expect that I should rank what is intended for its health and preservation, the hospitals themselves'.[81]

Of 44 deaths at the lunatic asylum in 1895–6, 17 were from 'thoracic disorders', though there is no indication of the original place of infection.[82]

Up to the end of this period doctors continued to attribute the problem of pulmonary (and other respiratory disorders) to the 'overcrowded houses of the humbler classes, poor ventilation and insanitary house surroundings'.[83] High on the list of illnesses were 'fevers', which referred, for the most part, to malarial fevers. It was not until the end of the century that a definite breakthrough was made which identified the *anopheles* mosquito as the vector of malaria which is characterised by high fever, chill, ague, rapid pulse, fall in blood pressure, delirium, nausea, and headaches. Debility, disability, and death are features of the disease, the elimination of which requires the control or preferably the elimination of the mosquito. Remittent and intermittent fever associated with malaria were most prevalent between October and December, and between December and February, respectively. Malarial fever was associated with sugar and banana plantation workers primarily because they worked on the coasts and close to swamp land where the mosquito bred profusely following periods of heavy rainfall. It is of interest to observe that remittent and intermittent fevers tended to coincide with the cane harvest.

The association between malarial fever and swampy land had long been made, but not necessarily the association between malaria and mosquitoes. Up to 1897 the standard medical explanation in Jamaica for malaria was still:

> The poison which excites 'ague' has long been known as malaria (or bad air), and unlike other special fevers is neither contagious nor infectious, but is conveyed to individuals probably from soil or water. It prevails especially in, and as a rule severely in marshy districts. Again the most virulent forms of malarial fevers have been in dry and barren regions; recent alluvial soils are likewise foci of the disease.[84]

There was significant variation in the incidence of malaria from year to year. In 1886–7, for example, only 1,235 cases of fever were treated at the General Hospitals, while in 1884–5 there had been 3,102. In 1892 there were 4,607 cases.[85] In 1906 malaria still produced a death rate of 1.62 per 1,000 living.[86]

In 1895 the Savanna-la-Mar hospital, located in the sugar belt of the island, treated over 830 patients for malarial fever, the Hordley hospital in eastern St Thomas in the banana plantation area treated 937 cases, while Annotto Bay hospital treated 851 cases.[87] These figures, from areas close to the coast, contrast sharply with the figures from the Mandeville hospital, located 2,000 feet above sea-level where there were only ten cases. Yet, Montego Bay which is a coastal city had no cases in that year. The explanation might be that a major swamp in the Montego Bay area had been filled from at least 1883.[88]

In 1895 there were only 25 deaths reported from the 4,028 cases treated throughout the island's hospitals.[89] The fact is that many people of African origin have abnormalities of the haemoglobin of the red blood cells which produce sickle-cell anaemia and act as a protection against mortality from malaria. It is not possible to ascertain the extent of sickle-cell anaemia or sickle-cell trait among the nineteenth century labouring classes, since anaemia itself was a consequence of several other conditions, including nutritional deficiencies. Malarial fever and yellow fever affected whites far more than blacks. The incidence of yellow fever significantly declined in the latter nineteenth century, though there were outbreaks in 1874, 1877 and 1896. Yet the seriousness of malaria among the labouring classes cannot be underestimated. Of 3,258 cases treated at the Kingston Public Hospital in 1899–1900 10 per cent or 329 were malaria cases, and 7 per cent of the patients died.[90]

Doctors of the period saw the growth of syphilis as one of the major challenges to public health. Reports for the period indicate an increase from 315 cases in 1880–1, to 458 cases in 1892.[91] The most pronounced presence of the disease in 1895 was in the seaport towns of Falmouth (53), Montego Bay (58), Hordley (66), Port Antonio (52), Annotto Bay (32) and Lionel Town (78 cases). In 1895 there were 489 cases outside Kingston and ten deaths.[92] In 1882–3 there were 111 cases treated at the Kingston Public Hospital (and seven deaths).[93] In 1899–1900 there were 79 cases of syphilis at that hospital and 159 cases of gonorrhea.[94] At the Lock hospital, where prostitutes were treated, there were in 1882–3 13 cases of syphilis, 83 cases of syphilis and gonorrhea, 11 cases of gonorrhea and one case of syphilis, gonorrhea and phthisis, who understandably died.[95]

It is possible that syphilis was sometimes confused with yaws (frembesia, pian, or bubas), a disease caused by a special micro-organism, the *treponema pertenue* – which is related to the *treponema pallidum*, the agent of syphilis.[96] In yaws there are growths all over the body, especially the face, feet, legs, hands and around the external genitals – growths which may become ulcerated. Yaws was endemic to certain parts of Africa, and was most probably brought to the Americas via the slave trade. In fact, Sheridan noted a decline in yaws after the abolition of the slave trade. Yaws is a highly contagious disease which thrives in crowded, insanitary conditions.[97] Yaws was a condition recognised as such during the slave plantation era, during which time the African methods of herbal healing proved more efficacious than European methods based on mercury.[98] Confinement in institutions such as the reformatories increased the incidence of yaws.

Hookworm, like yaws, could be contracted by picking up parasites through the thin parts between the toes. Barefooted labourers were therefore particularly susceptible to hookworm disease or *ankylostomiasis*. The island Medical Department's report of 1902–3 made the untrue claim that the disease had been introduced by East Indians.[99] Hookworm disease is mentioned by Sheridan for the slave period. 'There is reason to believe that 500–1,000 worms must be present for at least six months to produce well-marked *ankylostomiasis*. Because hookworms are anaemia-producing parasites themselves, the disease is exacerbated among people who eat coarse, bulky, non-nutritious food'.[100] The symptoms are: enormous appetite, extreme lethargy, generalised swelling, retarded mental, physical and among children, sexual growth.[101] Yaws and hookworm, as well as chigoe infections, could have been reduced significantly if shoes were worn.[102]

Whereas for the white population, fevers were the most fatal afflictions, for blacks fluxes or bowel complaints, and diseases of the intestinal tract were the most fatal illnesses.[103] Diarrhoea was one of the most common problems treated in hospitals. The highest number treated for this period was 259 in 1880–1.[104] The average of 144 per year treated in the hospitals clearly does not reflect the incidence of the problem. Of course, diarrhoea is a symptom of several other diseases; it may be caused by toxic substances, or food, alcohol, or highly spiced foods. It can also be a symptom of amebiasis, typhoid fever, dysentery, or cholera.[105] The disease, however, is generally associated with digestive disorders.

The list of digestive disorders among Jamaica's working class is formidable: dyspepsia, peritonitis, hypertrophy of the spleen, gastritis, colic, constipation and haemorrhoids. Colic and constipation were probably more generalised than the hospital figures suggest. Annotto Bay hospital alone treated 97 cases of colic in 1895, significantly more than anywhere else – the total being 135 cases outside Kingston.[106] Constipation can result from inadequate amounts of essential materials and dehydration. The function of the bowel can be rendered less efficient through profuse sweating during hot weather, which leads to the reduction of the body's moisture levels.[107] Of 184 cases in 1895, outside Kingston, 98 cases were reported from the Buff Bay (46) and Lionel Town hospitals (52), low-lying coastal areas. There were 12 deaths from constipation.[108]

In 1895 there were some 1,096 cases of digestive disorders treated in hospitals outside Kingston, leading to 54 deaths. In Kingston's Public Hospital in 1899–1900 there were 360 cases of gastro-intestinal problems, and 37 deaths.[109] 11 per cent of cases treated at the Kingston Public Hospital in that year were for gastro-intestinal disorders.

The labouring classes were very vulnerable to respiratory diseases, often related in medical opinion to poor housing, in respect of inadequate ventilation. Respiratory diseases are also related to the reduced intake of animal proteins, minerals and vitamins.[110] There is another reason for the susceptibility of the labouring population to respiratory ailments, however. The abnormalities of the haemoglobin of the red blood cells which provides defence against malaria increases the risk of severe pneumococcal infections.[111] Bronchitis was the most common of respiratory ailments. The smallest number of patients treated for bronchitis in hospitals between 1880 and 1892 was 148 in 1882–3. The highest was 209 in 1892.[112] In 1882–3, 37 cases of pneumonia were admitted into the Kingston Public Hospital. 11

patients or 29.7 per cent of those admitted, died.[113] Asthma, pleurisy and bronchial catarrh were among the less common cases treated in public health institutions.[114]

Rheumatic diseases were common but not apparently a major cause of death. An average of 398 patients were treated for rheumatic problems between 1880 and 1892 with a high of 642 in 1892.[115] There were 773 cases outside Kingston in 1895 and five deaths.[116] The highest number of cases treated was at Annotto Bay hospital where 207 cases were treated. The next highest (71) was Lionel Town and Hordley.[117] Rheumatism was attributed to exposure to 'which labourers are subjected in their fields, and their carelessness when exposed at night and sudden alterations of temperature'.[118] Older people were especially vulnerable.

Diseases of the 'cutaneous system' ranged from eczema, ulcers, onychia, framboesia (yaws), boils, impetigo, scabies, and chigoes. Skin infections mainly affected field labourers when minor wounds or insect bites left improperly attended became 'foul, sloughing ulcers'.[119] There were 1,027 cases of skin infections treated in 1902–3.[120] In 1882–3 some 179 ulcers were treated at the Kingston Public Hospital, compared to 1,553 island wide.[121] The average for the years 1880–92 was 1,568 cases per annum.[122] The incidence of ulcers was highest in the plantation areas, where the possibility of injury was probably higher than elsewhere. Ulcers led in several cases to amputation.

The Lepers' Home in Spanish Town accommodated just over a hundred patients, inflicted with leprosy, yaws or elephantiasis. The East Indian population was most vulnerable to leprosy. Elephantiasis (or filariasis) had long been a health problem among blacks. It is a tropical disease in which the legs and other parts of the body become grossly swollen. The disease is transmitted by mosquitoes. Happily, it was not widespread.

There were outbreaks of cerebro-spinal meningitis on a regular basis, and usually during the colder months of the year, between December and February.[119] Children were especially affected, though the disease was not confined to them. The disease could reach epidemic proportions, as it did in Duncans, Trelawny, in 1882–3. The disease, which proved generally fatal, was considered to be the result of 'exceptional atmospheric conditions, but little understood'.[120] The Senior Medical Officer confessed that in this instance there was no proof that the disease was 'aggravated or promoted by insanitary features' such as impure water and overcrowding. In fact, the disease is a consequence of inflammation of the *meninges*, the membranes of the brain and the spinal column. The cerebro-spinal column is attacked by pneumococcus, and staphylococcus. Cerebro-spinal meningitis 'is a sporadic or epidemic form of meningitis caused by a germ, the meningococcus. The disease is in fact most common during the cold months, and children are highly vulnerable. Overcrowding and insanitary conditions are in fact aggravating factors'.[122]

In an earlier section we discussed the incidence of infant mortality which was extremely high between 0–5 years. Children were especially vulnerable to epidemics of whooping cough, measles, and the lethal cerebro-spinal meningitis, yaws, bowel disorders, tetanus, colic and worms while whooping cough affected all classes of children. Mortality was highest among the children of the peasantry.[123] There were 2,297 deaths from whooping cough in 1878–81 and 3,686 between 1889–91.[124] Medical practitioners were disturbed by the unacceptable levels of infant mortality, 231 per 1000 in 1905–6 and 244 per 1000 in 1906–7.[125] Infant mortality was, in their view, a consequence of the lifestyle of parents, living conditions, sanitation and so on. But illegitimacy was also blamed.

In fact, an attempt was made to compare the mortality of illegitimate children with that of legitimate children. The usefulness of the comparison lies not in the proof of the legitimacy/illegitimacy thesis but in the fact that it is the closest to a comparison of mortality among the labouring classes compared to the middle and upper classes among whom there was a greater incidence of marriage. It is clear from Table 9.4 that mortality among illegitimate or working class children was, not surprisingly, higher than among legitimate children.

Table 9.4   *Proportion of deaths of legitimate and illegitimate children under one year to each 100 births, 1899–1900*

Parish	Legitimate	Illegitimate	Mean
Kingston	14.83	22.74	19.9
St Andrew	12.65	20.57	16.9
St Thomas	13.57	22.25	19.9
Portland	13.91	19.56	17.4
St Mary	11.84	17.08	15.2
St Ann	13.10	20.90	17.8
Trelawny	16.63	24.79	22.0
St James	12.66	23.30	19.6
Hanover	12.21	20.64	18.0
Westmoreland	11.40	20.21	16.8
St Elizabeth	12.05	19.02	16.1
Manchester	10.58	14.00	12.5
Clarendon	12.73	15.95	14.9
St Catherine	14.48	18.40	17.2
	12.78	19.46	17.0

Source: *JDR*, 1899–1900, p. 213.

Richard Lobdell concludes that 'parishes dominated by peasant organisation of production had higher fertility and lower infant and general mortality than their plantation and/or staple counterparts'.[126] Sheridan thinks that the growth of a free peasantry coincided with the retreat of the sugar monoculture and the establishment of a more balanced ecosystem in the post-emancipation period. And so he concludes that there was a rise in the birth rate and a fall in the death rate in Jamaica. Higman also noted that mortality was highest on sugar plantations in the period before 1834.[127] These conclusions are borne out by the lower levels of infant mortality in parishes such as Manchester and St Elizabeth, and the relatively high figures for Hanover, St James and St Thomas. It is possible, though, that mortality in plantation parishes was partly related to the disease environment in those areas.

Doctors generally concluded that Jamaican Creoles were reluctant to go to hospital, and that too often doctors were faced with patients in the terminal stages of a particular disease; that the Afro-Jamaican population exhausted home remedies first, and that those remedies sometimes aggravated rather than cured the ailment. While there is no good reason to doubt the truth of these conclusions, we must be careful to place the conclusions in a broader historical context. Firstly, doctors reported on home remedies which did not work, not on those which did, on those which aggravated illnesses, not on those which eased them. It was a Jesuit priest, Rev. Emerick, who conceded from his experience among the Afro-Jamaican population that 'it was common for the bush doctor to succeed where the professional doctor had failed'. He related the story of 'Granny' who cured a doctor's son of dysentery. When the doctor made inquiries about Granny's cures, her answer was simple and to the point: 'Docta! you medicine fe you, me medicine fe me!'[128] If the labouring classes regarded peanut tea as a good tonic, or cerasee as a good substitute for quinine, or lilac spikes mixed with lemon grass and taken with hot water as a cure for fever,[129] they may have done so not because of 'native superstition' but because they believed in the efficacy of these medicines or because official relief agencies were not always readily available. Traditions, like addictions and habits, are difficult to break, and the tradition of African folk medicine had become ingrained in a society where for centuries oligarchs had themselves encouraged cultural lines of division between themselves and their slaves by refusing to offer to the latter European education or religious or other training.

Sheridan observed for the earlier period that:

> The white doctor was both a technician and a coloniser who confronted a colonised and enslaved patient who was reluctant to entrust his life to a stranger. Slaves were generally alienated from

colonial society and tended to fear and mistrust the white doctors
who treated their illnesses.[130]

Such attitudes would not disappear by an act of emancipation. Furthermore,
black medics were able to communicate with their patients in their native
tongue, to make them feel better and thus speed recovery by caring for the
whole patient.[131] Doctors themselves admitted to another major problem
which would not have escaped the notice of the labouring population.
Hospitals were themselves a source of disease.

It is interesting to note by way of comparison that when the North
Americans occupied Haiti in 1915 they identified yaws, malaria, intestinal
parasites and tuberculosis as the major health disorders of that republic.

Of course whether in Haiti or Jamaica, the shortfall in nutrition,
especially 'of calories and proteins, affects working capacity visibly'. The
impression of laziness or lethargy is easily given. If lazy Quashie was really
sickly Quashie, the Jamaican oligarchy in the late-nineteenth century persisted in accepting the idea of Quashie being unwilling to work. R.M.
Hartwell, in his study of the economic history of medical care, has dared to
suggest that advances in health and in longevity that took place in Europe
before the industrial revolution were caused by a breakthrough in the
production of food while medical care had no effect at all'.

While we would not suggest that there were no important developments in medicine – there was the germ theory of disease, the use of
vaccines to combat and to immunise against disease – the reality was that
there were problems of health whose solution dictated social policy initia-
tives towards the improvement of housing, improvement of sanitation,
water supplies, and diet. Medical facilities could not solve problems which
were deeply rooted in a policy of social exploitation which cynically and
callously imposed taxes on the poor for their own poor relief, or taxed
imported protein foods used by the poor.

There were some general measures adopted which during this period
may have served to reduce epidemics. Important sanitation programmes
were launched. For example, there were new regulations for the sanitary
burial of the dead, a sewerage system for Kingston, and regulations for
cleaning the capital city. We could add the centralising of slaughter house
facilities and the isolation of smallpox patients.

Overall there was no significant increase in mortality during the
period, but there was not a decline, either. In a non-epidemic year the death
rate per thousand hovered at about 22 per thousand (compared to the United
Kingdom, 17.8 per thousand). In an epidemic year, for example 1879–80
and 1889–90 the mortality rate climbed to 27.8 and 28.0 respectively, per
thousand.

Doctors working in Jamaica among the poor were acutely aware of the problem of the limitations of their powers in an environment of poverty. It was Dr Donovan who made the point before the 1897 WIRC:

> When diseases such as these, so various, and dependent on such diverse causes, prevail to a very marked degree, attention must naturally be directed to the general life and hygienic surroundings of the people. If we take in order the conditions of life which surround the labourer, and which are essential to his well-being, we would have to consider the air he breathes, the soil he lives on, the water he drinks, the food he uses, the clothes he wears, his social and sexual relations, and many other complex questions.

Notes

1   CO, 137/526, 1886. Attorney General's Report, 21 April, 1886.
2   *JG* (Supplement) Vol. XII, No. 13, 16 May, 1889.
3   *JG*, Vol. XVIII, 1895, p. 1287. 'Number of Paupers to Population'.
4   *JG*, Vol. XII, 16 May, No. 13, 1889. 'Report of Board of Supervision'.
5   Department of State, C8 1/44, 3615/63. Miscellaneous Correspondence 11 January, 1892 – 21 Nov, 1892. Colonial Secretary to Mr Dent, re 'Information for your Government on the charitable societies referred to. A Memorandum by the Secretary of the Board of Supervision of Poor Relief on this Island, dealing with the questions put by you as regards poor relief and the pauper class in this colony'. 8 April, 1892.
6   *Ibid.* Section 6.
7   CO, 137/514, Vol. 2, March-April 1884. 'Report on Lunatic Asylum as of 30th Sept. 1882'.
8   Dept. of State, C8 1/44 Memorandum, *op. cit.* Section 8.
9   CO, 137/518. Governor Norman to Derby, (No. 488) 18 Nov, 1884.
10 *JG*, Vol. XVIII. 1895. Appendix 19, p. 1287. Annual Report of Board of Supervision.
11 *HBJ*, 1880–1900.
12 Jessica Gerard, 'Lady Bountiful: Women of the landed classes and rural Philanthropy', *Victorian Studies*, Vol. 30, No. 2, 1987, pp. 183–209.
13 Jamaica Archives, 'Upward and Onward Society of the Women of Jamaica. Second Annual Meeting and Report', March, 1905. Kingston Educational Supply and Printers. See also *DG*, 17 December, 1904. Report of address of Mrs James Watson, President of Upward and Onward Society.
14 *DG*, 13 Jan, 1886, 'Women's Self Help Society'.
15 *DG*, 17 Dec, 1904, 'Report of address, of Mrs James Watson'.
16 Richard Sheridan, *Doctors and Slaves, A Medical and Demographic History of Slavery in the British West Indies, 1680–1834*, Cambridge: Cambridge University Press, 1985, p. 335.
17 William A. Green, *British Slave Emancipation. The Sugar Colonies and the Great Experiment 1830–1865*, Oxford: Clarendon Press, 1982, p. 310–311.
18 *JBB*, 1889–91 and Frank Cundall, *Jamaica in 1912*, p. 62.
19 Sheridan, *Doctors and Slaves*, p. 342.
20 *HBJ*, 1880–1900.

21   *JBB*, 1889–1891. Report of Registrar-General, and *HBJ*, 1881, 1893–4, and 1899–1900.

22   Sheridan, *Doctors and Slaves*, p. 79.

23   Green, *British Slave Emancipation*, p. 311.

24   J.H. Reid, 'The People of Jamaica Described'. p. 91

25   Keith McDonald, 'Professional Formation: The case of Scottish Accountants' in *British Journal of Sociology*, Vol. 35, 1984, pp. 174–5.

26   *HBJ*, 1894.

27   *DG*, 1 Nov, 1889, 'Poison' to Editor. 'Poison' also observed that apart from competition faced from doctors who ran their own dispensaries, there was competition from merchants 'who with no qualifications [were] dispensing poisons'.

28   *JA*, 6 June, 1896 'Physicians and Dispensers'.

29   *JDR*, 1895–6.

30   *JDR*, 1905–7.

31   *JG*, Vol. XIII, 21 August, 1890. Petition of citizens of Leeward Districts of Hanover.

32   *Ibid*. Petition of inhabitants of Porus.

33   *JDR*, 1891–2, p. 122.

34   *HBJ*, 1894, p. 183. The attendance of medical officers at the houses of patients 'is no longer required'.

35   CO, 137/510. 1883. Mr Gamble (Administrator) No. 270 to Derby, enclosing Rev. John Stuart to Colonial Secretary, 28 March, 1883.

36   *Ibid*.

37   *JDR*, 1885–6. 'Annual Report of the Collector General for year 1885–86 (St James)', p. 89.

38   WIRC, 1897. Evidence of Rev. W.M. Webb, p. 349.

39   CO, 137/520. Report of SMO, Dr Ross, on Public Hospital. Enclosure to Norman, 7 March, 1885.

40   *HBJ*, 1908, p. 171.

41   *JDR*, 1900. 'Report on the Lunatic Asylum for the year ended 31 March, 1900', Dr Plaxton. Table 9: Total No. of Patients under Treatment from 1872–3 to 1899–1900.

42   CO, 137/514 (XC/A 012699). See Table 12, 'Causes of Insanity' in Dr Allen's Report, and Table 9 of the same report for Ages, Occupations of Patients admitted 1882–3.

43   *JDR*, 1900. 'Report on Lunatic Asylum', Table 5 *Causes of Death.*

44   *JDR*, 'Report on the Lunatic Asylum, 1900' Table 8, p. 149; and CO, 137/520. Enclosure to Despatch No. 85, 10 March, 1885.

45   CO, 137/514. Report of Dr Allen on Lunatic Asylum.

46   *JDR*, 1900, 'Report' p. 147, Tables 3 and 4.

47   *Ibid*. p. 153 (Table 11) and CO, 137/520, No. 85, 10 March, 1885, Table 6: *Return of Criminal Lunatics.*

48   Mary C. Karasch, *Slave Life in Rio de Janeiro 1808–1850*, Princeton, New Jersey: Princeton University Press, 1987, p. 175.

49   Sir Sibbald David Scott, Bart. *To Jamaica and Back*, London: Chapman and Hall, 1876, p. 79.

50   WIRC, 1897. Memorandum (No. 780) of Dr J. Donovan to Assistant Colonial Secretary, 24 March, 1897, p. 401/409.

51   *Ibid*. Evidence (5 April, 1897) of Dr Joseph Cargill, p. 326.

52   *DG*, 24 December, 1903, 'Housing for the Poor' by Dolly.

53   WIRC, 1897. Dr Donovan's Memorandum.
54   Jamaica Archives, *Jamaica Memories, Essay of Miss May Jeffrey Smith.*
55   *DG*, 20 December, 1902.
56   Rev. C.A. Wilson, *Men with Backbone and other Pleas for Progress*, p. 20.
57   B.W. Higman, 'Domestic Service in Jamaica since 1750', in B.W. Higman (ed.) *Trade, Government and Society in Caribbean History, 1700 — 1920*, Kingston: Heinemann Educational Books, 1983, p. 130.
58   Report of the Royal Commission upon the Conditions of the Juvenile Population of Jamaica, 1879. Evidence of Enos Nuttall, p. 13.
59   *Ibid*. p. 13.
60   NLJ, MST 209, No. 30, *Bishop's Letter Book*. Rev. King to Rev. Collymore.
61   WIRC, 1897. Dr Donovan's Memorandum.
62   WIRC, 1897. Dr F.A. Sinclair's Memorandum (Section 777) p. 399/409.
63   J.H. Reid, 'The People of Jamaica Described', p. 97–8.
64   Sheridan, *Doctors and Slaves*, p. 202.
65   *Ibid*. p. 206.
66   Mary Karasch, *Slave Life*, p. 179.
67   *Ibid*. p. 179.
68   Sheridan, *Doctors and Slaves*, p. 209.
69   *JDR*, 1882–3. Annual Report of Dr C.B. Mosse, SMO for financial year 1882–3, p. 100.
70   *JBB*, 1899–1900, and 1894–5.
71   *JDR*, 1890–1.
72   *Ibid*.
73   *Ibid*.
74   James Scott, Commissioner of Health, to Hon. H.J. King Kemble, Kingston. 'Papers relating to the present Sanitary State of Kingston', Kingston 1874, p. 23.
75   *JBB*, 1882–3, p. 20 AA. Kingston Public Hospital. 'Table of each kind of Disease treated in the Hospital in the year with the number of Deaths from each such cause'.
76   *JDR*, 1899–1900. Kingston Public Hospital.
77   *JDR*. Important cases 1883–4 to 1892.
78   *JDR*, 1905–1907. Annual Report of Dr Clare.
79   *Ibid*.
80   *JDR*, 1899–1900. Report of Dr J.W. Plaxton on Public General Hospital, Kingston, p. 174.
81   *JDR*, 1899–1900. Report on the Lunatic Asylum for the year ended 31 March, 1900, p. 145.
82   *JDR*, 1895–96. Report on Lunatic Asylum 'Causes of Death'.
83   *JDR*, 1902–3, p. 245.
84   WIRC, 1897. Memorandum of Dr Donovan, 24 March, 1897, p. 401/409.
85   *JDR*, 'Most Important Diseases', 1883–4 to 1892.
86   *JDR*, 1905–7. Dr Clare's Annual Report. 'Death Rates per 1,000 Living'.
87   *JBB*, 1895–6.
88   *HBJ*, 1883. 'Report on St James'.
89   *JBB*, 1895–6.
90   *JDR*, 1893–4. 'Most Important Diseases treated in Hospital'.
91   *Ibid*.
92   *JBB*, 1895–6.
93   *JBB*, 1882–3, p. 20 AA.

94   *JDR*, J.W. Plaxton, 'Report on Public General Hospital', p. 174.
95   *JBB*, 1882–3, p. 20 AA.
96   Morris Fishbein, (ed.) *The New Illustrated Medical and Health Encyclope-dia*, New York: Stuttman Co. 1974, Vol. 4, p. 1370.
97   Sheridan, *Doctors and Slaves*, p. 88 and Mary Karasch, *Slave Life*, p. 167.
99   *JDR*, 1902–3, p. 245.
100   Sheridan, *Doctors and Slaves*, p. 216.
101   *Ibid.* p. 216.
102   *Ibid.* p. 194.
103   *Ibid.* p. 186.
104   *JDR*, 1882–3. Statement of the Most Important Diseases treated in Hospital for the last three years noted in order of frequency, p. 103.
105   Fishbein (ed,) *The New Illustrated*, Vol. 2, p. 505.
106   *JBB*, 1895.
107   Fishbein, *The New Illustrated*, p. 434.
108   *JBB*, 1895.
109   *JDR*, 1899–1900, Kingston Public Hospital 1899–1900.
110   Sheridan, *Doctors and Slaves*, p. 202.
111   Mary Karasch, *Slave Life*, p. 173.
112   *JDR*, 1893–4. Most Important Diseases.
113   *JBB*, 1882–3, F. 20AA, Kingston Public Hospital.
114   *JDR*, 1893–4. Most Important Diseases, 1883–4 to 1892.
115   *Ibid.*
116   *JBB*, 1896. F. 28AA. Hospitals.
117   *Ibid.*
118   *JDR*, 1902–3, p. 247.
119   *Ibid.* p. 247.
120   *JDR*, 1882–3. Report of Dr Mosse, island Medical Dept., p. 100.
121   Fishbein (ed.) *The New Illustrated*, p. 332.
122   WIRC, 1897. Memorandum of Dr Jasper Cargill.
123   *JDR*, 1896–97, p. 42.
124   *JBB*, 1889–91. Report of island Medical Department, p. 458.
125   *JDR*, 1905–7. Dr Clare's Report.
126   Quoted in Sheridan, *Doctors and Slaves*, p. 341.
127   B.W. Higman, *Slave Population and Economy in Jamaica, 1807–1834*, Cam-bridge: Cambridge University Press, 1876.
128   Abraham J. Emerick, S.J., *Jamaica Superstitions: obeah and Duppyism in Jamaica*, Maryland (Woodstock Letters) 1915–16, p. 326 and p. 336.
129   Alice Spinner, 'Duppies'.
130   Sheridan, *Doctors and Slaves*, p. 335.
131   *Ibid.* p. 336.

CHAPTER 10 | Leisure and class in late-nineteenth century Jamaica

The use of leisure is influenced by the economic and social position of individuals.[1] In late-nineteenth century Jamaica the use of leisure emphasised the distinctions between classes, demonstrated the influences of metropolitan lifestyles on Jamaica's upper and middle classes, and highlighted the differences between the cultural practices of the upper and middle classes on the one hand and the working classes on the other. Leisure activity, which is not here narrowly defined to mean amusement, did bring about some limited interaction between rich and poor, and between ethnic groups, but usually on the basis of the assumption of white dominance and coloured/black subordination.

Among the working classes leisure activity was closely associated with traditions sometimes influenced by African culture, but definitely associated with the plantation Creole tradition. Plantation society in Jamaica had always assumed social distance between whites and blacks. The minority whites considered themselves socially isolated, but that isolation was one important reason for closer social intercourse between whites. This sense of isolation seems to have increased rather than decreased at the end of the nineteenth century, leading, it was claimed, to white emigration.

> A hundred years ago towns like Savanna-la-Mar, Montego Bay, Falmouth had a considerable white population. Their descendants today form a mere handful of white and coloured families who have inherited the prejudices but not the wealth of their ancestors. The young men . . . find themselves without congenial associates and without any social life.[2]

Frank Cundall also emphasises the isolation of the whites in a world of blacks:

> With the exception of the planters, government servants and professional men are almost the only cultured members of any community; for there are so few residents of leisure that they may be disregarded entirely. The only residents in any district are those who are there by necessity, engaged in agriculture or trade, the affairs of the Church, education, medicine, law or the collection of taxes, with the occasional retired naval or military officer, who from doing duty in the West Indies, has come to adopt it as his residence.[3]

From Cundall's point of view there were very few people in Jamaica with the proper endowment of 'culture' to make intelligent conversation, and talking is the most universal of pastimes. 'Whether we call it gossip, at which we sneer while engaging in it, or conversation, which is carried on in the drawing rooms as fine art . . . It has a place in every society . . . It enables one to identify with one's milieu'.[4] Visiting one's neighbours or friends for conversation was a regular feature of white Jamaican society, a practice which necessitated the possession of scores of calling cards. House calls, according to Alice Spinner, were 'the professional occupation of the English inhabitants out of business hours, and it is the invariable custom, as in most colonies, to send one's card before entering a house . . . In our little island so many cards are required that one would have to order them by the thousand, months in advance'.[5]

The reality of race in Jamaica facilitated a 'sham criteria of eminence',[6] partly because the social power of the elite rested on the belief that as whites they were the island's repositories of culture. The inequalities of Jamaican society made possible the existence at the top of the society of a minority whose way of life, it was thought, added tone to society. But a little leaven does not always leaven the whole lump. The relationship between elite status, inequality and culture is described in the following words by Tawney:

> Like an oasis which few can inhabit, but the very thought of which brings refreshment and hope to the sand-weary traveller, inequality it is argued, protects the graces of life from being submerged beneath the dust of its daily necessities. It perpetuates a tradition of culture, by assuring the survival of a class which is its visible embodiment, and which maintains that tradition in maintaining itself.[7]

Whatever the imperfections of the elite, they viewed themselves and were viewed as the natural 'centre of light and authority'.[8] The way in which the elite used their leisure emphasised the social and racial distinctions between them and 'plebeian' society. Since education was not intended to be, as Matthew Arnold would have liked to see it, for the pursuit of perfection within a broad humanising process,[9] the elite concept of distance could be maintained by aesthetic distance. Leisure was a mirror of social power and distance, a measure of cultural achievement, and at the same time a reflection of material possession. In Jamaica, the landed class, ruling class or social elite were in terms of persons, the same. Economic interest was pursued in tandem with the effort to maintain and advance social prestige. Leisure and social prestige were inseparable.

There were leisure pursuits in which all Jamaicans participated but in which participation was unequal, and which emphasised the distance between social, cultural and racial groups. One such example is gambling, a peculiar mixture of entertainment and business. The practice of gambling was considered to be the 'main cause of default in the higher stations of life'.[10] In 1890 it was reported that gambling was on the increase in Port Maria in the Billiard Saloons, either in the shape of Pin Pool at from 4/- to 20/- per game, 'which is played openly day and night, from 8.00 a.m. to 11.00 p.m., or at poker in a private room for unlimited stakes'. The report described how a young man 'of decent parentage' came to lose £27 in one gambling session.[11] There was gambling at the races, in the form of the French pool. One opinion was that the French pool was unbusinesslike and unprofitable.[12] It was a gambling issue which sparked off riots at Cumberland Pen in 1894 because the police, carrying out their orders against the illegal sport of gambling, arrested a young man, of presumably a lowly station in life, while leaving elite gamblers untouched.

> . . . the cause of these unseemly disorders can be found in the
> absurd attempt to stop young men in games – call them games of
> chance if you like – which they claim are carried on as a means
> of recreation more than for profit, while the better classes in high
> stations of life were free to hazard at the 'French pool' for the
> large sum of money stated. On such occasions it is far better not
> to see such things . . . But if it is desired that no such acts should
> be tolerated at race meetings, then examples should be sought
> for, without regard to persons. [At the Cumberland Pen Races]
> men occupying high positions were seen with others on the lower
> rung of the social ladder, shoulder to shoulder at the French pool,
> staking money on the different races ... Now we urge that crime
> can only be effectually repressed, and the law respected, if the
> people are made to understand that the laws will be administered
> in a spirit of equality and impartiality, but any attempt to seek out
> victims, as on the occasion at Cumberland Pen, is wrong, and
> must be fruitful of discontent.[13]

Clergymen and other social reformers viewed gambling as a practice which weakened the moral fibre of society. In 1893 the Jamaica Baptist Union and the Ministers Association issued a plea to Governor Blake to enforce more rigorously the laws against gambling in Jamaica.[14] It is probably this effort at more rigorous enforcement of the law which led to the climax at Cumberland Pen when arresting officers were beaten across the back with sticks, leading to the arrest of 51 people for rioting. Despite Blake's insistence that gambling was not on the increase, the arm of the law turned its attention to gambling. The statistics for 1893 reveal an increase in the number of prosecutions. The peak year for prosecutions was in 1900 when there were 173 prosecutions. Convictions were usually 50 per cent of those charged.[15]

In 1896 the *Jamaica Advocate* returned to the problem of gambling, protesting that the practice was so open that 'people ask if there is a law against gambling'.

> Newspapers cannot advertise the lottery. [But] a species of gambling called a lottery is being carried on in this city, every day in the week, in open day, on the street, and on special days until night, characterised by such scenes and such language as are incident to that particular species of evil.[16]

The *Advocate* was referring to the Chinese lottery, which was widely supported by the urban masses.

An article by 'Jacob Omnium' in a column which he called *Olla Podrida*, made a special issue of Chinese gambling which took place, he claimed, without secrecy, under the noses of the authorities, and attracting crowds of 'idle vagabonds' and 'slatternly women' – morning to night. In this game, 'Jacob Omnium' explains, 36 Chinese letters were used. 'The Celestial Banker' selected one of these letters which he recorded on a piece of paper. He 'wraps this up in a cloth and suspends it in sight, but out of reach of the persons present'. The participants take a guess at the number, in exchange for 3d. The prize for a correct guess was 7/3d.[17]

Racing Day was a gathering of all social classes and colours. At least one firm closed its doors at 1.30 p.m. to facilitate the attendance of its employees at the Kingston races on Tuesday, Wednesday and Thursday.[18] A major attraction of the races was that the 'fair sex' was expected to, and did, turn out in large numbers. Usually, on the last day of the races the Grandstand was full of the 'fashionable ladies' of St Andrew.[19] Racing was not confined to Kingston. St Mary, St Elizabeth and Manchester had their racing days as well. In its organisation the races were a true gentleman's sport. The list of Stewards in 1886, which included Louis Verley, prominent planter and businessman, R.H. Jackson, later a member of the Legislative Council, and George Stiebel, an extremely wealthy coloured Jamaican, indicates that organised racing was elite business.[20] The racing industry merged with the business of stud farms, one of them run by a very expert woman.

The period up to 1850 had been marked by the continuous importation of stallions and mares to replenish and improve stocks. (Probably, a good bit of emancipation compensation money went into this importation). Agualta Vale in St Mary, the property of the Hibbert family, appears to have been a very important stud farm. Manchester and St Elizabeth were also important horse-breeding parishes. In the 1880s a new iron stand was erected at the Kingston course. The ADC to Governor Norman, Captain Coxhead, injected new life into racing and added some taste by putting his boys (jockeys) into uniform.[21] Other racers followed suit. In 1886, J.T. Palache (a member of the Legislative Council) entered the turf, adopting the banner of the Manchester Cricket Club (green and gold stripes) for his colours.[22] Captain Kavanagh (ADC to Governor Blake) encouraged racing and together with Mr Verley organised the Cumberland Pen meetings, which inaugurated the Eclipse Stakes.[23] The governors of Jamaica during this period patronised the races. Sir Augustus Hemming seemed dissatisfied with the level of organisation of the races and advocated a strong Racing or Jockey Club which should have the authority to put a stop to various malpractices.[24] The government, perhaps in consequence of retrenchment at the end of the century, withdrew the grants for the Queen's Guineas. (There had been three or four Queen's purses of 100 guineas each run on various parts of the island). Several race tracks at the end of the century reverted to scrub, but Kingston continued to hold its own.

Racing had an appeal for all sectors of the population. An account of racing in Jamaica in 1902 noted that the Afro-Jamaican masses 'found racing to be an affordable sport'. The essayist was probably correct when he also attributed the popularity of racing to the fact that 'in a country like this . . . every adult male owns or used to own a horse'.[25]

Horse racing also took place under the most informal of situations, including at picnics:

> One Christmas we went to a picnic, where the people indulged in all types of sports, including horse racing; the old fashioned kind, where two owners matched their horses, just to see which was fastest.[26]

Dancing was a widespread and popular form of passing leisure time. Among the elite balls could be formidable affairs. In December, 1899, a Bachelor's Ball attracted some 90 couples, dancing to the strains of the band of the Kingston Infantry Militia.[27] The Quadrille, Polka and Caledonia were the dances of the time.[28] These occasions were not always as sizable, however, and were occasionally spontaneous.

> On one hand we had horse-back riding and lavish home entertainment in the way of tennis parties, amateur theatricals, impromptu concerts, and above all dances. As always, for the young people, dance was most popular and I can remember still the large drawing room with its raftered roof, and with old mahogany furniture gleaming in the candle light, with half-a-dozen couples gliding round and round to the strains of an orchestra composed of piano, two violins, and a flute.[29]

The richer folks had their state balls, the poorer ones had their boothes, their dances accompanied by the village drum and fife band and the inevitable violin.[30]

Athletic meets and garden parties were popular forms of entertainment. The garden parties often embraced various miscellaneous sporting activities, geared for amusement rather than for Olympic style competition. The winning high jumper at the Port Royal games in July 1885 just made an anaemic 4ft 10.5in. There were menagerie races, mule races, three-legged races, obstacle races, cricket matches, wishing wells, recitational tableaux, minstrels, competitions for best floral designs, fireworks, merry-go-rounds, mazes, (in imitation of Hampton Court), bands of music, restaurants and bars.[31] A garden party at Winchester Park could attract up to 2,000 people. The garden party was an attractive way to raise funds, and was so used by churchmen and by the Jamaica Horticultural Society.

Cricket, whose rules, like football, had been reframed and revised, was among Jamaica's most popular sports. It was during the late-nineteenth century that Jamaica's cricket clubs came into being: the Kingston Cricket Club (300 members in 1903), the Melbourne Club, Lucas and Kensington, Manchester and St Elizabeth. They always seemed to have a precarious financial existence. Games were organised at the international level for the first time. The first West Indian Cricket Team was organised in the 1890s, funded by private subscription.[32]

Cricket had not yet become a major professional sport, but was an important mechanism for bringing about elite social gatherings. The match scheduled for New year's Day, 1900, to raise funds for the Melbourne Cricket Club pavilion, for example, was described as a 'Grand Fancy Costume Cricket Match'. There was, according to the advertisement, to be great fun, splendid costumes, clowns, gowns, and personages past and present. The Kingston Infantry Militia (KIM) Band was scheduled to perform.[33] While other cricketing occasions did not have the fanfare of this particular one, yet it seems that the sport was more an occasion for elite social gatherings than for the professional exercise of an art.

In 1888, a cricket team visited from the United States, and lost to the Kingston Cricket Club, but won three other matches. In 1895 the Slade Lucas team lost at Sabina Park to an all Jamaica team but won four matches outside Kingston. In 1897, the Priestly team defeated everyone in sight in Jamaica.[34] Cricket was encouraged among schoolboys in secondary schools. This was cricket with its focus on cosmopolitan standards, equipment, rules, texts, style, bats and balls and gloves and pads, which could be purchased at Ayre's in down-town Kingston.[35]

Cricket had another face. This was the cricket of interdistrict rivalry when students travelled from village to village, singing, with a standard bearer in front to give competition to a rival village. These matches took place on holidays and during weekends. Buns, cakes and lemonade sufficed for lunch. Cricket gear was crude, with home-made bats and balls, including those from bamboo root. The prize was sometimes a large and tasty cornpone.

These were mini-fairs in which women turned out not so much to watch the fun as to sell baked products, candies, and ginger beer to the onlookers. Cricket clubs were widely disseminated throughout the island.

Equipment was not expected, as we have said, to conform to British standards. But a boy who had a 'regular' bat could be teased 'You gwine play wid gentleman t'ing, mind rat cut you han' tonight!' The game of cricket is associated with an immaculate elegance, so many boys put on their Sunday best, their 'Sunday tweeds'. A day's cricket soiled that elegance. Hence the comment of a captain to his long-stop 'Das right, dutty you tweed an 'tap de ball!'[36] Cricket was widespread but the rifts in society showed up in cricket pitches, environment, and probably approach.

It should be mentioned, in passing, that the West Indian Regiment was very active in all sporting activities, and Up-Park-Camp was always an important venue for sports meetings. Not only in cricket but also in football the men of the Leicestershire Regiment and his Majesty's Men at Port Royal were important.

A leisure activity which was the province of both elite and mass was listening to band concerts. Brass orchestras and other bands had become popular in England, so popular in fact that the masses of that country virtually took them over as a mass amusement.[37] By the end of the nineteenth century the band had become more 'respectable' and composers began to write music specifically for brass bands. The flexibility as well as the ability of bands to stand up to unpredictable weather conditions made them ideal for public entertainment. In Jamaica, the introduction of bands was yet another example of metropolitan influences on colonial culture. The West Indian Regiment and the Kingston Volunteer Militia bands performed during intermission time at public functions, including the theatre and the races, at cricket matches and at the Victoria Market on Christmas morning. On Wednesday or Thursday afternoons there was band music in public parks. These concerts were well attended though subscriptions from the audience were less than the bands had hoped. Attempts to establish bands were made in Black River and Port Antonio. The Salvation Army, which made its appearance in Jamaica in 1886, also attracted much of its mass support by the stirring strains of its various bands.

Ensembles thrived in late-nineteenth century Jamaica. There were choral societies and singing groups, whose combination of the secular and the sacred particularly appealed to churchgoers. There was the Montego Bay Coloured Concert Troupe – presumably founded by non-whites, the Kingston Choral Union, the Dominion Concert Troupe, the Spanish Town Choral Union and the Philharmonic Association of Montego Bay.[38] The Kingston Choral Union was led and directed by a black Jamaican, it gave regular performances and early in the twentieth century carried off first prize in a public choral competition.[39] It was in existence from at least 1885.

A Kingston Choral Union concert in June 1895 performed 'Dip Dem Bedward in de Healing Stream', and their performance was followed by comedian W.C. Murray ('Funny' Murray) who rendered his 'Bedward in the 'Sylum', dancing himself off the stage 'amidst a chrous of boisterous mirth'.[40]

Among the middle and upper classes literary and debating societies were established. Here again, there is an inevitable social dichotomy. The Institute of Jamaica had been founded by Sir Anthony Musgrave, and during Sir Henry Norman's governorship the Victoria Institute was established. The Institute of Jamaica aimed for the intellectual improvement of its members, and the promotion and cultivation of a taste for literature, science and art in Jamaica generally. The Institute was inaugurated in celebration of the Victoria Jubilee with 156 members which grew to 367 (including 36 lady subscribers) by 1889. Among its members, we are told, were 'many of the principal inhabitants of Kingston and other parts of the island'. It issued a quarterly journal, made available to readers of British and American periodicals, and sponsored lectures on literary, scientific and economic matters.

Widespread illiteracy made access to the Institute of Jamaica library and to the Victoria Institute impossible for most Jamaicans. A survey of what Jamaicans read in 1894 is revealing. What people read was influenced by the English papers, but stories of 'local colour' were popular. One such work was Alice Spinner's *A Study in Colour*. Shakespeare held his own, and so did Thackeray, Dickens and Scott. Among the 'lower classes' the most popular work was Bunyan's *The Pilgrim's Progress*, and works of a semi-religious nature such as *The Dream Book, Cain and Abel, Life of Joseph, The Book of Fate, Peep O'Day, Basket of Flowers, Baxter's Forty Coming Wonders, Thorns and Orange Blossoms*.[41] One bookseller was of the view that the 'standard of popular reading in Jamaica is not perhaps too high but it is, I think, a good sign that the people are reading at all'. A scathing criticism of Jamaican reading habits came from the clergyman Rev. C.A. Wilson, though his critique showed his awareness of the weaknesses of the educational system itself.

> Love of literature is not a marked feature of the life of the average Jamaican. In towns and increasingly in rural districts, newspapers find a large number of readers. Magazines and third rate novels are eagerly grabbed by a few. The large majority read little or nothing. They lack the love for literature, not because of inability to appreciate, but because so little has been done to cultivate a taste for reading. School life is more or less drudgery, unpleasantly connected with the rod, and cannot be said on the whole to create a love of knowledge for its own sake. The

majority of teachers read little apart from the newspapers. Facilities for reading [are] few. Lack of means prevents many from purchasing books.[42]

Wilson suggests that when the novelty of the library of the Institute of Jamaica had worn off, the books remained untouched. Penny Dreadfuls were becoming very popular in Jamaica at the end of the nineteenth century.

Literature by Jamaican authors such as W. Adolphe Roberts, Tom Redcam and H.G. deLisser, was steadily making its appearance; short stories began to appear which detailed, interestingly enough, the life of pre-British Jamaica. The prototype of this kind of work is to be found in deLisser's *Arawak Girl*. Several stories made their first appearance in the pages of the *Daily Gleaner*.

Much of the literature on Jamaica at this period was written by expatriates visiting the West Indian colonies about which judgments, usually adverse, were made – with swiftness, certainty, and prejudice. J.A. Froude is only the most well known, and like Froude most writers were 'experts' on all the West Indian colonies, and probably the British empire as a whole. There was H. de R. Walker, *The West Indies and the Empire* based on 'study and travel' in the winter of 1900–1, published in 1902, Sir Sibbald David Scott, Bart. *To Jamaica and Back* (1876), a title which reflected, it seems, some concern for his safety, and John William Root, *The British West Indies and the Sugar Industry* (1899) which severely (unusually) criticised the social policy (or rather the lack of it) of the Crown Colony administration.

Dr James Johnston, who had taken up residence in Jamaica, wrote specifically to encourage tourism (*Jamaica: The New Riviera: a pictorial Description of the Island and its Attractions*). Augusta Zelia Fraser, writing under the pseudonym 'Alice Spinner', had come to Jamaica with her husband, the Surveyor-General and Inspector of the Railway, in the 1890s, and during her stay produced novels of the 'costumbrista' type. (*A Study in Colour* (1894); *A Reluctant Evangelist and Other Stories* (1896); *Margaret: a Sketch in Black and White; Lucilla: An Experiment*). Frazer's stories were less concerned with elaborately woven plots than with the exotic customs of Creole Jamaica-language, dress, courtship, marriage, colour and race. Grant Allen, who had been appointed Professor of Mental and Moral Philosophy in the College at Spanish Town, and was to publish fairly well-known detective/crime stories (such as *An African Millionaire*, (1897) wrote two stories which were influenced by his stay in the island. *Ivan's Great Master-Piece* (1893), and *A Woman's Hand* are stories about the fidelity of members of the coloured race to the white race.

In literary-cum-dramatic output the masses of the island were used to give 'local colour'. Even before Tom Redcam wrote his first poem in the

local 'dialect' at the turn of the century, or Claude McKay published his
Songs of Jamaica, W.C. Murray was using the local scene, local incidents,
and the Jamaican Creole. Most of Murray's work has not been preserved.
We have already noted his satirical comment on Bedward ('Bedward in de
'Sylum'); he also responded to the Montego Bay riots of 1902 with 'Hol' de
light; Rockstone da come'. In an introduction to one of his few extant works
(*A day with Joe Lennan, the Rosewell Duppy Doctor*, and *Tommy Silvera or
Suck O' Peas Sil*) in 1891, Murray insisted that no 'ill-will was intended in
his satirical humour'.

> Every race has its characteristic traits; those of the Anglo-African
> race are too well known throughout the West Indies to need
> enlarging upon . . . It may be, in fact it must be, that the growth
> of education will make a wide difference between the coming
> and the past generations of Jamaicans: but no amount of educa-
> tion, no acquired facility in the use of well-chosen words and of
> finely-rounded grammatical periods will, to my mind, quite atone
> for the loss of the quaintly quipped or unduly elongated words,
> the quick and often utterly illogical repartee, the strangely apt
> and frequently far-fetched similes and allusions which character-
> ise the conversation – or shall I call it the chatter? – of such men
> as Tommy Silvera, Lennan and Benjy. They are types of a
> generation that is passing away.

Murray insisted that his characters and incidents reflected real people and
situations.[43]

The Jamaican elite paid some attention to theatre. The first Theatre
Royal was built in 1838 by subscription of the House of Assembly and by
public subscription. It was rebuilt in 1900 and destroyed by the great
earthquake of 1907.[44] The Ward Theatre was donated to the city of Kingston by Colonel Ward, a wealthy planter, merchant and more or less a
founder of the contemporary firm of J. Wray and Nephew. The Ward
Theatre was the venue for various operettas, dramatic presentations by
foreign and local groups such as the McDowell Company and the Kingston
Dramatic Association, respectively. There were also pantomimes at Christmas, and the themes reflected a continued attachment to metropolitan
stories – 'Dick Whittington and his Cat' (at the Port Royal Naval Canteen
in 1899) and in 1898 'Aladdin'. The principal 'boy' was usually played by
a lady. Efforts were made to inject Aladdin with local 'colour'.[45]

Cycling was another popular pastime for the upper and middle class.
Cycling attracted thousands of fans per year in Britain, and seaside resorts
provided bicycles for those who could not afford to own them.[46] Even mass
production had not been able to place bicycles within the reach of most
Britons, but at least the seaside holiday helped to place them within tem-

porary reach of vacationers. There is no evidence of this level of 'democratisation' of cycling in Jamaica where it was for the most part an elite pastime. An unofficial tally of bicycles in Kingston in 1903 was 531.[47] Riding parties of cyclists supplemented horse-back riding as a leisure pursuit. Young men used the opportunity to tour the various parishes of the island by bicycle. In May, 1886, Captain Coxhead spearheaded the formation of the Jamaica Bicycle Club, under the patronage of Governor Norman. In 1886 there were twenty members who paid a quarterly subscription of 5/- per head.[48] By 1897 the Victoria Cycle Club had been established, inaugurating cycle races at a track in Newton Square.[49] In 1903 an effort was made to establish a Cycling Association.[50]

The average cost of a bicycle was £8, and the life span, it was claimed, was just about two years.[51] It was in this context that the imposition of a 10/- tax on bicycles in 1899 was vigorously condemned by the elite at public meetings. They had other objections, such as failure to make arrangements for tourists whose bicycles would also be taxed, and the adverse effects of the tax on 'a great number of clerks in shops etc. who rode to work'.[52] By the end of the nineteenth century the novelty of bicycle riding seems to have worn off, and the functional rather than the leisure value of the bicycle was coming to be exercised.

Women, whose leisure time activity was much more circumscribed than that of men, were among the more avid cyclists both in Jamaica and overseas. At first, it was thought indecorous for ladies to ride, and cycling was believed to be unhealthy for women contributing, it was thought, to unspecified gynaecological disorders.[53] The problem was partly solved by the invention of the Ladies Wheel and by the invention of the bloomers, for which both Americans and Frenchmen claim paternity. In Jamaica an associated pastime was the abuse (and sometimes assault) of women who rode.[54] Whatever the decline in popularity may have been cycle races became part of the activities at garden parties, and up to 1899 at least, Governor Hemming extended his patronage to cycle races in Kingston.[55]

Another leisure activity which was closely associated with the elite and in which women participated was lawn tennis, despite the restraints on their mobility imposed by their voluminous dresses.[56] Women also played golf.[57] The strong support given to the participation of women in tennis is demonstrated in the decision of Kings House to open its lawn tennis courts for a play-off between two young women.[58]

Another sport closely related to the elite strata of Jamaican society was hunting. It is true that Jamaica's wild life is, and was, limited. However, during this period there were still wild boars in the island, and the guns of hunters were trained upon them and upon bird life – white wings, baldplates, peadoves, blue pigeons, ring-tail pigeons, partridge and quail, shovel-bill ducks, the white-belly, the teal and snipe. The close season was from the end of March to the end of July. 'Three hundred birds to twelve guns' was no unusual bag in the morning.[59] Restrictions were placed on the destruction of the humming bird whose feathers had a high decorative value. Hunters also found some amusement in crocodile stalking and shooting, though the habitat of the crocodile was the malarial swamp. There were crocodiles 10 ft long.[60] Those who preferred to sport at sea fished for sharks, salmon, or callipera, snork, devilfish and snapper.[61] The mongoose, which had been introduced to destroy rats, became victim to hunters.[62]

Another sport, associated with the elite, was cockfighting, which was illegal. There was a rink on a Westmoreland sugar estate organised by the overseer and a local shopkeeper every Sabbath evening.[63] The sport was also well known in Arthur's Pen near Spanish Town.[64]

Jamaica is a tropical island, but the relationship between the island and a temperate to cold metropolis made the island a venue for ice sports, which were becoming popular in North America and Britain.[65] Once the technology of the skating rink had been perfected a rink was established at Marina Villa, Rae Town. Jamaicans added their own local colour by incorporating a 'Carnival' into the show – really a costume parade. A winning costume was A.S. Figueroa's King of Diamonds, and second place was Mr DaCosta's 'fancy dress girl'.[66] This performance was associated with the more general masquerade practice whereby 'respectable' young men dressed as Red Indians or in female attire, patrolling the streets, visiting the homes of friends, who would pretend not to know who they were. Each member of the troupe offered a weekly dance.[67]

Elderly ladies and gentlemen who could no longer undertake rigorous exercise by way of horse-back riding, bicycling or athletics could indulge themselves in horticulture or dog-rearing. The Jamaica Horticultural Society was active and there were regular exhibitions in Kingston and Mandeville. The Kendal Agricultural Show indicated, too, that dog-rearing was an important leisure pursuit. According to a report on the 1899 show there were present a wide variety of dogs – St Bernards, Newfoundlands, Bloodhounds, Mastiffs, Retrievers, Spaniels, Bull-terriers, Daschunds, and Fox-terriers.[68]

The common interests of individuals and their shared social, cultural and economic interests can be expressed in an informal way: but these relationships can be formalised in the establishment of organisations or clubs which reflect those common interests. The club is more or less an association of equals meeting on common ground, and probably contributing a fee of some kind which is regulated by the equal economic and social standing of the individuals. The late-nineteenth century saw the establishment of various clubs and societies, which reinforced the economic and social cleavages, and sometimes directly, at other times indirectly, the racial cleavages of Jamaican society.

It was during this period, for example, that the St Andrew Lawn Tennis Association was founded. The older Manchester Club combined tennis, golf, and other sporting activities such as cricket. They were exclusive clubs. In 1885, the Yacht Club (later the Royal Jamaica Yacht Club) was organised with Captain Forwood (Manager of the Atlas Steamship Company) as Commodore. In mid-May 1885 the Yacht Club had 50 members, and the first race entered vessels ranging from canoes to 4 ton boats.[69] Mr George Stiebel, described as a gentleman of considerable wealth, great social standing,[70] and ample leisure, bought a boat (*Maggie*) for £135.[71] Stiebel was viewed by some as the wealthiest man in Jamaica. Starting life as a carpenter the coloured youth made his fortune overseas and returned to Jamaica to invest his acquired income in real estate, racing, and other enterprises.[72] Another coloured Jamaican who was a member of the Yacht Club, and was later to be a commodore was the Solicitor-General of Jamaica, William Baggett-Gray, the nephew of the founder of Gray's Charity. The Yacht Club held annual regattas, and was the gentleman's sport, par excellence, at Easter Tide or when the royal navy visited the island. The first annual regatta so dubbed was conducted on the Anniversary of the Queen's Birthday in 1886. But the Yacht Club was more than an association of people dedicated to yachting. The headquarters of the club boasted a billiard room, whist tables, and a cool and airy reading room.[73] As a matter of fact, the *Daily Gleaner* concluded in 1894 that yachting was a farce and that the Jamaica Yacht Club had practically no connection with yachting, apart from one or two genuine enthusiasts. 'Yachtsmen among the several hundred members cannot justify the institution using the indicative prefix before 'club'. We suggest that the word 'Yacht' be omitted. The 'Royal' would distinguish it from the other social club on Hanover Street'.[74]

It is not improbable that the golf clubs of Constant Spring, Mandeville, Kingston and St Andrew behaved in very much the same way – socialising rather than sporting. Entry into the Kingston Cricket Club required an invitation by a member.[75]

There are other activities which, because they create new obligations and can be time consuming, may seem to deny their inclusion within the framework of leisure activity. But since, as Dumazadier has noted, 'Individuals are free to decide how to use their free time',[76] the assumption of duties within mutual aid societies, freemasonry associations, charity organisations, Temperance Societies, Christian Endeavour Societies, and so on, must be viewed as ways in which people used their leisure in Jamaica at the end of the nineteenth century. It is an error to assume that leisure is tantamount to self-indulgence and cannot be used for the benefit of society as a whole.

In the thirty years between 1870 and 1900 several associations were established – Friendly Societies, Masonic Lodges, Provident Societies.

Most rested on the principle of mutual aid. Of the associations established the Masonic fraternity was perhaps the one most closely associated with elite life and leisure. Masonic lodges are very selective in their recruitment, a factor which makes it possible for them – on the principle of the brotherhood of all men before God – to ignore, if they wish, social and racial cleavages in a society.

Masonic fraternities were not racially exclusive, and included men of varied occupations – from Governor Sir Henry Blake to wealthy banana merchants, doctors, and lawyers.[77] William Baggett-Gray, the Solicitor-General was simultaneously a Steward of Mark Master Provincial Grand Lodge of Jamaica, and Master of Sussex Mark Lodge, No. 42. Colonel Ward was a leading member of the Ancient Order of Foresters, Dr A.A. Robinson was District Grand Treasurer of District Lodge of Jamaica, as well as Junior Deacon of the Mark Master Provincial Grand Lodge of Jamaica.[78] The venerable Archdeacon George William Downer (1837–1912), Archdeacon of Surrey and Rector of Kingston Parish Church, was a Freemason who belonged 'in his early days' to the Jamaica Lodge No. 1771. He was a founder of the United Service Lodge No. 1873 (this lodge did not survive) and from 1883–6 he was District Grand Chaplain of the district Grand Lodge of English Freemasons in Jamaica. His commitment to Freemasonry was demonstrated in 1883 when the 'foundation stone of the extension to the Parish Church was laid with masonic honours with the Deputy District Grand Master and representatives of all Lodges being present 'at what was probably one of the biggest public occasions in the history of Freemasonry in Jamaica'. In 1891 there was another important masonic ceremony at the Parish Church when a stained glass window was dedicated as a memorial to Dr Robert Hamilton, MD 'a famous former District Grand Master after whom the present Hamilton Lodge is named'.[79]

An extremely active group in late-nineteenth century Jamaica was an International Order of Grand Templars (IOGT) which unlike the Freemason fraternity which was entirely an organisation of men, included women in their membership and among their office holders. The IOGT was an ardent advocate of temperance, and in this respect was part of that expanding group of temperance societies, some of which were linked to the Churches. Strong drink was forbidden at their meetings. The independent Order of Good Samaritans and Daughters of Samaria was a women's Lodge association.[80]

Dr J. Robert Love, editor of the *Advocate*, established a branch of the Spark's Lodge in Jamaica, with himself as master, and the poet Thomas McDermot as one of the principal officers.[81]

Lodges were among the middle and upper class organisations in late-nineteenth century Jamaica involved simultaneously with mutual aid, works of charity, and social intercourse. They were neither racially nor occupationally exclusive. The black stockraiser and member of the Parochial Board of Spanish Town, Joseph Gordon, held office in the Hamilton Lodge in 1885.[82] In an interview with a coloured merchant of Port Antonio an American visitor reported:

> In speaking of the colour problem, the merchant affirmed that whites, Cubans, blacks and browns were members of the several secret societies to which he himself belonged. As to the real social intercourse between the races there is a line drawn, although not as definable as in the United States, he confessed.[83]

The implication was that while Freemasonry or secret societies were racially integrated, lodges did not represent the 'real social intercourse between the races', at the general social level.

Twenty-five societies were established between 1863 and 1903 under the Friendly Societies Act. Most provided for poor relief, funeral expenses, illness, old age, disability and distress. Others were designed to assist specific occupational groups among Jamaica's working class – such as the Cigarmakers Friendly and Benevolent Society.[84] The Chinese and the Jewish segments of the population also established their benevolent associations.

The Jamaican elite seemed, from this perspective in time, to have had much to do by way of passing their times of leisure: home entertainments, balls, outings to Rockfort and Port Henderson, horse-back and bicycle riding, sea-bathing, impromptu concerts, choral singing, literary and debating societies, hunting, sports, charity work, Freemasonry, horticulture, gambling, billiards, reading.

We now turn to the way in which other groups, outside the middle and upper classes, used their leisure time. Workers and labourers have less time for leisure, the very possession of which is an indication of social rank. One of the suggestions made about working class leisure time is that it is spent passively – watching events rather than participating in them – a period in which the batteries are recharged for renewed work the following day. One of the factors making for clear differences between working class and elite leisure is the financial incapacity of workers to participate in such activities as require investment in sports infrastructure – tennis, golf, yachting. Other leisure activities are out of the reach of workers because of what we might term the absence of cultural preparation.

Middle and upper class leisure pursuits were, as we have noted, sometimes geared towards the masses as objects of charity, or moral upliftment – the YMCA, Women's Self-Help Society, The Upward and Onward Society. In these activities they were not the actors but those acted upon, without, understandably, consultation. Patronising attitudes are part of the elite ambience but do not always receive the unqualified support of the beneficiaries. An angry correspondent to the *Gleaner* in May 1885 showed his feelings about a YMCA meeting in May 1885, at which there was a

> considerable number of the aristocracy, who are the patrons of the movement, whilst the body of the room was thickly occupied by the democracy or plebeians or by whatever name you please, who are to be patronised, reformed, and rescued from the intoxicating cup, the gambler's den, in a word, from the evils which Rev. D.J. East found to exist in large Dry Goods establishments. The idea conveyed to Spectator's mind was that the Institution should more appropriately be styled 'Young Man's Reformatory Association' for the implications of the speeches (are) that so many of the young men of Kingston are given to drink, thieving and other immoralities.[85]

The extent to which people can indulge in leisure activity is partly related to the availability of public holidays. In Jamaica, specifically, there were no provisions for general public holidays until 1893. It was in 1870 that a bill was introduced into the British Parliament designed to offer holidays to British bank employees. That item of legislation had tremendous utility for Englishmen in terms of leisure.[86] From Governor Blake's Despatches in 1893 it appears that the only compulsory public holidays in Jamaica at that time were Good Friday and Christmas. The other holidays such as the Great Storm (28 August), New Year's Day, Ash Wednesday, Easter Monday, Queen's Birthday, Great Earthquake (7 June) were described by Blake as optional, and were essentially holidays 'kept in public offices and not the public's general holidays prescribed by law'.[87] A bill introduced into the Jamaican Legislature to liberalise the holidays law was opposed by some members. Blake himself thought that the bill, if passed into law, would deprive of their employment a large number of the labouring population, thus creating (so Blake argued) possible disaffection. Moreover, the interruption of regular telegraphic services and communications could adversely affect merchants.[88]

The bill was passed into law (Law 36, 1893: The Public General Holidays Law) and allowed the following holidays:

> New Year's Day
> Ash Wednesday
> 1 August (First Monday in August)
> Day after Good Friday
> Easter Monday
> Monday in Whitsun week
> Day after Christmas Day
> Day appointed by the Governor to be kept as Birthday of the reigning sovereign.

(February 2–6 had, since 1886, been denominated as Chinese holidays).[89] When the Law came up for revision in 1895, Robert Love suggested that 1 August be confirmed among the holidays 'because it has tender associations for the majority of the people whose wishes are not to be despised'. The *Advocate* also pleaded that the legislation include not only clerks of mercantile houses and other such establishments, but the cook, housemaid, footman, and toiler on the estate.[90] The principle of public holidays had been accepted, however, since 1893. In Jamaica, Sunday had for long been a day away from work, and only the Atlas Steamship Company employed on the Sabbath. Jamaica, unlike England, had no need of a Sabbatarian lobby to keep the Lord's Day a day of rest.

Churchgoing performed an important religious and social function for the rural population. Churches attracted large congregations from miles around. Church services were expected to be and were long, and between morning service, Sunday School and Evensong church attendance was an all-day affair.[91] The Bishop of Sierra Leone, who visited Jamaica between 1891–2, was wryly impressed by the stamina of the Jamaican peasant congregation. Referring to a district in Clarendon in particular, the Bishop concluded that Church gatherings combined 'features of a religious meeting, a horseshow, and picnic'.[92] The church, he claimed, was crammed to suffocation. (The heavy attendance at church, in this case, may have been attributable in part to the desire of Afro-Jamaicans to hear news of Africa).[93] The benefits of Church were clearly not only of the spirit, however, for 'vendors of all sorts of cakes and fruit and ginger beer, bent on enabling the good folk to make a day of it' were in large attendance outside the church doors. Three hour services and in one case a five hour service did not dampen the ardour of the congregation.[94]

During Easter the Churches hosted sacred cantatas to the glory of God but also for the wholesome leisure of the population, and for raising funds. Where the Church was not hosting lantern slides and garden parties, the local schools (usually linked with the Churches) offered concerts which drew large crowds, providing audiences with songs, recitations and dramatic presentations.

The Churches were the major link or bridge between Afro-Jamaica and Euro-Jamaica, and between urban and rural life. These functions of the Church were important if for no other reason than that Afro-Jamaican leisure activity was so often associated with religious practice.

There were aspects of Afro-Jamaican leisure which the Church frowned upon – such as the tea meeting which was an entirely secular affair among Afro-Jamaicans. It was designed both for entertainment and for fundraising:

> The person keeping the tea-meeting would buy a crown bread
> and when the people gather they would bid for pieces of the

bread. Sometimes a piece of bread would be sold for 2/6, 1/6, 2/-. This would go on until the bread finished. Next they would go on until the break of day. In some cases they would dance after cutting of the bread until day-light.[95]

Archbishop Nuttall was scandalised when one of his clergymen (at Birnam Wood in Buff Bay) was reported to have conducted a tea meeting all night at the church. The Bishop, always suspicious of all-night meetings and of the 'immoral' things which could take place under cover of darkness, testily demanded an explanation from the erring priest.[96] Below is a more elaborate description of a tea meeting:

Invitations [were] sent especially to about a dozen soldiers. A belle of the village was asked to be queen. This was an all-night affair and elaborate preparations were made. A boothe was erected with a platform at the one end and a decorated chair as the queen's throne. A man was employed as leader of the singing. The charge for admission was 3d. People arrived (at 7.00 p.m.). The soldiers would enter with their guns looking very impressive in their imitation uniforms – a cardboard cap with a red band and a yellow tassel attached to the centre and hanging behind, white blouse with decorative red bands in front, black pants with two yellow braids . . . down the sides and a pair of black boots. Singing would start and the people arranged themselves in ranks of six and then they go 'bragging' around the booth all singing lustily in answer to the leaders. It is so far away that I have almost forgotten, but one of the favourites was:

Ju [dew], ju rain a come
Jubba yearie day;
Ans.   Whai-o, Whai-o wha Julina

Jubba yearie tunder da roll
Jubba yearie dey.
Ans.   Whai-o, Whai-o, wha Julina

To this they go stamping in rhythm round the leader who shouts: Back! Back! and they all stamp backwards. It was fun. Midnight came and the queen arrived exquisitely dressed in silk gown with a crown of gold on her head. She would be escorted by two lines of soldiers to the tune 'Queen jus' arrive, oh money come show, show money, show like a queen bank a show'. Then started selling of the Crown Bread. The principal drink for the night was 'Santa' something like our Rum Punch but a little stronger. Morning dawns and then after the queen has changed her dress, the whole party parades through the main street of the village.[97]

So with the revels ended, and the flights of fancy terminated, the pageant left 'not a rack behind'.

Work and leisure are sometimes difficult to separate among workers. European Jamaica was always scandalised by the practice among Afro-Jamaicans of peeling ginger at night, an exercise which continued until daylight. They were prone to think that ginger peeling was yet another exercise in 'native' immorality leading to pregnancies among young working women, and to the aggravation of Jamaica's 'problem' of illegitimacy. Ginger peeling, was, however, part of the pattern of communal or reciprocal labour which could perhaps in this case be best offered at night after the day's work. To divert themselves from the tedium of the work a ginger-peeling match was organised. The work was accompanied by singing of folk melodies and Sankeys.[98]

On digging days the tedium of labour was relieved by the pleasure of communal singing. Between April and July the sound of blowing shells summoned fellow workers to a 'digging match'. From the fifty or so workers assembled a good singer was selected, and

> a rod in hand he stood before the diggers with hoes or pick axes in hand, he signalled the diggers, each stood ready; with a loud voice the singer sung their favourite digging song: 'Mi go ha wood', the diggers with raised tools replied 'boa, boa, boa', the singer again sung 'Me si one boa' and chorus, 'Boa, Boa, Boa'. At the last boa by the diggers every tool reached the earth and ascended the air, in unison.[99]

Archbishop Nuttall was impressed by the digging song as an expression of musical talent among Jamaican workers.[100]

Communal singing by boatmen hauling logwood was common on the partly navigable Black River. These songs were often based on local incidents. ('One had to be careful what they did [sic] for at a slip they would compose a song and then either dance to it or dig ground to it').[101] The following two songs of the boatmen referred to the Merry-go-round, and to the material improvement of a minister of religion:

> Ride for a ride you ride the go-round
> When you a go you pon right hand
> When you a come you come pon left hand
> Destant (Decent) gal them live a upstairs.

> Parson Cover buy buggy before us
> Oh poor us! poor us!

Talking assists labour as well, though among a large collection of workers the effect can be something like the Tower of Babel. United States Consul,

Mr Hoskinson, reported on his first experience at an orange packing depot in the following way:

> The scene in one of these [orange] packing houses is a novel one to the stranger, and is not calculated to impress one accustomed to witness the orderly and silent proceedings of manufactories that employ large numbers of people in the United States and Europe. Between the wrangling of the man who brings his fruit for sale and the superintendent of these establishments and the thousand and one discordant *laughs, yells and songs* of the wrappers you can with difficulty hear yourself speak . . . [It is not] an uncommon sight after the barrel has been filled with fruit and heaped up . . . preparatory to its being headed up, to see one of the 'dusky maidens' place a flat piece of board on top and throw her whole weight in a sitting posture on it, for the purpose of squeezing down the contents of the barrel; this operation I need hardly say has the effect of reducing the upper portion of the oranges in the barrel to pulp.[102]

The relationship between song and labour was also commented on by J.H. Reid in 1888:

> He [the rural worker] is not given to street brawls, but is rather noisy at his play of which he is very fond. Once fairly on the swing, he pours his whole nature into that, and for the time is willing to forego a great deal else . . . See him at his toil singing his 'bambaho'. He works to the astonishment of the beholder, as long as he is excited by his song, by the use of which he has succeeded in reducing his toil to amusement.[103]

Christmas, Easter, and August were the high season of entertainment. There were in the 1880s ex-slaves who continued year after year to celebrate emancipation in their own way.

> When I was a boy many old slaves in Negril were alive, and it was customary for the slaves to assemble at the Presbyterian chapel in the village on 1 August each year to celebrate the anniversary of emancipation. [There were hymns and prayers] and the Catechist explained the disadvantages of slavery and the benefits of emancipation. When he had finished the slaves present ascended the platform and each alternately in crude vernacular related personal experiences of slavery life. Some tales [were] ludicrous some pathetic, but one could easily see that they were cruelly ill-treated by masters. After this service . . . the congregation moved on to Negril Square to join the bigger crowd. There was feasting and dancing under the spreading sea-grape tree.

The dancing (which the author found to be governed by 'grotesque motions') continued until evening when some 'were led home intoxicated'.[104]

It was thought that John Canoe (Jancoonoo, Jan Cannu) was dying out, and was confined to the 'least enlightened' segment of the population. Such was the view of J.H. Reid, a black Jamaican of liberal and progressive cast of mind:

> A Jancoonoo is a miniature of a mansion, constructed of cardboard. From its windows a number of miniature ladies looking out upon the scenes around . . . Music for the occasion issues forth from the voices of the set girls who sing in chorus in response to the 'maam' accompanied by beating the 'cocoo' drum and the 'goombay' . . . it would appear as if the object of a Jancoonoo play originally was praise of the master or owner of the slaves concerned and the condemnation of all others. But this kind of amusement has lost its charm for the intelligent peasantry and is deservedly discouraged by them. Hence it only exists in the most unenlightened parts.[105]

School entertainments, dancing and concerts were common during the holiday seasons.

But it was perhaps the combination of business and pleasure which most marked life for the poor. Markets were viewed as 'the clubs of the poor'. No lady went to market and she did not expect her domestics back till noon.[106] A visit to the market was not only a meeting with friends; in Half-Way-Tree's market 'Sagwa' took the stage. In between the sale of 'wonderful potions' such as 'soaps that will transform black cheeks to the bloom of peach, ointments to cure the most obstinate sore', for the sum of 3d. Sagwa offered entertainment on market day. The versatile Sagwa sang, told tall stories, ate fire, performed sleight of hand tricks, offered amusing anecdotes about people. In his entourage were four little boys who performed wonders as bun-eaters. He told the Cinderella story in a series of moving pictures. The verdict of the 'tall old Negro' suggested that Sagwa's antics had healing properties: 'Him can cure the min' as well as de body; ah declare I don' feel me rumatiz since ah hab sich a good laugh'.[107] Sagwa sometimes teamed up with 'Seaquaw', an American travelling salesman, specialising in patent medicines, chiefly derived from herbs. They also extracted teeth free of charge, with the expectation that patients would purchase a bottle of lotion to stop the bleeding and heal the gums quickly. To keep the audiences interested, speeches extolling the merits of their wares were interspersed with popular songs and wise-cracks by two coloured American guitarists.[108]

Idiosyncrasy, when it becomes eccentric, is amusement for the idle. Urban Jamaica offered an impressive list of eccentrics, who provided passive amusement for onlookers:

Tom Pang, Wooden Foot Buckra, Badnight, Fowler, Wingie, Sam Leg, Red Mouth Higgins. Sam Leg was a burglar who kept Kingston's residents on the alert for months. He wrote [to] householders informing them of when to expect him. Despite careful watching Sam Leg continued to prove himself the invisible burglar. Charlie (Red Mouth) Higgins drew crowds at the northern entrance of Victoria Park on Sunday afternoons. He rode a large grey horse, carried a sword at his side, and wore an admiral's hat. He raved and abused public men, and condemned all established religion. His language was usually of the kind which was indictable in law. Then there was 'Mackerel Fat' a newspaper and race book vendor – and bill sticker, who on working days wore patchwork pants, but on Sundays and public holidays dressed in the height of fashion, his hair well combed and brushed, shining in the sun – the lustre of the hair was attributable to the use of mackerel fat. Then there was 'Wingie' a slim brown-skinned virago, with respectable family connections, who spent most of her time in jail, but only for disorderly conduct, due to her allowing her nasty temper to get the better of her after too many big jills of 'whites' [white rum]. She loved to fight, and her speciality was the butt ('Kate'). Finally, there was the melancholy retired school teacher, who dressed 'à la Bond Street', complete with top hat, morning coat, lavender pants, gloves, patent leather boots with spats, who sat all day in a secluded spot in the Park, communicating with no one.[109]

Patterns of leisure definitely demonstrated rifts along class and colour lines, but this fact did not make less valid the reality that in terms of sport, for example, the Jamaican people had much in common – even if not on the same cricket pitch. There were organisations to which the middle and upper classes dedicated their leisure time and which were exclusive to those classes and dedicated in some cases to social work. Among the working classes the distinction between leisure and work was not always clear cut. The distinctions in the use of leisure also showed a continuation of Afro-Jamaican Creole culture in which the middle and upper classes watched but did not participate, or condemned outright. Leisure activity of Jamaicans was inevitably a reflection of station in life, but also of strong metropolitan influences on colonial culture.

Notes

1   Jeffrey Dumazedier, *Sociology of Leisure*, trans. from French by Morea A. McKenzie, New York: Elsevier, 1974, p. 15.
2   *DG*, 'Why our young men leave the island', Paper by Mr Joyce, 19 December, 1903.
3   Frank Cundall, *Jamaica in 1912*.
4   Mels Anderson, *Man's Work and Leisure*, Leiden: E.J. Brill, 1974, p. 94.

5   Alice Spinner, *Lucilla: An Experiment*, London: Kegan Paul, 1896, p. 5.
6   Raymond Williams, *Culture and Society, 1780–1950*, Harmondsworth: Pelican, 1961, p. 24.
7   R.H. Tawney, *Equality*, p. 79.
8   Raymond Williams, *Culture and Society 1780–1950*, p. 129.
9   L. Johnson, *The Cultural Critics, From Matthew Arnold to Raymond Williams*, Routledge and Kegan Paul 1979, p. 28.
10   Rev. C.A. Wilson, *Men With Backbone*, p. 27.
11   *DG*, 11 February, 1890. 'J' to Editor.
12   *DG*, 1886.
13   *DG*, 31 May, 1894.
14   Blake to Secretary of State No. 179, 15 May, 1893, 3310/93, enclosing memorial of JBU and No. 237, 9 June, 1893, enclosing memorial of Ministers' Association of Kingston.
15   *JDR*, 1905–7. Report of the Inspector General of Police.
16   *JA*, 7 March, 1896 'Supression of Gambling'.
17   *JA*, 4 July, 1896 'Olla Podrida' by 'Jacob Omnium'.
18   *DG*, 12 December, 1899. The firm was Metropolitan House.
19   *DG*, 15 December, 1899.
20   *DG*, 27 April, 1886.
21   J.T. Palache, *The Jamaica Stud Book*, Kingston 1891, p. xxv.
22   *Ibid*. p. xxv.
23   *Ibid*. p. xxv.
24   *DG*, (Christmas Number) 20 December, 1902. Interview with Sir Augustus Hemmings.
25   *DG*, 31 December, 1901.
26   Dr John Alexander Somerville, *Man of Colour. An Autobiography. A Factual Report on the Status of the American Negro Today*, Los Angeles, 1949, p. 33.
27   *DG*, 14 December, 1899.
28   *Jamaica Memories*.
29   *JM*, V.M. Clarke (Montego Bay).
30   *JM*, N.W. Fletcher.
31   *DG*, 6 January and 7 January, 1886.
32   *DG*, 15 December, 1899. 'Cricket Conference'.
33   *DG*, 23 December, 1899.
34   *DG*, 9 December, 1899.
35   *JM*, R.J. Blake, Bog Walk.
36   *DG*, 10 May, 1894.
37   James Walvin, *Leisure and Society 1830–1950*, London and New York: Longmans, 1978, p. 105.
38   *DG*, 1 May, 1896, J. Ruddock to Editor.
39   W.P. Livingstone, *Black Jamaica*, p. 158.
40   *JA*, 8 June, 1895.
41   *DG*, 30 May, 1894 'What Jamaicans Read. Literature in Jamaica'.
42   Rev. C. Wilson, *Men With Backbone*, p. 89.
43   W.C. Murray, *A Day with Joe Lennan, the Rosewell duppy doctor, and Tommy Silvera or Suck o' Peas Sil*, Kingston: Vendryes and Co. 1891 (Introduction).
44   NLJ, MS II, *Casserly Papers*. Item 10.
45   *DG*, 21 December, 1900 and 23 December, 1899.
46   James Walvin, *Leisure and Society*, p. 18.
47   *DG*, 24 December, 1903.

48   *DG*, 7 May, 1886.
49   *Jamaica Memories*, Mrs Melba Crosswell (Kingston).
50   *DG*, 24 December, 1903.
51   *DG*, 6 May, 1899. 'Bicycle Tax'.
52   *Daily Telegraph*, 27 April, 1899. 'M' to Editor.
53   James Walvin, *Leisure and Society*, p. 93.
54   *DG*, 21 April, 1897.
55   *DG*, 21 December, 1899.
56   *JM*, Jeffrey-Smith and James Walvin, *Leisure and Society*, p. 93.
57   National Library of Jamaica, Postcard Collection.
58   *DG*, 27 March, 1886.
59   James Johnston, MD, *Jamaica, The New Riviera. A Pictorial Description of the Island and its Attractions*, London: Cassel and Co. 1903, p. 35.
60   James Johnston, *Jamaica*, p. 35. See also *Livingstone Collection, 1898–1903*. 'Extract from Chicago News from the pen of Mr W.J. Thorp, formerly of Jamaica'.
61   *Ibid.* p. 35.
62   *DG*, Advertisement, 22 April, 1886. 'Wanted: Well-cured Mongoose Skins', Wm. Schiller and Co.
63   *DG*, 22 March, 1886.
64   Interview with Dr Mullings, March 1986; and W.A. Furtado, *A Forty-five year Reminiscence of the Characteristics and Character of Spanish Town.*
65   James Walvin, *Leisure and Society.*
66   *DG*, 12 December, 1899.
67   *JM*, C.D. Rowe.
68   *DG*, 18 December, 1899.
69   *DG*, 13 May, 1885.
70   J.T. Palache, *The Jamaica Stud Book*, p. xxv.
71   *DG*, 27 April, 1886.
72   *JA*, 4 October, 1902.
73   James Johnston, *Jamaica*, p. 35.
74   *DG*, 11 June, 1894.
75   James Johnston, *Jamaica*, p. 35.
76   Dumazadier, *Sociology of Leisure.*
77   *DG*, 'Centenary Celebration of The Royal Lodge'. 16 May, 1894.
78   *Handbook of Jamaica* (HBJ).
79   Lindsay Downer, *Memoirs of George William Downer, 1837–1912.*
80   *DG*, Announcements of Meetings, e.g. 11 May, 1885.
81   *DG*, 11 December, 1902.
82   *DG*, 22 May, 1885.
83   Julius Moritzen, 'Has Jamaica Solved the Color Problem?', p. 38.
84   *JBB*, 1906–7. 'Friendly Societies'.
85   *DG*, 19 May, 1885.
86   James Walvin, *Leisure and Society.*
87   Jamaica Archives, Blake to Colonial Secretary. No. 201, 25 May, 1883.
88   Same to Same, No. 164, 15 May, 1893 (4016/903).
89   *JG*, 27 January, 1886.
90   *JA*, 'Public Holidays Law', 2 March, 1895. The Legislation of 1893 was intended to be experimental for two years (See Blake No. 164, 15 May 1893 (4016/903).
91   *JM*, R.A.L. Knight.
92   E.G. Ingham, *The African in the West Indies*, 1892(?), p. 19.

93   *Ibid.* p. 20.
94   *Ibid.* p. 19.
95   *JM*, Julia Mullings.
96   MS 209, Vol. 30, 3 January, 1893 to 29 June, 1893. *Bishop's Letter Book.* Nuttall to Rev. A. Cole, 14 January, 1893.
97   *JM*, A.A. Grant (Innswood).
98   *JM*, Mrs Sarah Carter.
99   *JM*, E.A. Gardiner.
100 Enos Nuttall, 'Characteristics of the Negro', in Rev. J. Ellison (ed.) *Church and Empire*, London: Longmans, 1907.
101 *JM*, Henrietta Campbell (Gregory Park, born 1889).
102 Hoskinson to Dept. of State No. 296, 24 July, 1882. Report on the Fruit Trade. Department of State National Archives and Record Services Microcopy T31-Roll 28.
103 J.H. Reid, 'The People of Jamaica Described', in Rev. R. Gordon *et al. Jamaica's Jubilee: Or What we are and What we hope to be by Five of themselves*, London, S.W. Partridge and Co. 1888, p. 92.
104 *JM*, Daniel Tait (Born in Negril in 1874).
105 J.H. Reid, '*The People of Jamaica*, p. 101–102.
106 *JM*, May Jeffrey Smith.
107 NLJ, MST 59. Livingstone Collection, 1898–1903.
108 *JM*, C.D. Rowe (Maeven Ave. Kingston).
109 *JM*, C.D. Rowe.

CHAPTER 11 | The black middle class

Between the mass of rural labourers and small-scale cultivators on the one hand, and the white and coloured elite who dominated ownership of the island's major resource – land – there was an evolving strata which constituted part of the island's middle class. This middle class has been described by R.T. Smith as two-tiered, drawing a distinction between a middle class of traders and a middle class of professionals some black, some brown.[1] Occupational status and the possession of European cultural attributes were important variables in definitions of class but the status associated with an occupation could, in the Jamaican milieu, be modified by race and colour divisions. It is always difficult to draw rigid lines of division between classes given that there is an almost infinite gradation associated with material well-being, place and type of residence, cultural attainments, and occupation. At the same time, it is not only that occupation determines class but that class determines occupation. The extent to which heterogeneity can exist within classes and yet permit the application of the homogenising term 'class', is partly a question of philosophical outlook, and partly a question of how much weight we attach to the differences which people, within an objectively defined class, perceive between themselves. The factor of race was an important division within this middle class; there is also a significant division in occupation, income, and probably in education as well. The traders of Jamaica also constituted a diverse element in Jamaican economic and social life. Among the traders themselves there were substantial ethnic divisions, as well. The use of the term 'class', therefore, corresponds more with the need to find a convenient term to define a large group of people spread between the minorities and the masses, than with the accurate or scientific description of a group which shared common interests, aspirations, or a common consciousness.

The respectable peasantry

In rural Jamaica there was a layer of wealthy peasants and farmers who were generally termed 'respectable'. A respectable farmer was not, in the Jamaican context, the same thing as a 'gentleman farmer' who would have the term 'esquire' attached to his name. The respectable farmer was often of limited educational attainment, sometimes entirely illiterate, but his status was based on landownership and on his ability to employ labour. A rural farmer who attracted some attention and admiration was Mr Hibbert of Clarendon, who had acquired 150 acres of land. Hibbert was described by the *Daily Gleaner* as an 'enterprising black man from the superior of his class to be found in the colony'. He produced coffee, owned a mill, a pulping house, tanks and barbeques, a machine for preparing arrowroot and cassava starch. He had 15,000 hills of yams valued at £400. He had, we are told, no problem with labour, or with praedial larcenists and worked along with his employees with his pick and hoe. His income was estimated to be about £1,000 per year.[2]

Another prosperous black agriculturist and penkeeper was J.M. Gordon, who sat on the St Catherine Parochial Board.[3] Over a three year period, Gordon had been able to purchase approximately £2,000 worth of cattle from Mr George Sturridge, a large penkeeper near Mandeville. Gordon, described by his lawyer Mr Vendryes as a black man who had 'lifted himself to his position through integrity, industry, and ability', became a member of the Parochial Board of St Catherine in 1889. He received some dubious public attention in 1889 because of a charge made against him of theft of a steer. Gordon in the magistrate's court, insisted that he had been framed by men in league against him, and who desired to ruin him and hated him 'because I possess a certain amount of influence and respect among my people which they wish to destroy for their political ends . . . who affect to despise me because of my success, who think it an injudicious and dangerous thing for a man of my class at all to succeed and to possess property, and who hate me because I prefer to stand by the respected custos of my parish, in his desire to keep things straight, and to discountenance robbery and dishonesty'.

Gordon was committed to stand trial in any case, but the jury unanimously agreed to release him 'amidst the deafening and prolonged cheering from the large number of spectators assembled in and outside the courtroom'. It was also established, by way of poetic justice that his accuser, Henriques, had been in the habit of selling his employer's stock for a commission of 33⅓ per cent in exchange for selling below market value. But it was so tragically clear that had Gordon not had strong character references the case may have gone differently. Gordon's own statement illustrated the vulnerability of this segment of the middle class because of race.

In an earlier chapter we referred to black rural farmers who leased land to tenants. The evidence points to an evolving layer of black society whose lifestyle differed from the mass of rural labourers and tenants. One of the major comments made on this group came from Sir Anthony Musgrave in

1880. In his lecture to the Royal Colonial Institute Musgrave reproduced comments made on the standard of housing of this class. From Manchester, Rev. Panton described those who 'in material prosperity there is a large class now in the country whose means warrant their social elevation. But they are below the mark in education and taste'. Rev. Panton, one of the closest associates of Enos Nuttall, and a man much venerated in South Manchester, declared:

> We want a good middle class of black population. To a certain extent we have this in Manchester – men who will appreciate education, morality, social rules, among themselves, and the ordinary customs of civilized life. Such men would see the necessity for taxation, and not grudge their quota.[5]

Rev. Webb, reporting from Stewart Town in Trelawny, referred to the improvement in the construction of cottages 'in the Gibraltar District where people are small settlers and growers of coffee'. In Watt Town, he reported, no less than 'fifteen houses had been built in the previous ten years, and others were being constructed on an improved scale, neat, commodious, peasant-family cottages. Webb described the cottages as having a solid base wall, 25 ft by 15 ft; 7–8 ft high. There were normally two rooms below, the sons occupied one as a sleeping room, and one was used as a lock-up for coffee or ground provisions for market. Upstairs, there were two sleeping rooms, one for parents, the other for the daughters. There was a hall, with a few pieces of mahogany furniture . . . Upon a corner table there were cups, saucers, and mugs all of the latest and most approved designs, more for show and ornament than use. There was another hall for dining and general family chit-chat. There was a front portico. Comparable descriptions of homes among well-to-do small settlers in Westmoreland, North Manchester, and St Elizabeth confirm the existence of a middle group of black farmers whose daily life differed fundamentally from that of the rural workers and tenant farmers and small peasantry.[6]

   This middle group of black farmers would no doubt have been among those 3,766 'Africans' mentioned in a tabulation of voters made in 1886. In the latter year, of 7,443 qualified and registered voters 51 per cent or 3,766 were listed as 'African', 35 per cent or 2,578 as of mixed race, 13 per cent or 1,001 Europeans or Europeans born in Jamaica, and 1 per cent or 98 East Indians. The franchise was not particularly liberal. For a householder to qualify to vote he had to occupy a floored and roofed dwelling, and pay a tax on a horse and nine acres of cultivated land. In the 1890s the franchise was limited by the imposition of a literacy qualification, while the economic hardships in the twilight years of the nineteenth century contributed to the removal of several people from the voters list as a consequence of inability to pay taxes.

One source for the emergence of the middle group of farmers was the migrants returning from Panama, though it is probably true that several Panama migrants had been farmers before leaving for Panama 'with God as their compass' (as one migrant so ably and picturesquely explained the migration). For the thousands who did not succeed financially or even survive the experience of emigration, there were a few, who having returned to the island became small settlers and shopkeepers. Newton speculated that 'in Jamaica and the Windward Islands, the recipients were probably also the main purchasers of the several hundred acres of Crown Lands which the governments of these islands sold during the first two decades of the twentieth century'.[7] A report of an officially appointed commission in 1888 suggested, however, that even before the government made Crown Lands available, returned migrants were purchasing land and establishing shops.[8] Several of the emigrants to Panama had been artisans in Jamaica. In 1886 they were able to earn, as tradesmen in Panama, between $2 and $2.75 per day if they reported directly to the Compagnie Universelle, or between $4 and $5 per day if they were employed to contracting firms. Dr Gayleard, who had been despatched by Governor Norman in 1887 to report on conditions in the Canal Zone, reported that tradesmen on the line (masons and carpenters) earned $3 to $4 per day. They were also supplementing their income by their small farm tenements, 'raising corn, bananas and fowls'.[9]

The rural middle class farmer sometimes had common interests with larger farmers, especially in relation to labour supplies. In 1890 small proprietors of Canoe Valley in Clarendon petitioned the Governor on the labour question. This particular group of proprietors shared some of the most reactionary views of the elite on the educational system which, they claimed, spoiled labour.

> Dependent on the soil for our livelihood, we cannot express too strongly our disappointment at the present system of education. Most young men and women leave school, despise the soil, and regard agriculture as beneath them, and so strongly has this sentiment influenced the less informed that we find it difficult to obtain labour in our District even for high wages.[10]

Clearly, however, there was a distinction between education of one's own children, and the education of other people's children. For example, some small proprietors, also from Clarendon, complained that the education of their children was being hampered by the need to utilise their labour for conveying water for household use.[11]

Clarendon farmers grouped themselves into the Clarendon Agricultural Association, of which the President was George Douet. The association pleaded for 'practical training in agriculture, assistance to hardworking cultivators; some means to provide agricultural implements and machinery so as to economize labour'. The petition called for industrial schools, co-operative associations on the central factory principle, amendment of the Immigration Law, in respect of payment for immigrants so as to 'put it within the reach of a large number of those who want labour to avail themselves of East Indians, protection to certain of our exports from unscrupulous dealers'.[12]

The response to petitions such as the above was really the formation of the Jamaica Agricultural Society, which, founded in 1895, was to be the foremost organisation colonywide of small settlers. But the Jamaica Agricultural Society (JAS) was not a small farmers association in the sense that the initiative for its establishment came from the farmers themselves. It was organised by the colonial leadership, and its leadership remained in the hands of the country's elite. In the year of its formation the JAS had just over 150 members who paid 4/- for membership. The Board of the Society consisted of fourteen persons chosen from the Legislative Council, fourteen nominated by the Governor, and another fourteen elected by the membership. The Governor was president. There were to be four vice-presidents elected by members from among the Board. The Governor appointed the secretary and treasurer. The objective of the JAS, according to Governor Blake was to improve the small stock of the people by importing breeds of pigs, goats and fowls. 'By this means I hope to confer immediate benefits upon small proprietors and cultivators to *win their confidence* and support in the general movement which must of course be slow'.[13] The Hon. John Pringle, of banana fame, and one of Blake's Privy Councillors was one of the vice-presidents of the society. A Board of Agriculture would serve as the executive body of the JAS.

The structure of the JAS was designed to ensure that agricultural policy would remain distinctly the business of the colonial bureaucracy and the Legislative Council. While providing a voice for black farmers it was intended to provide a platform whereby small-farmer production could more easily be influenced by the agricultural policies of the colonial state. Thus the JAS was expected to help redirect the energies of small farmers into export production. Small farmers were to be exposed to the use of more modern implements of agriculture, to be lectured on methods of cultivation, to be provided with practical demonstrations in the methods of planting and pruning crops such as cacao, kola and coffee. The architect of the organisation, Governor Sir Henry Blake, made it clear that his optimism was much modified by the supposed inferiority of the black population:

> What the ultimate result will be I cannot say. A black population not very intelligent and saturated with suspicion of any attempt to interfere with their crude and wasteful system is not easily influenced.[14]

The JAS was an organisation of black farmers, by the colonial administration for the advancement of small-scale agriculture, under the paternal guidance of the Governor and the Legislative Council. In this respect it differed fundamentally from the Jamaica Union of Teachers, a professional organisation of teachers, established by black teachers, for the welfare of education and teachers in general.

The teachers

The middle-farming sector of the Afro-Jamaican population was always keen to provide education for their children. For this sector of the population the elementary school was the most probable avenue for learning basic literacy and numeracy.

> The system of elementary education was aimed at the lower class of ex-slaves, but it found its principal support among the more prosperous small and medium-sized farmers engaged in the production of 'minor', that is to say non-plantation crops. Its existence also led to the creation of a lower middle class of primary school teachers who became a reservoir of black leaders. Whatever its shortcomings, elementary school teaching was almost the only means by which poor blacks could escape manual labour . . . However, in the rural communities where church and school were most effective, particularly among the middle farmers who could make enough money to maintain a respectable style of life, the school-teachers were the local elite.[15]

Many teachers had been born to farming families, and in the absence of pensions until definitely the end of the nineteenth century, retirement often dictated a return to the soil. Indeed, many teachers left the schoolroom for the farm long before retirement, or became shopkeepers. One such example was Mr Josiah Smickle who, after nineteen years, left teaching and devoted his time to his shop and to his grazing property in one parish and cultivation in another. He had about 160 acres of land in all. Smickle became a member of the Parochial Board, and of the Legislative Council.[16] Rev. C.A. Wilson also observed the tendency of teachers to abandon the classroom for more gainful occupation in farming.[17]

We should be careful not to exaggerate the importance of elementary education as a factor in social mobility, insofar as elementary education in itself was unable to provide that. Basic numeracy and literacy, while of themselves important, cannot offer a general preparation for a lifetime occupation. The majority of children left school and were abandoned as far as educational institutions were concerned for the rest of their lives unless deviant behaviour brought them under the umbrella of reformatories, which ironically did more to prepare children for occupations as masons, carpenters, tailors and other artisan-based occupations. An elementary education, however, did provide an opening for further education, especially for those who excelled and were able to move on to training colleges, and in a few cases to study overseas.

The black rural middle class, among whom we include the teachers, were not yet a stable social group, moving as they did from teaching, to the religious ministry, to farming, or combining these occupations. However, teachers were among the first of the professional groups in the island to establish associations designed to further the interests of the profession and of individuals within it. Beginning in about 1883, a series of parish associations of teachers were set up under Church of England auspices.[18] The strongest and most vibrant of these teachers' associations was the North Manchester Teachers' Association operating out of Mount Olivet.

The main function of these early associations was to improve the 'intellectual culture' of teachers. Some meetings conducted essay readings, lectures (called 'orations'), written and oral discussion. They also purchased books and periodicals for members. These organisations were strictly for Church of England teachers. Archbishop Nuttall explained this apparent exclusiveness:

> While embracing some points of general interest, they are to a great extent such as only church teachers can benefit by. We are trying in various ways to train our teachers and catechists and improve their status. But much of this work is done on Church of England lines, so require these separate associations. But our teachers are at liberty to join general associations, and where these exist and work well it will be a benefit to our men to belong to both. You will therefore understand that we have not formed our teachers' associations in a spirit of exclusiveness but simply for the purpose of doing some needed work in our own way.[19]

So, then, the Anglican associations were being set up in 1883 to improve schoolmasters and catechists, and to elevate their status. The Westmoreland and Mountain Teachers' Association typically declared their objectives to be the 'promotion of the interests of teachers, and the advancement of their profession, the increase of efficiency of their work and a general furtherance of the course of elementary education. The Inspector of Schools, Mr Thomas Capper, associated the work of the associations with the improved training of teachers and higher standards in schools, and particularly the efforts of teachers towards "self-culture"'.[20]

Parallel to the teachers' associations which catered primarily for the professional development of teachers was a somewhat more subdued movement in the 1880s which began to agitate for the improved material welfare of teachers. The improvement of salaries was related, firstly, to the degree to which the government of the island was prepared to invest funds in education. It was related, secondly, to the more subjective factor of race. The late-nineteenth century witnessed an increased desire on the part of the Churches to encourage greater participation of government in education, in accordance with the experience of England, and in response to the reality that the Churches were experiencing financial difficulties in maintaining current establishments, at a time when the demand for more schools in the countryside was increasing. As far as the racial factor is concerned, most of the elementary school teachers were black and coloured, and they were probably correct when they argued that low pay and poor housing conditions emerged out of the low esteem in which blacks were held in the society.[21] Teachers clearly regarded themselves as an upwardly mobile section of the black population and were coming to demand incomes commensurate with their 'middle class' status. Current salaries, they argued, did not allow them to lead lives of dignity.

The Association of Schoolmasters established in 1884, at the instigation of Mr Matthew Joseph, was concerned with the economic interests of teachers as well as with the competence of teachers. On behalf of the Association Mr Joseph sent a long memorandum to the Colonial Office. It is not clear how long the Association lasted, but of interest are the issues raised in the memorandum of Mr Joseph.[22] His long memorandum can be summarised as follows:

Firstly, with all due respect to the wonderful work which the Churches had done, it was time for the Government to take a more active interest in education.

Secondly, the educational system was not providing facilities whereby the 'peasantry could be thoroughly civilised and enlightened'. The consequence was that the great majority of the black and coloured people who formed three-fourths of the population of this country are in a state of deplorable ignorance.

Thirdly, a proper system of education was particularly important in an island such as Jamaica 'inhabited by different races of people, with but little sympathy among them, such a state of gross ignorance is baneful to its peace and prosperity'.

Fourthly, there should be compulsory education, which would be the 'greatest boon' to the country since emancipation.

Fifthly, it was not true that such a system of universal education would lead to discontent among Negroes as 'put forth by strangers and others who have no real interest in the welfare and prosperity of our country and in the progress of its people. Rather, it would increase the loyalty of the people to the Crown'. 'Your memorialists who are all black men and coloured men and are natives of different parts of the Island, are the best judges in this matter; and we assert, that should the system of education which we are now advocating be introduced here, for the civilisation and enlightenment of our people it will greatly add to their love for our Most Gracious Queen and their loyalty to her throne'.

Turning to the question of conditions of work, the memorandum pointed out that teachers were often driven to migrate to Panama, or to join the Constabulary, or to become time keepers and 'bosses' at the Canal. Others became schoolmasters 'among the people of their own race in the southern USA'. Addressing itself specifically to salaries, the memorandum expressed the view that 'the great majority of trained schoolmasters are of the view that their pay is small because they are black men. The saying "Any pay will do for a Negro being a proverb in this Country"'. On the question of professionalism the memorandum noted that there was 'a false economy by which these incompetent men are employed at starving salaries, to pretend to educate the peasantry of this country . . . waste of public money and an act of injustice to the people themselves'. The memorandum also called for a pension scheme and a widows and orphan fund on the basis of monthly deductions from salary.

The memorandum is instructive because it views education as the road to 'civilisation' of the peasantry; it associated race as a factor in the slow mobility of blacks; it emphasises the need for a professional and properly trained corps of teachers. It advocates a widows and orphan fund, and hints at the movement outside the profession, of migration and change of profession. The Association viewed itself as a spokesman for the rural constituency, and makes a political point: education would reinforce rather than weaken loyalty to the Crown.

It is probably this trend among teachers which the Jamaica Union of Teachers (JUT) continued from its formation in 1894 – the idea of teaching as a profession of respectable black people; the dedication to the civilisation of blacks by blacks within an unreformed status quo. The JUT, as an organisation of black schoolmasters (and schoolmistresses), spoke in the same tones of education of the peasantry, and threw their support behind Legislative Council candidates who advocated educational causes.

In his history of the JUT, one of its founders, W.F. Bailey, emphasises this professional outlook.[23] In 1891 guest speakers had been invited from the United States to speak to teachers 'to widen the outlook of those who were destined to mould or mar the lives of as many tender ones'. According to Bailey 'with aspirations kindled and outlook widened, *teachers as a class* soon found that the environment which surrounded elementary education in Jamaica did not lend itself to progress'. The thinking behind the formation of the JUT was partly that since the Government, the general public and the planter class cared little for mass education, this particular class of blacks had to take the initiative. Education had to be undertaken as a responsibility by teachers themselves grouped in a countrywide professional association.

The JUT was modelled on the National Union of Teachers in Britain. It was to act as an advisory body to teachers who were moving to districts which were not known to them; it was designed to co-ordinate all the various local associations of school teachers throughout the island in order to facilitate the expression of the opinions of teachers. The JUT also committed itself to founding a Provident Benevolent Annuity Fund in connection with the Union, for the benefit of the scholastic profession.[24] Eventually a Teachers' Mutual Aid Society was formed.[25]

Black teachers and spokesmen, such as J.H. Reid, an ardent advocate of black racial unity, viewed the JUT as one of the columns of such unity. Even more he saw racial unity as cutting across class and occupational lines. In his response to the dockworkers strike in 1895 he expressed the view that the formation of the JUT and the wharf strike were indicators of growing ethnic unity:

Is the sentiment of race affinity so completely disrupted in the Negro race as to render it powerless in bringing about a coherence of its members? Objects of ostracism by other races, why should each stand aloof from the other, when numbers so greatly preponderate in their favour? United we stand divided we fall.

Reid was going beyond the idea that black teachers were responsible for the 'civilisation' of rural black workers, to the more revolutionary idea of a cross-class black alliance.[26]

While the religious bodies never ceased to show creative interest in the growth of educational facilities in the country, the JUT was associated with an expansion of secular education at the end of the nineteenth century – a factor which was of some concern to the Church which feared the growth of agnosticism and even atheism if there were not a strong religious input in the schools of a non-denominational nature. The JUT was, at the same time, an important organisation of black Jamaican professionals, many of them highly educated not by means of local institutions but through the acquisition of libraries. They would have constituted part of what was called the 'coloured aristocracy' of the country. Their intellectual respectability rather than their possession of wealth made them 'respectable'.

The priesthood was another important middle strata profession for coloured and black men. The path to the priesthood was often via the road of teaching, and in fact, the two professions were at some points inseparable. The Minister of the Gospel enjoyed considerable prestige in rural Jamaican society, partly because of the old tradition of close association between preacher and labourer, the former often acting as surrogate for the interests of the latter; partly because the Church and/or the school was often the social centre of life in rural Jamaica. The origins of the black minister of religion also rested in the rural smallholding class. In 1881 the census listed 261 ministers of religion and in 1891 it recorded 329 fairly evenly spread throughout rural Jamaica. In comparison there were approximately 1,000 schoolmasters in the country between 1881 and 1891, not including governesses, music teachers and dancing tutors of which there were a few dozens.

Such prestige which the black minister of religion or catechist enjoyed among his flock was modified by his race. Coloured clergymen were given, as a matter of course, the less prominent cures. The fact that, inevitably, the majority of Jamaican congregations were black led some churchmen to conclude that there was no discrimination in Churches. The 'Little Kirk' in 1896 committed the blunder which revealed the truth. A Presbyterian clergyman (black) Rev. Dingwall was refused burial at the Little Kirk. Dingwall had served at the Little Kirk and was a member of that congregation. It is true that Rev. Dingwall had died in the mental asylum, but that hardly seemed grounds for disqualifying the uncomplaining corpse of Rev. Dingwall from burial in Holy ground. Rev. T.M. Geddes of Coke Chapel (Methodist) came to the rescue of the deceased minister.[27] Dingwall, it should be noted here, made forthright remarks (in print) on sexual license in Jamaica and had associated loose sexual behaviour with white society. His had also been an extremely forceful African consciousness.[28] Little Kirk tried to punish his soul by not burying the body.

Rev. P.F. Schoburgh, a local Baptist minister, was discriminated against on board Captain Walker's ship. He had been refused a clean cabin on board though there were clean ones available. The remark of the Captain was: 'And what do you expect, better?' The *Jamaica Advocate* described Rev. Schoburgh as 'one of the foremost black men in the Colony, in education, character, social standing'.

> A denial of his rights not only wakes but startles, us all. If he is treated with indignity, what must be the lot of the many unfortunates of his race who travel on these boats?[29]

These two experiences demonstrate that social prestige as measured by cultural attainments was no barrier to discrimination on the grounds of race.

The artisans

An important social group in the country whose members constituted a substantial number of blacks outside the agricultural sector were the artisans. It is essential to observe, however, that while there were men who dedicated themselves entirely to the trades, there were others who supplemented the tilling of the soil with work in one of the trades.

The artisan group proved mobile in two respects: first they were among the Jamaicans who migrated most; secondly, it was the segment which perhaps experienced most downward social mobility. What may appear puzzling in late-nineteenth century Jamaica is that there were regular expressions of regret at the absence of skilled artisans, while the reality was that poor opportunities at home encouraged an outward movement of artisans. The fact is that declining opportunities for artisans in rural Jamaica, particularly in the sugar industry, drove many artisans overseas. Secondly, the competition faced by artisans from cheap imported goods reduced opportunities for some categories of artisans.

In 1870, for example, the West End Foundry in Kingston had employed an average of 120 mechanics, including apprentices, in addition to outdoor hands. Approximately £80 per week were paid in wages. In the decade of the 1870s the West End Foundry drew from the parish of Vere alone, for foundry and estate work, some £1,500 to £2,000 per annum. By the 1890s these contracts were not being renewed, and in 1897 the future appeared dim.

> We got work only to the value of £26 from Vere in 1895 compared with £1,500 to £2,000 per year in 1870–80. In 1869 contracts were worth only £80. The staff had therefore been reduced significantly, from 120 in the 1870s to 38 in 1897; that is eight good mechanics and 30 lads (not apprentices).

The decline in sugar was the main cause of the problem, but the banana industry 'has not given us one pound of work in ten years'.[30]

The possession of artisan skills was no longer viewed with the respect once enjoyed. As Mr Lazarus noted:

> The intelligent and respectable lads, as a rule, do not take readily to mechanical trades, nor are their families inclined to place them out. Their first object is to put them to the Civil Service examination, and if they should fail, they then make an attempt to put them to a trade; the lad is so spoilt and so above himself, that he becomes overbearing and has to be dismissed, for such an example would become a curse to any establishment.[31]

This statement confirms the view that browns and whites saw the civil service as the target of their aspirations. But their aspirations for civil service positions must have become associated with the decline in the standard of living of artisans and therefore with the view that artisans' work of any kind was beneath their social status. From the conduct of 'respectable lads' who were recruited, it was clear that foundry work was moving towards an occupation dominated by blacks – a movement comparable to that in the domestic service.[32]

The decline in demand for their services in the sugar industry combined with foreign competition to make the occupations of artisans hazardous during this period. W. Clarke Murray who had intimate knowledge of the artisan strata, having himself been a carpenter at Port Royal before his distinguished occupation as an educator in the island began, noted that the 'importation of entire buildings and parts of them, and also of dress lumber of every description, as well as ready-made clothing, boots, etc. have reduced the earnings of this class considerably, so that comparatively few of the youths see any prospect for making a living by trades, and do not seek instruction in them'.[33]

In 1898, two members of the Legislative Council (Mr Leyden, representative for St Elizabeth, and Dr Johnson of St Ann) presented petitions from artisans and tradesmen showing that their 'several trades were being ruined by the large importation of ready-made goods, and were consequently on the verge of starvation and could not find the means to pay their taxes and dues'.[34]

Earnings from the trades had, in the past, provided the cash for investments in land or in shopkeeping. The Custos of Westmoreland described the fall in status and fall in income as follows:

> [Artisans] used to occupy a much more respectable position than the ordinary labourer, and had accumulated some means which as a rule, they put into the savings bank or with which they purchased a mule and cart, or built a good house and bought a few acres of land and cultivated it, who are now worse off. This class of people who derived all their progress at the time from the sugar estates in my neighbourhood now scarcely exists at all.[35]

Looking at artisan occupations over the period 1871–91 there was, according to census returns, a decline in the number of blacksmiths from 1,432 in 1871 to 1,377 in 1881, and to 1,185 in 1891, or a 17 per cent decline between 1871 and 1891. The figures for coopers who were probably most affected by the decline of the sugar industry are not as clear. According to the 1871 census there were 2,089 coopers and 92 carpenters. In 1891 there were 8,982 carpenters and 1,487 coopers. In 1881 carpenters and coopers were linked; there were then 10,701 carpenters and coopers. It is not improbable that coopers took up carpentry. Shoemaking remained stable: 1,710 in 1871; 1,830 in 1881; 1,765 in 1891. There was a decline of hatmakers from 487 in 1871 to 412 in 1881, and 370 in 1891; a 24 per cent decline in 20 years.[36]

But there were definite increases in the number of bricklayers and masons, from 1,058 to 2,527, and 2,502 for the period 1871–91. There was an increase in the number of tailors (1,939 and 2,422) and in the number of painters – from 152 in 1871 to 300 in 1881 and to 426 in 1891. The suggestion is that artisans and tradesmen associated with the construction industry still found their occupations among the most viable, though Clarke Murray had observed that pre-fabricated buildings were being imported. There is good reason to believe that the carpenter, bricklayer and mason were fully occupied in the late-nineteenth century in the construction of housing. The number of dwellings with shingle, metal or concrete roof and flooring increased from 44,027 in 1891 to 91,183 in 1911, while the number of dwellings with thatch roof and flooring increased from 35,683 in 1891 to 47,637 in 1911. In 1891 the number of dwellings with metal roofs was only 994. In 1911 there were 18,135.[37] It is true, however, that these figures must be treated with caution since there was no census in 1901 and there must have been much more feverish building after the earthquake of 1907.

In spite of foreign competition, milliners and seamstresses increased in number from 14,565 to 18,966 in 1891. These figures do not, however, say anything about the quality of life of milliners and seamstresses, and the large numbers found in this category are probably a more significant comment on the limited occupational opportunities for women than on the economic viability of such occupations.

The Blue Book indicates that in 1888–9 tradesmen earned between 2/6 and 6/- per day. Painters earned between 1d to 1.5d per superficial yard, per coat.[38]

Many tradesmen were probably of dubious skill. Young men were in the habit of setting themselves up in business as soon as they had 'picked up the merest smattering of their business, carpenters who cannot drive a nail, bricklayers who cannot lay a brick, set up for themselves as skilled labourers without the slightest qualification'.[39] The Royal Commission of 1879 complained that these youths had been 'spoiled' for agriculture, but were no good for anything else. The scepticism concerning the skills of many of the young tradesmen continued to be vibrant in the late-nineteenth century:

> Notwithstanding we have some good, hardworking, intelligent tradesmen, who are doing well and have brought up their families decently, who own their own houses; we have against these, a large number of incompetent, insolent, ignorant, lazy and worthless lot of grown-up tradesmen, who are really in the way of good men.[40]

The point is, though, that many of them continued to receive jobs because 'they were encouraged by gentlemen who give out work to be done, because they think it is cheap, and when a little experience teaches them that they have been deceived, they abuse the whole rank and file of tradesmen and call them worthless'.[41]

The system of apprenticeship had evidently broken down. Mothers apparently often expected their sons to receive an income as apprentices.[42] Masters found it difficult to maintain discipline among apprentices, so they claimed, because the boys continued to 'live in their parents' yards and spending their leisure time away from restraint, are not sufficiently separated from the demoralising associations, and do not readily submit to the control of their employers'.[43] One cabinetmaker had been taken to court for strapping an apprentice, a sure indication of the conditions under which apprentices learned their trade.

Artisan's work, where it was closely linked to the sugar industry, witnessed a decline in the demand for skills; where there was demand, particularly in the building industry, the artisan situation was not as precarious. There was a decline in the prestige of the mechanical trades as they fell increasingly into the hands of black juveniles, and as 'lads' of higher 'social standing' agitated for employment in the more prestigious civil service.

The artisans did not confine themselves to employment in the trades. They often invested in land, partly because of the security arising out of investment in real estate, but more importantly for the income which good farm land could bring. In some respects, the artisans of the countryside were part of the small farmer complex. They cultivated their own land, but also engaged in carpentry, shingle splitting, sawing wood. In response to the reduction of opportunities in the sugar industry in Hanover one mason reported that he had converted full time to farming his twenty acres of land (three acres in coffee, and the rest in pasture and provisions).[44] Another carpenter divided his time between carpentry and cultivating eleven acres of his own land.[45] Of course, opportunities for artisans arose from the construction of railroads and from the programme of bridge building during the 1890s.

The artisans were regarded as leading a precarious existence. One response was to seek opportunities overseas, thereby depriving the colony of experienced artisans. In this context, there were serious discussions on 'free trade' versus 'protectionism'. There were some Jamaicans who regarded free trade as an 'economic law', there were others who advocated a tariff to protect local industries.[46] Spokesmen such as W. Clarke Murray, despite his sympathy for the class of artisans, thought it would be unwise to offer protection to the possible disadvantage of other groups in terms of increased costs:

A goodly number whom I represent would seek a protective duty on such imported articles, but I would myself hesitate in recommending such a course lest in seeking to advantage a class, though large, a much larger number be made to suffer additional payments for necessary articles and work . . . [47]

In any event Jamaica was not in the most favourable position to utilise the policy of protective tariffs. The colony's leverage was much reduced by the pressures placed on it by British and American trading policies – most favoured nation clauses on the one hand, and reciprocity conventions on the other. The US market absorbed, up to the end of the nineteenth century, considerable quantities of Jamaican sugar, and was in addition a favourable market for bananas, citrus, and cacao. Jamaica's small market also favoured British manufactured goods. There was little prospect that artisans would win legislative sanctions of the type which would make their goods competitive with cheaper manufactured imports or processed goods such as dressed lumber and pre-fabricated buildings. Meanwhile the increase in imports of clothing, footwear, and furniture supports the view that local production was faced with increased competition.[48]

There was not only a wide range of skills within the artisan layer, but differing levels of competence. The ambivalent attitudes of artisans is demonstrated by the fact that their 'attitudes and living standards had as much in common with lower middle class attitudes and living standards as with the attitudes of the unskilled'.[49] In Jamaica, some artisans supported industrial education for the sake of greater technical efficiency and a sense of professionalism. Others were hesitant to support educational policies which would have the effect of swelling the number of artisans.

Faced with severe competition from imports, the lower middle and middle class artisans were forced to support the Government's restrained approach to technical training in order to protect their small share of the local market. Those of the higher classes who were in favour of more vigorous action based their preference more on the supposed effectiveness of technical training in developing desirable attitudes to work than on marketable skills that could be gained.[50]

The artisans were not a united group, yet they were to establish one of the first occupational unions in the colony. One of the major divisions between the artisans rested on the existence of those who desired to maintain some degree of professionalism within the crafts and those who, poorly trained, set themselves up as skilled labourers, and, so it was argued, brought all tradesmen into disrepute. At the lower level of artisanry the line between the skilled worker and the hustler could only have been a thin one, merging at the bottom with the vagabonds, vagrants, and, in Kingston, 'the dangerous classes'. At the upper level the artisan groups were a part of the emergent middle class. In 1897 one of the island's most well-known artisans showed strong support for technical education, which he thought should be given at least the same importance as elementary education. Once that was done, Mr Lazarus argued, the 'disabilities from which the mechanical arts and crafts suffered, would be removed'.[51]

It is not that the upper levels of the artisan class were preoccupied with 'credentialism' or with the control of a market for their expertise, but definitely with the collective social status of respectable artisans.[52] Occupational role can become 'an integral part of a person's self-image', and it was with this self-image that the upper level of the artisan group was concerned.

It is in this spirit that we understand the formation of the Artisans' Union in 1899, an organisation determined on a collective level to defend the rights of the profession, and to discourage the intrusion into the profession of untrained artisans who discredited the profession, in their view at least. It was not a labour union organisation directed towards extracting concessions from capital, but an association of professionals to protect the integrity of the occupation by leaving membership open only to those who could prove their relevant skills.

When the Artisans' Union met in mid-December, 1899, it is significant that the *Daily Gleaner* referred to the 'weekly general meeting of the Carpenters, Bricklayers and Painters Union' – the artisans of the construction industry.[53] The meeting of 11 December, 1899, 'deprecated the system by which contracts were awarded', and recommended that the building public be cautioned against the 'instability of the lumber market and also the rule of thumb methods adopted by certain untrained and incapable builders and contractors in making valuation for building work, resulting in the detriment of the working man, sub-contractors and merchants'. At its meeting on 20 December, 1899, the Union called for the establishment of a Technical School Workshop in connection with the Union for 'training of hand and eye of both women and boys, so that "botchers" may learn to have ambition'.[54]

Yet, despite its concern with professional integrity, the Union was to make strong comments on various social issues which did not affect artisans only. The Union, for example, protested against poor wages and 'in many instances labour minus wages'. It sent circulars to the Parochial Boards seeking information 'as to the rate of wages etc. for artisans and labourers . . . ' It addressed itself to the unhappy state of affairs at the St Catherine District Prison, and 'deprecated' the action of the St Ann, St James, and Manchester Parochial Boards in withholding information asked for in connection with social conditions of the people whom they represented. 'This union is entirely indignant at this treatment in trying to trample under their feet the intelligence of the Artisans' Union'. The Union also called for the abolition of taxes which now 'oppress labour and hamper production'. Taxes should be placed on land instead. Workmen should be given the opportunity to be 'producers of wealth for the social advancement of the community'.[55]

The strength/weakness of the Union was partly demonstrated by the resolution that 'Rule 55 be suspended to enable delinquent members to become financial'. The tendency of the Union to express itself in strong language prompted the *Daily Gleaner* to plead with the Union to 'bear and forbear; grievous words stir up anger'.[56]

Professional women

Dr Robert Love, editor of the *Jamaica Advocate*, spoke strongly in favour of women's education, without which the Negro race as a whole could not rise. In April 1895 the redoubtable editor spoke of the 'culture of our women' as the 'key to the whole problem'.

> We have concentrated on the elevation of our men – clergymen, lawyers, etc. – but not on our daughters. The race must rise by families not by individuals. Men are still despised in spite of their achievements. The race rises as its women rise. They are the true standard of its elevation. We are trying to produce cultured men without asking ourselves where they are to find cultured wives. We forget that cultured families constitute a cultured race and that a cultured race is an equal race. The elevation of women to equality with [their] white counterparts is the Condition *Sine Qua Non* of the elevation of the Negro race.[57]

Returning to the same theme later that year the *Advocate* declared:

> Every pound spent to educate the black boy tends to elevate a class only, but every pound spent to educate a black girl, tends to elevate the whole race. Fathers and mothers, bear these facts in mind, and send as many of your black daughters to England as you can. Some tell you that your girls can be just as well educated here. Ask them, why then do they send theirs to England.[58]

By the end of the nineteenth century efforts to educate girls had begun to reap their reward. There was clearly a decline in illiteracy among women. The number of women signing the marriage register with a 'mark' declined even more rapidly than men.[59]

Table 11.1   Comparison of literacy between men and women as indicated by the marriage register.

Year	Men	Women	Mean
1883–4	49.6	68.8	59.2
1886–7	46.8	64.8	55.8
1889–90	47.6	64.9	56.3
1892–3	45.3	60.0	52.6
1895–6	41.5	55.5	48.6
1899–1900	41.1	51.6	—

It is not clear why employment requiring skills in shorthand, typing and telegraph operation is dominated by women, but such posts were filled in Jamaica by women rather than by men. In the 1890s Miss Maud M. Barrowes, principal of Wolmer's Girls School, added to the usual curriculum of French, English, Latin and German, a commercial syllabus which included shorthand, typing, book-keeping and French and English business correspondence. Miss Barrowes, so claims one grateful beneficiary, 'might be said to have put Jamaican girls on the map'.[60]

The health services also provided more occupation for women. The census gives only 20 nurses for the whole island in 1881, and 129 for the whole island in 1891, including three men.

Through the Deaconess programme the Anglican Church sought to develop a corps of nurses, though, as Nuttall indicated, the preference was for coloured women:

> As regards nursing even more had been accomplished. In this work one real difficulty to contend with has been the prejudice against it on the part of many, especially among the coloured people to whom we chiefly look for volunteers, but who have not been in the habit of considering the vocation of nurse a very honourable one.[61]

Black Jamaican women took up the profession of nursing, which became open to them because coloured women did not think it prestigious enough, and because of increased educational facilities for women. In 1904 the Jamaican Nurses Union was established, with the encouragement of the Anglican Church, and its objectives were to facilitate communication between nurses and medical men as well as patients who required their services.[62] For those who, in their dedication to the cult of 'true womanhood', preferred women to be "Queen of the Home" the nursing profession could be explained as an extension of the nurturant role played by women at home.

There was a concerted effort to encourage women to take up the teaching profession. In 1883 ministers of religion came together to draft a memorandum to the acting Governor advocating the establishment of a training college for women. As the clergymen saw it, the young women were to come from a 'grade in life higher than that of most of the students who enter training colleges . . . they would be persons of a higher social culture and of more general intelligence'. The ministers also thought that women were more efficient teachers than men. Their claim rested on British and United States authorities who claimed that females had a 'greater natural aptitude for teaching children and bearing with their ignorance and restlessness'.[63] Female teachers were also expected to exercise a healthy moral influence on their charges:

In view of the social condition of the people, the moral influence of well-trained female teachers upon scholars of their own sex would be of incalculable value.

Finally, the memorialists argued that such a programme 'would have a beneficial effect on the community by opening careers of such honorable employment to young women'.

There was one other pressing consideration, and that was the lack of moral restraint on the part of male teachers with respect to their older female pupils; though the Inspector of Schools admitted that 'under temptation, more or less severe, the moral stamina of several teachers has given way'.

The most painful feature of the matter is the fact that in several instances the change of teacher has been rendered necessary under Government Regulation respecting the maintenance of moral character . . . Among them, I regret to say, are some whom I have heretofore had occasion to commend highly for efficient work in the schoolroom.[64]

The Inspector commented on the 33 per cent turnover of teachers for that particular year, a turnover closely associated with the larger problem of sexual immorality. The introduction of more women into the classroom would stabilise staff, offer an ideal role model for girls, introduce gentler forms of discipline, and provide honourable work for women.

Women played an active role in the Jamaica Union of Teachers and from that platform tackled, in a practical manner, issues relating to women. Firstly, they asked for equal salaries; secondly, they protested against restrictions imposed on the professional mobility of women. Impediments to mobility arose precisely because of the policy of the Churches to employ men who could serve as catechists, according to the assumptions of the time.

Women were also employed as telegraph clerks. In 1889 they earned 10/- per week, and apparently were expected to pay rent, provide their own furniture, and to present a 'respectable appearance'.

> I think myself that when the Government can stoop to insult a class of respectable females who carry on the work of a responsible and paying institution, by paying them six-pence per day, allowing only for the first hour one shilling for working after official hours, it is time the matter was taken up by the new representatives of the country and set right.[65]

Artisans, teachers, nurses, constables, and prosperous small farmers represented a diffuse group of occupations standing between the minorities and the masses. They constituted the 'respectable' blacks of colonial society and probably represented a fair number of people who emigrated to seek superior opportunities elsewhere, for the obvious reason that their material circumstances could not support their 'respectability'. It was sometimes noted that many of the emigrants came from the 'middle walks of life' in Jamaica.

Out of this group has emerged the professional strata of black Jamaicans, whose 'respectability' and status rested upon education and professional attainments, rather than upon ownership of the means of production. Within this group can be identified the black intelligentsia which for a long time had been in formation. The ideas of the intelligentsia form the subject matter of the following chapter.

Notes

1   R.T. Smith, 'Race and Class in the Post-Emancipation Caribbean', in Robert Ross (ed.) *Racism and Colonialism: Essays on Ideology and Social Structure*, Leiden: Martinus Nijhoff 1982, p. 108.
2. *DG*, 28 March, 1886.
3   *DG*, 6 September, 1889.
4   Sir Anthony Musgrave, *Jamaica*.
5   *Ibid.* p. 14.
6   *Ibid.* p. 13.
7   Velma Newton, *The Silver Men. West Indian Labour Migration to Panama 1850–1914*, Kingston: ISER 1984, p. 106.
8   *JG*, Vol. XI, 1888. Report of Committee on Immigration, p. 686. The Committee consisted of Messrs. Neale Porter, Michael Solomon, W. Bancroft Espeut, Charles Mosse.
9   CO, 137/532, 1887. Norman (No. 364), 25 October, 1887. Enclosure Dr Gayleard's report on conditions in Panama.
10 CO, 137/541, Vol. 1, 1890. Blake (No. 47), 1890. Enclosing petition of Clarendon farmers.
11 CO, 137/542, 1890. Blake (No. 59), 10 February, 1890 reporting on tour of the

island and enclosing petition of farmers.

12   *JG*, Vol. 17, No. 39, 22 March, 1894. Address to Blake by Clarendon Agricultural Association.

13   Jamaica Archives, 1B/5/18, Vol. 50. Blake (No. 234), 3 July, 1895. 'Jamaica Agricultural Society'.

14   *Ibid*. Blake (No. 326).

15   R.T. Smith, *Race and Class*, p. 109.

16   WIRC, 1897. Evidence of Mr Thomas Smickle, 5 April, 1897, p. 325/333.

17   Rev. C.A. Wilson, *Men with Backbone*, p. 8.

18   MST 209, *Bishop's Letter Book*, Vol. 7, 14 July, 1883. Nuttall to Mr Asbourne.

19   *Ibid*. Nuttall to Mr Asbourne, 14 July, 1883.

20   *JCM*, 1887 Appendix XVIII. Annual Report of Inspector of Schools to 30 September, 1886.

21   *DG*, 9 March, 1885, 'A Son of Africa' to Editor.

22   CO, 137/514, 1884. Memorandum signed by Mr Matthew Josephs 'for and on behalf of the Meeting of the General Association of Schoolmasters in the Island of Jamaica'.

23   W.F. Bailey, *History of the Jamaica Union of Teachers*, Kingston: Gleaner Co. Ltd. 1937.

24   *Ibid*. p. 12.

25   C.A. Wilson, *Men of Vision*, p. 86.

26   *JA*, 22 June, 1895, J.H. Reid, 'Negro Isolation'.

27   *JA*, 27 June, 1896, 'The Little Kirk and the Rev. Robert Dingwall'.

28   Rev. R. Dingwall, 'Outlook for Jamaica and her People' in Rev. R. Gordon, *et al. Jamaica's Jubilee*, 1888, especially pp. 119–128.

29   *JA*, 21 September, 1895.

30   WIRC, 1897. Written testimony of Charles P. Lazarus (West End Foundry, Kingston, Jamaica) for the information of the West Indian Royal Commission, pp. 405/413 to 406/414.

31   *Ibid*. 406/414.

32   B.W. Higman, 'Domestic Service in Jamaica since 1750', in B.W. Higman, *Trade, Government and Society in Caribbean History, 1700–1920*, Kingston: Heinemann Educational Books, 1983, p. 126.

33   WIRC, 1897. W. Clarke Murray D.D., Vice-President, Wesleyan Conference, to the secretary of Her Majesty's Commission, pp. 388/396 to 389/397.

34   Jamaica. *Legislative Council Proceedings*, 4 May and 11 May, 1898.

35   WIRC, 1897. Evidence of Hon. W. Ewen, Custos of Westmoreland, p. 337/345.

36   See Jamacia Censuses of 1871, 1881, 1891.

37   Census, 1911. Housing, p. 5.

38   *JBB*, 1889.

39   Report of Royal Commission upon the Condition of the Juvenile Population of Jamaica (RCJ), 1879, p. 16.

40   WIRC, 1897. Testimony of Charles P. Lazarus.

41   *Ibid*.

42   RCJ, 1879. Evidence of Mr Alexander Berry.

43   *Ibid*.

44   WIRC, 1897. Evidence of Andrew Little, p. 330.

45   *Ibid*. Evidence of James Cox, p. 340/348.

46   *DG*, 27 March, 1886, and 'O.P.Q'. to Editor, *DG*, 22 March, 1886 and 4 April, 1886.

47   WIRC, 1897. Evidence of W. Clarke Murray.

48   Trevor Turner, 'Social Objectives in the Educational Thought of Jamaicans 1870–1920', Ph. D. University of Toronto, 1975, p. 124.
49   E.H. Hunt, *British Labour History 1815–1914*, New Jersey: Humanities Press, 1981, p. 39.
50   Trevor Turner, *Social Objectives*, p. 401.
51   WIRC, 1897. Testimony of Charles Lazarus.
52   Keith McDonald, 'Professional Formation: the case of Scottish Accountants' in *British Journal of Sociology*, Vol. 35, 1984, pp. 174–5.
53   *DG*, 13 December, 1899, 'Artisans Union'.
54   *DG*, 20 December, 1899, 'Artisans Union'.
55   *Ibid.*
56   *DG*, 21 December, 1899.
57   *JA*, 6 April, 1895, 'The Condition *Sine Qua Non* of the Complete Elevation of the Negro Race'.
58   *JA*, 14 September, 1895. 'Truths to be Remembered'.
59   *JDR*, 1895–6. 'Proportionate Numbers of Bridegrooms and Brides who signed by Mark, per 1,000 Persons Married'.
60   *JM*, Essay of Mrs Enid Pilgrim (née Carrington).
61   NLJ, MST 209a, Vol. 29, *Bishop's Letter Book*. Nuttall to Jamaica Church Ladies' Association in England, 9 August, 1892.
62   F. Cundall, *Jamaica in 1912*, p. 62.
63   *JG*, 18 October, 1883. Memorial from Ministers of Religion to Major-General Gamble (Acting Governor).
64   JCM, 1887. Appendix XVIII, Report of George Hicks, Inspector of Schools.
65   *DG*, 11 March, 1889. 'Fair Play' to Editor.

CHAPTER 12 | The black intelligentsia

The purpose of this chapter is to discuss the perspectives developed by educated black men on insular colonial society, on race and racism and on Africa.

Basic numeracy and literacy were offered to the rural population through the evolving system of primary education, primarily through the Churches. Primary education, along with teacher education, amounted to almost the full range of education available to the black rural family. Others, following the example of the well-to-do, sought education overseas.

The members of the colonial intelligentsia whom we discuss in this chapter emerged out of the class of prosperous rural farmers, out of the artisan layer of the society, or occasionally out of families who had already become members of the teaching profession. They were clearly men of above average ability, and in some cases, had access to large personal libraries. Claude McKay, for example, had the advantage of a large library possessed by his brother, an elementary school teacher. Marcus Garvey also had access to a good library owned by his father. A.A. Barclay won a scholarship to University College, and passed London Matriculation in the first division. In 1904, at age 28 years, Barclay entered the Presbyterian Mission Theological Hall at Woodlands. He taught at New Broughton and Ebenezer School, both in the parish of Manchester.

Rev. R. Gordon attended the Presbyterian Mission School and the Montego Bay Academy. As a schoolmaster he taught classics, maths and English; but then left the schoolroom for the ministry. He was pastor at Mt Horeb, Mt Herron, and Misgah. Sometime after 1890 he left Jamaica for the United States where he became a Bishop of the African Methodist Episcopal Church.

William Frederick Bailey, whose parents were teachers, was born in 1863. He grew up in the home of his grandfather, a 'highly respected' officer of the Moravian Church at Fairfield (in Manchester). He entered the Government college at Spanish Town, and graduated from there in 1885, 'prize-man of the year'. He was appointed to Mt Olivet School in northern Manchester, where he remained for ten years. His influence on the younger generation of students was reputedly considerable.[1] He was regarded as having a 'larger view' of the teachers' calling.

He set himself to inspire and uplift the entire community. He kept special classes for pupil teachers and paying scholars in the afternoons, and on Fridays. He purchased an American organ and instructed many in instrumental music . . . He trained the Church choir, was superintendent of one of the best Sunday Schools in the land. His annual school entertainments drew crowds, and did not a little to produce many an eloquent speaker. He cultivated a field and taught the dignity of labour, and gave the lie to croakers, who were urging the unwisdom of the education of the masses, because it was turning the youth of the country from the soil.[2]

Rev. Samuel Josiah Washington was born in 1844 of parents who had been slaves. After attending primary school in Savanna-la-Mar he was apprenticed to his brother and worked as a mason. He later went to the Calabar Normal College, a Baptist institution. He was then employed at the Stewart Town Baptist School, Washington, successfully turning the school into a first class one, relinquished teaching and entered the Calabar Theological College in 1875. He served as minister at the Green Island Baptist Church; he served in Port Antonio and Porus as well.[3]

Joseph Henry Reid was born in Westmoreland in 1851, left school at 12 years old following the death of his father. It is not clear how Reid completed his education, but he became a lay preacher, and a master of a choir which became well known, rendering 'services of songs and entertainments' in the Montego Bay area. He taught at New Road, Moravia, and subscribed several articles to Robert Love's *Jamaica Advocate*. He died in 1921.[4]

Robert Dingwall was born at New Broughton in South Manchester, and is described as a student of 'exceptional ability'. He attended the Theological College of the Presbyterian Church where he was taught by Dr Alexander Robb. His mind became unhinged, and he spent a short time in the asylum. He resumed his career but Dingwall's heart was 'broken' by the depravity of the island, which unstrung his mind. He died in the asylum.[5]

Since Mr Matthew Joseph has written his own autobiographical sketch we will let him speak for himself:

My father was the eldest son of Agullon, a prince of one of the Eboe tribes inhabiting a tract of country nearly bordering on the Gulf of Guinea, who, as he told my father, had been a general in his own land, before he was stolen thence – which was about the year 1780 and brought over the vast Atlantic, with many others of his countrymen and countrywomen, and sold as slaves on a plantation (Rose Hill). Reflecting often on the high position he had occupied in his native country, he bore the yoke of slavery with much uneasiness; and from the turbulent spirit he frequently exhibited he was always considered by his owner as a dangerous slave. He died at an advanced age two years before the emancipation. My father's mother – from whom I received some information respecting the customs and manners of her country, Dahomey, lived much longer . . .

During the period of my childhood there was no school in the country districts, to which the children of my race could be sent to receive the elements of useful learning; but my father, having been taught to read by a kind bookkeeper on the plantation on which he was 'headman', endeavoured to teach my brothers and myself to read . . .

In the year 1839, the Church Missionary Society established a mission and school at Woodford, two miles distant from my native place. That school I attended for about a year when my father left that part of the parish to settle in another district [there were certain problems with his schooling but by 1847 he was at the Government Normal School then recently established near Spanish Town, to be trained as a teacher]. [I took] charge of Woodford School, on the mastership becoming vacant in July 1849.

After labouring at Woodford for seven years . . . I obtained the more important situation of the mastership of the Church School, Trinity Ville, Blue Mountain Valley . . . It was while residing in this place, where Nature is seen in all her loveliness and sublimity, that I felt an ardent desire to express in verse the thoughts I had always, from my childhood, so strangely entertained of Nature, of Nature's God, and of the cruel wrongs inflicted on my race. In 1862 I published *The Slave and Minor Poems*, and two years after, *Time and Eternity*. These little publications having met with much success, I have been induced and advised to collect all my principal poetical writings and publish them in a single volume.

Joseph's poem *The Wonders of Creation and other Poems* is 'one of our first native long poems [231 pages]'.[6] Joseph was born in 1831. After his retirement from teaching he returned to farming. At some point Joseph journeyed to London where his work was published.[7]

Dr Theophilus E.S. Scholes grew up in Stewart Town, St Ann; he left Jamaica in 1873, and returned in 1885 fully qualified in medicine from the University of Edinburgh. He travelled to Africa as a medical missionary, wrote two books on the problems of empire and on the situation of coloured people within the British Empire. He was a contributor to Dr Robert Love's

Jamaica Advocate. Dr Love was born in Nassau, arrived in Jamaica during the 1890s, and founded the *Jamaica Advocate*, a weekly paper. He had spent a long time in the southern United States and in Haiti. A strong advocate of social causes, and a stern critic of the inequalities of Jamaican society, Love's *Advocate* provided a platform for the voice of black Jamaicans.[8]

The following two biographical sketches are of 'coloured' Jamaicans rather than 'black' Jamaicans, and they are included primarily because of their close identification with black education. They are Rev. William Webb, and William Plant. The former was born in January 1839. His father, the overseer of a property, later acquired two pieces of property of his own, and doubled as a building contractor. At the age of 15 years Webb attended Mico College where he obtained a first-class certificate after three years. After two years in the classroom he entered Calabar. Rev. Jonathan East, the founder of that institution, wished to send him to Stewart Town but the congregation was unwilling to accept a coloured minister, though in truth he did also have a reputation for preaching sermons of one hour. In 1901 Webb won a seat in the Legislative Council where he served two terms. He died in 1912.

William Plant was born in the vicinity of Mandeville, Manchester in 1860. His mother was a 'full-blooded Negress, his father an Englishman'. He attended Mandeville Free School and since 'enlightened folks of all colours did not wish to have a coloured man for their pastor', Plant decided to be a schoolmaster instead. At the age of 19 years, he entered the Government Training College in Spanish Town. He taught at Ebenezer school, and was transferred from there to Titchfield on the recommendation of Bishop (later Archbishop) Nuttall in 1886. In 1891 he attended the University Branch of the Jamaica High School to 'fit himself' for the secondary department at Titchfield. He was one time president of the Jamaica Union of Teachers, visited the Tuskegee Institute on the occasion of the International Negro Conference. In his retirement, he became Secretary of the Trustees of Wolmer's School, and was an active member of the Jamaica Agricultural Society. He was Chairman of the Teachers Mutual Aid Society, and sat on various Church committees.[9]

So far we know very little of the life-story of Rev. C.A. Wilson, the major source of much of the biographical material above. He was a minister of the Presbyterian faith, and comes to our attention as co-author of *Jamaica's Jubilee* in 1888. Wilson wrote two other books, *Men of Vision*, and *Men with Backbone*.

How did men such as these, more or less self-made, respond to the situation around them? Intellectual qualities are, after all, as Barrington Moore points out 'not merely a matter of individual endowment. They are also a product of the entire social and cultural environment in which a young person has grown up'.[10] It is Mannheim's view that when 'solitary individuals move between existence in two different cultural contexts, they become marginal and have no single worldview . . . The common frame of reference disappears when two or more groups or cultures exist side by side, each having its own approach to things'. He suggests that for socially mobile intellectuals the necessity becomes greater to comprehend 'different points of view' given the existence of 'multiple realities'.[11] To what extent can the intellectual, in terms of action do anything more than articulate the interests of various antagonistic social groups, for or against social change?

The content of their education was consciously formulated to steer them away from 'folk-culture', to anglicise them, and thereby remove them from the cultural, intellectual, even spiritual world of the Jamaican masses. On the one hand, personal progress demanded distance between them and the Afro-Jamaican masses. On the other hand, their own merits were assessed not only in terms of their ability to manipulate European culture, manners, religion, but in terms of their membership of a race which was viewed negatively. The process is often seen as one of 'alienation'.

> The process of alienation was waged on an additional front . . . The literary one. Through stereotype, white society depersonalized the black man's possible selves, aborted his fulfilment, and distorted his real self, making him an unreal thing. This method of psychological alienation has been considered to be the worst . . . Blacks viewed themselves as being in the community but not of it . . . Such a realization may bring varied responses. One response might be a falling back on the distinct culture which blacks have fashioned and which can provide some measure of security against alienation . . . Another might be a move towards integration with the dominant group, which not only involves a cultivation of prevailing cultural values but also an internalization of the prevailing attitudes towards blacks . . . Many black writers in the past [had] no firm cultural base in the reality of either the black world or white.[12]

We think that the above definition constituted the most pessimistic explanation of 'alienation'. In a society undergoing a continuous Creolisation process the world of whites and the world of blacks were never sharply divided in any absolute sense. It can also never be clear the extent to which whites believe in their superiority as a race, as opposed to their certainty of superiority as a caste or class within a specific social formation. It is known that cultural gaps can be bridged, racial ones cannot. Herein lies the importance of racism as a force for social control.

Racism forces upon its victims a consciousness of race, so that 'cultural' progress or lack of it, becomes synonymous with racial progress or lack of it. The achievement or lack of achievement of one becomes the achievement or lack of achievement of all. Educational and cultural progress in a society of materially deprived blacks was an important yardstick for measuring the progress of the race. The absorption of the cultural values of the dominant group did not therefore assume, not all the time anyway, the internalisation of prevailing prejudices towards blacks. It is for this reason that men such as we have just described were simultaneously men of thought and men of action, particularly in the realm of education. They accepted the prevailing Christian religious orthodoxy – some were Baptists, others Anglicans and Presbyterians – and they viewed society through the lenses of Christian humanitarianism. Their ability to act as surrogates for the oppressed classes was restrained by the fact that among the most formative influences on young Jamaicans were the school and the Church. That constraint was, however, one of method, not of strategy.

Claude McKay, the poet from the hills of Clarendon, conceded the thoroughly English foundations of his education, and demonstrated a kind of dual personality, one which insisted that Jamaica was the 'nigger's home', the other side which yearned for England, the cultural metropolis.[13] The formative influence of the Church was crucial to the creation of an intelligentsia which viewed the world from a Christian perspective, and rested the hope of all humanity upon the victory of Christian principles in daily life. The biographical sketches which we have given above illustrated the centrality of Church and school. Even Scholes, the most secular and most sophisticated of Jamaican born intellectuals of the period was constrained to see the hope of humanity in the readiness with which the world's citizens were prepared 'to do unto others what ye would that they should do unto you'.[14] Despite Scholes's growing secularism, and the secularism and pragmatism of Dr Robert Love, they were yet influenced by basic Christian philosophy.

Christianity, rather than blunting the ideology of freedom among black Jamaican slaves actually, in the Christmas Rebellion of 1831, gave that ideology more of a cutting edge.[15] The Morant Bay Rebellion of 1865 was led by Paul Bogle, a black Baptist Deacon. Just as forceful, and more comprehensive a statement on the methods of colonial domination is the view that there was a 'complete internalization of the history of the settlers [which] ensures yielding acceptance of the colonized's alleged social, cultural and intellectual inferiority'.[16] While it is true that westernization and all its appurtenances is an important mode of social control, we need not assume that rejection of the history of the settlers, of intellectual inferiority and so on will yield defiance, any more than an acceptance of Christianity presumes submissiveness.

The black intellectual had perhaps been co-opted, and his co-optation did not lead to social acceptance because of racism. Nor did his occasional ambivalence lead him to isolate himself from the destiny of the black masses of the population. Their own claim to be 'civilised' depended for its validity partly upon the number of blacks in the community who were also 'civilised'. Furthermore, as clergymen or men closely associated with the Christian Church they were part of a tradition of missionary, amelioratory work. In that sense they were concerned with social reform.

The land question

The black intelligentsia were particularly critical of the distribution of economic resources, particularly land, which was methodically kept out of the hands of rural farmers. Since land was Jamaica's major economic resource, landownership was a critical factor in the definition of classes. Rev. Dingwall pointed to the limited access of black farmers to land, compared with the favour shown to East Indians as an example of social injustice.[17] J.H. Reid noted that black farmers cultivated the hills for want of more cultivable land. Without compensation for his services during slavery, Reid argued, the Jamaican farmer should have been offered more land rather than the small patches he had obtained which did not afford him 'standing room'.[18] W.F. Bailey, writing in 1888, commented on the relationship between land tenure and demoralisation. 'That their services might be secured for these estates, land is not sold to them by the proprietors, and all the mean and demoralising results consequent upon living in this condition stand plainly out, to the disgust and annoyance of all who love the country's weal'.[19]

Theophilus Scholes placed the problem of land tenure in the broader context of an imperial system of appropriation of 'native resources'. The British Empire 'systematically deprived the coloured races of access to the land', and in Jamaica's case and that of the West Indies, the virtues of equality under British Law, missionary work and education were counterbalanced by such 'hindering influences as the dearth of cultivated lands'.[20] Indeed, empire amounted to a transfer of the resources of the coloured peoples to the metropolitan centre, like a 'giant sponge' applied to a 'pail of water'. Land ownership was illustrative in Scholes's view of 'class government'. Like Bailey and Love, Scholes saw landownership as part of a conspiracy on the part of planters, for example, to continue to tie labourers to the estates. In order to make the peasantry mere dependents on the estates 'the sugar interest . . . pursued the policy of withholding its lands from that portion of the community'. He identified land hunger, high taxation, and ignorance of scientific agriculture as hindrances to the contributions which farmers could make to the country's economic growth.[21] Scholes, who believed that failure to institute measures which would adjust the inequalities of empire would lead ultimately to socialist revolution, took the view that the Empire could be strengthened by a more enlightened approach to land policy. 'If the freedmen had been settled on small plots of land at the time of emancipation, and had schools been erected in a few centres for instructing them in agriculture, not only would British taxpayers have been saved the grants-in-aid with which from time to time they have assisted the West Indian colonies . . . but it is our conviction that . . . the imports of British goods into these colonies would at least have been double that amount. So that this melancholy record of 178 years of failure . . . is a failure that the Beet Sugar Bounty has only brought into bolder relief. This record is surely the fullest conceivable condemnation of the system of class government'.[22] There is a suggestion here that 'class government' is economically irrational because it failed to release land to the productive energies of an educated yeoman class of coloured farmers. The plantation economy of the West Indies weakened the Empire by enfeebling the outposts of empire. Scholes's critique of empire did not envisage, yet, a destruction of empire, but a readjustment of class relations within the empire. Subsequent history has, if anything, emphasised that with the removal of the formal institutions of empire, the essentials of empire have remained.

Now, one of the major charges made against black Jamaican workers was that they despised the soil, and shunned agricultural pursuits. The accusation was made and believed despite the fact that the majority of black Jamaicans worked on the soil as smallholders or as agricultural labourers. But for sections of the elite agriculture was equivalent to large-scale commercial plantation enterprise, and it is true that where small farmers had an option they preferred agriculture on their own account, or to share their time between plantation work and independent cultivation. The views of the black intelligentsia on this question illustrate their fundamental sympathy with the tendency of many labourers to keep away from the plantation sector. They frankly saw continued plantation labour as a constraint on the social and economic progress of the black population. For Scholes, the sugar plantation worker was 'only a bit of machinery, as long as he lives on an estate. He has no chance of developing himself in any way'. For C.A. Wilson, the movement away from plantation work demonstrated ambition on the part of labourers, not laziness:

> The favoured gentry have expressed the opinion that sons of the soil look with disdain on agricultural pursuits and clamour for clerkships and professions . . . [But] nobody will blame a man for desiring to be respectable. The man with the machete and the fork does not earn nearly as much as the man with the yardstick and pen. Dissatisfaction in the bright son of a labourer may well

be regarded as a hopeful sign . . . Men are seeking remuneration commensurate with their output of labour.[23]

Bailey described sugar estate work as semi-serfdom and thraldom.[24] In 1888, Rev. Gordon, responding to the 'uncharitable' things which the gentry had to say about black workers, pointed to the limited wages available to agricultural workers. 'One shilling a day [is] too little to serve as an incentive to help him up'. The introduction of East Indian labour forced free black workers to compete with semi-slave labour on the sugar estates. A spokesman before the Commission of 1897 lamented that East Indian labour violated the principle of a 'free labour market'.[25]

These spokesmen were entirely consistent in viewing poverty among the black population as a consequence of exploitation and unequal distribution of resources. The 'rich few', argued Wilson, 'who would hound to death the lazy peasant, and whip him with the cat-o'-nine who steals a hand of banana, are indirectly helping to pauperize and to criminalize'. Wilson was acutely aware of the protection which the law gave to the privileged, and of the adverse application of the law to labourers and to the poor. Poverty was a consequence of social injustice, and particularly of the inequitable distribution of land:

> Peasants need more land . . . As a rule, they occupy one or two properties cut up into scores of smallholdings, whilst around them are thousands of acres of the favoured few partly lying fallow or ruinate. Some refuse to rent one acre. Tenants give trouble no doubt. But one man should not be allowed to hold hundreds of acres he cannot utilize, when scores of his fellows might be cultivating it for the good of the community. A man with land valued over £1,000 is privileged. The law protects him. He does not pay his fair share of taxation. The favoured few should be forced to sell some of the surplus acreage. Why should a man be encouraged to purchase well-nigh inaccessible back-lands whilst wide acres in popular centres are lying unculti-vated?[26]

Wilson also commented on the loss of land by small cultivators to the 'privileged caste' who exploited the ill-fortune and ignorance of poorer men. Wilson made his statement in response to Governor William Manning who had said that 'people' should not 'covet' other people's land:

> On the platform beside him were men who had been adding property after property by a clever system of mortgage, men who had ruthlessly turned off their tenants and all but pauperized whole communities . . . Adverse circumstances always are at work compelling men to mortgage their smallholdings . . . to men

> whom fortune has favoured with abundant cash . . . Jamaica's
> best business is done by the man who can afford to prey on his
> fellows in difficulties.[27]

Contrary to what the gentry wished to suggest, namely that the sugar
plantation was the means whereby the black man would be 'civilised' by
living in close proximity to whites (the identical argument used for the
encomienda system) the plantation was viewed as a major nucleus of
depravity, immorality and demoralisation.[28]

Most black spokesmen challenged the adverse conditions under which
labourers worked on sugar plantations – inadequate housing, low wages, the
competition with contracted East Indian labour. But few, like Scholes,
offered a comprehensive condemnation of the plantation system. Most did
not go much beyond the white clergyman Rev. Henry Clarke of Westmoreland, and Governor Sir Anthony Musgrave, in their criticisms of the sugar
planters and the self-centred pursuit of their interest. Dingwall restricted
himself to saying that Jamaica suffered more from her 'soft times' when the
plantocracy 'prospered' than from her 'hard times',[29] a view echoed by
Governor Sir Henry Blake. Scholes questioned the myth that the primary
problem of the sugar industry was the beet bounties. Rather, he argued, the
structural weakness of the sugar industry had simply been aggravated by the
beet bounties:

> Was the Beet Bounty the cause of the problem in 1772 and 1791
> when as we know the owners being embarrassed, 318 of their
> estates passed from their hands, whilst the indebtedness of the
> industry was £22,563,786? Has not the Beet Bounty rather ac-
> centuated the malady already in existence than produced it? Can
> an industry which after two centuries of an unbroken record of
> failure, notwithstanding exceptional advantages and privileges,
> and supplemented by Parliamentary grants, be said still to have
> any claim to exceptional advantage and treatment?[30]

Scholes concluded that sugar was a 'paralytic and parasitic industry'. He
took strong exception to the Government granting financial assistance to an
industry which 'contributed practically nothing to its support'. The revenues of government were derived, Scholes argued with much evidence to
support him, from the peasantry not from the sugar planters. Rev. Henry
Clarke, had argued similarly in 1884:

> During the last 50 years they [the planters] have been constantly
> receiving vast sums out of the public revenue of the island to
> import coolies for their private and exclusive use under the name
> of immigrants but who are really slaves; and in the face of this
> fact their present outcry against bounty-fed sugar seems to me

rather inconsistent . . . Taxation has been removed from their estates and imports, and placed chiefly on the food and raiment of the Negroes . . . The sugar estates hitherto managed have been a hindrance to the progress of the emancipated people in wealth as well as morals. As a rule they are centres of vice and poverty. As the Negroes have no chance of speaking for themselves I feel sure you will give me this opportunity of speaking for them.[31]

We cannot assume that all educated blacks thought in this way about land, though the reality is that all those who discussed the matter in print were antagonistic to the prevailing system of land tenure. And as the quotation from Rev. Henry Clarke, above, demonstrated, there were sectors of the white group who criticised the planter class severely. In truth, the land question was ultimately a political question.

It was Dr Robert Love who gave most attention to the political question, though it is clear that he was articulating views shared with others. Love's response to the 1895 dockworkers' strike showed that his views on political development were not bound solely to blacks winning seats in the Legislative Council. Love envisaged the establishment of labour clubs or labour unions all over the colony, associations of workers which would exercise the kind of lobbying power which would enable the causes of the masses to be represented in the Council. Love's approach, while favouring black candidates, was more concerned with supporting candidates who addressed themselves to those social and economic issues with which Love and the *Jamaica Advocate* were most concerned. The Jamaica Union of Teachers was also envisaged as playing the role of surrogate of black interests.[32] But reform was to be achieved through greater control of the institutions of government rather than through a change of institutions.

Race and civilisation

The negative, contemporary image of blacks forced spokesmen to defend blacks not only as labourers (or as a class) but also as members of a race. They were aware that the misfortunes of independent Haiti were gleefully noted as 'proof' that blacks had no capacity for self-government. But Scholes recognised that the Haitian example was used as an argument in favour of the perpetuation of the current racial and class structure in Jamaica:

The planter, anxious to perpetuate his rule of absolutism by cutting off or obstructing the prospects of success that may be opening to the Negro, points to Hayti. The civil servant who looks upon the Negro as a rival, by whom he may probably be

ousted, points to Hayti. The political jobber, dreading the elevation of the Negro, by means of the franchise, to a position of
corresponding equality, points to Hayti.[33]

The question of race was not openly discussed in Jamaica for tactical
reasons and racist comments on the black race came more from overseas
than from Jamaica itself. But whatever the origin of racial slants black
spokesmen had to find suitable responses. White society had international-
ised race.

An obvious target for criticism was J.A. Froude who visited the
Caribbean in the 1880s and published his book *The English in the West
Indies: Or the Bow of Ulisses*.[34] Froude was really no worse than most
expatriate observers of the West Indies, and in some respects he was more
generous. In referring to black workers he says: 'We, too, only work as
much as we like or as we must, and we prefer working for ourselves to
working for others'.[35] His observation that 'social exclusiveness was increasing with political equality' in Jamaica was a shrewd and accurate
one.[36] Froude, however, like so many other whites, assumed the 'natural
superiority' of whites, and found the idea of self-government for the West
Indies in which there would be provision for a black Parliament untenable,
if not ridiculous. It was J.J. Thomas who wrote a systematic rebuttal of
Froude in his well known work *Froudacity*.

Scholes's attack on Froude was polemical:

> Mr Froude's attitude in his book . . . is not that of a great historian
> who, conscious of his responsibility as the conveyancer of truth
> to his generation and to generations yet unborn, seeks to dis-
> charge his duty fearlessly and impartially; neither is it the attitude
> of a great traveller . . . and a man of letters, but it is the attitude
> of a lawyer, and one not of the highest professional standing who,
> with little compunction, goes down into the gutter to collect the
> slime, and garbage of contempt, disdain and scorn, and conscious
> superiority, with which under the dominance of a diseased van-
> ity, he proceeds to . . . besmear and plaster the adversary of his
> client.[37]

Another of Scholes's targets was Dr E.A. Freeman whom he describes as a
historian 'of some repute', a scholar of Trinity College, Oxford. Freeman
had argued that:

> You may give [the black man] the rights of citizenship by law;
> you can never make him the real equal, the real fellow, of citizens
> of European descent . . . The Negro may be a man and a brother
> in some secondary sense; he is not a man and a brother in the
> same full sense in which every western Aryan is a man and a

brother . . . He cannot be assimilated; the laws of Nature forbid it.[38]

Scholes's response was to outline the relationship between the growth of European civilisation and the contributions of the ancient world when, in Scholes's view, there had been a substantial black contribution. This aspect of his thought he developed more fully in his larger work *Glimpses of the Ages*, which sought to establish that European civilisation evolved out of ancient Egypt, and that Europe was once as barbarous or more so than contemporary Africa which was, as a matter of course, viewed as barbaric. The early Egyptians who built the pyramids were blackmen:

> Had [Dr Freeman] been rightly influenced by his great historical knowledge . . . he would have asked whether the progressive races have always held their present position . . . And their progress would have been found to have grown into the blaze of European progress and advancement . . . were originally produced in Africa [Egypt]. And that in connection with the birth of science and art, the African, the Negro was no idle spectator, but an active and enthusiastic originator and participator.[39]

Furthermore, among the contemporary tribes of Africa 'there will not probably be found one occupying a place so low as that which in their earlier years the Greek race occupied . . . Egypt was the mine in which the metal, civilisation, was dug and cast into bullion and ingots'. In order to dismiss, once and for all, the myth of black inferiority, Scholes resorted to one of his acerbic syllogisms:

> So, then, unless it can be proved that when these Egyptians were the greatest civilised power in the world they were white, and when the white races of today were barbarians they were black or brown, the theory that the white skin is associated with progress and greatness cannot be sustained, neither can the obverse, that the dark skin is associated with littleness, be maintained.[40]

The Christianisation of Africa

The black colonial intelligentsia clearly saw that their immediate function was to counter myths of inferiority, and to do so they delved into the history of civilisation, which evolved through various phases, starting from Africa, to the highest phase as it currently existed in Europe. At the same time, to adopt such a position was to prove that blacks were capable of civilisation, and in that sense were equal to the white race. To adopt such a definition of the growth of civilisation meant that black intellectuals were in duty bound to concede that contemporary Africa was, objectively, backward, but could rise to prominence once again, when the 'light' of western civilisation was transferred to that continent. Black nationalism, the antithesis of white racism, logically sought a telluric base on the African continent itself.

We noted in an earlier part of this chapter that black intellectuals were in large part the products of a clerical education, whether because the schools they attended were established and run by the Churches of the island, or because they themselves became pastors in the Christian Churches. Scholes was a medical practitioner and a Baptist missionary. Dr Love was also a pastor of the Anglican Church. The other men whom we have mentioned vacillated between Church and school. They did not necessarily see the relationship between the role of the Christian Churches and the spread and maintenance of empire. If they did they saw a positive value in the connection. In this age, the end of the nineteenth century, religion and imperialism, associated with the *Pax Britannica*, were stronger allies than ever – resembling in some respects the alliance between Church and state in the Spanish conquest and colonisation of the Americas, in the sixteenth century. In Jamaica itself, the forceful Anglican Archbishop Nuttall was a sincere representative of that association between Church and imperialism.[41]

Educated blacks were to become proselytisers for the Christian Church in Africa. Dr Johnson, a Scottish medical practitioner in St Ann went on an evangelising mission to southern Africa with a group of Jamaicans.[42] The argument which he used to justify the expedition in 1891 was the one used by other cultural imperialists – the black West Indian having been exposed to western civilisation and Christianity had the additional advantages of racial 'empathy' and being able to cope with the climate. When Dr Scholes returned to Jamaica from Scotland in 1885 and reported that his immediate plan was to go to Africa, the Baptist community in Stewart Town was elated:

> Twelve years ago, you left home, a Christian lad, hardly knowing whither you would go, actuated by a laudable desire to develop the faculties of your mind, whereby you might be of greater service to your fellowmen in the service of God . . . Downright hard work has made you member of an honourable profession, but more important . . . is [your] desire to do missionary work – to bring glad tidings of salvation to benighted millions of Africa. For this above all other considerations we bless God for you . . . evangelise the fatherland under the auspices of the lately organised Missionary Society of the Western Churches of our coloured brethren. You have thereby won the highest esteem of your fellow-countrymen and you stand out as a bright example of the

mental culture and moral and religious standards to which our
black boys can attain . . . when higher educational advantages are
offered to them.[43]

The Basel Mission (later the Gold Coast Presbyterian Church) had
originally contacted Chief Addo Dankwa who, in an expansive frame of
mind, had declared his willingness to listen to black Christians:

> When God created the world he made a Book for the Whiteman
> and Fetish or Juju for the Blackman; but if you could show us
> some Blackmen who could read the Whiteman's Book then we
> would surely follow you.[44]

Dankwa was taken seriously. The use of West Indian labour in the mission-
fields was to be a demonstration of the capacity of blacks to live like
Christians. The words of Jamaican missionaries bring out the spirit of West
Indian evangelism in Africa:

> God, who knows the end of all things from the beginning, had in
> His Providence, caused to be removed from the Gold Coast to the
> West Indies some Africans to be taught and be made to accept the
> truth of the Gospel of Jesus Christ.
>
> Wicked men induced by shameful motives inhumanly and
> cruelly dragged many Africans from their land and inheritance
> into forced slavery in a strange country . . . It is a wonder before
> our eyes . . . that the Lord caused Joseph's servitude to be the
> source of deliverance of his family.
>
> We must not all necessarily be preachers or teachers but every-
> one according to his capacity and in his sphere of labour, whether
> with his brains or hands, is expected to do something for the
> elevation of Africa spiritually or bodily.[45]

The view that the slave trade (and slavery) was an act of Providence to
enable the transfer of the torch of Christianity to Africa was, apparently,
widely held. So was the view that the British Empire itself was an instrument of Divine Providence to make possible the enlightenment of
'benighted' Africa. The idea that Joseph's servitude was ultimately a means
of liberation for his family was used by analogy to predict the consequences
of the enslavement of Africans in the Egypt of the West Indies.

Yet the scar of slavery sat heavily on these men, despite their optimis-
tic outlook:

> The children of Ham are universally regarded as accursed by
> God . . . For centuries the track of the slave ship across the
> Atlantic was unquestionably marked by blood, by a species of

suffering then first developed, by the shark in his scent for human
flesh, by degradation and death, by blasphemy braving the heavens, by a consummation of misery never told, and never to be
revealed till the depths of the ocean shall speak, and the records
of God in the miseries of the damned shall be read in that great
day, when those who were actors in the tragedies of the slave
trade, and perpetrated the horrors and miseries and woes of the
notorious 'middle passage' shall cry out in their eternal ago-
nies.[46]

But the myth of empire, of the virtues of Christianisation, and of the
superiority of western civilisation had been thoroughly internalised by
educated blacks. Fundamentally, the standards which these men aspired to
were false or at least artificial; artificial because they were reflections of
idealised western civilisation and Christianity which most whites in
Jamaica separated from their daily lives. Education, and religion, too,
offered to the black intelligentsia a cosmopolitan vision, while the Creole
society, of which they were supposedly a part, was but a distorted fragment
of that vision. The black intellectuals were alienated from the Creole society
which gave them birth.

It was Scholes who commented upon the double standards of Christian
'societies', or as he expressed it the 'lack of truth'.[47] Beyond doubt, Scholes
suffered from deep disillusionment, and in his 1907 work lashed out at the
Protestant Christian Churches, which in his view were a major buttress of
the contemporary views which Europeans cherished about coloured people.
Membership of Christian Churches can and does exist with malignant
prejudice and the practice of discrimination, precisely because members of
a Church are more closely identified with the prejudices of their societies
than with the Church's message of brotherhood.[48] Scholes commented on
the contradiction between the preaching of brotherhood and the practice of
racism:

> Spurned by politics and hounded by literature, surely in the all-
> embracing arm of the Church of Christ, the Ethiopian may wipe
> his tears away, assuage his grief and rejoice in his full welcome
> as a man and a brother! In theory, the Ethiopian does receive
> Christian protection. But the Church fails to carry her theory
> fully into practice . . . And this is especially true of the Protestant
> section of the Church. If the Church had fully recognised the
> Ethiopian as a 'man and a brother' politics and literature would
> have done likewise, for in this respect at least they would reflect
> the action of the Church. We must not be thought to mean that
> Christians, on both hemispheres, hold and practise the un-Chris-
> tian sentiments of race hatred and race distinctions, but we do

wish to state our conviction that a solid mass of them do . . . the Negro is not allowed to hold leading office in Church because of his skin . . . Some will say that it is natural for a white congregation to be presided over by white ministers. But do they think it unnatural for a black congregation to be presided over by a white minister?[49]

Scholes then turned to the 'frenzied hatred' of the 'southern' Church towards blacks, but side by side with that frenzied hatred was the anomalous effort by the same southern Churches in the United States to send missionaries 'to teach Negroes in Africa that God is no respecter of persons'.[50] The attack by Scholes on the Protestant missions coincided with a period in which there was a more pronounced tendency for leadership in the mission stations of Africa to be white, as the new imperialism became associated with the 'white man's burden'.

Claude McKay also grew up in the Baptist faith, but later rejected the Baptist fundamentalism of his parents, and described himself as a free thinker who found religious fundamentalism too inhibiting.[51] Later, McKay returned to the Church – the Catholic Church – genuinely believing, like Scholes and George Blyden, that the Catholic Church placed greater emphasis on the brotherhood of all men. This folly may be excused on the grounds that there were no imperialist Catholic powers, with the exception of the ageing Empires of Spain and Portugal.

Black perspectives on Africa

A discussion of the role of West Indian missionaries in the Christianisation of Africa cannot be separated from a general overview of black perspectives on Africa. This is partly because in the late-nineteenth century – at least after 1884 – the African continent became subject to systematic colonisation from Europe; the 'Dark Continent' had become the focus of western attention and greed. At the same time, the fortune or misfortune of Africa was a psychological aspect of how blacks in the diaspora viewed themselves. The carving up of Africa by the various nations of Europe was symbolic of black powerlessness and a reassertion of the European viewpoint of the inconsequential nature of 'black' civilisation. To political powerlessness was added the history of three hundred years of servitude, and destruction of self-esteem, of what Orlando Patterson has called 'social death'.[52] For Africa had been invented the tradition of 'ethnicity', 'tribe', and racism.[53] The degradation of slavery had survived emancipation, and the colour of the skin had become alone the cause of degradation.

Educated, which is to say anglicised, blacks had no firm foothold in the culture of Africa either on the continent itself or at home, with its proportionately large African population. There was a tendency to distance themselves from the culture of Africa, but not from Africa as homeland. Their identification was with the future of Africa. Profound consciousness of Africa merged with a rejection of contemporary African culture, and the determination to bring the 'light' of civilisation to the continent. Racial pride was strong. Jamaicans still had a great affinity for Africa. It was reported, with some surprise by a visiting clergyman, that Jamaicans had no objections to being called African![54] It was also reported that the large attendance at missionary meetings in Jamaica was partly attributable to the great curiosity which Jamaicans still had for Africa. Matthew Joseph was obviously proud of those origins, and so too was Rev. Washington who was reported to have been a student of 'racial lore, and possessed a knowledge of African tribes, their customs and tribal peculiarities'.[55]

In his earlier years, Claude McKay demonstrated the ambivalence of an anglicised black:

> As an educated youth of black peasant origin, McKay . . . displayed to a painful degree the psychological ambivalence inculcated among West Indians under British colonialism. Both the strength and weakness of his dialect poetry flowed from this attempt to embrace his black Jamaican origins, while simultaneously clinging to Britain as a spiritual homeland.[56]

McKay, like most of the black intelligentsia, had thoroughly internalised the concept of a backward, uncivilised Africa. In his poem, 'Cudjoe Fresh from de Lecture', McKay has Cudjoe reporting as follows:

> No 'cos say we get cuss mek fe we 'kin come so . . .

> Talk 'bouten Africa, we would be deh till now,
> Maybe same half-naked – all day dribe buccra cow,
> An' tearin' t'rough de bush wid all de monkey dem,
> Wile an' uncivilise', an' neber comin' tame.

> Yes, Cous' Jarge, slabbery hot fe dem dat gone befo':
> We gettin' better times, for those days we no know;
> But I t'ink it do good, tek we from Africa
> An' lan' us in a blessed place as dis a ya.[57]

The message is clear. It is not the curse of Ham which has given the black man his skin colour; Africa is wild and uncivilised, and it is a blessing to have been taken out of Africa and placed in Jamaica.

While McKay speaks of England as 'our home' (in a poem written in honour of Inspector W.E. Clark) he yet sees Jamaica as Home (My Native Land, My Home'):

> Jamaica is de nigger's place,
> No mind whe' some declare;
> Although dem call we 'no land race'
> I know we home is here.[58]

Rev. Dingwall, while expressing hope for a revitalised Africa, insists that Africa had not progressed significantly since the first days of civilisation. But 'Jamaica is emphatically ours'.[59]

McKay expressed his ideas originally using the Jamaican Creole but later in the interest of 'universality' he adopted the use of standard English, and employed the sonnet form.[60] The black and the colonial problem were universal. In his earlier poetry he concentrated less on the international problems of race, and more on the social and economic conditions of blacks in the country:

> You hab all t'ings fe mek life bles'
> But buccra 'poil de whole
> Wid gove'mint an' all de res',
> Fe worry naygur soul.[61]

As a constable he was concerned about the brutal application of the law ('Strokes of the Tamarind Switch'), and with the plight of prostitutes driven to their trade by poverty and bad example.[62]

The relationship with Africa was not purely sentimental, and it ran deep. Rev. Dingwall looked for guidance from the Psalms, particularly Psalm 68: 'Princes shall come out of Egypt; Ethiopia shall soon stretch out her hands to God', and he spoke with some passion on the future of Africa and of Africa's past:

> We may not hope for any political revolution that shall set Egypt and the other tribes of Africa at the head of the nations; but we confidently expect for her sons and daughters that moral regeneration that makes men noble, majestic, princely . . . Internal righteousness shall rule the world . . . Two of these sons of Ham, Cush and Mizrain – Asyro-Babylonia and Egypt – were the first rulers of the world, the most civilised and intellectual in early days. The children of Ham . . . only want the Gospel to make them a people. God has blest us. Nay, rather, O ye sons and daughters of Africa, may we not now turn the scales against those blind and perverse maligners of our race, and say in the language of Scripture, 'Cursed is he that curseth us, and blessed is he that blesseth us? 10,000,000 of Africa's children transplanted in these western lands by human avarice . . . [We] are to become lightbearers to our still benighted fatherland . . . every man and woman and child whose veins are filled with Afric blood remember that

for us there is but one road to success here and bliss hereafter, and that the safest road and best [is] 'Ethiopia shall soon stretch forth her hands unto God'.[63]

With the expansion of European imperialism in Africa, blacks in the diaspora began to discuss black colonisation of Africa, consistent, however, with their belief that black colonisation from the Americas would contribute to the growth of a strong Africa. In Jamaica the first known attempt to resettle Africa from the Americas came from a Barbadian Dr Albert Thorne who had settled in Jamaica. In December 1899, Dr Thorne conducted a meeting chaired by the Baptist minister, Rev. T. Gordon Somers. Thorne proposed a colonising scheme (which he had apparently first advocated in 1893) which would have established a town in Nyasa in Africa, involving the provision of plots of land to black West Indian settlers.[64] A fortnight later Thorne held another meeting at the Hanover Street Baptist Church; this time the meeting was chaired by Rev. W.D. Brown, pastor of the Church. The objects of 'The African Colonial Enterprise' as set forth by Dr Thorne were:

1   To assist enterprising members of the African race now resident in the Western Hemisphere to return and settle down in their father-land, Nyasaland, British Central Africa, being the site selected.
2   To develop agricultural, commercial and other available resources of the country.
3   To give the natives a suitable and profitable education.
4   To extend the Kingdom of God in those vast regions, by leading such as are in darkness and error or superstition to Jesus Christ.
5   To improve the status of the African race.
6   To foster and cement the bonds of friendship and brotherhood between all races of mankind, without respect to colour or creed.

The *Gleaner* reported that Thorne's presentation was well received, and the meeting ended with the presentation by the Choir of 'Precious Fountain' composed by Bishop Small and set to music by Dr Thorne.[65]

Thorne's objectives combined the desire to provide land for enterprising West Indians, and other blacks in the Americas, with a missionising function, educational and religious. The aim was, too, to 'improve the status of the African race' and to contribute to the economic growth of at least one part of the continent. Just as striking was the commitment to the universal brotherhood between all races. There can be little doubt that Thorne had some influence on Marcus Garvey who was born in 1887, in St Ann, the parish where Thorne had settled and established an industrial school.

In some respects the colonial black intelligentsia of Jamaica were comparable to their Haitian counterparts, and the similarity is not purely coincidental. Of course, Haiti was regularly used as an example of black incapacity for self-rule; and Jamaicans who had a positive view of Haiti would have been few and far between: 'speak to a Jamaican Negro of average intelligence about Hayti and the Haytians and he at once professes allegiance to the Queen'.[66] The Haitian intelligentsia responded to the same stimulus, the emergence of quasi-scientific racism. The outlook of Haitian intellectuals was informed by a rejection of African culture, by the expectation that Africa would emerge when European civilisation was transferred to Africa; and was conditioned by the view that slavery was the means by which blacks in the diaspora had been selected to spread civilisation to Africa. Hannibal Price argued, for example, that 'In working for the white man the Negro received from him the light. This was not the intention of the slave owner, it was the will of God'.[67] Firmin insisted that 'Egyptian civilisation is the fountainhead from which sprang the Greek and Latin cultures, and that the development of the arts and sciences among white people of the West rested upon African foundations'. Caucasian presumption, he observed, could not abide the idea that the whole development of human civilisation originated with a race which they considered to be 'radically inferior to themselves'. The Egyptians were black Africans.[68]

The vision of Africa's past was employed by the Jamaican and Haitian intelligentsia to counter the myth of the inferiority of members of the black race. Dingwall dreamed of a political Africa in which there would be a regime of internal righteousness, a moral regeneration 'that makes men noble, majestic, princely'. Thorne more pragmatically spoke of a colonising scheme in which Africa would be brought into the 'modern world' with the help of colonising and Christianising blacks from the diaspora.

Ideas such as these were to become absorbed into the Pan-African movement, which was directed towards reform, and which was the political expression of the Christian plea for justice and the recognition of the universal brotherhood of man. The Pan-African Association was founded in 1897 by Sylvester Williams, a Trinidadian of Barbadian parentage. Williams, like Malcolm Nurse (better known as George Padmore) was of Barbadian background.[69] To a considerable extent the late-nineteenth century black intelligentsia (and the Pan-African Association) continued to believe in European justice and fair play. Scholes, in his own forceful way, was issuing a warning that the British Empire could last only as long as the coloured people continued to believe in British justice. The difference between the Pan-Africanists and the later Garveyite movement was that Garvey was a powerful advocate of black independence, achievable through black initiative, and black self-reliance. Yet, Garveyism unquestionably has its roots in the black intellectual ambience of the late-nineteenth century.

The irony was that Pan-Africanism and its advocates used much of the language of the paternal imperialists. While Archbishop Nuttall agitated for a universal Christendom linked to Anglo-Saxon cultural domination, Scholes and others saw African redemption as linked to the growth of the dominant civilisation of the age in Africa itself. Working from two apparently different premises, the Archbishop and some members of the black intelligentsia had much in common. The redemption or evangelisation of Africa was inseparable from the status, identity and self-esteem of blacks in the diaspora. In this way, British imperialism became linked with African redemption, through Christianity. And this is true, despite Scholes's rejection of the view that the coloured races needed the benevolence of the 'colourless race' and his view that the Empire was ruled by force.

It is easy to assume that the black intelligentsia blindly believed in the good-will of Europe's civilising mission, and even that they found nothing wrong with imperialism and colonialism.[70] While it may be true that they would have appeared satisfied with a reformed imperialism, they showed themselves anti-colonialist in their concern with economic and social issues within the structure of empire. Scholes, Love, Wilson and others were obviously aware of the class bias of Jamaica's political institutions.

This chapter has been concerned mostly with the ideas and concerns of the black intelligentsia, and has taken the position that they articulated important mass concerns, promoted the concept of black equality, attacked social injustices, and patterns of land utilisation. Their advocacy of political representation for blacks and black interests, utilising the existing structures of government and the media, demonstrates an important level of political consciousness, even if they never donned the mantle of revolution. Their energies were focused on the educational and cultural development of the black population. The role of men such as Webb in establishing educational institutions for the girls of the island, of Plant in his important work at Titchfield, may seem of relatively minor importance if we apply political or revolutionary criteria, until we recognise that such actions were often carried out against opposition or in face of disinterest among the leadership of the Jamaican community. Rev. Washington, apart from being an educator and pastor, looked with concern upon the exploitative role played by middlemen in the purchase of peasant crops. Washington took the step of establishing a marketing organisation to facilitate the earning of the best prices for small farmers. He 'realized the value of co-operative marketing, collected the produce of many, and shipped it to England, and obtained an enhanced price'.[71] Mr. A.A. Barclay, a teacher, mobilised the people of western St Mary parish – with the assistance of other teachers, ministers of religion, some businessmen and planters – to organise the purchase of properties and division of land into lots for the use of small settlers.[72] The politics of the JUT was to encourage the election of men who had an interest in education, and that organisation saw education as the key to black progress, particularly in the countryside. They fought against the regular efforts to reduce the budget for education.

By the end of the century, the People's Convention had been established. This association discussed issues of island-wide significance, e.g. in 1901 the issues of women's rights, registration of voters, abuse of Jamaican migrant workers, the use of flogging as an instrument for the elimination of praedial larceny. They deliberately focused their activities around Emancipation Day, 1 August. The People's Convention was clearly a black organisation designed to discuss and alleviate the social and economic conditions of blacks in the island:

> The first of August anniversary of the great day, when, to the African bond-slave, in the British West Indies, the blessing of personal liberty was given not by Act of Parliament only, but in *reality*, is approaching . . . it is the intention . . . of the People's Convention to celebrate the day in a manner befitting the event and the obligation of the children of the emancipated. For the last three years the observance of this anniversary has taken place in Spanish Town . . . We have had to combat the stupidity put forth by certain impostors, who pretend to have an unnecessary care of Society, and an unnecessary fear that our motive, or the results of our movement, would unhinge the settled order of peace and goodwill. Their idle prattle is of no value . . . The People's Convention has decided to make the celebration of this day an occasion of intellectual, and patriotic improvement . . . It is a day on which to recall the history of our Fathers, and to contemplate the destinies of our children. It should be utilized *to the end* that the Negro subjects of the British Crown will eventually rise to the full dignity of their national privileges, and *enjoy without any distinction* the full political manhood embraced in British citizenship.[73]

The People's Convention decided, as well, to work more closely with 'forces and influences outside of Jamaica'. Presumably, they meant the Pan-African Association.

In his study on Jamaica for the period 1830–65 Philip D. Curtin noted that among the 'coloured people' of the island there was a growing nationalism. They (the coloured people) were Europeanised, self-conscious, real natives of Jamaica, and visibly different from the Creole whites.[74] In the late-nineteenth century, the coloured community continued to display an intense identification with Jamaica. Alongside them, however, there was emerging a black nationalism which combined an attachment to the soil, with an international association with blacks. The People's Convention was in that tradition. Ever so slowly, the 'native' of Jamaica was coming to be identified with Afro-Jamaicans in whose hands the destiny of the island would rest. Indeed, as Curtin noted, that observation had been made as far back as the middle of the nineteenth century. At that time it was a prophecy, a truth acceptable only by faith. The end of the nineteenth century had not seen a fulfilment of the prophecy, but a Jamaican community was taking shape. Black spokesmen viewed racism as the major hindrance to patriotism and a sense of community. The pro-slavery ideological tradition was far from dead.[75] There was no telluric base for Jamaican nationalism but a sense of community was evolving despite rifts in the society. The 'black' position was perhaps best stated by Henderson's black medical practitioner who described himself as 'an Imperialist, a Protectionist [who] believed in God, and Jamaica and the Negro race'.[76]

Black involvement in Crown Colony politics was limited by the strictures imposed by the colonial state on black participation. A second constraint on black political action was the ambivalent position of the black leadership, bestriding two worlds – that of their origins and that of their middle class aspirations. Yet, the significance (we might almost say the achievement) of black intellectual development of the period lies in its accurate recognition that the position of blacks in Jamaica society was part of a world-wide conception of blacks, of Africa, and of African civilisation, past and present.

Black leaders operated within the confines of the colonial state apparatus, and through the voices of Robert Love and others mounted a moral crusade, seeking to use the conscience of empire to correct its social injustices. Position and respectability, gained sometimes at great personal sacrifice, could not be placed on the line by non-legal agitation. Thus black leaders such as Love could endorse strike action by workers but could never initiate it. At the same time, their own claim to respectability was jeopardised by the 'uncivilised' conduct of their ethnic counterparts. The solution was in part education, but as they understood very well, the availability of education was reduced by the declining resources of Churches and by elite attitudes which circumscribed educational opportunity. Black spokesmen such as Robert Love, therefore, viewed access to political decision-making as a crucial variable in black progress. And herein rested the eternal circle. Black influence on political decision-making was reduced by their lack of education (and by their poverty) but there was never enough education because the colonial system did not view education as a priority.

Black progress was also frustrated by the system of land tenure. Land was an important political issue for black leaders who sensed that blacks could be more effectively controlled by denying them access to land. For Love, Reid and others, black progress was incompatible with the prevailing plantation system, with the oppressive structure of the laws, and with general land tenure arrangements. But the political change which would or could have altered the status quo proved too difficult to achieve as long as British policy, especially during the Chamberlain years, gave military, political, and constitutional support to the white oligarchy.

Finally, trapped in their middle class status – measured by culture, speech, dress, occupation or income – black leaders would give no more than unqualified moral support to mass movements, protests, strikes, demonstrations or riots. Ethnicity had its limits.

Notes

1 These biographical sketches are derived principally from Rev. C.A. Wilson's, *Men of Vision: Biographical Sketches of Men who have made their mark*, Kingston: The Gleaner Co., 1929, pp. 96–100.
2 *Ibid.* p. 99.
3 WIRC, 1897. Evidence of Rev. S.J. Washington, 5 April, p. 329/337.
4 Wilson, *Men of Vision*, p. 109.
5 *Ibid.* p. 119.
6 This account I have obtained thanks to Professor Edward Kamau Brathwaite. It is taken from Joseph's major work.
7 WIRC, 1897. Evidence of Matthew Josephs, 5 April, 1897, p. 315–6/323–4.
8 *DG*, 21 October, 1885. 'Address to Rev. Dr Theophilus Scholes, Stewart Town: John Edward Bruce, Dr Theophilus Scholes, MD'. in *The Voice of the Negro*, Vol. IV, No. 7, March 1907, pp. 114–115; Joy Lumsden, 'Dr Robert Love and Jamaican Politics', Ph. D. UWI, Mona,, 1988.
9 Wilson, *Men of Vision*, pp. 3–15, and pp. 61–86.
10 Barrington Moore, Jr. *Reflections on the Causes of Human Misery and upon certain proposals to eliminate them*, Boston: Beacon Press, 1972, p. 101 and p. 105.
11 John Heeren, 'Karl Manheim and the Intellectual Elite', *British Journal of Sociology*, Vol. 22, March 1971, p. 9.
12 Roosevelt Williams, 'Modes of Alienation', in Roy S. Bryce-Laporte and Claudewell S. Thomas, (ed.) *Alienation in Contemporary Society. A Multidisciplinary Examination*, New York: Praeger 1979, p. 74.
13 Wayne Cooper, (ed.) *The Passion of Claude McKay*, New York: Schocker Books, 1973, p. 5.
14 T.E.S. Scholes, *Glimpses of the Ages or the 'Superior' and 'Inferior' Races, so-called, discussed in the light of Science and History*, (2 Vols.) London: John Long, 1905, Vol. 2, p. 6.
15 Mary Turner, *Slaves and Missionaries: The Disintegration of Jamaican Slave Society, 1787–1834*, Urbana: University of Illinois Press 1982, p. 153; and Edward Kamau Brathwaite, *Wars of Respect, Nanny, Sam Sharp and the Struggle for People's Liberation*, Kingston, 1977, pp. 20–28.
16 Aggrey Brown, *Color, Class and Politics in Jamaica*, New Jersey: Transaction Books, 1979, p. 89.
17 R. Dingwall, 'Outlook for Jamaica', in R. Gordon, *Jamaica's Jubilee*, p. 112.
18 J.H. Reid, 'The People of Jamaica Described', in R. Gordon, *Jamaica's Jubilee*, p. 91.
19 W.F. Bailey, 'Jamaica of Today contrasted with Jamaica as Freedom found it', p. 72.
20 T.E.S. Scholes, *The British Empire and Alliances, or Britain's Duty to her*

colonies and Subject Races, London: Elliot Stock, Paternoster Row, 1899, p. 366.

21   Ibid. p. 368.
22   Ibid. p. 373.
23   Wilson, Men with Backbone, p. 7–8.
24   W.F. Bailey, 'Jamaica of Today', p. 72.
25   WIRC, 1897. Evidence of Mr Smickle, 5 April, 1897, p. 326/334.
26   Wilson, Men with Backbone, p. 26.
27   Wilson, Men with Backbone, p. 30.
28   D.J. East, Minority Report on Report of the Royal Commission upon the Condition of the Juvenile Population of Jamaica, 1879, p. 37. Yet five years later the Colonial Standard and Jamaica Despatch (9 October, 1884) reasserted the claim that the 'sugar plantation was the nucleus of civilised life'. East and others saw 'civilised life' as centred in the population of rural farmers. A similar position was adopted by black spokesman J.H. Reid.
29   Dingwall, 'Outlook for Jamaica', p. 106.
30   Scholes, The British Empire, pp. 345–6.
31   Rev. Henry Clarke to the Editor, London Times, reproduced in Colonial Standard, 7 October, 1884.
32   JA, 22 June, 1895. 'Negro Isolation' by J.H. Reid.
33   Scholes, The British Empire, p. 268.
34   J.A. Froude, The English in the West Indies or the Bow of Ulisses, New York: Negro Universities Press, 1969. It should be noted, in passing, that Froude's book did not offend only black Jamaicans.
35   Ibid. p. 211–12.
36   Ibid. p. 213.
37   Scholes, The British Empire, p. 272.
38   Ibid. p. 273.
39   Ibid. p. 277.
40   Ibid. p. 279 and p. 399.
41   The ideas of Enos Nuttall have been discussed in Chapter 4.
42   HBJ, 1921 (Obituaries) p. 647. Dr Johnson came to Jamaica from Scotland in 1874 for his health. He practised as a physician in Brown's Town. He also established the 'Jamaica Evangelic Mission' in the Dry Harbour Mountains along with nine supplementary churches, which he directed until his death in 1920. He represented St Ann in the Legislative Council. He did much, the Handbook reports, to make Jamaica well known in England and elsewhere. 'In 1891 he was inspired by the idea that black men from Jamaica by reason of their more ready adaptability to climatic conditions and supposed racial sympathy, could be advantageously employed in Christianisation and civilisation of the African savage tribes. He accordingly fitted out an expedition and during a period of 20 months crossed South Central Africa from Benguella on the west mouth of the Zambezi on the east coast. He published the result of his journeying in Reality vs. Romance in South Central Africa.
43   DG, October, 1885.
44   Rev. Koramora, Centenary Report re the West Indian assistant founders of the erstwhile Basel Mission Church which is now known by the name Gold Coast Presbyterian Church, 1843–1943, Ghana, 1943.
45   Ibid. 'It is a wonder before our eyes . . . that the Lord caused Joseph's servitude to be the source of deliverance of his family'.
46   R. Gordon, 'Glance at the Past, the Present and the Road to the Future', in R. Gordon, et. al. Jamaica's Jubilee, p. 13–14.

47 Scholes, *Glimpses of the Ages*, Vol. 1, pp. xiii–xv.
48 David O. Moberg, *The Church as a Social Institution*, p. 447.
49 Scholes, *The British Empire*, pp. 288–89.
50 *Ibid.* p. 292–4.
51 Wayne Cooper, *The Passion*, p. 3.
52 Orlando Patterson, *Slavery and Social Death: A Comparative Study*, Cambridge Mass: Harvard University Press, 1982.
53 See Eric Hobsbawm (ed.) *The Invention of Tradition*, Cambridge: Cambridge University Press, 1983.
54 W. Collins, *The Church in Jamaica*.
55 Wilson, *Men of Vision*, p. 108.
56 Wayne Cooper, *The Passion*, p. 5.
57 Claude McKay, *Songs of Jamaica*, Florida 1969, 'Cudjoe Fresh from de Lecture', pp. 56–7.
58 *Ibid.* 'My Native Land, My Home', p. 48.
59 Dingwall, 'Outlook for the Jamaican People', in R. Gordon, *Jamaica's Jubilee*, p. 111.
60 Edward Kamau Brathwaite, *History of the Voice, The Development of Nation Language in Anglophone Caribbean Poetry*, London and Port of Spain, 1984, p. 20.
61 McKay, 'My Native Land', in *Songs of Jamaica*.
62 McKay, *Songs of Jamaica*, 'A midnight Woman to the Bobby', 'A Country Girl', p. 119, 'Strokes of the Tamarind Switch', p. 111.
63 Dingwall, 'Outlook for the Jamaican People', in R. Gordon, *Jamaica's Jubilee*, pp. 122–8.
64 *DG*, 16 December, 1899.
65 *DG*, 21 December, 1899.
66 Julius Moritzen, 'Has Jamaica Solved the Color Problem?' *Gunton's Magazine*, January 1901, NLJ, Jamaica Pamphlets No. 49, p. 16.
67 David Nicholls, *From Dessalines to Duvalier: Race, Colour and National Independence in Haiti*, WUCS, London: Macmillan Publishers Ltd., 1989 p. 130.
68 *Ibid.* p. 130.
69 Bridget Brereton, *Race Relations in Colonial Trinidad, 1870–1900*, Cambridge and London: Cambridge University Press, 1979, p. 92.
70 Rupert Lewis, 'Review of J.R. Hooker, *Henry Sylvester Williams: Imperialist Pan Africanist*, in *Jamaica Journal*, Vol. 11 Nos. 1 and 2, p. 57.
71 Wilson, *Men of Vision*, p. 109.
72 *Ibid.* p. 35.
73 *JA*, 27 July, 1901.
74 Philip D. Curtin, *Two Jamaicas: The Role of Ideas in a Tropical Colony 1830–65*, Cambridge, Mass: Harvard University Press, 1955, p. 176.
75 Gordon K. Lewis, *Main Currents in Caribbean Thought, The Historical Evolution of Caribbean Society in its Ideological Aspects, 1492–1900*, Kingston and Port of Spain: Heinemann Educational Books, 1983, pp. 94–170, *passim*.
76 John Henderson, *Jamaica*, p. 103.

CHAPTER 13 | Riots and social disturbances

For the mass of blacks, the struggle was not against racism defined as such but against class oppression, heavy taxation, and injustice. Yet, there is evidence, as in the case of the Morant Bay Rebellion of 1865, of the Bedwardian movement, in the insistence by St Mary's farmers that 'God had given the land to the Black Man', that ethnicity served as 'the encompassing principle of social perception'.[1]

One of the creative ideas of the twentieth century has been that workers should be allowed the right, in law, to challenge deplorable working conditions and to demand higher wages. Such a principle did not exist in nineteenth century Jamaica, and had only limited acceptance in industrialised societies. In Jamaica workers' protests were described significantly enough as 'labour revolts' in other words as protests against the principle of authority itself, and a violation of accepted modes of social conduct. Thus there were 'labour revolts' in 1867 on several estates in St Thomas, Portland and St Elizabeth, for higher wages during crop time. There were strikes (revolts) in 1868 in St James and Hanover, in 1878 in St James for which Mr W.E. Espeut, a conservative legislator and sugar planter, blamed the language of the Governor, Sir Anthony Musgrave. Labour revolts were definitely used as an excuse for introducing East Indian labour.[2] Protests were usually in response to the inadequacy of wages or to irregularity in the payment of wages or the failure to pay them at all.

In 1884, a particularly bad year for sugar, there were several strikes on various estates in St Ann.[3] The frequent and major protests were blamed on the stevedores and on agents recruiting labour for Panama. The Inspector of Police (industrial conflict fell under the watchful eye of the police), reporting on the strikes, blamed the 'evil disposed' among the stevedore class. The workers

> . . . demand higher wages and go so far as to threaten those willing to work. While on most estates strikes have been common, and notices have been posted advising the gangs to strike for higher wages, and the consequence has been strikes – most of them have proved abortive owing to increased wages, and judicious action on the part of overseers and attorneys.

The Inspector's idiosyncratic definition of an abortive strike – as one which evokes the concession of higher wages to striking workers – need not detain us. In 1884, both stevedores and sugar workers were working together to secure higher wages. But the Inspector of Police also blamed the agitation on one, Mr Young, whom he described as a recruiting agent for Panama, and who had created disaffection contingent upon the announcements made by recruiters for Panama that higher wages could be obtained there, 'sowing seeds of discontent among hitherto quiet and contented labourers of this Parish, as St Ann's has been the headquarters of the Crimps and the vessels have been despatched from here'. Workers converged on St Ann's Bay from the Leeward parishes of Hanover, St James, Trelawny (the main sugar producing parishes), 'crowding' the town while waiting to embark.

Not all workers were seeking the route of embarkation to Colon, no matter how excited the town of St Ann's Bay had become as a result of the convergence of workers, meeting in the rum shops to discuss the labour, wages and Colon questions. Workers put up posters stating clearly what the purpose of their agitation was. The poster, reproduced below, not only presented the problem of wages, or of the scarcity of labour, but underlined the legal orientation of the workers' action:

TAKE NOTICE!

All person or persons having shop? store? Estate? [sic] and all others do do [sic], and out of the Town, whether Master or Manager we the undersign do give you legal notice, that from and after this 6 day of February 1884, that if there is no work for us to do, and better wages, whether mechanic or labourers, landsmen or Seamen, We the undersign, do resolved as soon as Sunny come if there is no progress are [sic] better times that are [sic] to be made for our benefits, we the undersign, do resolved to visit you, and all those who are determine to oppress us:

Sgd. Fire Arms
      Fire Ship
      Flaming Satan
      Incubate?
      March

as we may determine.

The prospect of losing labourers to the DeLesseps Canal was probably the factor which most persuaded planters to concede on wage benefits.[4] September 1884 also saw serious riots among Chinese workers at the Gray's Town Estate in St Mary.[5]

In 1884, as in 1878, the agitation of workers was attributed to the fiery language of some member, or members, of the elite. In 1878 it was the language of Sir Anthony Musgrave, in 1884 it was the language of the constitutional reformers.[6] Both incidents reveal the assumption of Jamaica's white leadership that blacks were 'combustible' or 'easily led away' by irresponsible language used by an elite which ought to recognise that black labourers on their own did not have the capacity to revolt against oppressive conditions. Such revolts, it was assumed, came about much as a revolver shot had the effect of stampeding cattle. Or as the Colonial Secretary expressed the point in 1884: 'the general tendency of such language when used by gentlemen of position is to induce the poorer portion of the community to resist and contemn constituted authority'.[7]

There were no formal labour organisations in the island, but strike action was coming to be seen by workers as a legitimate method of protest against conditions – both inside and outside the sugar industry. At the end of May 1895 wharf labourers went on strike in Kingston, an action which Robert Love approved as a 'new chapter' in the social history of Jamaica. For four days the dock workers 'continued to maintain, with more or less obstinacy, their hostile attitude . . . Strikes are in reality the mode of warfare adopted by the labourers against the capitalist. It is the former's method of bringing the latter to terms'.[8] In a letter to the *Daily Gleaner*, one of the strikers explained the benefit which would accrue to the whole island should the difficult conditions under which workers operated be examined with more sympathy:

> I ask you to occupy a space in your paper concerning the striking of the labourers. We the labouring classes do strike for higher wages, for we are under the advantage of the Agents of ships, we asked for more wages so that we may be able to sustain ourselves and families in a respectable manner. We have to support our families, pay rent, and tax and water rates. Our Island will increase more. It will enable us to spend more, and the merchants will receive more, for we will be able to pay our tax, and in a better way. We won't be having to trouble the Governments often for coffins, and hole for the burial of the dead; we will be able to bury them ourselves if we get suitable wages. The Alms House won't be having so much paupers on the list. All those owing from the want of more wages. Look at our sister island of Trinidad, where the labouring classes are getting 5/- per day and feeding, then why we Jamaicans can't do the same, we are not behind hand, we been suffering a long time under the tyranny of small wages, so it is time now we look around ourselves . . . We mean to be determined for good wages, in our Island – and everybody will inherit the benefit thereof. Three and two shillings are no pay at all for a working man. There are more stealing going on now than if we were getting good wages, if we got good pay, there is no need for us to steal; but on account of the wages

is so small, we have to steal, we are going to prison and disgrace ourselves.[9]

Somewhere between 800 and 1,000 men were involved in the strike. An attempt was made to break the strike by employing men from the Sailors Home at 6/- per day. Those sailors refused to co-operate partly as a gesture of solidarity, but mainly out of fear of reprisals from angry workers. The strike had arisen out of the refusal of the wharfinger, Mr Polack, a functionary of Mr Forwood's Atlas Steamship Co., to carry out Mr Forwood's instructions that double pay should be given to workers for a public holiday, and his determination to pay regular wages. The protest then escalated into a generalised demand for higher wages of 5/- to 6/- per day. Love's *Jamaica Advocate* was ecstatic, praising the 'pluck', audacity and self-restraint of workers, and their 'manliness', ending with the exhortation 'Well done men!'[10]

In 1886 Dr John Hall referred to the hydra of anarchy in Jamaica and pleaded for the expansion of educational facilities to 'put an end to the loss and misery of strikes and lockouts and boycotting'. While Dr Hall did not give details, the impression derived from his statement was that in 1886 at least there were industrial incidents of some significance.

Apart from group action, there were cases of assault and of arson in instances when workers' wages had been withdrawn in whole or in part. Fire on estates was sometimes accidental but trash houses or cane fields were sometimes (as a result of wage disputes) set afire by outraged workers.[11]

Robert Love had hoped that workers would 'organise themselves everywhere into Labour Clubs, or Labour Unions (or whatever else they may choose to call it)'. Such groupings he envisaged as directed towards the formation of a collective labour voice which could have an impact on the membership structure of the Legislative Council.[12] It was another forty years before that vision became reality.

Labour disturbances provided the rationale for continuing the programmes of importation of East Indian labour which contributed to the depression in wages. That programme was, in short, useful for securing maximum control over the Afro-Jamaican labour force.

The orientation of the vagrancy laws, praedial larceny laws and those laws which endeavoured to strengthen the police force and make it more efficient during this period, demonstrate the anxiety of the colonial state to maintain law and order at any cost; and that coercion was viewed as an extremely important mode of social control. The balance of white fear was beginning to shift from rural Morant Bay to urban Kingston.

The police had a few riots to deal with during this period, and in 1894 the riots at Cumberland Pen, before the eyes of the Governor, convinced the latter that a more serious riot would have been beyond the capacity of the force to handle. (The riot had been sparked off by the attempt of a police officer to arrest a young man of lowly social status for illegal gambling at the races). It is true that Governor Blake enjoyed an ardent belief in 'black combustibility' and that his response may have constituted an over-reaction. Blake was able to play upon white fears of a race war to obtain permission to 'improve the efficiency' of the constabulary. The law in its new guise authorised the Governor to appoint members of the Royal Irish Constabulary (RIC) to be sergeant-majors and sergeants of the force in Jamaica, that is to say deepening the white leadership of the force.[13] The law specified not more than 30 men from the RIC, at salaries not exceeding £140 and £90 per annum for sergeant-majors and sergeants respectively. (It was reported that the officers of the constabulary had run for cover when the rioting started).

On 9 August, 1894, special instructions were issued to the Kingston Constabulary in case of riot or serious disturbances of the peace by soldiers or other organised or armed parties. The instructions were to shoot, aiming low at the ring leaders if other methods, including the reading of the riot act, had failed.[14]

Riots were sometimes a consequence of conflict between the West India Regiment and the Jamaica Constabulary, usually when the constabulary attempted to detain or arrest a soldier of the WIR for disorderly conduct or some relatively minor offence. The WIR on at least one occasion were associated in their rioting with women of the town. When on 8 June, 1894, soldiers of the WIR attacked police stations at Fletcher's Land and Sutton Street, wrecking the former station and roughly handling the police, they were accompanied by a crowd of 'loose women and other idlers of the town'. 13 soldiers and 13 women were eventually tried for rioting.[15] In 1900 Fletcher's Land and Allman Town again became the battleground between soldiers and constables, who in a pitched battle utilising sticks and stones, proceeded to beat each other.[16] Rioting brought about by conflicts between the police and the WIR was one additional reason for educating the Jamaica Constabulary in the art and craft of riot control.

Between 1901 and 1902 the police force were to put into practice what they had been taught. On 14 May, 1901 'men and women armed with sticks and stones attacked some draymen on the road. No reason was given for the attack'. The draymen were badly injured. Of the 20 accused and tried, 11 were sent to prison without the option of a fine. In 1901 20 persons were convicted in Portland of riot and five were imprisoned, while 15 were bound over to keep the peace for six months. A dispute over the sale of bananas had sparked off the riot and only the timely intervention of the police prevented a more serious situation emerging. Again in 1901 a riot in St Mary led to the conviction of at least four persons charged with rioting.

This riot arose out of a wage dispute. The rioters combined to compel other persons, who were working for the Public Works Department, not 'to work for less wages than they (the rioters) demanded, and afterwards attacked persons who worked in contravention of their wishes'.[17]

St Mary, one of the major banana producing parishes, was the centre of several land disputes in 1901–2. In 1901, small settlers and others seized and attempted to keep forcible possession of lands owned by the Hon. Dr John Pringle. The police Blue Book report for 1901–2 indicates that the seizure of Pringle's property was only one of several attempts which had been made by 'unscrupulous' persons to seize the land of large proprietors. 'The persons so acting in all cases try to put forward some bogus title, and incite the more ignorant portion of the peasantry by telling them that the lands in St Mary were belonging to the black people'.

In 1902 the taxation issue was attracting more and more attention, partly because of efforts being made by the government to impose a property tax. On the very day of the major riot which took place in Montego Bay, the *Jamaica Advocate*, which could not have been aware of the possibility of an explosion at Montego Bay that same day, editorialised on the burning issue of taxation. It was almost prophetic:

> If advantage is taken of their ignorance, their patience, and sub-missiveness, to push them to the wall, they may place their backs against it, and may take a hand in settling the problem of excessive and unendurable taxation . . . Accustomed to the oppression of those in authority, they bear unmurmuringly the heavy impositions placed upon them. They have grown to think it is their lot and thus pass on submissively from bad to worse. But their sufferings are not less intense for that.

The editorial referred to the 'accumulated weight of exactions which may well be omitted when we see absolute Destitution dragged before the Courts of Law (not courts of Justice . . . no, not courts of Justice, for Justice is even-handed, and gives as well as takes)'.[18]

The government had deferred the property tax, but imposed additional taxes on land by Law 9 of 1901. There were also misunderstandings created by the method of tax collection, for example, 'the system by which a runner is precluded from giving an official *interim* receipt for a part of payment of taxes'.[19]

About a week or two before the riot in Montego Bay there had been relentless attempts to collect taxes. A large number of poverty-stricken taxpayers were taken 'before the resident magistrate for the non-payment of taxes, and given the alternative of either paying their obligations in full within a certain period – or going to prison'. Unable to pay, but unwilling to go to prison, or to be charged with contempt of court, the taxpayers of

Montego Bay borrowed money from friends and neighbours to pay their taxes. 'The effect was to produce indignation and discontent in many circles besides that of the poverty stricken people who were summoned before the court'. A public meeting in Montego Bay had also stirred passions. There had also been protest against taxes by leaders of the community, such as Mr Hart, the Chairman of the Parochial Board.[20]

No doubt, the whole island faced the same kind of problem as Montego Bay, however, the major challenge to 'public order' came from this seaport town, which had been only lightly policed. The Kingston and St Andrew area had a higher proportion of police per capita than any other township, and it is clear that this policy rested on the assumption that an upsurge in violence would occur in Kingston.

Montego Bay was a growing town, its population increasing in the 19 years between 1881 and 1900 from 4,651 to 7,000.[21] From the 1880s the town was regarded as the second most important township in the country with respect to size, population, and commerce. While Kingston continued to be the major nucleus of export and import, Montego Bay was gaining importance as a centre for the export trade to the United States. From 1883, Montego Bay was described as enjoying regular visits from steamers trading with the United States and was a port of call for coastal steamers. 'The increased fruit trade has converted almost useless property into valuable property'.[22] With the depression in the sugar industry workers attempted to secure more employment in the banana industry.

From 1895 reports began to flow in regarding the problem of unemployment in Montego Bay, with crowds of labourers hanging around the wharves, and standing in groups about the street eagerly endeavouring to 'catch a job'.[23] According to the *Daily Gleaner* some irritation was felt by 'Stalwart ruffians of Meagre Bay' who objected to 'not being summoned like gentlemen, concerning the payment of taxes, but arrested or threatened with arrest like vagabonds'.[24]

The town was wracked by rioting for two days, beginning on market day, 5 April, 1902, when the town was full, not only with residents from Montego Bay, but from the environs of Montego Bay, including Meagre Bay, a small port. 'A horde of the worst and most depraved', claimed the *Daily Telegraph*, 'joined the rush against law and order. Specially does it seem that Meagre Bay poured its men to the fray. The women of the pavement, loose, vile as corruption, hideous and shameless, egged on the men to violence'.[25] The *Daily Telegraph*, which supported the thesis that the riots were strictly against the police, admitted that feeling against taxation 'helped to bring a larger crowd on the spot on Sunday'.

The spark which ignited the riot was the arrest by a constable of a drunken sailor, Cooper, at 5.00 p.m., and the brutal treatment of two unoffending women by the police. Cooper, in his drunken state resisted arrest and was joined by his companions 'who were a rather rough class of men from the wharf and from Meagre Bay, a little fishing village, contiguous to Montego Bay'. A crowd of about 2,000, according to the *Daily Telegraph*, hung around the Court House threatening to kill the Sergeant-Major if they could catch him. 'In fact, the personal feeling against this officer was one of the main causes of the riot. He is the most efficient officer and a terror to the evildoers of the town, and in spite of the efforts which have been made to remove him by a certain class he has been kept at his post and protects the interest of the town'.[26]

At the Court House a hail of stones and missiles of all kinds rained against the windows and smashed them to pieces. Mr Hart tried to address the crowd but quickly sought refuge from the hail of stones which welcomed him. In the darkened streets the crowd went wild. Elsewhere, the mob attacked the home of the Sergeant-Major and smashed all the upstairs windows in the building.[27]

In response to the fury of the rioters the police released Cooper. The release of the man, whose incarceration had sparked off the riot in the first place, did not soothe the rioters. Two hours later police on beat duty were attacked by a 'mob of young men and loose women' who virtually obtained possession of the town, 'their animus being directed solely against the police'.[28] The police made some further arrests but 'owing to the threatening nature of the mob', the prisoners had to be released from the guardroom whither the Sergeant-Major and his seven men had to retreat to escape the stoning of the mob. Police sent to reconnoitre again retreated to their barracks before the hostile mob. The Custos addressed the people, special constables were nominated, and rioting ceased for the night.[29]

Reinforcements arrived the following day, consisting of the Inspector-General himself, three Inspectors, a Sergeant-Major and 60 armed men.[30] All was quiet during the day but rioting started again after Church services, after 8.00 p.m., Sunday night. Renewed rioting took place when Adjutant Simons of the Salvation Army addressed the crowd. Simons was described as one who did work among the 'poorest and worst of the community, especially in Meagre Bay, whence the rioters came, and has great influence with the people'.[31] Simons, it was claimed, was seeking not to inflame but to quieten the people, placing 'himself over them in the hope of diverting attention from the police'.[32] While there is no good reason to doubt the peaceful intentions of the Salvation Army Adjutant, it does seem strange that the tactic he employed was to stage a march to the tune of 'Onward Christian Soldiers'. (36 years later the same tune was to be used by marching rioters). Simons was followed by a 'great mob down the street', which proceeded to attack the police on beat. The police took shelter in houses, the crowds attacked the police barracks and assaulted the Inspector-General.

The police resorted to armed force. An Inspector 'cleared the square with 40 men by means of bayonets and shot (some 25 rounds)'. When the riot ended two and a half hours later, one person had been shot dead, and a second died subsequently from injuries received. Clearly some rioters were attacking the police at close range since one person was wounded by a bayonet and another by a baton. Of 70 policemen, only 31 were able to report for duty the following morning. Three or four police officers had been severely injured.

One of the fullest accounts of the riots was offered by the *Daily Telegraph*:

> Everything was quiet yesterday until in the evening when knots of men began to collect on the streets. The town was policed by strange constables. They did not wear arms, and this was especially done in order that no cause of annoyance might be given to the people. The constables behaved well and took no notice of the jeers which were directed . . . on all sides. After the services in the Churches were over some constables were attacked and were badly beaten . . . Seeing the state of affairs the Inspector-General ordered Inspector Thomas to proceed from the gaol with a squad of armed constables and to clear the streets with fixed bayonets and to resort to firing with ball cartridges if necessary. This was done but the force was met by a fusillade of stones and bottles. Inspector Thomas then ordered his men to fix bayonets, fire and charge. This order was immediately carried out, and before the shower of bullets the crowd melted away, and disappeared in the back streets, or into houses, from the windows of which they threw volleys of stones down on the police. One man, not a rioter, was . . . shot dead. In the meantime another mob seized the drum and trumpet belonging to the Salvation Army, and they passed the Gaol, playing the hymn 'Onward Christian Soldiers, Marching on to War'. They had stones and other weapons in their hands as well as musical instruments and as they passed the building they stoned it, and the constables standing in front of it. The latter charged the mob with clubbed rifles. This only made the rioters furious and they repeated the attack, but were met this time by Sub-Inspector Toole and his men with fixed bayonets and ball cartridges. This had the desired effect and the mob dispersed. Toole was knocked senseless by a bottle.[33]

The security forces took no chances. *HMS Tribune* arrived from Port Royal with 300 'blue jackets', increasing the peace-keeping force in Montego Bay to 750 armed men.[34]

The fury of the rioters was deep, and the events in Montego Bay brought to mind – at least to the *Daily Telegraph*'s mind – the Morant Bay upheaval of 1865. 'Not since Morant Bay' had there been such a rising against constituted authority, claimed the newspaper.[35]

The inevitable Commission of Enquiry was held, and concluded as the elite wished it to conclude, that the riots were a consequence of hostility to the police, and especially to one police officer.

A week before the riots, the correspondent of the *Daily Telegraph* had issued warning of impending trouble in Montego Bay. 'It was partly on the assurances we received from this quarter that we ventured to hint to the Government that all was not well, and that if trouble arose it had had fair warning'.[36] An editorial of the *Telegraph* commented that 'the conditions of a conflagration were present in Montego Bay: unpopularity of the police force, government taxes, and the spark in the form of police conduct'.

The *Jamaica Advocate* editorialised on the Montego Bay events on 12 April, 1902, and placed the blame for the disturbances squarely on the 'chronic irritation and discontent which have for some time existed among the poorer classes as the consequence of the grinding, crushing, weight of the taxes which they are unable to pay, and of the prosecutions which have been recently instituted against them for not being able to pay'.[37] The *Advocate* quite correctly viewed the riots as having 'predisposing' causes in unequal and heavy taxation, relative to income, and in the brusque efforts of the authorities to enforce collection.

Among the arrests made by the security forces were Alfred Solomon, Ralph Thompson, and one Mr Mullings. Solomon had been charged with 'criminal connection with the recent riot in that town'.[38] Jamaican official-dom was obviously anxious to isolate members of the 'better-off' classes in order to establish that the masses of the population had, as usual, been led by 'designing men' into massive rioting. All three men were eventually released. The *Advocate* responded with the suggestion that a 'strong desire on the part of some officials to make victims and to re-enact some of the features of the Morant Bay disturbance has been painfully evident'.[39]

Indications are that oppressive taxation, doubts about the impartiality of justice and harsh economic conditions were among the objective factors leading to the riots. Not to be ignored is that the resident magistrate of St James, Mr Maxwell Hall, was also an unpopular figure 'in the sense that people rightly or wrongly don't feel they can rely upon his judgements'.[40] The venues of the riots were the police station and the court house. Analysts of the period focused upon crowd antagonism to the police without pointing out that the police were simply the uniformed symbol of a system of justice which was unduly oppressive on the poor. Those analysts who drew a parallel with the Morant Bay Rebellion of 1865 made the comparison only in terms of the size and scale of the riot. The most significant point of all was missed, and it was that the Morant Bay Rebellion, like the Montego Bay Riot, centred around protests against the system of justice; Paul Bogle had directed his wrath against the Court House at Morant Bay. The Montego Bay Riots once again showed the importance of imperial forces in the country as a last resort in the maintenance of order.

The Jamaica Constabulary which had been created following the Morant Bay upheaval precisely in order to suppress comparable riots were to receive paeans of praise for their restraint and effectiveness in Montego Bay. The constabulary had come under severe pressure, and there was no repetition of episodes such as had occurred during the Falmouth riots of 1859 when fire was opened without instructions. The constabulary had been roughly handled by the rioters, it is true, and to all appearances fire power was used only under severe pressure. Yet the action of the constabulary was highly lauded for another important reason. In a society obsessed with race and caste distinctions, and haunted by Morant Bay, it was never clear whether a black constabulary would be willing to turn its gun on black people. In Montego Bay professionalism triumphed over race. Inspector Thomas, who took part in the suppression of the riot, observed that the black constabulary were willing to 'use their weapons against their kith and kin. I am proud to have had the honour of thus "blooding" the Jamaica Constabulary, especially in such trying circumstances . . . They proved their loyalty to the hilt on the night of 6 April, 1902; and they have done so repeatedly since then'.[41] The Montego Bay Riots demonstrated that the paramilitary constabulary could be relied upon to defend the white dominated status quo. More could not have been expected, or more demanded.

All societies must of necessity be concerned with law and order. In an ethnically divided community in which a minority race is also economically and politically dominant over a majority race or ethnic group, the law is informed partly by ethnic divisions in that community, precisely because it is thought that ethnic loyalties can cut across class divisions. The law was an instrument for the maintenance of the social authority of the dominant white ethnic segment.

Notes

1   Magnus Morner, 'Economic factors and Stratification in Colonial Spanish America with Special Regard to Elites'. *Hispanic American Historical Review*, **63**:2, May 1983, p. 357.
2   Wesley Roberts, 'The Jamaican Plantocracy', p. 194.
3   Prices dropped from 25/6d per cwt in 1873 and 19/- in 1883 to 13/3d in 1884.
4   CO, 137/513, Vol. 2, 1884. Enclosure: Report of Inspector of Police (St Ann) to Custos of St Ann, 9 February, 1884, 'State of Feeling in St Ann's Parish'.
5   *Colonial Standard*, 24 September, 1884. The riots took place on 8 September, 1884, at the Gray's Town Estate in St Mary, among recently imported Chinese labourers resulting in the death of one and five injuries. 'It appears that they

refused to do certain work on the estate, whereupon they were tried by the Inspector of Immigrants for the district and sentenced to prison. On the police attempt to escort them they made a raid on them with bottles, sticks, etc. and assistance of coolie and Creole labourers had to be sought. This made matters worse and affairs assumed such a serious aspect that the ringleader had to be shot down . . . In the mêlée, Inspector Coward and Sgt.-Major Allen received severe injuries'.

6   See Chapter 2.
7   CO, 137/513, Vol. 2, 1884. Colonial Secretary to Custos of St Ann.
8   *JA*, 1 June, 1895, 'Wharf Labourers' Strike in Kingston'.
9   *Ibid.*
10 *Ibid.* 8 June, 1895. 'Dock Labourers' Strike'.
11 CO, 137/534, Vol. 1, 1888. Norman to CO, No. 59, 21 February, 1888. 'A few years ago a trifling dispute over wages frequently led to the proprietor having his trash house or canefields burnt'.
12 *JA*, 1 June, 1895. 'Wharf Labourers'.
13 Jamaica Archives, 1B 5/18, Vol. 48. Blake to CO, No. 145, 9 April, 1894; No. 279, 14 August, 1895.
14 *Ibid.* No. 279, 14 August, 1895.
15 Frank Cundall, *Political and Social Disturbances in the West Indies. A Brief Account and Bibliography*, Jamaica: 1906, p. 20.
16 *DG*, 17 December, 1900.
17 *JBB*, 1901–2, p. 60, p. 103.
18 *JA*, 5 April, 1902, 'Taxing the People'.
19 *Daily Telegraph*, 31 May, 1902.
20 *JA*, 5 April, 1902. Pluck's Column (dateline Montego Bay, 1 April, 1902).
21 *HBJ*, 1883, Section VII: 'Parishes' and Frank Cundall, *Political and Social Disturbances*. The population census gives figures of 4,803 in 1891 and 6,616 in 1911.
22 *HBJ*, 1883, Section VII: 'Parishes': St James, p. 228.
23 *JA*, 15 July, 1895.
24 *DG*, quoted by *JA*, 12 April, 1902.
25 *Daily Telegraph*, 31 May, 1902.
26 *DG*, 7 April, 1902.
27 *Ibid.*
28 Cundall, *Political and Social Disturbances*.
29 *Ibid.*
30 *Ibid.*
31 *JA*, 12 April, 1902. 'Riots at Montego Bay'.
32 Cundall, *Political and Social Disturbances*.
33 *DG*, 8 April, 1902.
34 *Ibid.*
35 *Daily Telegraph*, 3 April, 1902.
36 *JA*, 5 April, 1902. 'Pluck' reporting from Montego Bay, 1 April, 1902.
37 *JA*, 12 April, 1902.
38 *JA*, 30 August, 1902.
39 *JA*, 1 November, 1902, 'Montego Bay Riot Case'.
40 *Jamaica Times*, 12 April, 1902.
41 Herbert Thomas, *Story of a West Indian Policeman*, p. 122.

Epilogue

The period of this study begins, chronologically, in 1884, the year when the constitution of 1866 was modified by the reintroduction of the electoral principle, and ends in 1900–2 which saw the implementation of the 'constitutional retrogression' spearheaded by Joseph Chamberlain. The constitutional order should be congruent with the reality of social power as the local oligarchy and the Colonial Office perceived that reality. During the 1890s in particular, anxieties concerning the need to ensure white leadership were vigorously expressed in face of the more zealous demands for black and coloured representation in the Legislative Council. Secondly, the constitutional order in Jamaica was intended, by Chamberlain at least, to be a mirror of power relations in the Empire as a whole. British policy at the end of the nineteenth century did not envisage coloured domination of political administration anywhere in the Empire. There was always a clear distinction, for example, between the white colonies (dominions) such as Australia and Canada on the one hand, and the coloured colonies in the Caribbean, India and Africa. The former could enjoy responsible government, the latter at best semi-representative government, corresponding, presumably, to the lesser or greater degree of political evolution achieved. Social, political and economic power in Jamaican society, with race as an important component, was the microcosm of the structure and ideas of Anglo-Saxon imperial administration. The fact that Chamberlain reasserted the dominance of the metropolis in the partnership between Whitehall and the local oligarchy does not disprove the fact that there was a coincidence between the social structure of empire and that of the island colony of Jamaica. Both realities assumed white hegemony and coloured subordination.

The social realities of Jamaica were determined, however, not only by the island's links with British industrial society (as important as those were), but also by the internal logic of the Creole plantation order, born in the late-seventeenth century. In a society dedicated to inequality as a principle of life, class inequalities were reinforced by the social distance which the elite maintained on cultural and on racial grounds. A continued narrowing of the cultural gap by social reformers could not, and was not intended to, bridge the racial gap, but it could encourage equilibrium.

278

In Jamaica, socio-racial subordination had been created by the system of slavery in which blacks were the 'property' of whites. As Eugene Genovese has observed for the United States South, 'wherever racial subordination exists, racism exists', and 'racial distinction between master and slave heightened the tension inherent in an unjust social order'.[1] Emancipation could remove legal bondage but it could not dismiss the socio-racial differences which had determined who was bound to whom. The pattern of social relationships between white and coloured transcended the legal ownership of black 'property'. The social system rested during and after slavery on the assumption that superiority or inferiority of social position were physically or philosophically congruent with superiority or inferiority of race.

White superordination and black subordination, rested both on force and on consensus. As important as the forces of coercion might have been for the maintenance of order, however, the internalisation of beliefs in white supremacy and white leadership was perhaps in the long run more important than the British Navy, or the Jamaica Constabulary, in facilitating social control.

In the late-nineteenth century white supremacy was given firmer ideological justification in positivism and social Darwinism. Black people who had been emancipated between 1834–38 now became the 'subject people', and their environment the 'mission frontier'. Social Darwinism is susceptible to extremely crude and racist interpretation. If subordinated human elements survived oppression, then they had been 'selected' to survive. If they died, they simply proved, predictably, that they were not fit to survive, and therefore deserved to die. Michael Banton has suggested that social Darwinism 'contributed an important element to the ideology of late-nineteenth and early-twentieth century white imperialism and may have been partly responsible for the vicious streak often apparent in it'.[2]

Yet, social Darwinism, with its emphasis on evolution, as applied to social institutions, and to the idea that society was 'evolving towards a more highly developed individuality of units, and towards their closer co-ordination [and towards] a more generous brotherhood, a more real equality, a fuller liberty', was to be one of the steps towards the development of British socialism.[3] Positivism, which also constituted part of the intellectual background of British socialism, was essentially a body of ideas which envisaged the gradual evolution of society, but sought to reconcile that progress with the maintenance of order and the order of society. Part of positivism's appeal rested in its belief that the moral basis of society could be transformed by rooting out ingrained habits of selfishness, together with the laws and institutions which sustained them, while stimulating the growth of social sympathies and altruism. Mankind could be regenerated only through altruism and social sympathy. This process could gradually infuse society with social duty from top to bottom. Positivism reaffirmed many Christian values in face of the challenges posed by Marxism and social Darwinism to the existing socio-economic and political order on the one hand and to biblical fundamentalism on the other. At the same time the traditional social distance could be maintained between white and black, hope of improvement generated, class oppression justified, works of charity performed and moral equality coexist with class, race, and cultural inequalities and differences.

Both positivism and social Darwinism were to have some influence on the leaders of opinion in Jamaica – such as Archbishop Enos Nuttall, W.P. Livingstone, the editor of the *Daily Gleaner* in the 1890s, churchmen of different denominational persuasions, and assorted members of the Legislative Council. It is also true, though, that as a British colony Jamaica absorbed not only ideas but laws and institutions, which had emerged out of British positivist thought. The passion for the creation of a new moral order was evident in policies that encouraged stable family life and legitimacy; it was also evident in prison reform, juvenile laws and charity institutions. Social and cultural structures and processes were evolving in relation to the 'modernising' impulses coming form Britain and acting upon Creole social and cultural processes. The metropolis was expected to set the standards for colonial society and there was a genuine conviction that the adoption of British institutions would confer upon Jamaica and Jamaicans the varnish of 'civilisation'.

In the period after mid-century, but perhaps more pronounced in the last two decades of the nineteenth century, segments of the Jamaican leadership (but especially churchmen) waved the banner of civilisation, moral reform, and religious reorientation. That outlook closely resembled that of the Spanish Catholic Church in the sixteenth century when the indigenous population was taught to live like 'Christian Spaniards', when the policy was to 'extirpate idolatry', and to assure Indian subordination to the culture of the dominant Spanish-European element. Paradoxically, the persistence of a world view distinct or partly distinct from that of the European segment in Jamaica, had resulted from the earlier policy (up to about 1800) of the whites to 'preserve the cultural distance separating them from their slaves'.[4]

Blacks would now be allowed a place in 'civilised' society provided that they rejected their 'mental construction' and their African religious world view. The social bonus for cultural whiteness was respectability. African religion or any other manifestation of non-European culture was the surest sign of barbarism. The noble savage was now pointed on the path of salvation and perfection of self by turning his back on his gods, and seeing God face to face. The converted heathen of Jamaica would also become God's instrument for the spread of Christianity and Anglo-Saxon culture to Africa.

Meanwhile, for those on Jamaica's mission frontier, African cultural expression became synonymous with lower class practices, to the extent that the educated black middle class decisively distanced themselves from uneducated blacks. The very clever J.H. Reid who confessed the need for ethnic unity among blacks voiced his own position of hard-earned respectability: 'in every commonwealth the masses occupy a position corresponding to that of children in a household, and as children of the State, they claim such consideration from the State'.[5] For the brilliant Dr Theophilus Scholes, a most severe critic of empire, and of the social and economic exploitation of coloured people, it was important to draw a line of distinction between the civilised and uncivilised elements of the race.[6]

The black intelligentsia adopted the theory of evolution for its own ends, using that theory to elaborate a theory of the history and evolution of civilisation which originated in Africa (Egypt) and then spread to Europe. Now that civilisation which had evolved to its most advanced state in Europe would be used by the children of the African slaves to launch Africa into the evolving mainstream of western civilisation. The analogy was Joseph's captivity in Egypt. Black advancement was a function of education. Pride in blackness was a function of African redemption. Black intellectuals such as Robert Love and other contributors to the *Jamaica Advocate* sharply criticised racism in Jamaican society, at the risk, of course, of being dubbed agitators, and arousers of 'class' and 'racial' discord. Their position stood in contrast to the views of the white oligarchy that Jamaica had long ago buried its racial antagonisms. The vigorous denial of white society that racism existed in Jamaica was to be an ironical indication of the existence of the problem. Black intellectuals were rendered politically impotent by the constitutional order, and by their own social and cultural distance from the masses. But they were highly critical of land distribution, racism, and what Robert Love called 'class legislation'.

One of the primary targets of Dr Love was the law or the system of justice which he considered discriminatory. In contrast, the white establishment argued that the law was a primary instrument for the civilisation of blacks. However, rioting blacks in Montego Bay in 1902 clearly viewed the law as at the centre of the system of class oppression.

Jamaica's social order and systems of social control assumed white leadership, paternalism, control of land resources, a measure of cultural integration and the negative view of Africa and of the black race. The essence of Garveyism which emerged two decades later was its recognition of the significance of racism as a factor in retarding black social, economic and cultural progress. Garveyism was a logical development from the late-nineteenth century experience. In many respects Garveyite radicalism was not so much in thought as in political action. It was logical that a movement directed to mass organisation in Jamaica should develop outside the existing political/constitutional framework which had methodically limited black involvement in decisions pertaining to their own welfare. The movement challenged the white hegemony which had been so meticulously cultivated at the end of the nineteenth century, a hegemony which Garvey, like Scholes, recognised to be a part of the world order.

Chronologically, the period 1880–1900, is the background to Garveyism, which in many respects was a massive and radical response to the social structure and conscious white hegemony of the period. The Garveyite challenges to racism, to black underprivilege, to the idea of black inferiority and conversely its belief in black capability and self-worth are products of the late-nineteenth century. In one sense, Garvey had been shaped by the same social forces that had shaped the views of the black intelligentsia; in another, the emerging critique of the system of social control voiced by black intellectuals was adopted by Garvey and turned into political action. Garvey's plans for closer association with Africa were anticipated by Albert Thorne and his Nyasaland scheme; his plans for money-making black enterprises are reminiscent of Robert Love's insistence that it was money that made the world go round; his view of history and of the African role within it go back to T.E.S. Scholes and the Pan-Africanists. To suggest, therefore, that 'Garvey self-consciously departed from the past'[7] is to deny that Garvey was part of a whole tradition, in Jamaica, of African and ethnic consciousness. In more practical terms, it was the social conditions in Jamaica's countryside that, by forcing thousands of black Jamaicans into the Spanish Caribbean, Panama, and Central America, provided in part, the territorial base for Garvey's Universal Negro Improvement Association.

Notes

1   Eugene D. Genovese, *Roll Jordan Roll. The World the Slaves made*, New York: Vintage Books, 1976, p. 4.

2   Michael Banton, '1960: A Turning Point in the Study of Race Relations', in Sidney W. Mintz, *Slavery, Colonialism, and Racism*, New York: W.W. Norton and Co. Inc., 1974, p. 34.

3   Willard Wolfe, *From Radicalism to Socialism. Men and Ideas in the Formation of Fabian Socialist Doctrines, 1881–1889*, New Haven and London: Yale University Press, 1975, p. 263.

4   Richard Sheridan, *Doctors and Slaves*, p. 78.

5   J.H. Reid, 'Educating the Peasantry' *JA*, 18 March, 1895.

6   Scholes, *Glimpses of the Ages*, Vol. 1, p. 355.

7   Judith Stein, *The World of Marcus Garvey: Race and Class in Modern Society*, Baton Rouge and London: Louisiana State University Press, 1986, p. 4.

Select bibliography

Primary Sources

Public Record Office, London CO 137 Vols. 508–549, Governor's Despatches, 1883–91.
Jamaica Archives 1B/5/18 Governor's Despatches to Secretary of State, 1890–1900.
Parliamentary Papers West Indian Royal Commission, Report and Evidence (1897)
Report of the Royal Commission upon the Condition of the Juvenile Population of Jamaica, 1879.
National Archives, Washington. National Archives and Records Service Despatches from US Consulate, Kingston, 1729–1906. Microcopy, T–31.
Department of State C8.1/44 Miscellaneous Correspondence.

Manuscripts

National Library of Jamaica:
    Nuttall Papers MS 209a
    Livingstone Collection 1898–1903
    Casserly Papers

Jamaica Government Publications

Handbook of Jamaica, 1881–1908.
Blue Books of Jamaica, 1881–1900.
Governor's Reports on the Blue Books of Jamaica and Departmental Reports, 1880–1900.
Jamaica, *Council Minutes*, 1886–1900.
Laws of Jamaica, 1886–1906.
Censuses of Jamaica, 1871, 1881, 1891, 1911.
Jamaica Gazette, 1883–1899.

Newspapers

Daily Gleaner, 1884–1903.
Colonial Standard and Jamaica Despatch, 1883 – 1890.
Jamaica Advocate, 1891–1902.
Jamaica Times, 1902.
Daily Telegraph.

Contemporary Works

Aspinall, A.F., *The British West Indies, Their History, Resources and Progress*, London: Pitman and Sons, 1912.

Bailey, W.F., *History of the Jamaica Union of Teachers*, Kingston: Gleaner Co. Ltd., 1937.

Betton, W.G. Melbourne, *The Black Man at Home. Dr Johnson on 'some of his little ways'. Correspondence between W.G. Betton and Hon. and Rev. J. Johnson*, Bethune Bros., 1901.

Blake, Sir Henry, 'The Awakening of Jamaica', NLJ, *Jamaica Pamphlets*, No. 22, 1890.

Brooks, A.A. 'History of the Jamaican Native Baptist Church', Kingston: *Daily Gleaner*, (no date).

Caldecott, A., *The Church in the West Indies*, London: Cass and Co. Ltd., 1970.

Church of England, Jamaica (Synod), *Memorial to H.E. Sir Henry Wylie Norman, Governor of Jamaica. Primary Education in Jamaica*, Kingston, 1885.

Church of England, Jamaica, *Proposals for a Church of England Training College*, Kingston, 1874.

Collins, W., 'The Church in Jamaica', *1900*, NLJ, *Jamaica Pamphlets*.

Cooper Wayne, *The Passion of Claude McKay*, New York: Schocken Books, 1973.

Cundall, Frank, *Jamaica in 1912. A Handbook of Information for intending Settlers and Visitors with some account of the Island's History*, Kingston, 1912.

Historic Jamaica, London, 1915.

Political and Social Disturbances in the West Indies. A Brief Account and Bibliography. Kingston, 1906.

DeLisser, H.G., 'White Man in the Tropics', *New Century Review*, February 1900, NLJ, Pamphlet 44.

'The Negro as a Factor in the Future of the West Indies', *New Century Review*, January 1900, NLJ Pamphlet, 43.

Twentieth Century Jamaica, Kingston: The Jamaica Times, 1913.

Dingwall, Rev. R., *Jamaica's Greatest Need*, London: Lemmont and Co. 1892.

'Outlook for Jamaica and her People', in R. Gordon *et al. Jamaica's Jubilee: Or What we are and What we hope to be*, London: S.W. Partridge and Co., 1888.

Dodsworth, Francis (ed.) *The Book of Jamaica*, Sollas and Cooking, 1904.

Downer, Lindsay P., *Memoir of George William Downer, 1837–1912. Archdeacon of Surrey and Rector of Kingston*, Kingston, 1937.

East, D.J., *Elementary Education: Report on the Royal Commissioners. A Review*, Kingston: *Daily Gleaner*, 1884.

Ellison, Rev. J. (ed.) *Church and Empire*, London: Longman, 1907.

Emerick, Abraham, (S.J.) *Jamaica Superstitions: Obeah and Duppyism in Jamaica (1915) Jamaica Mialism (1916), Jamaica Duppies (1916)*, from the Woodstock Letters, Woodstock, MD. 1915 and 1916.

Feurtado, William A., *A Forty-five year Reminiscence of the Character and Characteristics of Spanish Town*, Kingston, 1890.

The Jubilee Reign of Queen Victoria in Jamaica, 1837–1887, Kingston, 1890.

Froude, J.A., *The English in the West Indies: Or the Bow of Ulisses*, New York: Negro Universities Press, 1969.

Gardner, W.J., *History of Jamaica*, London, 1873.

Gaunt, Mary, *Where the Twain Meet*, New York: Dutton and Co., 1922.

Gordon, Rev. R. *et al.*, *Jamaica's Jubilee: Or what we are and what we hope to be*, London: S.W. Partridge and Co., 1888.

Graham, Rev. William, *Woman: Her Sphere and Opportunities*, Kingston: Educational Supply Co., 1899.
Grant, Allen, 'A Woman's Hand', NLJ, Pamphlet, Vol. 22, Item 36.
Ivan's Great Masterpiece, 1893.
Henderson, John, *Jamaica*, London: Adam and Charles Black, 1906.
Ingram, E.G., *The African in the West Indies*, c. 1892.
James, Winnifred, *The Mulberry Tree*, London: Chapman and Hall, 1913.
Livingstone, W.P., *Black Jamaica: A Study in Evolution*, London: Sampson Low, Marston and Co., 1900.
McKay, Claude, *Songs of Jamaica*, (intro. by Walter Jekyll), Kingston: Aston Gardner, 1912.
McLean, Isabel, *Children of Jamaica*, Edinburgh and London: Oliphant, Anderson and Ferrier, 1910.
Murray, W.C., *A Day with Joe Lennan, The Rosewell duppy doctor and Tommy Silvera or Suck O' Peas Sil*, Kingston: Vendryes and Co., 1891.
Musgrave, Sir Anthony, *Jamaica: Now and fifteen years since*, Proceedings of the Royal Colonial Institute, 1879–80, Vol. XI.
Nuttall, Enos, 'The Negro Race', in Rev. J. Ellison (ed.) *Church and Empire*, London: Longman, 1907.
'Characteristics of the Negro', in Rev. J. Ellison (ed.) *Church and Empire*, London: Longman, 1907.
Some Present Needs of Jamaica as specified in an address delivered at the opening meeting of the Diocesan, Kingston, February, 1897.
Price, Ernest (Rev.) *Banana Land: A Missionary chronicle: Pages from the Chronicles of an English Minister in Jamaica*, London: the Carey Press, 1930.
Radcliffe, Rev. John, *Lectures on Jamaican Proverbs*, Kingston: Henderson and Savage, 1859.
Reid, J.H. 'The People of Jamaica Described' in R. Gordon *et al. Jamaica's Jubilee: Or what we are and what we hope to be*, London: Partridge and Co., 1888.
Root, John W., *The British West Indies and the Sugar Industry*, Liverpool, 1899.
Scholes, T.E.S., *The British Empire and Alliances: Or Britain's Duty to her Colonies and Subject Races*, London, 1899.
Glimpses of the Ages or the 'Superior' and 'Inferior' Races so-called, discussed in the light of Science and History, 2 Vols., London: John Long, 1905.
Scotland, Horace (Rev.) 'Modern Infidelity considered in respect to the middle and lower classes in the West Indies'. *West Indian Quarterly*, 1886–7.
Scott, James, (Commissioner of Health) *Papers Relating to the Present Sanitary State of Kingston*, Kingston, 1874.
Scott, Sir Sibbald David, *To Jamaica and Back*, London: Chapman and Hall, 1870.
Spinner, Alice, 'A West Indian Fairy Story', in Alice Spinner, *A Reluctant Evangelist and other stories*, London: Edward Arnold, 1896.
A Study in Colour, London, T. Fisher Unwin, 1894.
Lucilla: An Experiment, London: Kegan Paul, 1896.
'Margaret: A Sketch in Black and White' in Alice Spinner, *A Reluctant Evangelist and other Stories*, London: Edward Arnold, 1896.
Thomas, Herbert T., *The Story of a West Indian Policeman or 47 years in the Jamaica Constabulary*, Kingston: *Daily Gleaner*, 1927.
Untrodden Jamaica, Kingston: Aston Gardner and Co., 1896.
Walker, H. de R., *The West Indies and the Empire. Study and Travel in the Winter of 1900–1921*, New York and London: Fisher Unwin, 1902.
Williams, Joseph (S.J.) *Whisperings of the Caribbean: Reflections of a Missionary*, New York, Benziger Bros., 1925.

Wilson, C.A. (Rev.) *Men With Backbone and other Pleas for Progress*, Kingston: Educational Supply Co., 1913.
    Men of Vision: Biographical Sketches of Men who have made their mark upon our time, Kingston: Gleaner Co., 1929.

Books

Abrahams, Roger D., *The Man of Words in the West Indies. Performance and the Emergence of Creole Culture*, Baltimore and London: Johns Hopkins University Press, 1983.

Allen, Ann and Morton, Arthur, *This is your Child: The Story of the National Society for the Prevention of Cruelty to Children*, London: Routledge and Kegan Paul, 1961.

Anderson, Mels, *Man's Work and Leisure*, Leiden: EJ Brill, 1974.

Andic, F.M. and Matthews, T.E., *The Caribbean in Transition*, Rio Piedras, Institute of Caribbean Studies, 1965.

Azarya, Victor, *Aristocrats Facing Change: The Fulbe in Guinea, Nigeria and Cameroon*, Chicago and London: University of Chicago Press, 1978.

Baker, Margaret, *Wedding Customs and Folklore*, New Jersey: David and Charles, 1977.

Beachey, R., *The West Indian Sugar Industry in the late 19th century*, Oxford: Basil Blackwell, 1957.

Becker, Howard and Barnes, Harry, *Social Thought from Lore to Science*, Vol. 3, New York: Dover Publications, December, 1961.

Black, Clinton (ed.), *Jamaica's Banana Industry. A History of the Banana Industry with particular reference to the part played by the Jamaica Producers Association*, Kingston: 1984.

Brathwaite, Edward, *The Development of Creole Society in Jamaica: 1780–1820*, London: Oxford University Press, 1971.
    History of the Voice. The Development of Nation Language in Anglophone Caribbean Poetry, London, Port of Spain: New Beacon, 1984.
    Contradictory Omens: Cultural Diversity and Integration in the Caribbean, Kingston: Savacou Publications, 1985.

Brathwaite, Lloyd, 'Social Stratification in Trinidad', *Social and Economic Studies 2 and 3*, 1953.

Brereton, Bridget, *Race Relations in Colonial Trinidad, 1870–1900*, Cambridge: CUP, 1979.

Brodber, Erna, *Perceptions of Caribbean Women: Towards a documentation of stereotypes*, Barbados: ISER, 1982.
    Life in Jamaica in the early Twentieth Century, Kingston: ISER, 1980.

Bryce-Laporte, Roy and Thomas C.S., (ed.) *Alienation in contemporary Society: A Multidisciplinary Examination*. New York: Praeger, 1976.

Buisseret, David and Pawson, Michael, *Port Royal, Jamaica*, Oxford: Clarendon Press, 1975.

Burns, E.B. *The Poverty of Progress. Latin America in the Nineteenth Century*, Berkeley: University of California Press, 1980.

Caldecott, A. *The Church in the West Indies*, London: Frank Cass Reprint, 1970.

Cargill, Morris, *Jamaica Farewell*, New Jersey: Lyle Stuart Secaucus, 1978.

Casmir-Liautaud, Jean, 'Haitian Social structure in the nineteenth century' in Sidney Mintz (ed.) *Working Papers in Haitian Society and Culture*, New Haven: Antilles Research Programme, Yale University, 1975.

Cooper, Wayne, (ed.) *The Passion of Claude McKay*, New York: Schocken Books, 1973.

Crahan, Margaret and Knight, Franklin, *Africa and the Caribbean: The Legacies of a Link*, Baltimore and London: Johns Hopkins University Press, 1979.

Cronin, James E. and Schneer, Jonathan, *Social Conflict and the Political Order in Modern Britain*, London and Canberra: Crown Helm, 1982.

Cundall, Frank, *Life of Enos Nuttall*, London: Macmillan, 1922.

Curtin, Philip D., *Two Jamaicas. The Role of Ideas in a Tropical Colony, 1830–1865*, Harvard University Press, Cambridge: 1955.

The Image of Africa. British Ideas and Action 1780–1850, Madison: University of Wisconsin Press, 1964.

Davis, H.E., *Latin American Social Thought*, Washington, DC: University Press of Washington DC, 1963.

Downer, Lindsay P., *Memoirs of George William Downer, 1837–1912. Archdeacon of Surrey and Rector of Kingston*, Kingston, 1937.

Dyer, T.G., *Theodore Roosevelt and the Idea of Race*, Baton Rouge and London: Louisiana State University Press, 1980.

Eisenstadt, S.N., *The Political Systems of Empire*, New York: The Free Press of Glencoe, 1963.

Eisner, Gisela, *Jamaica 1830–1930. A Study in Economic Growth*, London: University of Manchester Press, 1961.

Ellis, J.B., *The Diocese of Jamaica. A Short Account of its History, Growth and Organisation*, London: SPCK, 1913.

Enloe, Cynthia, *Police, Military and Ethnicity: Foundations of State Power*, New Brunswick and London: Transaction Books, 1980.

Evans, Bishop E.L., *A History of the Diocese of Jamaica*, Kingston c. 1976.

Flynn, M.W. and Smout, T.C. (ed.), *Essays in Social History*, Oxford, Clarendon Press, 1974.

Fuchs, Racheal, *Abandoned Children: Foundlings and Child Welfare in nineteenth century France*, Albany: SUNY Press, 1984.

Gordon, Donald, *The Dominion Partnership in Imperial Defense, 1870–1914*, Baltimore: Johns Hopkins University Press, 1965.

Gordon, Shirley, *A Century of West Indian Education. A Source Book*, London: Longman, 1963.

Harrison, Lawrence, *Underdevelopment is a State of Mind: The Latin American Case*, Maryland and London, c. 1985.

Henry, Paget, *Peripheral Capitalism and Underdevelopment in Antigua*, New Brunswick and Oxford: Transaction Books, 1985.

Hunt, E.H., *British Labour History, 1815–1914*, New Jersey: Humanities Press, Atlantic Highlands, 1981.

Jervier, Wills S., *Educational Change in post-Colonial Jamaica*, New York: Vantage Press, 1977.

Kerr, Madeline, *Personality and Conflict in Jamaica*, London: Collins, 1963.

Knight, Franklin, *The Caribbean: Genesis of a Fragmented Nationalism*, New York: Oxford University Press, 1978.

Levin, Jack and Levin, William, *The Function of Discrimination and Prejudice*, Cambridge, Philadelphia: Harper and Rowe, 1982.

Lewis, Gordon, *Main Currents in Caribbean Thought*, Kingston: Heinemann Educational Books, 1983.

Marcuse, H., *Reason and Revolution, Hegel and the Rise of Social Theory*, Boston: Beacon Press, 1961.

Maunier, Rene, *The Sociology of Colonies: An Introduction to the Study of Race*

Contact, (ed. and trans. E.O. Lorimer) London and Boston: Routledge and Kegan Paul, 1949.

Mazrui, Ali A. *World Culture and the Black Experience*, Seattle and London: University of Washington Press, 1974.

Moberg, David O. *The Church as a Social Institution: The Sociology of American Religion*, New Jersey: Prentice Hall 1962.

Moore, Barrington (Jr.) *Reflections on the Causes of Human Misery and Upon Certain Proposals to Eliminate Them*, Boston: Beacon Press, 1972.

Newton, Judith, *et al.* (ed.) *Sex and Class in Women's History*, London and Boston: Routledge and Kegan Paul, 1983.

Newton, Velma, *The Silver Men. West Indian Labour Migration To Panama, 1850–1914*, Kingston, ISER, 1984.

Post, Ken, *Arise ye Starvelings: The Jamaican Labour Rebellion of 1938 and its Aftermath*, The Hague, Boston and London: Martinus Nijhoff, 1978.

Roberts, Kenneth, *Leisure*, London: Longman, 1970.

Roberts, W. Adolphe, *Six Great Jamaicans*, Kingston: Pioneer Press, 1952.

Rodney, Walter, *History of the Guyanese Working People, 1881–1905*, Baltimore and London: Johns Hopkins University Press, 1981.

Ross, Robert, (ed.) *Racism and Colonialism: Essays on Ideology and Social Structure*, Leiden: University Press, Martinus Nijhoff, 1982.

Saggarra, Eda, *A Social History of Germany, 1648–1914*, New York: Holmes and Meir Publishers, 1977.

Salaman, Graeme, *Community and Occupation: An Exploration of Work/Leisure relationships*, London: Cambridge University Press, 1974.

Schuler, Monica, *Alas! Alas! Kongo: A social history of indentured African immigration to Jamaica 1841–1865*, Baltimore and London: Johns Hopkins University Press, 1980.

Sheridan, Richard, *Doctors and Slaves. A Medical and Demographic History of Slavery in the British West Indies*, Cambridge: Cambridge University Press, 1985.

Sorum, Paul Clay, *Intellectuals and Decolonisation in France*, Chapel Hill: University of North Carolina Press, 1977.

Spackman, Ann, *Constitutional Development of the West Indies, 1922–1968. A Selection from the major Documents*, Kingston: Caribbean Universities Press, No date.

Stevenson, John, *British Society 1914–45*, Harmondsworth: Pelican Books, 1984.

Stone, Carl, *Power in the Caribbean Basin: A Comparative Study of Political Economy*, Philadelphia: Institute for the Study of Human Issues, 1986.

Tawney, R.H., *Equality*, New York: Capricorn Books, 1961.

Thane, Pat, (ed.) *The Origins of British Social Policy*, London: Croom Helm, 1978.

Turner, Mary, *Slaves and Missionaries. The Disintegration of Jamaican Slave Society, 1787–1834*, Urbana: Chicago and London: University of Chicago Press, 1982.

Walvin, James, *Leisure and Society, 1830–1950*, London and New York: Longman, 1978.

Will, H.A. *Constitutional Change in the British West-Indies, 1880–1903*, Oxford, 1970.

Williams, Eric, *British Historians and the West Indies*, London: Andre Deutsch, 1966.

Williams, Rev. Joseph (S.J.) *Whisperings of the Caribbean: Reflections of a Missionary*, New York, Benniger Bros., 1925.

Wolfe, Willard, *From Radicalism to Socialism: Men and Ideas in the Formation of*

Fabian Socialist Doctrines, 1881–1889, New Haven and London: Yale University Press 1975.

Unpublished theses and dissertations

Brodber, Erna, 'A Second Generation of Freemen in Jamaica', Ph. D., UWI, 1984.
Brown, Beryl, 'A History of Portland, 1723–1917', M.A., UWI, 1974.
Burt, Arthur, 'The Development of Self-Government in Jamaica, 1884–1913', Ph. D., University of Toronto, 1960.
Goulbourne, Harry, 'Teachers and Pressure Group Activity in Jamaica, 1894–1967', Ph. D., University of Sussex, 1975.
Roberts, Wesley A, 'The Jamaican Plantocracy' A Study of Their Economic Interests, 1866–1914'. Ph. D., University of Guelph, 1972.
Satchell, Veront, 'Land Transactions in Rural Jamaica, 1866–1900', M. Phil., UWI, 1985.
Shepherd, Verene, 'Separation vs. Integration. The Experience of the East Indian Group in the Creole Society of Jamaica', M. Phil., UWI, 1984.
Stewart, Robert, 'Religion and Society in Jamaica', Ph. D., UWI, 1983.

Articles

Allen, Beryl, 'The Contribution of Enos Nuttall to the Development of Education in Jamaica', *International Journal of Lifelong Education*, **3**. No. 4, 293–303.
Augier, F.R., 'Before and After 1865', *New World Quarterly*, **2**, No. 2, 1966.
Blaug, M., *'The Myth of the Old Poor Law and the Making of the New'*, in M.W. Flynn and T.C. Smout, (eds.) *Essays in Social History*, Oxford: Clarendon Press, 1974.
Brathwaite, L.E.S., 'Problems of Race and Colour in the Caribbean', *Caribbean Issues*, **1**, No. 1.
Brereton, Bridget, 'The Foundations of Prejudice. Indians and Africans in Nineteenth Century Trinidad', *Caribbean Issues* **1**, No. 1.
Brown, John, '"Social Control" and the Modernisation of Social Policy, 1890–1929', in Pat Thane, (ed.), *The Origins of British Social Policy*, London: Croom Helm, 1978.
Campbell, Carl, 'Social and Economic Obstacles to the Development of Popular Education in Post-Emancipation Jamaica', *Journal of Caribbean History*, **1**, Nov. 1970; 'Towards an Imperial Policy for the Education of Negroes in the West Indies after Emancipation', *Jamaica Historical Review*, **7**, 1967.
Cronin, James E., 'Social History and Politics in Britain', in James Cronin and Jonathan Schneer, (eds.) *Social Conflict and the Political Order in Modern Britain*, London and Canberra: Croom Helm, 1982, pp. 7–20.
Cumper, George E., 'A Modern Jamaican Sugar Estate', *Social and Economic Studies*, **3**, No. 2, 1954, pp. 119–160; 'Labour Demand and Supply in the Jamaican Sugar Industry, 1830–1850', *Social and Economic Studies*, **2**, No. 4, 1954.
Curtin, Philip D., 'The Black Experience of Colonialism and Imperialism', in Sidney Mintz, (ed.) *Slavery, Colonialism and Racism*, New York: W.W. Norton and Co., 1974, pp. 17–29.
Downes, David and Rock, Paul, 'Social Reaction to Deviance and its Effects on Crime and Criminal Careers', *British Journal of Sociology*, **XX11**, No. 4, 1971.

Durrans, P.J., 'A Two-edged sword: The Liberal Attack on Disraeli Imperialism', *Journal of Imperial and Commonwealth History*, X, No. 3, 1982, pp. 262–284.

Duthie, John, 'Some further Insights into the Working of mid-Victorian Imperialism: Lord Salisbury and Anglo-Afghan Relations, 1874–78', *Journal of Imperial and Commonwealth History*, VIII, No. 3, May 1980.

Gordon, William E., 'Imperial Policy Decisions in the Economic History of Jamaica, 1664–1934', *Social and Economic Studies*, 6, No. 1, March 1957.

Green, Thomas, 'The Work-Leisure Conflict in the American Tradition', in Roye S. Bryce-Laporte and Claudewell S. Thomas, (eds.) *Alienation in Contemporary Society: A Multidisciplinary Examination*, New York: Praeger, 1976.

Hall, Douglas, 'The Flight from the Estates Reconsidered: the British West Indies 1838–42', *Journal of Caribbean History*, 10 and 11, 1978.

Hart, Ansell, 'The Banana in Jamaica', *Social and Economic Studies*, 3, No. 2, Sept. 1954, pp. 212–29.

Hay, J.R., 'Employers' Attitude to Social Policy and the Concept of "Social Control", 1900–1920', in Pat Thane, (ed.) *The Origins of British Social Policy*, London: Croom Helm, 1978, pp. 107–125.

Heerem, John, 'Karl Manheim and the Intellectual Elite', *British Journal of Sociology*, 22, 1971.

Hobsbawm, Eric J., 'From Social History to the History of Society', in M.W. Flinn and T.C. Smout, (eds.) *Essays in Social History*, Oxford: Clarendon Press, 1974.

Hoetink, H., 'The Dominican Republic in the Nineteenth Century: Some Notes on Stratification, Immigration, and Race', in Magnus Morner, (ed.) *Race and Class in Latin America*, New York and London: Columbia University Press, 1971, pp. 96–121.

Houston, Susan, 'Victorian Origins of Juvenile Delinquency: A Canadian Experience', in Michael B. Katz and Paul Mattingly, (eds.) *Education and Social Change*, University Press, 1975.

Jacobs, H.P., 'Port Royal in Decline', *Jamaica Historical Review*, 8, 1971.

Jones, Edwin, 'Class and Administrative Development Doctrines in Jamaica', *Social and Economic Studies*, 30, No. 3, 1981, pp. 1–20.

Coalitions of the Oppressed, Jamaica: ISER, 1987.

Johnson, Howard, 'Social Control and the Colonial State: The Reorganisation of the Police Force in the Bahamas 1888–1893', in *Slavery and Abolition*, Vol. 7, No. 1, May 1986, pp. 46–58.

Karch, Cecilia, 'Class Formation and Class and Race Relations in the West Indies', in Dale L. Johnson, (ed.) *Middle Classes in Dependent Countries*, London and New Delhi: Sage Publications, 1985.

Keith, Novella and Keith, Nelson, 'Rise of the Middle X Class in Jamaica', in Dale L. Johnson, (ed.) *Middle Classes in Dependent Countries*, London and New Delhi: Sage Publications, 1985.

Levy, Jacqueline, 'The Economic Role of the Chinese in Jamaica. The Grocery Retail Trade', *Jamaica Historical Review*, XV, 1986, pp. 31–49.

Marshall, Woodville, 'Peasant Development in the West Indies since 1838', in P.I. Gomes, (ed.) *Rural Development in the Caribbean*, Kingston: Heinemann Educational Books, 1985, pp. 1–14.

McCreery, David, 'Prostitution in Guatemala City, 1880–1920', *Journal of Latin American Studies*, 18, 2, November 1986.

McDonald, Keith, 'Professional Formation: the Case of Scottish Accountants', *British Journal of Sociology*, 35, 1984.

Mintz, Sidney, 'The Jamaican Internal Marketing Pattern: Some Notes and Hypotheses', *Social and Economic Studies*, 4, No. 1, March 1955; 'Caribbean Nationhood in Anthropological Perspective', in S. Lewis and T.G. Matthews, (eds.) *Caribbean Integration: Papers on Social, Political and Economic Integration*, Rio Piedras, 1967.

Miller, J., 'Women and Weak Ties. Difference by Sex in the Size of Voluntary Organisations'. *American Journal of Sociology*, 87, No. 4, Jan. 1982.

Mörner, Magnus, 'Economic Factors and Stratification in Colonial Spanish America with Special Regard to Elites', *Hispanic American Historical Review*, 63, No. 2, May 1983, pp. 335–369.

Mullings, Leith, 'Uneven Development. Class, Race and Gender in the USA before 1900', in Eleanor Leacock, Helen Safa, *et al. Women's Work: Development and the Division of Labor by Gender*, Massachusetts: Bergin and Garvey Publishers, 1986.

Pryce, Ken, 'Towards a Caribbean Criminology', *Caribbean Issues*, 2, No. 2, August 1976.

Schreuder, D.M., 'The Cultural Factor in Victorian Imperialism. A Case Study of the British Civilizing Mission', *Journal of Imperial and Commonwealth History*, 4, No.3, May, 1976.

Senior, Carl, 'German Immigration in Jamaica, 1834–38', *Journal of Caribbean History*, 10 and 11, 1978.

Sires, Ronald V., 'The Jamaican Constitution of 1884', *Social and Economic Studies*, 3, No. 1, June, 1954.

Smith, Raymond T. 'Race and Class in the Post Emancipation Caribbean', in Robert Ross, (ed.) *Racism and Colonialism: Essays on Ideology and Social Structure*, Leiden: Martinus Nijhoff, 1982.

Staples, Robert, 'Masculinity and Race: The Dual Dilemma of Black Men', *Journal of Social Issues*, 34, No. 1, 1978.

Strauss, George, 'Professionalism and Occupational Associations. Industrial Relations', *Journal of Economy and Society*, 2, No. 3, May, 1963.

Sutton, John R., 'Social Structure, Institutions and the Legal Status of Children in the USA', *American Journal of Sociology*, 88, Nos. 4–6, 1983.

Weare, Walter B., 'The Idea of Progress in Afro-American Thought, 1890–1915', in Ralph M. Alderman, (ed.) *The Quest for Social Justice*, Madison: University of Wisconsin Press, 1983.

Weiss, Robert S., 'Growing up a little faster: The Experience of Growing up in a Single-Parent Household', *Journal of Social Studies*, 35, No. 4, 1979.

Wiarda, Howard, 'Law and Political Development in Latin America: Toward a Framework of Analysis', in Howard Wiarda, (ed.) *Politics and Social Change in Latin America: The Distinct Tradition*, University of Massachusetts Press, 1982. Reprint from *American Journal of Comparative Law*, 19. No. 3, 1971.

Index